Aux martyrs de l'Holocauste
Aux révoltés des Ghettos
Aux partisans de forêts
Aux insurgés des camps
Aux combattants de la résistance
Aux soldats des forces alliées
Aux sauveteurs de frères en peril
Aux vaillants de l'immigration clandestine
A l'éternité

Inscription at *Yad Va-shem* Memorial,
Jerusalem

JUST AND UNJUST WARS

A MORAL ARGUMENT WITH HISTORICAL ILLUSTRATIONS

FOURTH EDITION

Michael Walzer

BASIC
BOOKS

A Member of the Perseus Books Group
New York

Library of Congress Cataloging-in-Publication Data
Walzer, Michael.
    Just and unjust wars.
    Includes bibliographical references and index.
    1. War.   I. Title.
U21.2W345   355.02   77-75252
Fourth Edition: ISBN-13: 978-0-465-03707-0; ISBN-10: 0-465-03707-0

DESIGNED BY VINCENT TORRE

EBM   21 20 19 18 17 16 15

CONTENTS

PART THREE
THE WAR CONVENTION

CONTENTS

PREFACE TO THE FOURTH EDITION

Regime Change and Just War

I

The year 2005 was the sixtieth anniversary of the end of World War Two and the beginning of regime change and democratization in Germany. The allies confirmed their commitment to democratization at Potsdam in July of 1945, where the British provided an admirable example of what democracy means. Elections were held in the United Kingdom while the conference was going on; Winston Churchill, the great wartime leader of his country, was defeated—and immediately replaced at the meetings (Stalin must have been astonished) by Clement Atlee, the leader of the Labor party. This was a classic democratic moment: The ability of the opposition to challenge and possibly defeat a powerful leader is surely the crucial test of a democratic constitution.

The political reconstruction of Germany was an effort, at least in the western occupation zones, to enable the German people to enact moments like that. It is important to notice that what was planned was a restoration of democracy, not a creation ex nihilo—the Weimar republic lay only 12 years in the past, and old political parties like the Christian Democrats and the Social Democrats were quickly reconstituted. For that reason (and for others too) the German case isn't a good precedent, as is sometimes claimed, for what the United States has recently been trying to do in Iraq. Still, this was a restoration-by-force, the consequence of military victory and military occupation. And so it raises the question of when or whether forcible democratization can be justified. Or, in the language of contemporary debates: Is "regime change" a just cause for war? This is a question that is only indirectly addressed in *Just and Unjust Wars*; it seems right to deal with it now.

In the case of Nazism, regime change was the consequence, not the cause, of the war fought by the allies. It wasn't the aim of the wars declared in 1939 by Poland, France, and Britain to transform the German state. Rather, these were paradigmatic just wars; their cause was resistance to armed aggression. And according to the just war paradigm, resistance to aggression stops with the military defeat of the aggressor. After that, presumably, there is a negotiated peace, and in the course of the negotiations, the victims of aggression and their allies may legitimately look for material reparations and political guarantees against any future attack, but regime change is not part of the paradigm. It is a feature of just war theory in its classic formulations that aggression is regarded as the criminal policy of a government, not as the policy of a criminal government—let alone a criminal system of government. Individual leaders may be brought to trial after the war; the governmental system is not at issue. But if we understand aggression as an act that follows from the very character of the system—which is how we came to understand Nazi warmaking—then regime change will seem a necessary feature of the post-war settlement.

Of course, it wasn't only the aggressive wars fought by the Nazi regime but also the genocidal policies it pursued that justified the demand first for unconditional surrender and then for political reconstruction. A negotiated peace with Hitler or his associates was not a morally imaginable outcome of the second World War, as it might have been with the Kaiser in the first, had his regime not been overthrown from within. The Nazis had to go, whether or not their German opponents were capable of seeing them out. There is a general argument here, which applies most clearly to cases of "humanitarian intervention." When a government is engaged in the mass murder of its own people, or some subgroup of its own people, then any foreign state or coalition of states that sends an army across the border to stop the killing is also going to have to replace the government or, at least, to begin the process of replacement. It isn't only aggressiveness, then, but also murderousness that makes a political regime a legitimate candidate for forcible transformation. Still, the primary aim of the intervention is to stop the killing; regime change follows from that purpose. An authoritarian regime that is capable of mass murder but not engaged in mass murder is not liable to military attack and political reconstruction.

Imagine that there had been, as there surely should have been, an African or a European or a United Nations intervention in Rwanda in 1994. The initial purpose of the military action would have been to stop the massacre of Tutsi men and women (and their Hutu sympathizers), but in order to do that and to protect the survivors, it would have been necessary to overthrow the Hutu Power regime. And whoever was responsible for that overthrow would also have taken on, willy-nilly, some degree of responsibility for the creation of an alternative government. It would have been wise to share that responsibility with local political forces and also with international agencies, but there would have been no way, no just way, of shedding it entirely.

And once the intervening forces are engaged in the work of political reconstruction, there are good reasons why they should aim at democracy or, at least, open the way for the practice of democracy. The reasons have to do with the legitimacy of democratically based regimes, which are established through a literal (and on-going) self-determination, and also with their relative benevolence. Genuine democracies have not engaged in the mass murder of their own citizens (even if their record abroad is less satisfactory). But what if there are other traditions of legitimacy in the invaded country—involving, for example, a dominant role for religious leaders? What if there is strong traditionalist opposition to the legal equality that democracy requires—most crucially (and commonly), opposition to the equality of women? I can imagine cases where democratization might have to be a gradual process or where democratic principles might have to be compromised in one way or another. Even when a humanitarian crisis has rightly triggered intervention, we can still hope to minimize the coercive imposition of foreign ideas and ideologies. The intervening forces have a mandate for political, but not for cultural, transformation. In any case, it isn't easy to imagine how they might set about changing the customs and beliefs of the people they are (temporarily) ruling. Negotiation and compromise are almost certainly better than the coercion that would be necessary for a project like that.

Nonetheless, just wars and humanitarian interventions will often be an occasion for forcible and justifiable democratization—and that will sometimes require an attack upon traditional hierarchies and customary practices: The exclusion of women from the political sphere is an obvious example. So consider the other case of post-World War Two regime change: the American occupation of Japan. The constitution imposed by the occupation authorities provided that all laws governing gender relations "shall be enacted from the standpoint of individual dignity and the essential equality of the sexes." Sixty years later, there is pressure from the right to repeal this article—in defense, it is claimed, of traditional Japanese values. But one might say that the very possibility of repeal vindicates the American imposition. The Japanese now have to argue about the structure of gender relations in their society, and they will get whatever structure a majority of them are prepared to support. Even imposed democracy is defensible in this sense: It is more open-ended than any other regime change would be.

II

So we have what we might think of as the World War Two occasions for justified regime change, and we have the (unrealized) Rwandan occasion. Is there, was there, an Iraqi occasion?

Note that in the first Gulf War of 1991, the United States and its allies fought in strict accordance with the classic just war paradigm: They stopped fighting once the invasion of Kuwait had been decisively defeated. They did not march on Baghdad; they did not aim at the overthrow and replacement of the Baathist regime; nor did they do anything to make it possible for the Iraqi people to turn Saddam Hussein out of office. On the contrary, having called for rebellions against Saddam's rule, they failed to come to the aid or, much worse, to the rescue, of the rebels. Though US officials compared Saddam to Hitler, the allies did not act on the comparison; it was propaganda and nothing more. They did seek constraints on the future behavior of the Baathist regime, and these constraints were predicated on a fairly grim view of the regime. Still, what we might think of as the constitutional character of the Iraqi state—whether it was autocratic or democratic, secular or religious; whether it recognized or violated human rights; whether its bureaucrats acted arbitrarily or were legally constrained—all this was judged irrelevant to the decisions about war and peace made by the American-led coalition.

By 2003 the position of the United States and its allies, a smaller number now, had changed dramatically. To be sure, the second Bush administration gave a variety of reasons for its decision to go to war: another day, another reason. But all the reasons suggested the need, this time, to march on Baghdad and replace the Baathist regime. The most important reason was the danger that Iraq possessed, or in the near future would be capable of producing, weapons of mass destruction. But the fact that France (say) possessed weapons of mass destruction was never imagined as an occasion for war. It was the character of its regime that made Iraq dangerous: The US government claimed that Saddam's regime was inherently aggressive and inherently murderous. Just as it had committed aggression in the past, so it had massacred its own people in the past, and American leaders insisted that, in this case, the past was prologue. What had happened before would happen again unless the regime was replaced.

So Iraq was not similar to the German or Japanese or the (hypothetical) Rwandan case: The war was not a response to aggression or a humanitarian intervention. Its cause was not (as in 1991) an actual Iraqi attack on a neighboring state or even an imminent threat of attack; nor was the cause an actual, ongoing massacre. The cause was regime change, directly—which means that the US government was arguing for a significant expansion of the doctrine of *jus ad bellum*. The existence of an aggressive and murderous regime, it claimed, was a legitimate occasion for war, even if the regime was not actually engaged in aggression or mass murder. In more familiar terms, this was an argument for preventive war, but the reason for the preventive attack wasn't the standard perception of a dangerous shift in the balance of power that would soon leave "us" helpless against "them." It was a radically new perception of an evil regime.

No one who has experienced, or reflected on, the politics of the twentieth century can doubt that there are evil regimes. Nor can there be any doubt that we need to design a political/military response to such regimes that recognizes their true character. Even so, I do not believe that regime change, by itself, can be a just cause of war. When we act in the world, and especially when we act militarily, we must respond to "the evil that men do," which is best read as "the evil that they are doing," and not to the evil that they are capable of doing or have done in the past. Aggression and massacre are legitimate causes of war, and we must learn, what we have not yet learned, to respond to each of these in a timely and forceful way. But the existence of regimes capable of aggression and massacre requires a different response.

The harsh containment system imposed on Iraq after the first Gulf War was an experiment in responding differently. Containment had three elements: The first was an embargo intended to prevent the importation of arms (which also affected supplies of food and medicine though it should have been possible to design a "smarter" set of sanctions). The second element was an inspection system organized by the UN to block the domestic development of weapons of mass destruction. The third element was the establishment of "no-fly" zones in the northern and southern parts of the country so that Iraq's air power could not be used against its own people. The containment system was, as we now know, highly effective. At least, it was effective in one sense: It prevented both weapons development and mass murder and therefore made the war of 2003 unnecessary. But in another sense it was a failure: It did not prevent the war.

The primary reason for the failure was, obviously, the ideologically driven policy of the Bush administration, which from the beginning favored regime change and war over containment. But there is another reason, less obvious, which needs to be stressed: The states that opposed the war on the grounds that containment was working were not themselves making it work. They were not participants in, or even supporters of, the containment system. The containment of Saddam's Iraq began as a multilateral enterprise, but in the end it was the Americans who were doing almost all the work. Had there been many states, or even just a few more states, enforcing the embargo, insisting on inspections, and flying planes over northern and southern Iraq, the unilateral abrogation of the containment system by the US government would not have been possible (or, at least, it would not have been as easy as it was). Had containment been an international project, American power might also have been contained within it.

There is a simple lesson here about the meaning of collective security. If measures short of war are to work against evil or dangerous regimes, they have to be the common work of a group of nations. They require multilateral commitment. Collective security must be a collective project. It won't be successful if the costs of security are assigned to one state while all the others pursue business as usual. The state bearing the costs can't be counted on to bear them indefinitely. Adventurous politicians will be tempted by the idea of a quick and radical alternative to containment. And regime change is the obvious alternative.

I have described the elements of the containment system as "measures short of war." In fact, they all involved the use (or, in the case of inspections, the threat) of force, which is why states eager for business as usual refused to participate. According to international law, embargoes (stopping ships on the high seas) and the enforcement of no-fly zones (bombing radar and anti-aircraft installations) are acts of war. But it is common sense to recognize that they are very different from actual warfare: Compare Iraq before and after March 2003. And certainly containment is much easier to justify than a full-scale attack. The arguments against preventive war canvassed in this book don't apply, it seems to me, to the preventive use of force-short-of-war—since short-of-war means without war's unpredictable and often catastrophic consequences. Forceful containment can be justified by a reasonable perception of the dangers posed by a regime like Saddam Hussein's.

But containment doesn't or, in the Iraqi case, didn't, bring the regime down. So why is it preferable to, let's say, a short war that produces a new regime? That is a hard question, even after the war has turned out not to be short. But I believe that patience would have been a better policy in 2003. Since containment rendered Saddam's regime harmless, it did in fact weaken it—for regimes of this sort cannot endure being harmless. But the full realization of this effect was still a long way off; in the short run, the regime survived containment. Hence the most plausible argument for going to war might have been that the containment system was costly and carried risks of its own, that it could not be sustained indefinitely, and that a decision to fight might well win out on a straightforward utilitarian calculation. The argument fails, however, because the calculation would only go that way if we took an optimistic view of the probable costs of the war, and it seems to me that we are not allowed that kind of optimism. I mean, morally allowed, given the nature of the risks that we are imposing on other people.

So, the Iraqi case invites us to think about the use of force-short-of-war; the containment regime of 1991–2003 that the UN endorsed and the United States enforced is only one possible example of this use. Despite the French argument at the UN in 2002 and 2003 that force must always come as a last resort, force-short-of-war obviously comes before war itself. The argument about *jus ad bellum* needs to be extended, therefore, to *jus ad vim*. We urgently need a theory of just and unjust uses of force. This shouldn't be an overly tolerant or permissive theory, but it will certainly be more permissive than the theory of just and unjust war. The immediate question for us is whether the permissions reach to regime change and democratization. As I have already suggested, this is closely connected to questions about prevention. Preventive war is not justifiable either in standard just war theory or in international law, but what we might think of as "preventive force" can be justified when we are dealing with a brutal regime that has acted aggressively or murderously in the past and gives us reason to think that it might do so again. In such cases, we aim at containment but hope for regime change. And we can legitimately design the containment policy to advance this further purpose whenever that is possible—which means that we can use force, in limited ways, for the sake of producing a new (and if new then also democratic) regime.

I will come back to the necessary limits on this use of force; before doing that, however, I want to consider how it stands vis-à-vis the classic principle of non-intervention, which holds that the regime of a country should reflect the history, culture, and politics of that country, and not of any other. A regime of freedom, as John Stuart Mill argued, requires men and women who value freedom enough to risk their lives in its defense. But regime change short-of-war leaves plenty of room for local valuations and local risk-taking. It is so indirect that it doesn't raise the questions I have already raised with regard to Japan in 1945. Consider, again, the no-fly zone in northern Iraq. This was certainly a kind of humanitarian intervention, in that it served to prevent a massacre of the Kurds, which there was good reason to expect after the massacre of Shi'ites in the south. That good reason, it seems to me, was sufficient to justify the preventive intervention. The no-fly zone also produced a kind of regime change in that it allowed the creation of an autonomous Kurdistan. Can this also be justified? Kurdish autonomy was not a regime imposed from the outside; though the containment system made autonomy possible, the new regime was first demanded, and then created and sustained, by the Kurds themselves. It may happen that containment anticipates rather than responds to local demands for self-determination. But this isn't an unjust anticipation, since the states organizing the containment don't themselves overthrow the old regime, and they don't establish the new one, if there is a new one. They are operating at the edge of the non-intervention principle but not in violation of it. If preventing aggression and mass murder is justified, then so is this indirect version of regime change.

But there are limits on the occasions when force-short-of-war can be used and also on the ways in which it can be used—limits that correspond to *jus ad bellum* and *jus in bello*. I have already discussed the two critical occasions, which have to do with the threat of aggression or of massacre. But what state or set of states is morally bound to recognize this threat and organize a containment system? Collective security depends on collective recognition. Right now, however, the capacity of international agencies and regional associations to respond to threats of aggression and massacre is probably even less developed than their capacity to respond to actual aggression and massacre. So we have to acknowledge the possible legitimacy of unilateral action in both cases. But unilateralism works less well in the first case than in the second. Force-short-of-war—especially when it involves trade sanctions or a weapons embargo—requires the cooperation of many nations if it is to be effective. I have said this already, but it bears repeating: The avoidance of war and massacre requires a committed collective, ready to use force. It is sadly true that Europe today does not display that commitment; nor do Europe and the United States together. And the United States alone has seemed more ready, these past several years, to go to war than to use force in restrained and politic ways.

When force-short-of-war is used, it should be limited in the same way that the conduct of war is limited, so as to shield civilians. This is especially important in the case of economic blockades, where the civilian population is inevitably at risk, even if the government and not the population is the target of the blockade. The policy that Colin Powell called "smart sanctions"—they are meant to be morally as well as politically smart—is supposed to reduce the risk; it should certainly be tried on the next legitimate occasion. There is no justification for a blockade that effectively deprives civilians of food and medicine. But what should we do if a barbarous government deliberately increases the privation of its own civilians in order to discredit the blockade, as Saddam did in the 1990s? The UN responded with its oil-for-food program, and I suppose something might be learned from that effort, if only about how to do it better. Some such response is clearly necessary, even if the hunger and disease attributed to the blockade are in fact the work of the targeted government—further evidence that the targeting is justified.

Force-short-of-war doesn't permit direct and forcible democratization. The German and Japanese examples are not relevant here. Nor is Iraq as it is at this moment, with forcible democratization proceeding, not very effectively. I have defended an alternative way of proceeding, which was wrongly rejected in 2003 but will certainly come up again. Containment opens a different path to democracy, where the actual work of democratization must be done by local political agents, taking advantage of the international condemnation, ostracism, and constraint of the brutal regime. But this suggests one further step in the regime change argument. War can lead directly to political reconstruction; the use of force-short-of-war can do this only indirectly. But there is another form of direct action, which involves what we might call "politics-short-of-force," non-coercive politics, the work of non-governmental organizations, like Human Rights Watch or Amnesty International, which also aim, in their own way, at regime change.

The most important work of groups like these is to foster the kind of civil society that democracy requires—the associational world of interest groups, labor unions, professional societies, social movements, and political parties. By opposing repression and censorship, they open space for organizations independent of the state, and their people on the ground train local men and women in the organizational skills that enable political action. These organizations, and these men and women, are at least potential contributors to a democratic political process. In the case of really brutal and dangerous governments, however, their actual contribution may wait upon a more coercive political intervention. Politics-short-of-force may depend on force-short-of-war. In fact, we have to sponsor and support this interaction—because these two together can help us avoid war itself.

Allied policy at the end of World War Two reminds us that regime change can be justified in the aftermath of a just war. I have argued that a more indirect approach to regime change can also be justified before (and instead of) a just war—indeed, the success of this approach would render war unnecessary and therefore unjust. And if we commit ourselves to that indirection, if we commit ourselves to the forceful containment of brutal regimes, to collective security, we may find that we can reach justice without the terrible destructiveness of war.

Michael Walzer

PREFACE

I did not begin by thinking about war in general, but about particular wars, above all about the American intervention in Vietnam. Nor did I begin as a philosopher, but as a political activist and a partisan. Certainly, political and moral philosophy ought to help us at those difficult times when we choose sides and make commitments. But it does so only indirectly. We are not usually philosophical in moments of crisis; most often, there is no time. War especially imposes an urgency that is probably incompatible with philosophy as a serious enterprise. The philosopher is like Wordsworth's poet who reflects in tranquility upon past experience (or other people's experience), thinking about political and moral choices already made. And yet these choices are made in philosophical terms, available because of previous reflection. It was, for example, a matter of great importance to all of us in the American anti-war movement of the late 1960s and early 1970s that we found a moral doctrine ready at hand, a connected set of names and concepts that we all knew—and that everyone else knew. Our anger and indignation were shaped by the words available to express them, and the words were at the tips of our tongues even though we had never before explored their meanings and connections. When we talked about aggression and neutrality, the rights of prisoners of war and civilians, atrocities and war crimes, we were drawing upon the work of many generations of men and women, most of whom we had never heard of. We would be better off if we did not need a vocabulary like that, but given that we need it, we must be grateful that we have it. Without this vocabulary, we could not have thought about the Vietnam war as we did, let alone have communicated our thoughts to other people.

No doubt we used the available words freely and often carelessly. Sometimes this was due to the excitement of the moment and the pressures of partisanship, but it also had a more serious cause. We suffered from an education which taught us that these words had no proper descriptive use and no objective meaning. Moral discourse was excluded from the world of science, even of social science. It expressed feelings, not perceptions, and there was no reason for the expression of feelings to be precise. Or rather, any precision it achieved had an entirely subjective reference: it was the domain of the poet and the literary critic. I don't need to rehearse this point of view (I shall criticize it in detail later on), though it's less prevalent now than it once was. What is crucial is that we disputed it, knowingly or unknowingly, every time we criticized American conduct in Vietnam. For our criticisms had the form at least of reports on the real world, not merely on the state of our own tempers. They required evidence; they pressed us, however trained we were in the loose use of moral language, toward analysis and investigation. Even the most skeptical among us came to see that they *could* be true (or false).

In those years of angry controversy, I promised myself that one day I would try to set out the moral argument about war in a quiet and reflective way. I still want to defend (most of) the particular arguments that underlay our opposition to the American war in Vietnam, but also and more importantly I want to defend the business of arguing, as we did and as most people do, in moral terms. Hence this book, which may be taken as an apology for our occasional carelessness and a vindication of our fundamental enterprise.

Now, the language with which we argue about war and justice is similar to the language of international law. But this is not a book about the positive laws of war. There are many such books, and I have often drawn upon them. Legal treatises do not, however, provide a fully plausible or coherent account of our moral arguments, and the two most common approaches to the law reflected in the treatises are both in need of extra-legal supplement. First of all, legal positivism, which generated major scholarly works in the late nineteenth and early twentieth centuries, has become in the age of the United Nations increasingly uninteresting. The UN Charter was supposed to be the constitution of a new world, but, for reasons that have often been discussed, things have turned out differently.[1] To dwell at length upon the precise meaning of the Charter is today a kind of utopian quibbling. And because the UN sometimes pretends that it already is what it has barely begun to be, its decrees do not command intellectual or moral respect—except among the positivist lawyers whose business it is to interpret them. The lawyers have constructed a paper world, which fails at crucial points to correspond to the world the rest of us still live in.

The second approach to the law is oriented in terms of policy goals. Its advocates respond to the poverty of the contemporary international regime by imputing purposes to that regime—the achievement of some sort of "world order"—and then reinterpreting the law to fit those purposes.[2] In effect, they substitute utilitarian argument for legal analysis. That substitution is certainly not uninteresting, but it requires a philosophical defense. For the customs and conventions, the treaties and charters that constitute the laws of international society do not invite interpretation in terms of a single purpose or set of purposes. Nor are the judgments they require always explicable from a utilitarian standpoint. Policy-oriented lawyers are in fact moral and political philosophers, and it would be best if they presented themselves that way. Or, alternatively, they are would-be legislators, not jurists or students of the law. They are committed, or most of them are committed, to restructuring international society—a worthwhile task—but they are not committed to expounding its present structure.

My own task is different. I want to account for the ways in which men and women who are not lawyers but simply citizens (and sometimes soldiers) argue about war, and to expound the terms we commonly use. I am concerned precisely with the present structure of the moral world. My starting point is the fact that we do argue, often to different purposes, to be sure, but in a mutually comprehensible fashion: else there would be no point in *arguing*. We justify our conduct; we judge the conduct of others. Though these justifications and judgments cannot be studied like the records of a criminal court, they are nevertheless a legitimate subject of study. Upon examination they reveal, I believe, a comprehensive view of war as a human activity and a more or less systematic moral doctrine, which sometimes, but not always, overlaps with established legal doctrine.

In fact, the vocabulary overlaps more than the arguments do. Hence I must say something about my own use of language. I shall always refer to the laws of international society (as these appear in legal handbooks and military manuals) as *positive* laws. For the rest, when I talk of law, I am referring to the moral law, to those general principles that we commonly acknowledge, even when we can't or won't live up to them. When I talk of the rules of war, I am referring to the more particular code that governs our judgments of combat behavior, and that is only partially articulated in the Hague and Geneva conventions. And when I talk of crimes, I am describing violations of the general principles or of the particular code: so men and women can be called criminals even when they cannot be charged before a legal tribunal. Since positive international law is radically incomplete, it is always possible to interpret it in the light of moral principles and to refer to the results as "positive law." Perhaps that is what has to be done in order to flesh out the legal system and render it more attractive than it presently is. But it is not what I have done here. Throughout the book, I treat words like aggression, neutrality, surrender, civilian, reprisal, and so on, as if they were terms in a moral vocabulary—which they are, and always have been, though most recently their analysis and refinement have been almost entirely the work of lawyers.

I want to recapture the just war for political and moral theory. My own work, then, looks back to that religious tradition within which Western politics and morality were first given shape, to the books of writers like Maimonides, Aquinas, Vitoria, and Suarez—and then to the books of writers like Hugo Grotius, who took over the tradition and began to work it into secular form. But I have not attempted a history of just war theory, and I quote the classical texts only occasionally, for the sake of some particularly illuminating or forceful argument.[3] I refer more often to contemporary philosophers and theologians (and soldiers and statesmen), for my main concern is not with the making of the moral world but with its present character.

Perhaps the most problematic feature of my exposition is the use of the plural pronouns: we, our, ourselves, us. I have already demonstrated the ambiguity of those words by using them in two ways: to describe that group of Americans who condemned the Vietnam war, and to describe that much larger group who understood the condemnation (whether or not they agreed with it). I shall limit myself henceforth to the larger group. That its members share a common morality is the critical assumption of this book. In my first chapter I try to make a case for that assumption. But it's only a case, it's not conclusive. Someone can always ask, "What is this morality *of yours*?" That is a more radical question, however, than the questioner may realize, for it excludes him not only from the comfortable world of moral agreement, but also from the wider world of agreement and disagreement, justification and criticism. The moral world of war is shared not because we arrive at the same conclusions as to whose fight is just and whose unjust, but because we acknowledge the same difficulties on the way to our conclusions, face the same problems, talk the same language. It's not easy to opt out, and only the wicked and the simple make the attempt.

I am not going to expound morality from the ground up. Were I to begin with the foundations, I would probably never get beyond them; in any case, I am by no means sure what the foundations are. The substructure of the ethical world is a matter of deep and apparently unending controversy. Meanwhile, however, we are living in the superstructure. The building is large, its construction elaborate and confusing. But here I can offer some guidance: a tour of the rooms, so to speak, a discussion of architectural principles. This is a book of practical morality. The study of judgments and justifications in the real world moves us closer, perhaps, to the most profound questions of moral philosophy, but it does not require a direct engagement with those questions. Indeed, philosophers who seek such an engagement often miss the immediacies of political and moral controversy and provide little help to men and women faced with hard choices. For the moment, at least, practical morality is detached from its foundations, and we must act as if that separation were a possible (since it is an actual) condition of moral life.

But that's not to suggest that we can do nothing more than describe the judgments and justifications that people commonly put forward. We can analyze these moral claims, seek out their coherence, lay bare the principles that they exemplify. We can reveal commitments that go deeper than partisan allegiance and the urgencies of battle; for it is a matter of evidence, not a pious wish, that there are such commitments. And then we can expose the hypocrisy of soldiers and statesmen who publicly acknowledge these commitments while seeking in fact only their own advantage. The exposure of hypocrisy is certainly the most ordinary, and it may also be the most important form of moral criticism. We are rarely called upon to invent new ethical principles; if we did that, our criticism would not be comprehensible to the people whose behavior we wanted to condemn. Rather, we hold such people to their own principles, though we may draw these out and arrange them in ways they had not thought of before.

There is a particular arrangement, a particular view of the moral world, that seems to me the best one. I want to suggest that the arguments we make about war are most fully understood (though other understandings are possible) as efforts to recognize and respect the rights of individual and associated men and women. The morality I shall expound is in its philosophical form a doctrine of human rights, though I shall say nothing here of the ideas of personality, action, and intention that this doctrine probably presupposes. Considerations of utility play into the structure at many points, but they cannot account for it as a whole. Their part is subsidiary to that of rights; it is constrained by rights. That is above all true of the classical forms of military maximization: the religious crusade, the proletarian revolution, the "war to end war." But it's true also, as I will try to show, of the more immediate pressures of "military necessity." At every point, the judgments we make (the lies we tell) are best accounted for if we regard life and liberty as something like absolute values and then try to understand the moral and political processes through which these values are challenged and defended.

The proper method of practical morality is casuistic in character. Since I am concerned with actual judgments and justifications, I shall turn regularly to historical cases. My argument moves through the cases, and I have often foregone a systematic presentation for the sake of the nuances and details of historical reality. At the same time, the cases are necessarily sketched in outline form. In order to make them exemplary, I have had to abridge their ambiguities. In doing that, I have tried to be accurate and fair, but the cases are often controversial and no doubt I have sometimes failed. Readers upset by my failures might usefully treat the cases as if they were hypothetical—invented rather than researched—though it is important to my own sense of my enterprise that I am reporting on experiences that men and women have really had and on arguments that they have really made. In choosing experiences and arguments for discussion, I have relied heavily on World War II in Europe, the first war of which I have memories and the paradigm, for me, of a justified struggle. For the rest, I have tried to pick out the obvious cases: those that have figured largely in the literature of war and those that play a part in contemporary controversies.

The structure of the book is explained in the second and third chapters, which introduce the main argument. Here I only want to say that my presentation of the moral theory of war is focused on the tensions within the theory that make it problematic and that make choice in wartime difficult and painful. The tensions are summed up in the dilemma of winning and fighting well. This is the military form of the means/ends problem, the central issue in political ethics. I address it directly, and resolve or fail to resolve it, in Part Four; and the resolution, if it works, must be relevant also to the choices faced in politics generally. For war is the hardest place: if comprehensive and consistent moral judgments are possible there, they are possible everywhere.

Cambridge, Massachusetts, 1977

ACKNOWLEDGMENTS

In writing about war, I have had the support of many allies, institutional and personal. I began my research during the academic year 1971–72, while working at the Center for Advanced Study in the Behavioral Sciences in Stanford, California. I wrote a version of the preface and of chapter 1 at Mishkenot Sha'ananim (Peaceful Habitations) in Jerusalem, Israel in the summer of 1974—a visit made possible by the Jerusalem Foundation; the bulk of the book was completed in 1975–76, while I was a Guggenheim Fellow.

Over the past nine years, I have gone to school with the members of the Society for Ethical and Legal Philosophy, and while none of them are responsible for any of the arguments in this book, they have collectively had a great deal to do with the writing of it. I am especially grateful to Judith Jarvis Thompson, who read the entire manuscript and made many valuable suggestions. With Robert Nozick I have quarreled amicably about some of the hardest issues in the theory of war and his arguments, hypothetical cases, queries, and proposals helped me shape my own presentation.

My friend and colleague Robert Amdur read most of the chapters and he often forced me to think about them again. Marvin Kohl and Judith Walzer read portions of the manuscript; their comments on matters of style and substance have often been incorporated into my pages. I am grateful also to Philip Green, Yehuda Melzer, Miles Morgan, and John Schrecker.

During a quarter at Stanford University and for several years at Harvard, I taught a course on the just war, and learned while I was teaching—from colleagues and students alike. I will always be glad of the cooling skepticism of Stanley Hoffmann and Judith Shklar. I also benefited from the comments and criticisms of Charles Bahmueller, Donald Goldstein, Miles Kahler, Sanford Levinson, Dan Little, Gerald McElroy, and David Pollack.

Martin Kessler of Basic Books conceived this book almost before I did, and has assisted and encouraged me at every stage of the writing of it.

When I was almost finished, Betty Butterfield undertook to type the final draft and set an astonishing pace, both for herself and for me; without her the completion of the book would have taken much longer than it did.

An early version of chapter 12, on terrorism, appeared in *The New Republic* in 1975. In chapters 4 and 16 I have drawn upon arguments first developed in *Philosophy and Public Affairs* in 1972. In chapters 14 and 15, I have used portions of an article published in 1974 in the Israeli philosophical quarterly *Iyyun*. I am grateful to the editors of the three journals for permission to reprint these materials.

I am grateful to the various publishers who have kindly permitted me to reprint material which first appeared under their auspices:

Rolf Hochhuth, "Little London Theater of the World/ Garden," lines 38-40, in *Soldiers: An Obituary for Geneva*. Copyright © 1968 by Grove Press, Inc. Reprinted by permission of Grove Press, Inc.

Randall Jarrell, "The Death of the Ball Turret Gunner," line 1, copyright © 1945 by Randall Jarrell. Renewed copyright © 1972 by Mrs. Randall Jarrell; and "The Range in the Desert," lines 21-24, copyright © 1947 by Randall Jarrell. Renewed copyright © 1974 by Mrs. Randall Jarrell. Both appeared in *The Complete Poems*. Reprinted by permission of Farrar, Strauss & Giroux, Inc.

Stanley Kunitz, "Foreign Affairs," lines 10-17, in *Selected Poems. 1928-1958*. Copyright © 1958 by Stanley Kunitz. This poem originally appeared in *The New Yorker*. Reprinted by permission of Little, Brown and Company in association with the Atlantic Monthly Press.

Wilfred Owen, "Anthem for Doomed Youth," line 1, and "A Terre," line 6, in *The Collected Poems of Wilfred Owen*, edited by C. Day Lewis. Reprinted by permission of the Owen Estate and Chatto and Windus Ltd. and New Directions Publishing Corporation.

Gillo Pontecoro, *The Battle of Algiers*, edited and with an introduction by PierNico Solinas. Scene 68, pages 79-80. Reprinted by permission of Charles Scribner's Sons.

Louis Simpson, "The Ash and the Oak" in *Good News of Death and Other Poems. Poets of Today II*. Copyright © 1955 by Louis Simpson. Reprinted by permission of Charles Scribner's Sons.

PART ONE

THE MORAL

REALITY OF WAR

1

Against "Realism"

For as long as men and women have talked about war, they have talked about it in terms of right and wrong. And for almost as long, some among them have derided such talk, called it a charade, insisted that war lies beyond (or beneath) moral judgment. War is a world apart, where life itself is at stake, where human nature is reduced to its elemental forms, where self-interest and necessity prevail. Here men and women do what they must to save themselves and their communities, and morality and law have no place. *Inter arma silent leges*: in time of war the law is silent.

Sometimes this silence is extended to other forms of competitive activity, as in the popular proverb, "All's fair in love and war." That means that anything goes—any kind of deceit in love, any kind of violence in war. We can neither praise nor blame; there is nothing to say. And yet we are rarely silent. The language we use to talk about love and war is so rich with moral meaning that it could hardly have been developed except through centuries of argument. Faithfulness, devotion, chastity, shame, adultery, seduction, betrayal; aggression, self-defense, appeasement, cruelty, ruthlessness, atrocity, massacre—all these words are judgments, and judging is as common a human activity as loving or fighting.

It is true, however, that we often lack the courage of our judgments, and especially so in the case of military conflict. The moral posture of mankind is not well represented by that popular proverb about love and war. We would do better to mark a contrast rather than a similarity: before Venus, censorious; before Mars, timid.

3

Not that we don't justify or condemn particular attacks, but we do so hesitantly and uncertainly (or loudly and recklessly), as if we were not sure that our judgments reach to the reality of war.

The Realist Argument

Realism is the issue. The defenders of *silent leges* claim to have discovered an awful truth: what we conventionally call inhumanity is simply humanity under pressure. War strips away our civilized adornments and reveals our nakedness. They describe that nakedness for us, not without a certain relish: fearful, self-concerned, driven, murderous. They aren't wrong in any simple sense. The words are sometimes descriptive. Paradoxically, the description is often a kind of apology: yes, our soldiers committed atrocities in the course of the battle, but that's what war does to people, that's what war is like. The proverb, all's fair, is invoked in defense of conduct that appears to be unfair. And one urges silence on the law when one is engaged in activities that would otherwise be called unlawful. So there are arguments here that will enter into my own argument: justifications and excuses, references to necessity and duress, that we can recognize as forms of moral discourse and that have or don't have force in particular cases. But there is also a general account of war as a realm of necessity and duress, the purpose of which is to make discourse about particular cases appear to be idle chatter, a mask of noise with which we conceal, even from ourselves, the awful truth. It is that general account that I have to challenge before I can begin my own work, and I want to challenge it at its source and in its most compelling form, as it is put forward by the historian Thucydides and the philosopher Thomas Hobbes. These two men, separated by 2,000 years, are collaborators of a kind, for Hobbes translated Thucydides' *History of the Peloponnesian War* and then generalized its argument in his own *Leviathan*. It is not my purpose here to write a full philosophical response to Thucydides and Hobbes. I wish only to suggest, first by argument and then by example, that the judgment of war and of wartime conduct is a serious enterprise.

Against "Realism"

The Melian Dialogue

The dialogue between the Athenian generals Cleomedes and Tisias and the magistrates of the island state of Melos is one of the high points of Thucydides' *History* and the climax of his realism. Melos was a Spartan colony, and its people had "therefore refused to be subject, as the rest of the islands were, unto the Athenians; but rested at first neutral; and afterwards, when the Athenians put them to it by wasting of their lands, they entered into open war."[1] This is a classic account of aggression, for to commit aggression is simply to "put people to it" as Thucydides describes. But such a description, he seems to say, is merely external; he wants to show us the inner meaning of war. His spokesmen are the two Athenian generals, who demand a parley and then speak as generals have rarely done in military history. Let us have no fine words about justice, they say. We for our part will not pretend that, having defeated the Persians, our empire is deserved; you must not claim that having done no injury to the Athenian people, you have a right to be let alone. We will talk instead of what is feasible and what is necessary. For this is what war is really like: "they that have odds of power exact as much as they can, and the weak yield to such conditions as they can get."

It is not only the Melians here who bear the burdens of necessity. The Athenians are driven, too; they must expand their empire, Cleomedes and Tisias believe, or lose what they already have. The neutrality of Melos "will be an argument of our weakness, and your hatred of our power, among those we have rule over." It will inspire rebellion throughout the islands, wherever men and women are "offended with the necessity of subjection"—and what subject is not offended, eager for freedom, resentful of his conquerors? When the Athenian generals say that men "will everywhere reign over such as they be too strong for," they are not only describing the desire for glory and command, but also the more narrow necessity of inter-state politics: reign or be subject. If they do not conquer when they can, they only reveal weakness and invite attack; and so, "by a necessity of nature" (a phrase Hobbes later made his own), they conquer when they can.

The Melians, on the other hand, are too weak to conquer. They face a harsher necessity: yield or be destroyed. "For you have not in hand a match of valor upon equal terms . . . but rather a consultation upon your safety . . ." The rulers of Melos, however, value freedom above safety: "If you then to retain your command, and your vassals to get loose from you, will undergo the utmost danger: would it not in us, that be already free, be great baseness and cowardice, if we should not encounter anything whatsoever rather than suffer ourselves to be brought into bondage?" Though they know that it will be a "hard matter" to stand against the power and fortune of Athens, "nevertheless we believe that, for fortune, we shall be nothing inferior, as having the gods on our side, because we stand innocent against men unjust." And as for power, they hope for assistance from the Spartans, "who are of necessity obliged, if for no other cause, yet for consanguinity's sake and for their own honor to defend us." But the gods, too, reign where they can, reply the Athenian generals, and consanguinity and honor have nothing to do with necessity. The Spartans will (necessarily) think only of themselves: "most apparently of all men, they hold for honorable that which pleaseth and for just that which profiteth."

So the argument ended. The magistrates refused to surrender; the Athenians laid siege to their city; the Spartans sent no help. Finally, after some months of fighting, in the winter of 416 B.C., Melos was betrayed by several of its citizens. When further resistance seemed impossible, the Melians "yielded themselves to the discretion of the Athenians: who slew all the men of military age, made slaves of the women and children; and inhabited the place with a colony sent thither afterwards of 500 men of their own."

The dialogue between the generals and the magistrates is a literary and philosophical construction of Thucydides. The magistrates speak as they well might have done, but their conventional piety and heroism is only a foil to what the classical critic Dionysius calls the "depraved shrewdness" of the Athenian generals.[2] It is the generals who have often seemed unbelievable. Their words, writes Dionysius, "were appropriate to oriental monarchs . . . but unfit to be spoken by Athenians . . ."* Perhaps Thucydides means us to notice the unfitness, not so much of the words but of the policies

---

* Even oriental monarchs are not quite so toughminded as the Athenian generals. According to Herodotus, when Xerxes first disclosed his plans for an invasion of Greece, he spoke in more conventional terms: "I will bridge the Hellespont and march an army through Europe into Greece, and punish the Athenians for the outrage they committed upon my father and upon us." (*The Histories*, Book 7, trans. Aubrey de Selincourt) The reference is to the burning of Sardis, which we may take as the pretext for the Persian invasion. The example bears out Francis Bacon's assertion that "there is that justice imprinted in the nature of men that they enter not upon wars (whereof so many calamities do ensue) but upon some, at least specious, grounds and quarrels." (Essay 29, "Of the True Greatness of Kingdoms and Estates")

they were used to defend, and thinks we might have missed it had he permitted the generals to speak as they probably in fact spoke, weaving "fair pretenses" over their vile actions. We are to understand that Athens is no longer itself. Cleomedes and Tisias do not represent that noble people who fought the Persians in the name of freedom and whose politics and culture, as Dionysius says, "exercised such a humanizing influence on everyday life." They represent instead the imperial decadence of the city state. It is not that they are war criminals in the modern sense; that idea is alien to Thucydides. But they embody a certain loss of ethical balance, of restraint and moderation. Their statesmanship is flawed, and their "realistic" speeches provide an ironic contrast to the blindness and arrogance with which the Athenians only a few months later launched the disastrous expedition to Sicily. The *History,* on this view, is a tragedy and Athens itself the tragic hero.[3] Thucydides has given us a morality play in the Greek style. We can glimpse his meaning in Euripides' *The Trojan Women,* written in the immediate aftermath of the conquest of Melos and undoubtedly intended to suggest the human significance of slaughter and slavery —and to predict a divine retribution:[4]

> How ye are blind
> Ye treaders down of cities, ye that cast
> Temples to desolation, and lay waste
> Tombs, the untrodden sanctuaries where lie
> The ancient dead; yourselves so soon to die!

But Thucydides seems in fact to be making a rather different, and a more secular, statement than this quotation suggests, and not about Athens so much as about war itself. He probably did not mean the harshness of the Athenian generals to be taken as a sign of depravity, but rather as a sign of impatience, toughmindedness, honesty—qualities of mind not inappropriate in miltary commanders. He is arguing, as Werner Jaeger has said, that "the principle of force forms a realm of its own, with laws of its own," distinct and separate from the laws of moral life.[5] This is certainly the way Hobbes read Thucydides, and it is the reading with which we must come to grips. For if the realm of force is indeed distinct and if this is an accurate account of its laws, then one could no more criticize the Athenians for their wartime policies than one could criticize a stone for falling downwards. The slaughter of the Melians is explained by reference to the circumstances of war and the necessities of nature; and again, there is nothing to say. Or rather, one can *say* anything, call necessity cruel and war hellish; but while

7

these statements may be true in their own terms, they do not touch the political realities of the case or help us understand the Athenian decision.

It is important to stress, however, that Thucydides has told us nothing at all about the Athenian decision. And if we place ourselves, not in the council room at Melos where a cruel policy was being expounded, but in the assembly at Athens where that policy was first adopted, the argument of the generals has a very different ring. In the Greek as in the English language, the word *necessity* "doubles the parts of indispensable and inevitable."[6] At Melos, Cleomedes and Tisias mixed the two of these, stressing the last. In the assembly they could have argued only about the first, claiming, I suppose, that the destruction of Melos was necessary (indispensable) for the preservation of the empire. But this claim is rhetorical in two senses. First, it evades the moral question of whether the preservation of the empire was itself necessary. There were some Athenians, at least, who had doubts about that, and more who doubted that the empire had to be a uniform system of domination and subjection (as the policy adopted for Melos suggested). Secondly, it exaggerates the knowledge and foresight of the generals. They are not saying with certainty that Athens will fall unless Melos is destroyed; their argument has to do with probabilities and risks. And such arguments are always arguable. Would the destruction of Melos really reduce Athenian risks? Are there alternative policies? What are the likely costs of this one? Would it be right? What would other people think of Athens if it were carried out?

Once the debate begins, all sorts of moral and strategic questions are likely to come up. And for the participants in the debate, the outcome is not going to be determined "by a necessity of nature," but by the opinions they hold or come to hold as a result of the arguments they hear and then by the decisions they freely make, individually and collectively. Afterwards, the generals claim that a certain decision was inevitable; and that, presumably, is what Thucydides wants us to believe. But the claim can only be made afterwards, for inevitability here is mediated by a process of political deliberation, and Thucydides could not know what was inevitable until that process had been completed. Judgments of necessity in this sense are always retrospective in character—the work of historians, not historical actors.

Now, the moral point of view derives its legitimacy from the perspective of the actor. When we make moral judgments, we try to recapture that perspective. We reiterate the decision-making process, or we rehearse our own future decisions, asking what we would have done (or what we would do) in similar circumstances. The Athenian generals recognize the importance of such questions, for they defend their policy certain "that you likewise, and others that should have the same power which we have, would do the same." But that is a dubious knowledge, especially so once we realize that the "Melian decree" was sharply opposed in the Athenian assembly. Our standpoint is that of citizens debating the decree. What *should* we do?

We have no account of the Athenian decision to attack Melos or of the decision (which may have been taken at the same time) to kill and enslave its people. Plutarch claims that it was Alcibiades, chief architect of the Sicilian expedition, who was "the principal cause of the slaughter . . . having spoken in favor of the decree."[7] He played the part of Cleon in the debate that Thucydides does record, that occured some years earlier, over the fate of Mytilene. It is worth glancing back at that earlier argument. Mytilene had been an ally of Athens from the time of the Persian War; it was never a subject city in any formal way, but bound by treaty to the Athenian cause. In 428, it rebelled and formed an alliance with the Spartans. After considerable fighting, the city was captured by Athenian forces, and the assembly determined "to put to death . . . all the men of Mytilene that were of age, and to make slaves of the women and children: laying to their charge the revolt itself, in that they revolted not being in subjection as others were . . ."[8] But the following day the citizens "felt a kind of repentance . . . and began to consider what a great and cruel decree it was, that not the authors only, but that the whole city should be destroyed." It is this second debate that Thucydides has recorded, or some part of it, giving us two speeches, that of Cleon upholding the original decree and that of Diodotus urging its revocation. Cleon argues largely in terms of collective guilt and retributive justice; Diodotus offers a critique of the deterrent effects of capital punishment. The assembly accepts Diodotus' position, convinced apparently that the destruction of Mytilene would not uphold the force of treaties or ensure the stability of the empire. It is the appeal to interest that triumphs—as has often been pointed out—though it should be remembered that the occasion for the appeal was the repentance of the citizens. Moral anxiety, not political calculation, leads them to worry about the effectiveness of their decree.

In the debate over Melos, the positions must have been reversed. Now there was no retributivist argument to make, for the Melians had done Athens no injury. Alcibiades probably talked like Thucydides' generals, though with the all-important difference I have already noted. When he told his fellow citizens that the decree was necessary, he didn't mean that it was ordained by the laws that govern the realm of force; he meant merely that it was needed (in his view) to reduce the risks of rebellion among the subject cities of the Athenian empire. And his opponents probably argued, like the Melians, that the decree was dishonorable and unjust and would more likely excite resentment than fear throughout the islands, that Melos did not threaten Athens in any way, and that other policies would serve Athenian interests and Athenian self-esteem. Perhaps they also reminded the citizens of their repentance in the case of Mytilene and urged them once again to avoid the cruelty of massacre and enslavement. How Alcibiades won out, and how close the vote was, we don't know. But there is no reason to think that the decision was predetermined and debate of no avail: no more with Melos than with Mytilene. Stand in imagination in the Athenian assembly, and one can still feel a sense of freedom.

But the realism of the Athenian generals has a further thrust. It is not only a denial of the freedom that makes moral decision possible; it is a denial also of the meaningfulness of moral argument. The second claim is closely related to the first. If we must act in accordance with our interests, driven by our fears of one another, then talk about justice cannot possibly be anything more than talk. It refers to no purposes that we can make our own and to no goals that we can share with others. That is why the Athenian generals could have woven "fair pretenses" as easily as the Melian magistrates; in discourse of this sort anything can be said. The words have no clear references, no certain definitions, no logical entailments. They are, as Hobbes writes in *Leviathan*, "ever used with relation to the person that useth them," and they express that person's appetites and fears and nothing else. It is only "most apparent" in the Spartans, but true for everyone, that "they hold for honorable that which pleaseth them and for just that which profiteth." Or, as Hobbes later explained, the names of the virtues and vices are of "uncertain signification."[9]

> For one calleth wisdom, what another calleth fear; and one cruelty what another justice; one prodigality, what another magnanimity . . . etc. And therefore such names can never be true grounds of any ratiocination.

"*Never*"—until the sovereign, who is also the supreme linguistic authority, fixes the meaning of the moral vocabulary; but in the state of war, *"never"* without qualification, because in that state, by definition, no sovereign rules. In fact, even in civil society, the sovereign does not entirely succeed in bringing certainty into the world of virtue and vice. Hence moral discourse is always suspect, and war is only an extreme case of the anarchy of moral meanings. It is generally true, but especially so in time of violent conflict, that we can understand what other people are saying only if we see through their "fair pretenses" and translate moral talk into the harder currency of interest talk. When the Melians insist that their cause is just, they are saying only that they don't want to be subject; and had the generals claimed that Athens deserved its empire, they would simply have been expressing the lust for conquest or the fear of overthrow.

This is a powerful argument because it plays upon the common experience of moral disagreement—painful, sustained, exasperating, and endless. For all its realism, however, it fails to get at the realities of that experience or to explain its character. We can see this clearly, I think, if we look again at the argument over the Mytilene decree. Hobbes may well have had this debate in mind when he wrote, "and one [calleth] cruelty what another justice . . ." The Athenians repented of their cruelty, writes Thucydides, while Cleon told them that they had not been cruel at all but justly severe. Yet this was in no sense a disagreement over the meaning of words. Had there been no common meanings, there could have been no debate at all. The cruelty of the Athenians consisted in seeking to punish not only the authors of the rebellion but others as well, and Cleon agreed that that would indeed be cruel. He then went on to argue, as he had to do given his position, that in Mytilene there were no "others." "Let not the fault be laid upon a few, and the people absolved. For they have all alike taken arms against us . . ."

I cannot pursue the argument further, since Thucydides doesn't, but there is an obvious rejoinder to Cleon, having to do with the status of the women and children of Mytilene. This might involve the deployment of additional moral terms (innocence, for example); but it would not hang—any more than the argument about cruelty and justice hangs—on idiosyncratic definitions. In fact, definitions are not at issue here, but descriptions and interpretations. The Athenians shared a moral vocabulary, shared it with the people of Mytilene and Melos; and allowing for cultural differences, they share it with us too. They had no difficulty, and we have none, in understanding the claim of the Melian magistrates that the invasion of their island was unjust. It is in applying the agreed-upon words to actual cases that we come to disagree. These disagreements are in part generated and always compounded by antagonistic interests and mutual fears. But they have other causes, too, which help to explain the complex and disparate ways in which men and women (even when they have similar interests and no reason to fear one another) position themselves in the moral world. There are, first of all, serious difficulties of perception and information (in war and politics generally), and so controversies arise over "the facts of the case." There are sharp disparities in the weight we attach even to values we share, as there are in the actions we are ready to condone when these values are threatened. There are conflicting commitments and obligations that force us into violent antagonism even when we see the point of one another's positions. All this is real enough, and common enough: it makes morality into a world of good-faith quarrels as well as a world of ideology and verbal manipulation.

In any case, the possibilities for manipulation are limited. Whether or not people speak in good faith, they cannot say just anything they please. Moral talk is coercive; one thing leads to another. Perhaps that's why the Athenian generals did not want to begin. A war called unjust is not, to paraphrase Hobbes, a war misliked; it is a war misliked for particular reasons, and anyone making the charge is required to provide particular sorts of evidence. Similarly, if I claim that I am fighting justly, I must also claim that I was attacked ("put to it," as the Melians were), or threatened with attack, or that I am coming to the aid of a victim of someone else's attack. And each of these claims has its own entailments, leading me deeper and deeper into a world of discourse where, though I can go on talking indefinitely, I am severely constrained in what I can say. I must say this or that, and at many points in a long argument this or that will be true or false. We don't have to translate moral talk into interest talk in order to understand it; morality refers in its own way to the real world.

Let us consider a Hobbist example. In Chapter XXI of *Leviathan*, Hobbes urges that we make allowance for the "natural timorousness" of mankind. "When armies fight, there is on one side, or both a running away; yet when they do it not out of treachery, but fear, they are not esteemed to do it unjustly, but dishonorably." Now, judgments are called for here: we are to distinguish cowards from traitors. If these are words of "inconstant signification," the task is impossible and absurd. Every traitor would plead natural timorousness, and we would accept the plea or not depending on whether the soldier was a friend or an enemy, an obstacle to our advancement or an ally and supporter. I suppose we sometimes do behave that way, but it is not the case (nor does Hobbes, when it comes to cases, suppose that it is) that the judgments we make can only be understood in these terms. When we charge a man with treason, we have to tell a very special kind of story about him, and we have to provide concrete evidence that the story is true. If we call him a traitor when we cannot tell that story, we are not using words inconstantly, we are simply lying.

Strategy and Morality

Morality and justice are talked about in much the same way as military strategy. Strategy is the other language of war, and while it is commonly said to be free from the difficulties of moral discourse, its use is equally problematic. Though generals agree on the meaning of strategic terms—entrapment, retreat, flanking maneuver, concentration of forces, and so on—they nevertheless disagree about strategically appropriate courses of action. They argue about what ought to be done. After the battle, they disagree about what happened, and if they were defeated, they argue about who was to blame. Strategy, like morality, is a language of justification.* Every confused and cowardly commander describes his hesitations and panics as part of an elaborate plan; the strategic vocabulary is as available to him as it is to a competent commander. But that is not to say that its terms are meaningless. It would be a great triumph

---

* Hence we can "unmask" strategic discourse just as Thucydides did with moral discourse. Imagine that the two Athenian generals, after their dialogue with the Melians, return to their camp to plan the coming battle. The senior in command speaks first: "Don't give me any fine talk about the need to concentrate our forces or the importance of strategic surprise. We'll simply call for a frontal assault; the men will organize themselves as best they can; things are going to be confused anyway. I need a quick victory here, so that I can return to Athens covered with glory before the debate on the Sicilian campaign begins. We'll have to accept some risks; but that doesn't matter since the risks will be yours, not mine. If we are beaten, I'll contrive to blame you. That's what war is like." Why is strategy the language of hard-headed men? One sees through it so easily . . .

for the incompetent if they were, for we would then have no way to talk about incompetence. No doubt, "one calleth retreat what another calleth strategic redeployment . . ." But we do know the difference between these two, and though the facts of the case may be difficult to collect and interpret, we are nevertheless able to make critical judgments.

Similarly, we can make moral judgments: moral concepts and strategic concepts reflect the real world in the same way. They are not merely normative terms, telling soldiers (who often don't listen) what to do. They are descriptive terms, and without them we would have no coherent way of talking about war. Here are soldiers moving away from the scene of a battle, marching over the same ground they marched over yesterday, but fewer now, less eager, many without weapons, many wounded: we call this a retreat. Here are soldiers lining up the inhabitants of a peasant village, men, women, and children, and shooting them down: we call this a massacre.

It is only when their substantive content is fairly clear that moral and strategic terms can be used imperatively, and the wisdom they embody expressed in the form of rules. Never refuse quarter to a soldier trying to surrender. Never advance with your flanks unprotected. One might construct out of such commands a moral or a strategic war plan, and then it would be important to notice whether or not the actual conduct of the war conformed to the plan. We can assume that it would not. War is recalcitrant to this sort of theoretical control—a quality it shares with every other human activity, but which it seems to possess to an especially intense degree. In *The Charterhouse of Parma*, Stendhal provides a description of the battle of Waterloo that is intended to mock the very idea of a strategic plan. It is an account of combat as chaos, therefore not an account at all but a denial, so to speak, that combat is accountable. It should be read alongside some strategic analysis of Waterloo like that of Major General Fuller, who views the battle as an organized series of maneuvers and counter-maneuvers.[10] The strategist is not unaware of confusion and disorder in the field; nor is he entirely unwilling to see these as aspects of war itself, the natural effects of the stress of battle. But he sees them also as matters of command responsibility, failures of discipline or control. He suggests that strategic imperatives have been ignored; he looks for lessons to be learned.

The moral theorist is in the same position. He too must come to grips with the fact that his rules are often violated or ignored—and with the deeper realization that, to men at war, the rules often don't seem relevant to the extremity of their situation. But however he does this, he does not surrender his sense of war as a human action, purposive and premeditated, for whose effects someone is responsible. Confronted with the many crimes committed in the course of a war, or with the crime of aggressive war itself, he searches for human agents. Nor is he alone in this search. It is one of the most important features of war, distinguishing it from the other scourges of mankind, that the men and women caught up in it are not only victims, they are also participants. All of us are inclined to hold them responsible for what they do (though we may recognize the plea of duress in particular cases). Reiterated over time, our arguments and judgments shape what I want to call *the moral reality of war*—that is, all those experiences of which moral language is descriptive or within which it is necessarily employed.

It is important to stress that the moral reality of war is not fixed by the actual activities of soldiers but by the opinions of mankind. That means, in part, that it is fixed by the activity of philosophers, lawyers, publicists of all sorts. But these people don't work in isolation from the experience of combat, and their views have value only insofar as they give shape and structure to that experience in ways that are plausible to the rest of us. We often say, for example, that in time of war soldiers and statesmen must make agonizing decisions. The pain is real enough, but it is not one of the natural effects of combat. Agony is not like Hobbist fear; it is entirely the product of our moral views, and it is common in war only insofar as those views are common. It was not some unusual Athenian who "repented" of the decision to kill the men of Mytilene, but the citizens generally. They repented, and they were able to understand one another's repentance, because they shared a sense of what cruelty meant. It is by the assignment of such meanings that we make war what it is—which is to say that it could be (and it probably has been) something different.

What of a soldier or statesman who does not feel the agony? We say of him that he is morally ignorant or morally insensitive, much as we might say of a general who experienced no difficulty making a (really) difficult decision that he did not understand the strategic realities of his own position or that he was reckless and insensible of danger. And we might go on to argue, in the case of the general, that such a man has no business fighting or leading others in battle, that he ought to know that his army's right flank, say, is vulnerable, and ought to worry about the danger and take steps to avoid it. Once again, the case is the same with moral decisions: soldiers and statesmen ought to know the dangers of cruelty and injustice and worry about them and take steps to avoid them.

Historical Relativism

Against this view, however, Hobbist relativism is often given a social or historical form: moral and strategic knowledge, it is said, changes over time or varies among political communities, and so what appears to me as ignorance may look like understanding to someone else. Now, change and variation are certainly real enough, and they make for a tale that is complex in the telling. But the importance of that tale for ordinary moral life and, above all, for the judgment of moral conduct is easily exaggerated. Between radically separate and dissimilar cultures, one can expect to find radical dichotomies in perception and understanding. No doubt the moral reality of war is not the same for us as it was for Genghis Khan; nor is the strategic reality. But even fundamental social and political transformations within a particular culture may well leave the moral world intact or at least sufficiently whole so that we can still be said to share it with our ancestors. It is rare indeed that we do not share it with our contemporaries, and by and large we learn how to act among our contemporaries by studying the actions of those who have preceded us. The assumption of that study is that they saw the world much as we do. That is not always true, but it is true enough of the time to give stability and coherence to our moral lives (and to our military lives). Even when world views and high ideals have been abandoned—as the glorification of aristocratic chivalry was abandoned in early modern times—notions about right conduct are remarkably persistent: the military code survives the death of warrior idealism. I shall say more about this survival later on, but I can demonstrate it now in a general way by looking at an example from feudal Europe, an age in some ways more distant from us than Greece of the city states, but with which we nevertheless share moral and strategic perceptions.

Against "Realism"

Three Accounts of Agincourt

Actually, the sharing of strategic perceptions is in this case the more dubious of the two. Those French knights so many of whom died at Agincourt had notions about combat very different from our own. Modern critics have still felt able to criticize their "fanatical adherence to the old method of fighting" (King Henry, after all, fought differently) and even to offer practical suggestions: the French attack, writes Oman, "should have been accompanied by a turning movement around the woods . . ."[11] Had he not been "overconfident," the French commander would have seen the advantages of the move. We can talk in a similar way about the crucial moral decision that Henry made toward the end of the battle, when the English thought their victory secure. They had taken many prisoners, who were loosely assembled behind the lines. Suddenly, a French attack aimed at the supply tents far in the rear seemed to threaten a renewal of the fighting. Here is Holinshed's sixteenth century account of the incident (virtually copied from an earlier chronicle):[12]

> . . . certain Frenchmen on horseback . . . to the number of six hundred horsemen, which were the first that fled, hearing that the English tents and pavilions were a good way distant from the army, without any sufficient guard to defend the same . . . entered upon the king's camp and there . . . robbed the tents, broke up chests, and carried away caskets and slew such servants as they found to make any resistance. . . . But when the outcry of the lackeys and boys which ran away for fear of the Frenchmen . . . came to the king's ears, he doubting lest his enemies should gather together again, and begin a new field; and mistrusting further that the prisoners would be an aid to his enemies . . . contrary to his accustomed gentleness, commanded by sound of trumpet that every man . . . should incontinently slay his prisoner.

The moral character of the command is suggested by the words "accustomed gentleness" and "incontinently." It involved a shattering of personal and conventional restraints (the latter well-established by 1415), and Holinshed goes to some lengths to explain and excuse it, stressing the king's fear that the prisoners his forces held were about to rejoin the fighting. Shakespeare, whose *Henry V* closely follows Holinshed, goes further, emphasizing the slaying of the English servants by the French and omitting the chronicler's assertion that only those who resisted were killed:[13]

> *Fluellen.* Kill the [b]oys and the baggage! 'Tis expressly against the
> law of arms. 'Tis as arrant a piece of knavery, mark you now, as
> can be offert.

At the same time, however, he cannot resist an ironical comment:

> *Gower.* . . . they have burned and carried away all that was in the
> king's tent, wherefore the king most worthily hath caused every
> soldier to cut his prisoner's throat. O, 'tis a gallant king!

A century and a half later, David Hume gives a similar account,
without the irony, stressing instead the king's eventual cancellation
of his order:[14]

> . . . some gentlemen of Picardy . . . had fallen upon the English
> baggage, and were doing execution on the unarmed followers of
> the camp, who fled before them. Henry, seeing the enemy on all
> sides of him, began to entertain apprehensions from his prisoners;
> and he thought it necessary to issue a general order for putting them
> to death; but on discovering the truth, he stopped the slaughter, and
> was still able to save a great number.

Here the moral meaning is caught in the tension between "necessary" and "slaughter." Since slaughter is the killing of men as if
they were animals—it "makes a massacre," wrote the poet Dryden,
"what was a war"—it cannot often be called necessary. If the
prisoners were so easy to kill, they were probably not dangerous
enough to warrant the killing. When he grasped the actual situation, Henry, who was (so Hume wants us to believe) a moral man,
called off the executions.

French chroniclers and historians write of the event in much the
same way. It is from them that we learn that many of the English
knights refused to kill their prisoners—not, chiefly, out of humanity,
rather for the sake of the ransom they expected; but also "thinking of the dishonor that the horrible executions would reflect on
themselves."[15] English writers have focused more, and more wor-
riedly, on the command of the king; he was, after all, their king. In
the later nineteenth century, at about the same time as the rules
of war with respect to prisoners were being codified, their criticism
grew increasingly sharp: "a brutal butchery," "cold-blooded wholesale murder."[16] Hume would not have said that, but the difference
between that and what he did say is marginal, not a matter of
moral or linguistic transformation.

To judge Henry ourselves we would need a more circumstantial
account of the battle than I can provide here.[17] Even given that
account, our opinions might differ, depending on the allowance we

were willing to make for the stress and excitement of battle. But this is a clear example of a situation common in both strategy and morality, where our sharpest disagreements are structured and organized by our underlying agreements, by the meanings we share. For Holinshed, Shakespeare, and Hume—traditional chronicler, Renaissance playwright, and Enlightenment historian—and for us too, Henry's command belongs to a category of military acts that requires scrutiny and judgment. It is *as a matter of fact* morally problematic, because it accepts the risks of cruelty and injustice. In exactly the same way, we might regard the battle plan of the French commander as strategically problematic, because it accepted the risks of a frontal assault on a prepared position. And, again, a general who did not recognize these risks is properly said to be ignorant of morality or strategy.

In moral life, ignorance isn't all that common; dishonesty is far more so. Even those soldiers and statesmen who don't feel the agony of a problematic decision generally know that they should feel it. Harry Truman's flat statement that he never lost a night's sleep over his decision to drop the atomic bomb on Hiroshima is not the sort of thing political leaders often say. They usually find it preferable to stress the painfulness of decision-making; it is one of the burdens of office, and it is best if the burdens appear to be borne. I suspect that many officeholders even experience pain simply because they are expected to. If they don't, they lie about it. The clearest evidence for the stability of our values over time is the unchanging character of the lies soldiers and statesmen tell. They lie in order to justify themselves, and so they describe for us the lineaments of justice. Wherever we find hypocrisy, we also find moral knowledge. The hypocrite is like that Russian general in Solzhenitsyn's *August 1914*, whose elaborate battle reports barely concealed his total inability to control or direct the battle. He knew at least that there was a story to tell, a set of names to attach to things and happenings, so he tried to tell the story and attach the names. His effort was not mere mimicry; it was, so to speak, the tribute that incompetence pays to understanding. The case is the same in moral life: there really is a story to tell, a way of talking about wars and battles that the rest of us recognize as morally appropriate. I don't mean that particular decisions are necessarily right or wrong, or simply right or wrong, only that there is a way of seeing the world so that moral decision-making makes sense. The hypocrite knows that this is true, though he may actually see the world differently.

Hypocrisy is rife in wartime discourse, because it is especially important at such a time to appear to be in the right. It is not only that the moral stakes are high; the hypocrite may not understand that; more crucially, his actions will be judged by other people, who are not hypocrites, and whose judgments will affect their policies toward him. There would be no point to hypocrisy if this were not so, just as there would be no point to lying in a world where no one told the truth. The hypocrite presumes on the moral understanding of the rest of us, and we have no choice, I think, except to take his assertions seriously and put them to the test of moral realism. He pretends to think and act as the rest of us expect him to do. He tells us that he is fighting according to the moral war plan: he does not aim at civilians, he grants quarter to soldiers trying to surrender, he never tortures prisoners, and so on. These claims are true or false, and though it is not easy to judge them (nor is the war plan really so simple), it is important to make the effort. Indeed, if we call ourselves moral men and women, we must make the effort, and the evidence is that we regularly do so. If we had all become realists like the Athenian generals or like Hobbists in a state of war, there would be an end alike to both morality and hypocrisy. We would simply tell one another, brutally and directly, what we wanted to do or have done. But the truth is that one of the things most of us want, even in war, is to act or to seem to act morally. And we want that, most simply, because we know what morality means (at least, we know what it is generally thought to mean).

It is that meaning that I want to explore in this book—not so much its general character, but its detailed application to the conduct of war. I am going to assume throughout that we really do act within a moral world; that particular decisions really are difficult, problematic, agonizing, and that this has to do with the structure of that world; that language reflects the moral world and gives us access to it; and finally that our understanding of the moral vocabulary is sufficiently common and stable so that shared judgments are possible. Perhaps there are other worlds to whose inhabitants the arguments I am going to make would seem incomprehensible and bizarre. But no such people are likely to read this book. And if my own readers find my arguments incomprehensible and bizarre, that will not be because of the impossibility of moral discourse or the inconstant signification of the words I use, but because of my own failure to grasp and expound our common morality.

2

The Crime of War

The moral reality of war is divided into two parts. War is always judged twice, first with reference to the reasons states have for fighting, secondly with reference to the means they adopt. The first kind of judgment is adjectival in character: we say that a particular war is just or unjust. The second is adverbial: we say that the war is being fought justly or unjustly. Medieval writers made the difference a matter of prepositions, distinguishing *jus ad bellum*, the justice of war, from *jus in bello*, justice in war. These grammatical distinctions point to deep issues. *Jus ad bellum* requires us to make judgments about aggression and self-defense; *jus in bello* about the observance or violation of the customary and positive rules of engagement. The two sorts of judgment are logically independent. It is perfectly possible for a just war to be fought unjustly and for an unjust war to be fought in strict accordance with the rules. But this independence, though our views of particular wars often conform to its terms, is nevertheless puzzling. It is a crime to commit aggression, but aggressive war is a rule-governed activity. It is right to resist aggression, but the resistance is subject to moral (and legal) restraint. The dualism of *jus ad bellum* and *jus in bello* is at the heart of all that is most problematic in the moral reality of war.

It is my purpose to see war whole, but since its dualism is the essential feature of its wholeness, I must begin by accounting for the parts. In this chapter, I want to suggest what we mean when we say that it is a crime to begin a war, and in the next I will try to explain why it is that there are rules of engagement that apply even to soldiers whose wars are criminal. This chapter introduces Part Two, where I will examine in detail the nature of the crime, describe the appropriate forms of resistance, and consider the ends that soldiers and statesmen may legitimately seek in fighting just wars. The next chapter introduces Part Three, where I will discuss the legitimate means of warfare, the substantive rules, and show how these rules apply in combat conditions and how they are modified by "military necessity." Only then will it be possible to confront the tension between ends and means, *jus ad bellum* and *jus in bello*.

I am not sure whether the moral reality of war is wholly coherent, but for the moment I need not say anything about that. It's enough that it has a recognizable and relatively stable shape, that its parts are connected and disconnected in recognizable and relatively stable ways. We have made it so, not arbitrarily, but for good reasons. It reflects our understanding of states and soldiers, the protagonists of war, and of combat, its central experience. The terms of that understanding are my immediate subject matter. They are simultaneously the historical product of and the necessary condition for the critical judgments that we make every day; they fix the nature of war as a moral (and an immoral) enterprise.

The Logic of War

Why is it wrong to begin a war? We know the answer all too well. People get killed, and often in large numbers. *War is hell.* But it is necessary to say more than that, for our ideas about war in general and about the conduct of soldiers depend very much on how people get killed and on who those people are. Then, perhaps, the best way to describe the crime of war is simply to say that there are no limits at either of these points: people are killed with every conceivable brutality, and all sorts of people, without distinction of age or sex or moral condition, are killed. This view of war is brilliantly summed up in the first chapter of Karl von Clausewitz's *On War*, and though there is no evidence that Clausewitz thought war a crime, he has certainly led other people to think so. It is his early definitions (rather than his later qualifications) that have shaped the ideas of his successors, and so it is worth considering them in some detail.

The Argument of Karl von Clausewitz

"War is an act of force," Clausewitz writes, ". . . which theoretically can have no limits."[1] The idea of war carries with it for him the idea of limitlessness, whatever actual restraints are observed in this or that society. If we imagine a war fought, as it were, in a social vacuum, unaffected by "accidental" factors, it would be fought with no restraint at all in the weapons used, the tactics adopted, the people attacked, or anywhere else. For military conduct knows no intrinsic limits; nor is it possible to refine our notions of war so as to incorporate those extrinsic moral codes that Clausewitz sometimes calls "philanthropic." "We can never introduce a modifying principle into the philosophy of war without committing an absurdity." The more extreme the battle is, then, the more general and intense the violence employed on one side and the other, the closer to war in the conceptual sense ("absolute war") it is. And there can be no imaginable act of violence, however treacherous or cruel, that falls outside of war, that is not-war, for the logic of war simply is a steady thrust toward moral extremity. That is why it is so awful (though Clausewitz does not tell us this) to set the process going: the aggressor is responsible for all the consequences of the fighting he begins. In particular cases, it may not be possible to know these consequences in advance, but they are always potentially terrible. "When you resorted to force," General Eisenhower once said, ". . . you didn't know where you were going . . . If you got deeper and deeper, there was just no limit except . . . the limitations of force itself."[2]

The logic of war, according to Clausewitz, works in this way: "each of the adversaries forces the hand of the other." What results is a "reciprocal action," a continuous escalation, in which neither side is guilty even if it acts first, since every act can be called and almost certainly is pre-emptive. "War tends toward the utmost exertion of forces," and that means toward increasing ruthlessness, since "the ruthless user of force who shrinks from no amount of bloodshed must gain an advantage if his opponent does not do the same."[3] And so his opponent, driven by what Thucydides and Hobbes call "a necessity of nature," does the same, matching the ruthlessness of the other side whenever he can. But this description, though it is a useful account of how escalation works, is open to the criticism that I have already made. As soon as we focus on some concrete case of military and moral decision-making, we enter a world that is governed not by abstract tendencies but by human choice. The actual pressures toward escalation are greater here, less there, rarely so overwhelming as to leave no room for maneuver. Wars no doubt are often escalated, but they are also (sometimes) fought at fairly steady levels of violence and brutality, and these levels are (sometimes) fairly low.

Clausewitz grants this, though without surrendering his commitment to the absolute. War, he writes, "may be a thing which is sometimes war in a greater, sometimes in a lesser degree." And again, "There can be wars of all degrees of importance and energy, from a war of extermination down to a mere state of armed observation."[4] Somewhere between these two, I suppose, we begin to say, all's fair, anything goes, and so on. When we talk that way, we are not referring to the general limitlessness of war, but to particular escalations, particular acts of force. No one has ever experienced "absolute war." In this or that struggle, we endure (or commit) this or that brutality, which can always be described in concrete terms. It is the same with hell: I cannot conceptualize infinite pain without thinking of whips and scorpions, hot irons, other people. Now, what is it that we think about when we say, war is hell? What aspects of warfare lead us to regard its initiation as a criminal act?

The same questions can be introduced in another way. War is not usefully described as an act of force without some specification of the context in which the act takes place and from which it derives its meaning. Here the case is the same as with other human activities (politics and commerce, for example): it's not what people do, the physical motions they go through, that are crucial, but the institutions, practices, conventions that they make. Hence the social and historical conditions that "modify" war are not to be considered as accidental or external to war itself, for war is a social creation. At particular points in time, it takes shape in particular ways, and sometimes at least in ways that resist the "utmost exertion of forces." What is war and what is not-war is in fact something that people decide (I don't mean by taking a vote). As both anthopological and historical accounts suggest, they can decide, and in a considerable variety of cultural settings they have decided, that war is limited war—that is, they have built certain notions about who can fight, what tactics are acceptable, when battle has to be broken off, and what prerogatives go with victory into the idea of war itself.* Limited war is always specific to a time and place, but so is every escalation, including the escalation beyond which war is hell.

The Limit of Consent

Some wars are not hell, and it will be best to begin with them. The first and most obvious example is the competitive struggle of aristocratic young men, a tournament on a larger scale and with no presiding officer in the stands. Examples can be found in Africa, ancient Greece, Japan, and feudal Europe. Here is a "contention by arms" that has often captured the imagination, not only of children, but also of romantic adults. John Ruskin made it his own ideal: "creative or foundational war is that in which the natural restlessness and love of contest are disciplined, by consent, into modes of beautiful—though it may be fatal—play . . ."[5] Creative war may not be terribly bloody, but that is not the crucial thing about it. I have read accounts of tournaments that make them sound brutal enough, but no such account would lead anyone to say that it was a crime to organize a tournament. What rules out such a claim, I think, is Ruskin's phrase "by consent." His beautiful aristocrats do what they choose to do, and that is why no poet ever described their deaths in terms comparable to those of Wilfred Owen writing of infantrymen in World War I:[6]

What passing-bells for these who die as cattle?

---

* This, of course, is exactly what Clausewitz wants to deny. In technical terms, he is arguing that war is never an activity constituted by its rules. War is never like a duel. The social practise of duelling includes and accounts for only those acts of violence specified in the rulebook or the customary code. If I wound my opponent, shoot his second, and then beat him to death with a stick, I am not duelling with him; I am murdering him. But similar brutalities in war, though they violate the rules, are still regarded as acts of war (war crimes). Hence there is a formal or linguistic sense in which military action is limitless, and this has undoubtedly influenced our understanding of such action. At the same time, however, "war" and related words are at least sometimes used in a more restrictive sense, as in the famous speech of Sir Henry Campbell-Bannerman, one of the leaders of the Liberal Party in Britain during the Boer War: "When is war not war? When it is fought by methods of barbarism . . ." We do still refer to the Boer War, but the argument is not idiosyncratic. I will provide other examples later on.

"To the youths who voluntarily adopt it as their profession," writes Ruskin, "[war] has always been a grand pastime . . ." We take their choice as a sign that what they are choosing cannot be awful, even if it looks that way to us. Perhaps they ennoble the brutal melee; perhaps not; but if this kind of war were hellish, these well-born young men would be doing something else.*

A similar argument can be made whenever fighting is voluntary. Nor does it matter a great deal if the men involved don't choose to fight, so long as they can choose to break off fighting without dire consequences. In certain primitive societies, whole age cohorts of young males go off to battle; individuals cannot avoid combat without exposing themselves to dishonor and ostracism. But there is no effective social pressure or military discipline on the battle-field itself. And then there takes place, as Hobbes says, "on both sides a running away."[7] When running away is acceptable, as it often is in primitive warfare, battles will obviously be short and casualties few. There is nothing that resembles "the utmost exertion of forces." Those men who don't run away, but stand and fight, do so not because of the necessities of their case, but freely, as a matter of choice. They seek out the excitement of battle, perhaps because they enjoy it, and their subsequent fate, even if it is very painful, can't be called unjust.

The case of mercenaries and professional soldiers is more complex and needs to be examined with some care. In Renaissance Italy, wars were fought by mercenary soldiers recruited by the great *condottieri*, partly as a business venture, partly as a political speculation. City-states and principalities had to rely on such men because the political culture of the time did not allow for effective coercion. There were no conscript armies. The result was warfare of a very limited sort, since recruits were expensive and each army represented a considerable capital investment. Battle became a matter largely of tactical maneuver; physical confrontation was rare; relatively few soldiers were killed. Wars had to be won, as two of the *condottieri* wrote, "rather by industry and cunning than by actual clash of arms."[8] Thus the great defeat of the Florentines at Zagonara: "no deaths occurred [in the battle]," Machiavelli tells us, "except those of Lodovico degli Obizi and two of his men, who, having fallen from their horses, were drowned in the mud."[9] But,

---

* We can glimpse the mood of the happy warrior in a letter that Rupert Brooke wrote to a friend at the very beginning of World War I, before he knew what it would be like: "Come and die. It'll be great fun." (Quoted in Malcolm Cowley, A Second Flowering, New York, 1974, p. 6.)

once again, I don't want to stress the limited character of the fighting but something prior to that, from which the limits follow: a certain sort of freedom in choosing war. Mercenary soldiers signed up on terms, and if they could not actually choose their campaigns and tactics, they could to some degree fix the cost of their services and so condition the choices of their leaders. Given that freedom, they might have fought very bloody battles and the spectacle would not lead us to say that war was a crime. A fight between mercenary armies is undoubtedly a bad way of settling political disputes, but we judge it bad for the sake of the people whose fate is being settled, not for the sake of the soldiers themselves.

Our judgments are very different, however, if the mercenary armies are recruited (as they most often are) from among desperately impoverished men, who can find no other way of feeding themselves and their families except by signing up. Ruskin makes this point well when he tells his aristocratic warriors: "Remember, whatever virtue and goodliness there may be in this game of war, rightly played, there is none when you . . . play it with a multitude of small human pawns . . . [when you] urge your peasant millions into gladitorial war . . ."[10] Then battle becomes a "circus of slaughter" in the midst of which no consensual discipline is possible, and those who die do so without ever having had a chance to live in another way. Hell is the right name for the risks they never chose and the agony and death they endure; the men responsible for that agony are rightly called criminals.

Mercenaries are professional soldiers who sell their services on the open market, but there are other professionals who serve only their own prince or people and, though they may earn their bread by soldiering, disdain the name of mercenary. "We're either officers who serve their Tsar and country," says Prince Andrey in *War and Peace*, "and rejoice in the success and grieve at the defeat of the common cause, or we're hirelings who have no interest in our master's business."[11] The distinction is too gross; in fact there are intermediate positions; but the more a soldier fights because he is committed to a "common cause," the more likely we are to regard it as a crime to force him to fight. We assume that his commitment is to the safety of his country, that he fights only when it is threatened, and that then he has to fight (he has been "put to it"): it is his duty and not a free choice. He is like a doctor who risks his life during an epidemic, using professional skills he chose to acquire but whose acquisition is not a sign that he hopes for epidemics. On the other hand, professional soldiers are sometimes exactly like those aristocratic warriors who relish battle, driven more by a lust for victory than by patriotic conviction, and then we may well be unmoved by their deaths. At least we will not say, they would not want us to say, what Owen says of his comrades in the trenches, that "one dies of war like any old disease."[12] They died instead of their own free will.

War is hell whenever men are forced to fight, whenever the limit of consent is breached. That means, of course, that it is hell most of the time; throughout most of recorded history, there have been political organizations capable of marshalling armies and driving soldiers into battle. It is the absence of political discipline or its ineffectiveness in detail that opens the way for "creative war." The examples I have given are best understood as limiting cases, establishing the boundaries of hell. We ourselves are old inhabitants—even if we live in democratic states where the government that decides to fight or not to fight is popularly elected. For I am not considering now the legitimacy of that government. Nor am I immediately interested in the willingness of a potential soldier to vote for a war he has been led to believe is necessary or to volunteer for it. What is important here is the extent to which war (as a profession) or combat (at this or that moment in time) is a personal choice that the soldier makes on his own and for essentially private reasons. That kind of choosing effectively disappears as soon as fighting becomes a legal obligation and a patriotic duty. Then "the waste of the life of the combatants is one which," as the philosopher T. H. Green has written, "the power of the state compels. This is equally true whether the army is raised by voluntary enlistment or by conscription."* For the state decrees that an army of a certain size be raised, and it sets out to find the necessary men, using all the techniques of coercion and persuasion at its disposal. And the men it finds, precisely because they go to war under constraint or as a matter of conscience, can no longer mod-

* Green is arguing against the proposition I have hitherto maintained: that no wrong is done in war if "the persons killed are voluntary combatants." He denies this on the grounds that a soldier's life is not merely his own. "The individual's right to life is but the other side of the right which society has in his living." But that, it seems to me, is only true in certain sorts of societies; it is hardly an argument that could have been made to a feudal warrior. Green goes on to argue, more plausibly, that in his own society it makes little sense to talk of soldiers fighting voluntarily: war is now a state action. The chapter on "The Right of the State over the Individual in War" in Green's *Principles of Political Obligation*, provides an especially clear description of the ways in which moral responsibility is mediated in the modern state; I have relied on it often in this and later chapters.

erate their battles; the battles are no longer theirs. They are political instruments, they obey orders, and the practice of war is shaped at a higher level. Perhaps they really are obligated to obey orders in this or that case, but war is radically changed by the fact that they do so generally. The change is best represented for the modern period (though there are historical analogues) by the effects of conscription. "Hitherto soldiers had been costly, now they were cheap; battles had been avoided, now they were sought, and however heavy were the losses, they could rapidly be made good by the muster-roll."[13]

Napoleon is said to have boasted to Metternich that he could afford to lose 30,000 men a month. Perhaps he could have lost that many and still have maintained political support at home. But he could not have done so, I think, had he had to ask the men he was about to "lose." Soldiers might agree to such losses in a war forced upon them by the enemy, a war of national defense, but not in the sorts of wars that Napoleon fought. The need to seek their consent (whatever the form in which it was sought and given or not given) would surely limit the occasions of war, and if there were any chance at all of reciprocity from the other side, it would limit its means too. This is the sort of consent I have in mind. Political self-determination is not, judging from twentieth century history, an adequate substitute, though it isn't easy to think of one that would be better. In any case, it is when individual consent fails that "acts of force" lose whatever appeal they previously had and become the constant object of moral condemnation. And after that, war also tends to escalate in its means, not necessarily beyond all limits, but certainly beyond those limits that ordinary humanity, as free of political loyalty as of political constraint, would establish if it could.

The Tyranny of War

War is most often a form of tyranny. It is best described by paraphrasing Trotsky's aphorism about the dialectic: "You may not be interested in war, but war is interested in you." The stakes are high, and the interest that military organizations take in an individual who would prefer to be somewhere else, doing something else, is frightening indeed. Hence the peculiar horror of war: it is a social practice in which force is used by and against men as loyal or constrained members of states and not as individuals who choose their own enterprises and activities. When we say, war is hell, it is the victims of the fighting that we have in mind. In fact, then, war is the very opposite of hell in the theological sense, and is hellish only when the opposition is strict. For in hell, presumably, only those people suffer who deserve to suffer, who have chosen activities for which punishment is the appropriate divine response, knowing that this is so. But the greater number by far of those who suffer in war have made no comparable choice.

I do not mean to call them "innocent." That word has come to have a special meaning in our moral discourse. It doesn't refer there to the participants but to the bystanders of battle, and so the class of innocent men and women is only a subset (though it is often a frighteningly large subset) of all those in whom war takes an interest without asking their consent. The rules of war by and large protect only the subset, for reasons I will have to consider later on. But war is hell even when the rules are observed, even when only soldiers are killed and civilians are consistently spared. Surely no experience of modern warfare has etched its horror so deeply in our minds as the fighting in the trenches of World War I —and in the trenches civilian lives were rarely at risk. The distinction of combatants and bystanders is enormously important in the theory of war, but our first and most fundamental moral judgment does not depend upon it. For in one sense at least, soldiers in battle and nonparticipating civilians are not so different: the soldiers would almost certainly be nonparticipants if they could.

The tyranny of war is often described as if war itself were the tyrant, a natural force like flood or famine or, personified, a brutal giant stalking his human prey, as in these lines from a poem by Thomas Sackville:[14]

> Lastly stood War, in glittering arms y-clad,
> With visage grim, stern looks, and blackly hued;
> In his right hand a naked sword he had
> That to the hilts was all with blood embrued,
> And in his left (that kings and kingdoms rued)
> > Famine and fire he held, and therewithal
> > He razed towns, and threw down towers and all.

Here is the Grim Reaper in uniform, armed with a sword instead of a scythe. The poetic image enters also into moral and political thought, but only, I think, as a kind of ideology, obscuring our critical judgment. For it is a piece of mystification to represent tyrannical power as an abstract Force. In battle as in politics, tyranny is always a relation among persons or groups of persons. The tyranny of war is a peculiarly complex relation because coercion is common on both sides. Sometimes, however, it is possible to distinguish the sides and to identify the statesmen and soldiers who first took the naked sword to hand. Wars are not self-starting. They may "break out," like an accidental fire, under conditions difficult to analyze and where the attribution of responsibility seems impossible. But usually they are more like arson than accident: war has human agents as well as human victims.

Those agents, when we can identify them, are properly called criminals. Their moral character is determined by the moral reality of the activity they force others to engage in (whether or not they engage in it themselves). They are responsible for the pain and death that follow from their decisions, or at least for the pain and death of all those persons who do not choose war as a personal enterprise. In contemporary international law, their crime is called aggression, and I will consider it later on under that name. But we can understand it initially as the exercise of tyrannical power, first over their own people and then, through the mediation of the opposing state's recruitment and conscription offices, over the people they have attacked. Now, tyranny of this sort rarely encounters domestic resistance. Sometimes the war is opposed by local political forces, but the opposition almost never extends to the actual exercise of military power. Though mutinies are common in the long history of war, they are more like peasant *jacqueries*, quickly and bloodily suppressed, than revolutionary struggles. Most often, real opposition comes only from the enemy. It is the men and women on the other side who are most likely to recognize and resent the tyranny of war; and whenever they do that, the contest takes on a new significance.

When soldiers believe themselves to be fighting against aggression, war is no longer a condition to be endured. It is a crime they can resist—though they must suffer its effects in order to resist it—and they can hope for a victory that is something more than an escape from the immediate brutality of battle. The experience of war as hell generates what might be called a higher ambition: one doesn't aim to settle with the enemy but to defeat and punish him and, if not to abolish the tyranny of war, at least to reduce the probability of future oppression. And once one is fighting for purposes of this sort, it becomes terribly important to win. The conviction that victory is morally critical plays an important part in the so-called "logic of war." We don't call war hell because it is fought without restraint. It is more nearly right to say that, when certain restraints are passed, the hellishness of war drives us to break with every remaining restraint in order to win. Here is the ultimate tyranny: those who resist aggression are forced to imitate, and perhaps even to exceed, the brutality of the aggressor.

General Sherman and the Burning of Atlanta

We are now in a position to understand what Sherman had in mind when he first announced that war is hell. He wasn't merely describing the awfulness of the experience, nor was he denying the possibility of moral judgment. He made such judgments freely, and he surely thought of himself as a righteous soldier. His maxim sums up, with admirable brevity, a whole way of thinking about war— a one-sided and partial way of thinking, I shall argue, but powerful nonetheless. In his view, war is entirely and singularly the crime of those who begin it, and soldiers resisting aggression (or rebellion) can never be blamed for anything they do that brings victory closer. The sentence *War is hell* is doctrine, not description: it is a moral argument, an attempt at self-justification. Sherman was claiming to be innocent of all those actions (though they were his own actions) for which he was so severely attacked: the bombardment of Atlanta, the forced evacuation of its inhabitants and the burning of the city, the march through Georgia. When he issued the order for the evacuation and burning of Atlanta, the city's aldermen and the Confederate commander, General Hood, protested his plans: "And now, sir," wrote Hood, "permit me to say that the unprecedented measure you propose transcends, in studied and ingenious cruelty, all acts ever before brought to my attention in the dark history of war." Sherman replied that war is indeed dark. "War is cruelty and you cannot refine it."[15] And therefore, he went on, "those who brought war into our country deserve all the curses and maledictions a people can pour out." But he himself deserves no curses at all. "I know I had no hand in making this war." He is only fighting it, not by choice but because he has to. He has been forced to use force, and the burning of Atlanta (so that the city could not again serve as a military depot for Confederate forces) is simply one more example of that use, one of the entailments of war. It is cruel, no doubt, but the cruelty isn't his own; it belongs, so to speak, to the men of the Confederacy: "You who, in the midst of peace and prosperity, have plunged a nation into war . . ." The Confederate leaders can easily restore peace by yielding obedience to federal law, but he can do so only by military action.

Sherman's argument expresses the anger that is commonly directed against those who begin a war and inflict its tyrannies on the rest of us. We disagree, of course, when it comes to giving the tyrants a proper name. But that disagreement is intense and heated only because we agree on the moral stakes. What is at issue is responsibilty for death and destruction, and Sherman is by no means the only general to take a lively interest in such matters. Nor is he the only general to think that if his cause is just he cannot be blamed for the death and destruction he spreads around him—for war is hell.

It is the Clausewitzian idea of limitlessness that is at work here, and if that idea is right, there would indeed be no response to Sherman's argument. But the tyranny of war is no more limitless than is political tyranny. Just as we can charge a tyrant with particular crimes over and above the crime of ruling without consent, so we can recognize and condemn particular criminal acts within the hell of war. When we answer the question, "Who started this war?" we have not finished distributing responsibility for the suffering that soldiers inflict. There are further arguments to make. That's why General Sherman, though he insisted that the cruelty of war could not be refined, claimed nevertheless to be refining it. "God will judge . . . ," he wrote, "whether it be more humane to fight with a town full of women [and children] at our back or to remove them in time to places of safety among their own friends and people." This is another kind of justification; and whether or not it is made in good faith, it suggests (what is certainly true) that Sherman had some responsibility for the people of Atlanta, even though he did not begin the war of which they were victims. When we focus exclusively on the fact of aggression, we are likely to lose sight of that responsibility and to talk as if there were only one morally relevant decision to be made in the course of a war: to attack or not to attack (to resist or not to resist). Sherman wants to judge war only at its outermost boundaries. But there is a great deal to be said about its interior regions, as he himself admits. Even in hell, it is possible to be more or less humane, to fight with or without restraint. We must try to understand how this can be so.

3

The Rules of War

The Moral Equality of Soldiers

Among soldiers who choose to fight, restraints of various sorts arise easily and, one might say, naturally, the product of mutual respect and recognition. The stories of chivalric knights are for the most part stories, but there can be no doubt that a military code was widely shared in the later Middle Ages and sometimes honored. The code was designed for the convenience of the aristocratic warriors, but it also reflected their sense of themselves as persons of a certain sort, engaged in activities that were freely chosen. Chivalry marked off knights from mere ruffians and bandits and also from peasant soldiers who bore arms as a necessity. I suppose that it survives today: some sense of military honor is still the creed of the professional soldier, the sociological if not the lineal descendent of the feudal knight. But notions of honor and chivalry seem to play only a small part in contemporary combat. In the literature of war, the contrast between "then and now" is commonly made —not very accurately, but with a certain truth, as in this poem by Louis Simpson:[1]

> At Malplaquet and Waterloo
> They were polite and proud,
> They primed their guns with billets-doux
> And, as they fired, bowed.
> At Appomattox too, it seems
> Some things were understood . . .
> But at Verdun and at Bastogne

The Rules of War

> There was a great recoil,
> The blood was bitter to the bone
> The trigger to the soul. . . .

Chivalry, it is often said, was the victim of democratic revolution and of revolutionary war: popular passion overcame aristocratic honor.[2] That draws the line before Waterloo and Appomattox, though still not quite correctly. It is the success of coercion that makes war ugly. Democracy is a factor only insofar as it increases the legitimacy of the state and then the effectiveness of its coercive power, not because the people in arms are a bloodthirsty mob fired by political zeal and committed to total war (in contrast to their officers, who would fight with decorum if they could). It is not what the people do when they enter the arena of battle that turns war into a "circus of slaughter," but, as I have already argued, the mere fact that they are there. Soldiers died by the thousands at Verdun and the Somme simply because they were available, their lives nationalized, as it were, by the modern state. They didn't choose to throw themselves at barbed wire and machine guns in fits of patriotic enthusiasm. The blood is bitter to their bones, too; they, too, would fight with decorum if they could. Their patriotism is, of course, a partial explanation of their availability. The discipline of the state is not merely imposed on them; it is also a discipline they accept, thinking that they have to for the sake of their families and their country. But the common features of contemporary combat: hatred for the enemy, impatience with all restraint, zeal for victory—these are the products of war itself whenever masses of men have to be mobilized for battle. They are as much the contribution of modern warfare to democratic politics as of democracy to war.

In any case, the death of chivalry is not the end of moral judgment. We still hold soldiers to certain standards, even though they fight unwillingly—in fact, precisely because we assume that they all fight unwillingly. The military code is reconstructed under the conditions of modern warfare so that it comes to rest not on aristocratic freedom but on military servitude. Sometimes freedom and servitude co-exist, and then we can study the difference between them in clinical detail. Whenever the game of war is revived, the elaborate courtesies of the chivalric age are revived with it—as among aviators in World War I, for example, who imagined themselves (and who have survived in the popular imagination) as airborne knights. Compared to the serfs on the ground, these were aristocrats indeed: they fought in accordance with a strict code of conduct that they invented themselves.[3] There was thralldom in the trenches, however, and mutual recognition took a very different form. Briefly, on Christmas Day 1914, German and French troops came together, drank and sang together, in the no-man's land between their lines. But such moments are rare in recent history, and they are not occasions for moral invention. The modern rules of war depend upon an abstract rather than a practical fellowship.

Soldiers cannot endure modern warfare for long without blaming someone for their pain and suffering. While it may be an example of what Marxists call "false consciousness" that they do not blame the ruling class of their own or of the enemy country, the fact is that their condemnation focuses most immediately on the men with whom they are engaged. The level of hatred is high in the trenches. That is why enemy wounded are often left to die and prisoners are killed—like murderers lynched by vigilantes—as if the soldiers on the other side were personally responsible for the war. At the same time, however, we know that they are not responsible. Hatred is interrupted or overridden by a more reflective understanding, which one finds expressed again and again in letters and war memoirs. It is the sense that the enemy soldier, though his war may well be criminal, is nevertheless as blameless as oneself. Armed, he is an enemy; but he isn't *my* enemy in any specific sense; the war itself isn't a relation between persons but between political entities and their human instruments. These human instruments are not comrades-in-arms in the old style, members of the fellowship of warriors; they are "poor sods, just like me," trapped in a war they didn't make. I find in them my moral equals. That is not to say simply that I acknowledge their humanity, for it is not the recognition of fellow men that explains the rules of war; criminals are men too. It is precisely the recognition of men who are not criminals.

They can try to kill me, and I can try to kill them. But it is wrong to cut the throats of their wounded or to shoot them down when they are trying to surrender. These judgments are clear enough, I think, and they suggest that war is still, somehow, a rule-governed activity, a world of permissions and prohibitions— a moral world, therefore, in the midst of hell. Though there is no license for war-makers, there is a license for soldiers, and they hold it without regard to which side they are on; it is the first and most important of their war rights. They are entitled to kill, *not anyone*, but men whom we know to be victims. We could hardly understand such a title if we did not recognize that they are victims too.

Hence the moral reality of war can be summed up in this way: when soldiers fight freely, choosing one another as enemies and designing their own battles, their war is not a crime; when they fight without freedom, their war is not their crime. In both cases, military conduct is governed by rules; but in the first the rules rest on mutuality and consent, in the second on a shared servitude. The first case raises no difficulties; the second is more problematic. We can best explore its problems, I think, if we turn from the trenches and the front lines to the general staff at the rear, and from the war against the Kaiser to the war against Hitler—for at that level and in that struggle, the recognition of "men who are not criminals" is hard indeed.

The Case of Hitler's Generals

In 1942, General von Arnim was captured in North Africa, and it was proposed by members of Dwight Eisenhower's staff that the American commander "should observe the custom of by-gone days" and permit von Arnim to visit him before he was sent into captivity. Historically, such visits were not merely matters of courtesy; they were occasions for the reaffirmation of the military code. Thus General von Ravenstein, captured by the British that same year, reports: "I was taken to see . . . Auchinleck himself in his office. He shook hands with me and said: 'I know you well by name. You and your division have fought with chivalry.' "[4] Eisenhower, however, refused to allow the visit. In his memoirs, he explained his reasons:[5]

> The custom had its origin in the fact that the mercenary soldiers of old had no real enmity toward their opponents. Both sides fought for love of a fight, out of a sense of duty or, more probably, for money . . . The tradition that all professional soldiers are comrades in arms has . . . persisted to this day. For me, World War II was far too personal a thing to entertain such feelings. Daily as it progressed there grew within me the conviction that, as never before . . . the forces that stood for human good and men's rights were . . . confronted by a completely evil conspiracy with which no compromise could be tolerated.

On this view, it doesn't matter whether or not von Arnim had fought well; his crime was to have fought at all. And similarly, it may not matter how General Eisenhower fights. Against an evil conspiracy, what is crucial is to win. Chivalry loses its rationale, and there are no limits left except "the limitations of force itself." That was Sherman's view too, but it does not account for the judgments that we make of his conduct, or of Eisenhower's, or even of von Arnim's and von Ravenstein's. Consider now the better-known case of Erwin Rommel: he, too, was one of Hitler's generals, and it is hard to imagine that he could have escaped the moral infamy of the war he fought. Yet he was, so we are told by one biographer after another, an honorable man. "While many of his colleagues and peers in the German army surrendered their honor by collusion with the iniquities of Nazism, Rommel was never defiled." He concentrated, like the professional he was, on "the soldier's task of fighting." And when he fought, he maintained the rules of war. He fought a bad war well, not only militarily but also morally. "It was Rommel who burned the Commando Order issued by Hitler on 28 October 1942, which laid down that all enemy soldiers encountered behind the German line were to be killed at once . . ."[6] He was one of Hitler's generals, but he did not shoot prisoners. Is such a man a comrade? Can one treat him with courtesy, can one shake his hand? These are the fine points of moral conduct; I do not know how they might be resolved, though I am sympathetic with Eisenhower's resolution. But I am sure, nevertheless, that Rommel should be praised for burning the Commando Order, and everyone who writes about these matters seems equally sure, and that implies something very important about the nature of war.

It would be very odd to praise Rommel for not killing prisoners unless we simultaneously refused to blame him for Hitler's aggressive wars. For otherwise he is simply a criminal, and all the fighting he does is murder or attempted murder, whether he aims at soldiers in battle or at prisoners or at civilians. The chief British prosecutor at Nuremberg put this argument into the language of international law when he said, "The killing of combatants is justifiable . . . only where the war itself is legal. But where the war is illegal . . . there is nothing to justify the killing and these murders are not to be distinguished from those of any other lawless robber bands."[7] And then Rommel's case would be exactly like that of a man who invades someone else's home and kills only some of the inhabitants, sparing the children, say, or an aged grandmother: a murderer, no doubt, though not one without a drop of human kindness. But we don't view Rommel that way: why not? The reason has to do with the distinction of *jus ad bellum* and *jus in bello*. We draw a line between the war itself, for which soldiers are not responsible, and the conduct of the war, for which they are responsible, at least within their own sphere of activity. Generals may well straddle the line, but that only suggests that we know pretty well where it should be drawn. We draw it by recognizing the nature of political obedience. Rommel was a servant, not a ruler, of the German state; he did not choose the wars he fought but, like Prince Andrey, served his "Tsar and country." We still have misgivings in his case, and will continue to have them, for he was more than just unlucky in his "Tsar and country." But by and large we don't blame a soldier, even a general, who fights for his own government. He is not the member of a robber band, a willful wrongdoer, but a loyal and obedient subject and citizen, acting sometimes at great personal risk in a way he thinks is right. We allow him to say what an English soldier says in Shakespeare's *Henry V*: "We know enough if we know we are the king's men. Our obedience to the king wipes the crime of it out of us."[8] Not that his obedience can never be criminal; for when he violates the rules of war, superior orders are no defence. The atrocities that he commits are his own; the war is not. It is conceived, both in international law and in ordinary moral judgment, as the king's business—a matter of state policy, not of individual volition, except when the individual is the king.

It might, however, be thought a matter of individual volition whether particular men join the army and participate in the war. Catholic writers have long argued that they ought not to volunteer, ought not to serve at all, if they know the war to be unjust. But the knowledge required by Catholic doctrine is hard to come by; and in case of doubt, argues the best of the Schoolmen, Francisco de Vitoria, subjects must fight—the guilt falling, as in *Henry V*, on their leaders. Vitoria's argument suggests how firmly political life is set, even in the pre-modern state, against the very idea of volition in time of war. "A prince is not able," he writes, "and ought not always to render reasons for the war to his subjects, and if the subjects cannot serve in the war except they are first satisfied of its justice, the state would fall into grave peril . . ."[9] Today, of course, most princes work hard to satisfy their subjects of the justice of their wars; they "render reasons," though not always honest ones. It takes courage to doubt these reasons, or to doubt them in public; and so long as they are only doubted, most men will be persuaded (by arguments something like Vitoria's) to fight. Their routine habits of law-abidingness, their fear, their patriotism, their moral investment in the state, all favor that course. Or, alternatively, they are so terribly young when the disciplinary system of the state catches them up and sends them into war that they can hardly be said to make a moral decision at all:[10]

From my mother's sleep I fell into the State.

And then how can we blame them for (what we perceive to be) the wrongful character of their war?*

Soldiers are not, however, entirely without volition. Their will is independent and effective only within a limited sphere, and for most of them that sphere is narrow. But except in extreme cases, it never completely disappears. And at those moments in the course of the fighting when they must choose, like Rommel, to kill prisoners or let them live, they are not mere victims or servants bound to obedience; they are responsible for what they do. We shall have to qualify that responsibility when we come to consider it in detail, for war is still hell, and hell is a tyranny where soldiers are subject to all sorts of duress. But the judgments we actually make of their conduct demonstrate, I think, that within that tyranny we have carved out a constitutional regime: even the pawns of war have rights and obligations.

During the past hundred years, these rights and obligations have been specified in treaties and agreements, written into international law. The very states that enlist the pawns of war have stipulated the moral character of their mutual slaughter. Initially, this stipulation was not based upon any notion of the equality of soldiers but upon the equality of sovereign states, which claimed for themselves the same right to fight (right to make war) that individual soldiers more obviously possess. The argument that I have made on behalf of soldiers was first made on behalf of states—or rather, on behalf of their leaders, who, we were told, are never willful criminals, whatever the character of the wars they begin, but statesmen serving the national interest as best they can. When I discuss the theory of aggression and of responsibility for aggres-

---

* But these young men, Robert Nozick argues, "are certainly not encouraged to think for themselves by the practice of absolving them of all responsibility for their actions within the rules of war." That is right; they are not. But we cannot blame them in order to encourage the others unless they are actually blameworthy. Nozick insists that they are: "It is a soldier's responsibility to determine if his side's cause is just . . ." The conventional refusal to impose that responsibility flatly and across the board is "morally elitist." (*Anarchy, State, and Utopia*, New York, 1974, p. 100.) But it isn't elitist merely to recognize the existence of authority structures and socialization processes in the political community, and it may be morally insensitive not to. I do agree with Nozick that "some bucks stop with each of us." A great deal of this book is concerned with trying to say which ones those are.

sion, I will have to explain why that is an inadequate description of what statesmen do.[11] For now, it is enough to say that this view of sovereignty and political leadership, which was never in accord with ordinary moral judgment, has also lost its legal standing, replaced in the years since World War I by the formal designation of war-making as a criminal activity. However, the rules of engagement have not been replaced but expanded and elaborated, so that we now have both a ban on war and a code of military conduct. The dualism of our moral perceptions is established in the law.

War is a "legal condition which equally permits two or more groups to carry on a conflict by armed force."[12] It is also, and for our purposes more importantly, a moral condition, involving the same permissiveness, not in fact at the level of sovereign states, but at the level of armies and individual soldiers. Without the equal right to kill, war as a rule-governed activity would disappear and be replaced by crime and punishment, by evil conspiracies and military law enforcement. That disappearance seems to be heralded by the United Nations Charter, where the word "war" does not appear but only "aggression," "self-defense," "international enforcement," and so on. But even the UN's "police action" in Korea was still a war, since the soldiers who fought in it were moral equals even if the states were not. The rules of war were as relevant there as in any other "conflict by armed force," and they were equally relevant to the aggressor, the victim, and the police.

Two Sorts of Rules

The rules of war consist of two clusters of prohibitions attached to the central principle that soldiers have an equal right to kill. The first cluster specifies when and how they can kill, the second whom they can kill. My chief concern is with the second, for there the formulation and reformulation of the rules reach to one of the hardest questions in the theory of war—that is, how those victims of war who can be attacked and killed are to be distinguished from those who cannot. I don't believe that this question must be answered in this or that specific way if war is to be a moral condition. It is necessary, however, that at any particular moment there be an answer. War is distinguishable from murder and massacre only when restrictions are established on the reach of battle.

The first set of rules does not involve any such fundamental issue. Rules specifying how and when soldiers can be killed are by no means unimportant, and yet the morality of war would not be radically transformed were they to be abolished altogether. Consider, for example, those battles described by anthropologists in which warriors fight with bows and unfeathered arrows. The arrows fly less accurately than they would if they were feathered; they can be dodged; few men are killed.[18] It is clearly a good rule, then, that arrows not be feathered, and we may fairly condemn the warrior who first arms himself with the superior and forbidden weapon and hits his enemy. Yet the man he kills was liable to be killed in any case, and a collective (intertribal) decision to fight with feathered arrows would not violate any basic moral principle. The case is the same with all other rules of this kind: that soldiers be preceded into battle by a herald carrying a red flag, that fighting always be broken off at sunset, that ambushes and surprise attacks be prohibited, and so on. Any rule that limits the intensity and duration of combat or the suffering of soldiers is to be welcomed, but none of these restraints seem crucial to the idea of war as a moral condition. They are circumstantial in the literal sense of that word, highly particularized and local to a specific time and place. Even if in practise they endure for many years, they are always susceptible to the transformations brought about by social change, technological innovation, and foreign conquest.*

The second set of rules does not seem similarly susceptible. At least, the general structure of its provisions seems to persist without reference to social systems and technologies—as if the rules involved were (as I think they are) more closely connected to universal notions of right and wrong. Their tendency is to set certain classes of people outside the permissible range of warfare, so that killing any of their members is not a legitimate act of war but a crime. Though their details vary from place to place, these rules point toward the general conception of war as a *combat between combatants*, a conception that turns up again and again in anthropological and historical accounts. It is most dramatically exemplified when war is actually a combat between military cham-

---

* They are also susceptible to the kind of reciprocal violation legitimized by the doctrine of reprisal: violated by one side, they can be violated by the other. But this does not seem to be true of the other sort of rules, described below. See the discussion of reprisals in chapter 13.

pions, as among many primitive peoples, or in the Greek epics, or in the biblical tale of David and Goliath. "Let no man's heart fail within him," says David, "thy servant will go and fight this Philistine."[14] Once such a contest has been agreed upon, soldiers themselves are protected from the hell of war. In the Middle Ages, single combat was advocated for precisely this reason: "Better for one to fall than the whole army."[15] More often, however, protection has been offered only to those people who are not trained and prepared for war, who do not fight or cannot: women and children, priests, old men, the members of neutral tribes, cities, or states, wounded or captured soldiers.* What all these groups have in common is that they are not currently engaged in the business of war. Depending on one's social or cultural perspective, killing them may appear wanton, unchivalrous, dishonorable, brutal, or murderous. But it is very likely that some general principle is at work in all these judgments, connecting immunity from attack with military disengagement. Any satisfactory account of the moral reality of war must specify that principle and say something about its force. I shall attempt to do both these things later on.

The historical specifications of the principle are, however, conventional in character, and the war rights and obligations of soldiers follow from the conventions and not (directly) from the principle, whatever its force. Once again, war is a social creation. The rules actually observed or violated in this or that time and place are necessarily a complex product, mediated by cultural and religious norms, social structures, formal and informal bargaining between belligerent powers, and so on. Hence, the details of noncombatant immunity are likely to seem as arbitrary as the rules that determine when battles should start and stop or what weapons may be used. They are more important by far, but similarly subject to social revision. Exactly like law in domestic society, they will often represent an incomplete or distorted embodiment of the relevant moral principle. They are subject, then, to philosophical criticism. Indeed, criticism is a crucial part of the historical process through which the rules are made. We might say that war is a philosophical creation. Long before philosophers are satisfied with it, however,

---

* The lists are often more specific and more picturesque than this, reflecting the character of a particular culture. Here is an example from an ancient Indian text, according to which the following groups of people are not to be subjected to the exigencies of battle: "Those who look on without taking part, those afflicted with grief . . . those who are asleep, thirsty, or fatigued or are walking along the road, or have a task on hand unfinished, or who are proficient in fine art." (S. V. Viswanatha, *International Law in Ancient India*, Bombay, 1925, p. 156.)

soldiers are bound by its canons. And they are equally bound, because of their own equality, and without reference to the content or the incompleteness of the canons.

The War Convention

I propose to call the set of articulated norms, customs, professional codes, legal precepts, religious and philosophical principles, and reciprocal arrangements that shape our judgments of military conduct *the war convention*. It is important to stress that it is our judgments that are at issue here, not conduct itself. We cannot get at the substance of the convention by studying combat behavior, any more than we can understand the norms of friendship by studying the way friends actually treat one another. The norms are apparent, instead, in the expectations friends have, the complaints they make, the hypocrisies they adopt. So it is with war: relations between combatants have a normative structure that is revealed in what they say (and what the rest of us say) rather than in what they do—though no doubt what they do, as with friends, is affected by what they say. Harsh words are the immediate sanctions of the war convention, sometimes accompanied or followed by military attacks, economic blockades, reprisals, war crimes trials, and so on. But neither the words nor the actions have any single authoritative source; and, finally, it is the words that are decisive—the "judgment of history," as it is called, which means the judgment of men and women arguing until some rough consensus is reached.

The terms of our judgments are most explicitly set forth in positive international law: the work of politicians and lawyers acting as representatives of sovereign states, and then of jurists codifying their agreements and searching out the rationale that underlies them. But international law arises out of a radically decentralized legislative system, cumbrous, unresponsive, and without a parallel judicial system to establish the specific details of the legal code. For that reason, the legal handbooks are not the only place to find the war convention, and its actual existence is demonstrated not by the existence of the handbooks but by the moral arguments that everywhere accompany the practice of war. The common law of combat is developed through a kind of practical casuistry. Hence the method of this book: we look to the lawyers for general formulas, but to historical cases and actual debates for those particular judgments that both reflect the war convention and constitute its vital force. I don't mean to suggest that our judgments, even over time, have an unambiguous collective form. Nor, however, are they idiosyncratic and private in character. They are socially patterned, and the patterning is religious, cultural, and political, as well as legal. The task of the moral theorist is to study the pattern as a whole, reaching for its deepest reasons.

Among professional soldiers, the war convention often finds advocates of a special kind. Though chivalry is dead and fighting unfree, professional soldiers remain sensitive (or some of them do) to those limits and restraints that distinguish their life's work from mere butchery. No doubt, they know with General Sherman that war is butchery, but they are likely to believe that it is also, simultaneously, something else. That is why army and navy officers, defending a long tradition, will often protest commands of their civilian superiors that would require them to violate the rules of war and turn them into mere instruments for killing. The protests are mostly unavailing—for instruments, after all, they are—but within their own sphere of decision, they often find ways to defend the rules. And even when they don't do that, their doubts at the time and justifications after the fact are an important guide to the substance of the rules. Sometimes, at least, it matters to soldiers just whom they kill.

The war convention as we know it today has been expounded, debated, criticized, and revised over a period of many centuries. Yet it remains one of the more imperfect of human artifacts: recognizably something that men have made, but not something that they have made freely or well. It is necessarily imperfect, I think, quite aside from the frailties of humankind, because it is adapted to the practise of modern war. It sets the terms of a moral condition that comes into existence only when armies of victims meet (just as the chivalric code sets the terms of a moral condition that comes into existence only when there are armies of free men). The convention accepts that victimization or at least assumes it, and starts from there. That is why it is often described as a program for the toleration of war, when what is needed is a program for its abolition. One does not abolish war by fighting it well; nor does fighting it well make it tolerable. War is hell, as I have already said, even when the rules are strictly observed. Just for that reason, we are sometimes made angry by the very idea of rules or cynical about their meaning. They only serve, as Prince Andrey says in that impassioned outburst that evidently also expresses Tolstoy's conviction to make us forget that war is "the vilest thing in life . . ."[16]

> And what is war, what is needed for success in war, what are the morals of the military world? The object of warfare is murder; the means employed in warfare—spying, treachery, and the encouragement of it, the ruin of a country, the plunder of its inhabitants . . . trickery and lying, which are called military strategy; the morals of the military class—absence of all independence, that is, discipline, idleness, ignorance, cruelty, debauchery, and drunkeness.

And yet, even people who believe all this are capable of being outraged by particular acts of cruelty and barbarism. War is so awful that it makes us cynical about the possibility of restraint, and then it is so much worse that it makes us indignant at the absence of restraint. Our cynicism testifies to the defectiveness of the war convention, and our indignation to its reality and strength.

The Example of Surrender

Anomalous the convention often is, but binding nonetheless. Consider for a moment the common practice of surrendering, the detailed features of which are conventionally (and in our own time, legally) established. A soldier who surrenders enters into an agreement with his captors: he will stop fighting if they will accord him what the legal handbooks call "benevolent quarantine."[17] Since it is usually made under extreme duress, this is an agreement that would have no moral consequences at all in time of peace. In war it does have consequences. The captured soldier acquires rights and obligations specified by the convention, and these are binding without regard to the possible criminality of his captors or to the justice or urgency of the cause for which he has been fighting. Prisoners of war have a right to try to escape—they cannot be punished for the attempt—but if they kill a guard in order to escape, the killing is not an act of war; it is murder. For they committed themselves to stop fighting, gave up their right to kill, when they surrendered.

It is not easy to see all this as the simple assertion of a moral principle. It is the work of men and women (with moral principles in mind) adapting to the realities of war, making arrangements, striking bargains. No doubt, the bargain is generally useful to captives and captors alike, but it is not necessarily useful in every case to either of them or to mankind as a whole. If our purpose in this particular war is to win as soon as possible, the spectacle of a prison camp must seem strange indeed. Here are soldiers making themselves at home, settling in for the duration, dropping out of the war before it is over, and bound not to renew the fighting, even if they can (through sabotage, harassment, or whatever), because they promised at the point of a gun not to do so. Surely these are promises that can sometimes be broken. Yet prisoners are not invited to calculate the relative utilities of keeping or of breaking them. The war convention is written in absolutist terms: one violates its provisions at one's moral, as at one's physical peril. But what is the force of these provisions? They derive ultimately from principles that I will take up later on, which explain the meaning of quarter, disengagement, and immunity. They derive immediately and specifically from the consensual process itself. The rules of war, alien as they often are to our sense of what is best, are made obligatory by the general consent of mankind.

Now that, too, is a consent given under a kind of duress. Only because there is no escape from hell, it might be said, have we labored to create a world of rules within it. But let us imagine an escape attempt, a liberation struggle, a "war to end war." Surely it would be foolish then to fight according to the rules. The all-important task would be to win. But it is always important to win, for victory can always be described as an escape from hell. Even the victory of an aggressor, after all, ends the war. Hence the long history of impatience with the war convention. That history is nicely summed up in a letter written in 1880 by the Prussian chief of staff, General von Moltke, to protest the Declaration of St. Petersburg (an early effort to codify the rules of war): "The greatest kindness in war," wrote von Moltke, "is to bring it to a speedy conclusion. It should be allowable, with that view, to employ all means save those that are absolutely objectionable."[18] Von Moltke stops short of a total denial of the war convention; he recognizes absolute prohibitions of some unspecified sort. Almost everyone does. But why stop short if that means falling short of the "greatest kindness"? This is the form of the most common argument in the theory of war and of the most common moral dilemma in its practice. The war convention is found to stand in the way of victory and, it is usually said, a lasting peace. Must its provisions, must this particular provision be obeyed? When victory means the defeat of aggression, the question is not only important; it is painfully difficult. We want to have it both ways: moral decency in battle and victory in war; constitutionalism in hell and ourselves outside.

PART TWO

THE THEORY
OF AGGRESSION

4

Law and Order in
International Society

Aggression

Aggression is the name we give to the crime of war. We know the crime because of our knowledge of the peace it interrupts—not the mere absence of fighting, but peace-with-rights, a condition of liberty and security that can exist only in the absence of aggression itself. The wrong the aggressor commits is to force men and women to risk their lives for the sake of their rights. It is to confront them with the choice: your rights or (some of) your lives! Groups of citizens respond in different ways to that choice, sometimes surrendering, sometimes fighting, depending on the moral and material condition of their state and army. But they are always justified in fighting; and in most cases, given that harsh choice, fighting is the morally preferred response. The justification and the preference are very important: they account for the most remarkable features of the concept of aggression and for the special place it has in the theory of war.

Aggression is remarkable because it is the only crime that states can commit against other states: everything else is, as it were, a misdemeanor. There is a strange poverty in the language of international law. The equivalents of domestic assault, armed robbery, extortion, assault with intent to kill, murder in all its degrees, have but one name. Every violation of the territorial integrity or political sovereignty of an independent state is called aggression. It is as if we were to brand as murder all attacks on a man's person, all attempts to coerce him, all invasions of his home. This refusal of differentiation makes it difficult to mark off the relative seriousness of aggressive acts—to distinguish, for example, the seizure of a piece of land or the imposition of a satellite regime from conquest itself, the destruction of a state's independence (a crime for which Abba Eban, Israel's foreign minister in 1967, suggested the name "policide"). But there is a reason for the refusal. All aggressive acts have one thing in common: they justify forceful resistance, and force cannot be used between nations, as it often can between persons, without putting life itself at risk. Whatever limits we place on the means and range of warfare, fighting a limited war is not like hitting somebody. Aggression opens the gates of hell. Shakespeare's *Henry V* makes the point exactly:[1]

> For never two such kingdoms did contend
> Without much fall of blood, whose guiltless drops
> Are every one a woe, a sore complaint
> 'Gainst him whose wrongs gives edge unto the swords
> That makes such waste in brief mortality.

At the same time, aggression unresisted is aggression still, though there is no "fall of blood" at all. In domestic society, a robber who gets what he wants without killing anyone is obviously less guilty, that is, guilty of a lesser crime, than if he commits murder. Assuming that the robber is prepared to kill, we allow the behavior of his victim to determine his guilt. We don't do this in the case of aggression. Consider, for example, the German seizures of Czechoslovakia and Poland in 1939. The Czechs did not resist; they lost their independence through extortion rather than war; no Czech citizens died fighting the German invaders. The Poles chose to fight, and many were killed in the war that followed. But if the conquest of Czechoslovakia was a lesser crime, we have no name for it. At Nuremberg, the Nazi leadership was charged with aggression in both cases and found guilty in both.[2] Once again, there is a reason for this identity of treatment. We judge the Germans guilty of aggression in Czechoslovakia, I think, because of our profound conviction that they ought to have been resisted— though not necessarily by their abandoned victim, standing alone.

The state that does resist, whose soldiers risk their lives and die, does so because its leaders and people think that they should or that they have to fight back. Aggression is morally as well as physically coercive, and that is one of the most important things about it. "A conqueror," writes Clausewitz, "is always a lover of peace (as Bonaparte always asserted of himself); he would like to make his entry into our state unopposed; in order to prevent this, we must choose war . . ."[3] If ordinary men and women did not ordinarily accept that imperative, aggression would not seem to us so serious a crime. If they accepted it in certain sorts of cases, but not in others, the single concept would begin to break down, and we would eventually have a list of crimes more or less like the domestic list. The challenge of the streets, "Your money or your life!" is easy to answer: I surrender my money and so I save myself from being murdered and the thief from being a murderer. But we apparently don't want the challenge of aggression answered in the same way; even when it is, we don't diminish the guilt of the aggressor. He has violated rights to which we attach enormous importance. Indeed, we are inclined to think that the failure to defend those rights is never due to a sense of their unimportance, nor even to a belief (as in the street-challenge case) that they are, after all, worth less than life itself, but only to a stark conviction that the defense is hopeless. Aggression is a singular and undifferentiated crime because, in all its forms, it challenges rights that are worth dying for.

The Rights of Political Communities

The rights in question are summed up in the lawbooks as territorial integrity and political sovereignty. The two belong to states, but they derive ultimately from the rights of individuals, and from them they take their force. "The duties and rights of states are nothing more than the duties and rights of the men who compose them."[4] That is the view of a conventional British lawyer, for whom states are neither organic wholes nor mystical unions. And it is the correct view. When states are attacked, it is their members who are challenged, not only in their lives, but also in the sum of things they value most, including the political association they have made. We recognize and explain this challenge by referring to their rights. If they were not morally entitled to choose their form of government and shape the policies that shape their lives, external coercion would not be a crime; nor could it so easily be said that they had been forced to resist in self-defense. Individual rights (to life and liberty) underlie the most important judgments that we make about war. How these rights are themselves founded I cannot try to explain here. It is enough to say that they are some-how entailed by our sense of what it means to be a human being. If they are not natural, then we have invented them, but natural or invented, they are a palpable feature of our moral world. States' rights are simply their collective form. The process of collectiviza-tion is a complex one. No doubt, some of the immediate force of individuality is lost in its course; it is best understood, nevertheless, as it has commonly been understood since the seventeenth cen-tury, in terms of social contract theory. Hence it is a moral process, which justifies some claims to territory and sovereignty and in-validates others.

The rights of states rest on the consent of their members. But this is consent of a special sort. State rights are not constituted through a series of transfers from individual men and women to the sovereign or through a series of exchanges among individuals. What actually happens is harder to describe. Over a long period of time, shared experiences and cooperative activity of many differ-ent kinds shape a common life. "Contract" is a metaphor for a process of association and mutuality, the ongoing character of which the state claims to protect against external encroachment. The protection extends not only to the lives and liberties of indi-viduals but also to their shared life and liberty, the independent community they have made, for which individuals are sometimes sacrificed. The moral standing of any particular state depends upon the reality of the common life it protects and the extent to which the sacrifices required by that protection are willingly accepted and thought worthwhile. If no common life exists, or if the state doesn't defend the common life that does exist, its own defense may have no moral justification. But most states do stand guard over the community of their citizens, at least to some degree: that is why we assume the justice of their defensive wars. And given a genuine "contract," it makes sense to say that territorial integrity and political sovereignty can be defended in exactly the same way as individual life and liberty.*

* The question of when territory and sovereignty can rightly be defended is closely connected to the question of when individual citizens have an obligation to join the defense. Both hang on issues in social contract theory. I have discussed the

54

It might also be said that a people can defend its country in the same way as men and women can defend their homes, for the country is collectively as the homes are privately owned. The right to territory might be derived, that is, from the individual right to property. But the ownership of vast reaches of land is highly problematic, I think, unless it can be tied in some plausible way to the requirements of national survival and political independence. And these two seem by themselves to generate territorial rights that have little to do with ownership in the strict sense. The case is probably the same with the smaller properties of domestic society. A man has certain rights in his home, for example, even if he does not own it, because neither his life nor his liberty is secure unless there exists some physical space within which he is safe from intrusion. Similarly again, the right of a nation or people not to be invaded derives from the common life its members have made on this piece of land—it had to be made somewhere—and not from the legal title they hold or don't hold. But these matters will become clearer if we look at an example of disputed territory.

The Case of Alsace-Lorraine

In 1870, both France and the new Germany claimed these two provinces. Both claims were, as such things go, well founded. The Germans based themselves on ancient precedents (the lands had been part of the Holy Roman Empire before their conquest by Louis XIV) and on cultural and linguistic kinship; the French on two centuries of possession and effective government.[5] How does one establish ownership in such a case? There is, I think, a prior question having to do with political allegiance, not with legal titles at all. What do the inhabitants want? The land follows the people. The decision as to whose sovereignty was legitimate (and therefore as to whose military presence constituted aggression) belonged by right to the men and women who lived on the land in dispute. Not simply to those who owned the land: the decision belonged to the landless, to town dwellers and factory workers as well, by virtue of

second question at length in my book *Obligations: Essays on Disobedience, War, and Citizenship* (Cambridge, Mass., 1970). See especially "The Obligation to Die for the State" and "Political Alienation and Military Service." But neither in that book nor in this one do I deal in any detail with the problem of national minorities —groups of people who do not fully join (or do not join at all) in the contract that constitutes the nation. The radical mistreatment of such people may justify military intervention (see chapter 6). Short of that, however, the presence of national minorities within the borders of a nation-state does not affect the argument about aggression and self-defense.

the common life they had made. The great majority of these people were apparently loyal to France, and that should have settled the matter. Even if we imagine all the inhabitants of Alsace-Lorraine to be tenants of the Prussian king, the king's seizure of his own land would still have been a violation of their territorial integrity and, through the mediation of their loyalty, of France's too. For tenantry determines only where rents should go; the people themselves must decide where their taxes and conscripts should go.

But the issue was not settled in this way. After the Franco-Prussian war, the two provinces (actually, all of Alsace and a portion of Lorraine) were annexed by Germany, the French conceding German rights in the peace treaty of 1871. During the next several decades, the question was frequently asked, whether a French attack aimed at regaining the lost lands would be justified. One of the issues here is that of the moral standing of a peace treaty signed, as most peace treaties are signed, under duress, but I shall not focus on that. The more important issue relates to the endurance of rights over time. Here the appropriate argument was put forward by the English philosopher Henry Sidgwick in 1891. Sidgwick's sympathies were with the French, and he was inclined to regard the peace as a "temporary suspension of hostilities, terminable at any time by the wronged state . . ." But he added a crucial qualification:[6]

> We must . . . recognize that by this temporary submission of the vanquished . . . a new political order is initiated, which, though originally without a· moral basis, may in time acquire such a basis, from a change in the sentiments of the inhabitants of the territory transferred; since it is always possible that through the effects of time and habit and mild government—and perhaps through the voluntary exile of those who feel the old patriotism most keenly—the majority of the transferred population may cease to desire reunion . . . When this change has taken place, the moral effect of the unjust transfer must be regarded as obliterated; so that any attempt to recover the transferred territory becomes itself an aggression . . .

Legal titles may endure forever, periodically revived and reasserted as in the dynastic politics of the Middle Ages. But moral rights are subject to the vicissitudes of the common life.

Territorial integrity, then, does not derive from property; it is simply something different. The two are joined, perhaps, in socialist states where the land is nationalized and the people are said to own it. Then if their country is attacked, it is not merely their homeland that is in danger but their collective property—though

I suspect that the first danger is more deeply felt than the second. Nationalization is a secondary process; it assumes the prior existence of a nation. And territorial integrity is a function of national existence, not of nationalization (any more than of private ownership). It is the coming together of a people that establishes the integrity of a territory. Only then can a boundary be drawn the crossing of which is plausibly called aggression. It hardly matters if the territory belongs to someone else, unless that ownership is expressed in residence and common use.

This argument suggests a way of thinking about the great difficulties posed by forcible settlement and colonization. When barbarian tribes crossed the borders of the Roman Empire, driven by conquerors from the east or north, they asked for land to settle on and threatened war if they didn't get it. Was this aggression? Given the character of the Roman Empire, the question may sound foolish, but it has arisen many times since, and often in imperial settings. When land is in fact empty and available, the answer must be that it is not aggression. But what if the land is not actually empty but, as Thomas Hobbes says in *Leviathan*, "not sufficiently inhabited"? Hobbes goes on to argue that in such a case, the would-be settlers must "not exterminate those they find there but constrain them to inhabit closer together."[7] That constraint is not aggression, so long as the lives of the original settlers are not threatened. For the settlers are doing what they must do to preserve their own lives, and "he that shall oppose himself against [that], for things superfluous, is guilty of the war that thereupon is to follow."[8] It is not the settlers who are guilty of aggression, according to Hobbes, but those natives who won't move over and make room. There are clearly serious problems here. But I would suggest that Hobbes is right to set aside any consideration of territorial integrity-as-ownership and to focus instead on life. It must be added, however, that what is at stake is not only the lives of individuals but also the common life that they have made. It is for the sake of this common life that we assign a certain presumptive value to the boundaries that mark off a people's territory and to the state that defends it.

Now, the boundaries that exist at any moment in time are likely to be arbitrary, poorly drawn, the products of ancient wars. The mapmakers are likely to have been ignorant, drunken, or corrupt. Nevertheless, these lines establish a habitable world. Within that world, men and women (let us assume) are safe from attack; once the lines are crossed, safety is gone. I don't want to suggest that every boundary dispute is a reason for war. Sometimes adjustments should be accepted and territories shaped so far as possible to the actual needs of nations. Good borders make good neighbors. But once an invasion has been threatened or has actually begun, it may be necessary to defend a bad border simply because there is no other. We shall see this reason at work in the minds of the leaders of Finland in 1939: they might have accepted Russian demands had they felt certain that there would be an end to them. But there is no certainty this side of the border, any more than there is safety this side of the threshold, once a criminal has entered the house. It is only common sense, then, to attach great importance to boundaries. Rights in the world have value only if they also have dimension.

The Legalist Paradigm

If states actually do possess rights more or less as individuals do, then it is possible to imagine a society among them more or less like the society of individuals. The comparison of international to civil order is crucial to the theory of aggression. I have already been making it regularly. Every reference to aggression as the international equivalent of armed robbery or murder, and every comparison of home and country or of personal liberty and political independence, relies upon what is called the *domestic analogy*.[9] Our primary perceptions and judgments of aggression are the products of analogical reasoning. When the analogy is made explicit, as it often is among the lawyers, the world of states takes on the shape of a political society the character of which is entirely accessible through such notions as crime and punishment, self-defense, law enforcement, and so on.

These notions, I should stress, are not incompatible with the fact that international society as it exists today is a radically imperfect structure. As we experience it, that society might be likened to a defective building, founded on rights; its superstructure raised, like that of the state itself, through political conflict, cooperative activity, and commercial exchange; the whole thing shaky and unstable because it lacks the rivets of authority. It is like domestic society in that men and women live at peace within it (sometimes), determining the conditions of their own existence, negotiating and bargaining with their neighbors. It is unlike domestic society in that every conflict threatens the structure as a whole with collapse. Aggression challenges it directly and is much more dangerous than domestic crime, because there are no policemen. But that only means that the "citizens" of international society must rely on themselves and on one another. Police powers are distributed among all the members. And these members have not done enough in the exercise of their powers if they merely contain the aggression or bring it to a speedy end—as if the police should stop a murderer after he has killed only one or two people and send him on his way. The rights of the member states must be vindicated, for it is only by virtue of those rights that there is a society at all. If they cannot be upheld (at least sometimes), international society collapses into a state of war or is transformed into a universal tyranny.

From this picture, two presumptions follow. The first, which I have already pointed out, is the presumption in favor of military resistance once aggression has begun. Resistance is important so that rights can be maintained and future aggressors deterred. The theory of aggression restates the old doctrine of the just war: it explains when fighting is a crime and when it is permissible, perhaps even morally desirable.* The victim of aggression fights in self-defense, but he isn't only defending himself, for aggression is a crime against society as a whole. He fights in its name and not only in his own. Other states can rightfully join the victim's resistance; their war has the same character as his own, which is to say, they are entitled not only to repel the attack but also to punish it. All resistance is also law enforcement. Hence the second presumption: when fighting breaks out, there must always be some state against which the law can and should be enforced. Someone must be responsible, for someone decided to break the peace of the society of states. No war, as medieval theologians explained, can be just on both sides.[10]

There are, however, wars that are just on neither side, because the idea of justice doesn't pertain to them or because the antagonists are both aggressors, fighting for territory or power where

---

* I shall say nothing here of the argument for nonviolent resistance to aggression, according to which fighting is neither desirable nor necessary. This argument has not figured much in the development of the conventional view. Indeed, it poses a radical challenge to the conventions: if aggression can be resisted, and at least sometimes successfully resisted, without war, it may be a less serious crime than has commonly been supposed. I will take up this possibility and its moral implications in the Afterword.

they have no right. The first case I have already alluded to in discussing the voluntary combat of aristocratic warriors. It is sufficiently rare in human history that nothing more need be said about it here. The second case is illustrated by those wars that Marxists call "imperialist," which are not fought between conquerors and victims but between conquerors and conquerors, each side seeking dominion over the other or the two of them competing to dominate some third party. Thus Lenin's description of the struggles between "have" and "have-not" nations in early twentieth century Europe: ". . . picture to yourselves a slave-owner who owned 100 slaves warring against a slave-owner who owned 200 slaves for a more 'just' distribution of slaves. Clearly, the application of the term 'defensive' war in such a case . . . would be sheer deception . . ."[11] But it is important to stress that we can penetrate the deception only insofar as we can ourselves distinguish justice and injustice: the theory of imperialist war presupposes the theory of aggression. If one insists that all wars on all sides are acts of conquest or attempted conquest, or that all states at all times would conquer if they could, then the argument for justice is defeated before it begins and the moral judgments we actually make are derided as fantasies. Consider the following passage from Edmund Wilson's book on the American Civil War:[12]

> I think that it is a serious deficiency on the part of historians . . . that they so rarely interest themselves in biological and zoological phenomena. In a recent . . . film showing life at the bottom of the sea, a primitive organism called a sea slug is seen gobbling up small organisms through a large orifice at one end of its body; confronted with another sea slug of an only slightly lesser size, it ingurgitates that, too. Now the wars fought by human beings are stimulated as a rule . . . by the same instincts as the voracity of the sea slug.

There are no doubt wars to which that image might be fit, though it is not a terribly useful image with which to approach the Civil War. Nor does it account for our ordinary experience of international society. Not all states are sea-slug states, gobbling up their neighbors. There are always groups of men and women who would live if they could in peaceful enjoyment of their rights and who have chosen political leaders who represent that desire. The deepest purpose of the state is not ingestion but defense, and the least that can be said is that many actual states serve that purpose. When their territory is attacked or their sovereignty challenged, it makes sense to look for an aggressor and not merely for a natural predator.

Hence we need a theory of aggression rather than a zoological account.

The theory of aggression first takes shape under the aegis of the domestic analogy. I am going to call that primary form of the theory the *legalist paradigm*, since it consistently reflects the conventions of law and order. It does not necessarily reflect the arguments of the lawyers, though legal as well as moral debate has its starting point here.[13] Later on, I will suggest that our judgments about the justice and injustice of particular wars are not entirely determined by the paradigm. The complex realities of international society drive us toward a revisionist perspective, and the revisions will be significant ones. But the paradigm must first be viewed in its unrevised form; it is our baseline, our model, the fundamental structure for the moral comprehension of war. We begin with the familiar world of individuals and rights, of crimes and punishments. The theory of aggression can then be summed up in six propositions.

1. *There exists an international society of independent states.* States are the members of this society, not private men and women. In the absence of an universal state, men and women are protected and their interests represented only by their own governments. Though states are founded for the sake of life and liberty, they cannot be challenged in the name of life and liberty by any other states. Hence the principle of non-intervention, which I will analyze later on. The rights of private persons can be recognized in international society, as in the UN Charter of Human Rights, but they cannot be enforced without calling into question the dominant values of that society: the survival and independence of the separate political communities.

2. *This international society has a law that establishes the rights of its members—above all, the rights of territorial integrity and political sovereignty.* Once again, these two rest ultimately on the right of men and women to build a common life and to risk their individual lives only when they freely choose to do so. But the relevant law refers only to states, and its details are fixed by the intercourse of states, through complex processes of conflict and consent. Since these processes are continuous, international society has no natural shape; nor are rights within it ever finally or exactly determined. At any given moment, however, one can distinguish the territory of one people from that of another and say something about the scope and limits of sovereignty.

3. *Any use of force or imminent threat of force by one state against the political sovereignty or territorial integrity of another constitutes aggression and is a criminal act.* As with domestic crime, the argument here focuses narrowly on actual or imminent boundary crossings: invasions and physical assaults. Otherwise, it is feared, the notion of resistance to aggression would have no determinate meaning. A state cannot be said to be forced to fight unless the necessity is both obvious and urgent.

4. *Aggression justifies two kinds of violent response: a war of self-defense by the victim and a war of law enforcement by the victim and any other member of international society.* Anyone can come to the aid of a victim, use necessary force against an aggressor, and even make whatever is the international equivalent of a "citizen's arrest." As in domestic society, the obligations of bystanders are not easy to make out, but it is the tendency of the theory to undermine the right of neutrality and to require widespread participation in the business of law enforcement. In the Korean War, this participation was authorized by the United Nations, but even in such cases the actual decision to join the fighting remains a unilateral one, best understood by analogy to the decision of a private citizen who rushes to help a man or woman attacked on the street.

5. *Nothing but aggression can justify war.* The central purpose of the theory is to limit the occasions for war. "There is a single and only just cause for commencing a war," wrote Vitoria, "namely, a wrong received."[14] There must actually have been a wrong, and it must actually have been received (or its receipt must be, as it were, only minutes away). Nothing else warrants the use of force in international society—above all, not any difference of religion or politics. Domestic heresy and injustice are never actionable in the world of states: hence, again, the principle of nonintervention.

6. *Once the aggressor state has been militarily repulsed, it can also be punished.* The conception of just war as an act of punishment is very old, though neither the procedures nor the forms of punishment have ever been firmly established in customary or positive international law. Nor are its purposes entirely clear: to exact retribution, to deter other states, to restrain or reform this one? All three figure largely in the literature, though it is probably fair to say that deterrence and restraint are most commonly accepted. When people talk of fighting a war against war, this is usually what they have in mind. The domestic maxim is, punish crime to prevent violence; its international analogue is, punish aggression to

prevent war. Whether the state as a whole or only particular persons are the proper objects of punishment is a harder question, for reasons I will consider later on. But the implication of the paradigm is clear: if states are members of international society, the subjects of rights, they must also be (somehow) the objects of punishment.

Unavoidable Categories

These propositions shape the judgments we make when wars break out. They constitute a powerful theory, coherent and economic, and they have dominated our moral consciousness for a long time. I am not concerned to trace their history here, but it is worth emphasizing that they remained dominant even during the eighteenth and nineteenth centuries, when lawyers and statesmen regularly argued that war-making was the natural prerogative of sovereign states, not subject to legal or moral judgment. States went to war for "reasons of state," and these reasons were said to have a privileged character, such that they needed only to be alluded to, not even expounded, in order to terminate all argument. The common assumption in the legal literature of the time (roughly from the age of Vattel to that of Oppenheim) is that states always have, like Hobbist individuals, a right to fight.[15] The analogy is not from domestic to international society, but from the state of nature to international anarchy. But this view never seized the popular imagination. "The idea of war and the launching of it," writes the foremost historian of the theory of aggression, "were for the ordinary man and for public opinion always loaded with moral significance, demanding full approval if waged with right and condemnation and punishment if without . . ."[16] The significance ordinary men attached was exactly of the sort I have been describing: they drew the terrifying experience of war, as Otto von Bismarck once complained, back to the familiar ground of everyday life. "Public opinion," Bismarck wrote, "is only too ready to consider political relations and events in the light of those of civil law and private persons generally . . . [This] shows a complete lack of understanding of political matters."[17]

I am inclined to think that it shows a deep understanding of political matters, though not always in its applications a knowledgeable or sophisticated understanding. Public opinion tends to focus on the concrete reality of war and on the moral meaning of killing and being killed. It addresses the questions that ordinary men cannot avoid: should we support this war? should we fight in it? Bismarck works from a more distant perspective, turning the people who ask such questions into pawns in the high game of *realpolitik*. But ultimately the questions are insistent and the distant perspective untenable. Until wars are really fought with pawns, inanimate objects and not human beings, warfare cannot be isolated from moral life. We can get a clear view of the necessary links by reflecting on the work of one of Bismarck's contemporaries and on one of the wars at which the German chancellor connived.

Karl Marx and the Franco-Prussian War

Like Bismarck, Marx had a different way of understanding political matters. He regarded war not merely as the continuation but as the necessary and inevitable continuation of politics, and he described particular wars in terms of a world historical scheme. He had no commitment to the existing political order, nor to the territorial integrity or political sovereignty of established states. The violation of these "rights" raised no moral problems for him; he did not seek the punishment of aggressors; he sought only those outcomes that, without reference to the theory of aggression, advanced the cause of proletarian revolution. It is entirely characteristic of Marx's general views that he should have hoped for a Prussian victory in 1870 because it would lead to German unification and ease the course of socialist organization in the new Reich and because it would establish the dominance of the German over the French working class.[18]

> The French need a drubbing [he wrote in a letter to Engels]. If the Prussians are victorious, then the centralization of state power will be favorable to the centralization of the working class. German preponderance will shift the center of the working class movement in Western Europe from France to Germany and . . . the German working class is theoretically and organizationally superior to that of France. The superiority of the Germans over the French . . . would mean at the same time the superiority of our theory over Proudhon's, etc.

But this was not a view that Marx could defend in public, not only because its publication would embarrass him among his French comrades, but for reasons that go directly to the nature of our moral life. Even the most advanced members of the German working class would not be willing to kill French workers for the sake of German unity or to risk their own lives merely in order to enhance the power of their party (or of Marx's theory!) within the ranks of international socialism. Marx's argument was not, in the most literal sense of the word, a *possible* account of the decision to fight or of the judgment that the war the Germans fought was, at least initially, a just war. If we are to understand that judgment, we would do better to begin with the simplistic assertion of a British member of the General Council of the International: "The French," said John Weston, "had invaded first."[19]

We know now that Bismarck worked hard and with all his usual ruthlessness to bring about that invasion. The diplomatic crisis that preceded the war was largely of his contrivance. Nothing that he did, however, can plausibly be said to have threatened the territorial integrity or political sovereignty of France; nothing that he did forced the French to fight. He merely exploited the arrogance and stupidity of Napoleon III and his entourage and succeeded in putting the French in the wrong; it was the tribute he paid to the public opinion he deplored. Hence it has never been necessary to correct the argument of John Weston or of those members of the German Social Democratic Workers' Party who declared in July 1870 that it was Napoleon who had "frivolously" destroyed the peace of Europe: "The German nation . . . is the victim of aggression. Therefore . . . with great regret, [we] must accept the defensive war as a necessary evil."[20] The "First Address" of the International on the Franco-Prussian War, drafted by Marx on behalf of the General Council, took the same view: "On the German side, the war is a war of defense" (though Marx went on to ask, "Who put Germany to the necessity of defending herself?" and to hint at the true character of Bismarckian politics).[21] French workers were called upon to oppose the war and to drive the Bonapartists from power; German workers were urged to join the war, but in such a manner as to maintain "its strictly defensive character."

Some six weeks later, the war of defense was over, Germany was triumphant at Sedan, Bonaparte a prisoner, his empire overthrown. But the fighting continued, for the chief war aim of the German government was not resistance but expansion: the annexation of Alsace-Lorraine. In the "Second Address" of the International, Marx accurately described the war after Sedan as an act of aggression against the people of the two provinces and against the territorial integrity of France. He did not believe that either the German workers or the new French republic would be capable of punishing that aggression in the near future, but he looked for punishment nonetheless: "History will measure its retribution, not by the extent of the square miles conquered from France, but by the intensity of the crime of reviving, in the second half of the nineteenth century, *the policy of conquest.*"[22] What is striking here is that Marx has enlisted history not in the service of the proletarian revolution but in the service of conventional morality. Indeed, he invokes the example of the Prussian struggle against the first Napoleon after Tilset and so suggests that the retribution he has in mind will take the form of a future French attack on the German Reich, a war of exactly the sort that Henry Sidgwick also thought justified by the German "policy of conquest." But whatever Marx's program, it is clear that he is working within the terms set by the theory of aggression. When he is forced to confront the actualities of war and to describe in public the possible shape of a socialist foreign policy, he falls back upon the domestic analogy and the legalist paradigm in their most literal forms. Indeed, he argued in the "First Address" that it was the task of socialists "to vindicate the simple laws of morals and justice, which ought to govern the relations of private individuals, as the rules paramount of the intercourse of nations."[23]

Is this Marxist doctrine? I am not sure. It has little in common with Marx's philosophic pronouncements on morality and little in common with the reflections on international politics that fill his letters. But Marx was not only a philosopher and a letter-writer; he was also a political leader and the spokesman of a mass movement. In these latter roles, his world-historical view of the significance of war was less important than the particular judgments he was called upon to make. And once he was committed to judgment, there was a certain inevitability to the categories of the theory of aggression. It was not a question of adjusting himself to what is sometimes condescendingly called the "level of consciousness" of his audience, but of speaking directly to the moral experience of its members. Sometimes, perhaps, a new philosophy or religion can reshape that experience, but this was not the effect of Marxism, at least not with regard to international warfare. Marx simply took the theory of aggression seriously, and so he placed himself in the front ranks of those ordinary men and women about whom Bismarck complained, who judged political events in the light of domestic morality.

The Argument for Appeasement

The war of 1870 is a hard case because, with the exception of those French liberals and socialists who challenged Bonaparte and those German social-democrats who condemned the annexation of Alsace-Lorraine, none of its participants are very attractive. The moral issues are muddy, and it would not be difficult to argue that the struggle was in fact an aggressive war on both sides, rather than on each in succession. But the issues are not always muddy; history provides wonderfully clear examples of aggression. The historical study of war virtually begins with such an example (with which I also began): the Athenian attack on Melos. But the easy cases raise problems of their own, or rather, one characteristic problem. Aggression most often takes the form of an attack by a powerful state upon a weak one (that is why it is so readily recognizable). Resistance seems imprudent, even hopeless. Many lives will be lost, and to what end? Even here, however, our moral preference holds. We not only justify resistance; we call it heroic; we do not measure the value of justice, apparently, in terms of lives lost. And yet such measurements can never be entirely irrelevant: who would want to be ruled by political leaders who paid them no mind? So justice and prudence stand in an uneasy relation to one another. Later on, I will describe various ways in which the argument for justice incorporates prudential considerations. But now it is important to stress that the legalist paradigm tends in a radical way to exclude them.

The paradigm as a whole is commonly defended in utilitarian terms: resistance to aggression is necessary to deter future aggressors. But in the context of international politics, an alternative utilitarian argument is almost always available. This is the argument for appeasement, which suggests that giving in to aggressors is the only way of avoiding war. In domestic society, too, we sometimes choose appeasement, negotiating with kidnappers or extortionists, for example, when the costs of refusal or resistance are greater than we can bear. But we feel badly in such cases, not only because we have failed to serve the larger communal purpose of deterrence, but also and more immediately because we have yielded to coercion and injustice. We feel badly even though all that we have yielded is money, whereas in international society appeasement is hardly possible unless we are willing to surrender values far more important. And yet the costs of war are such that the argument for surrender can often be put very strongly. Appeasement is a bad word in our moral vocabulary, but the argument is not morally obtuse. It represents the most significant challenge to what I have been calling the presumption in favor of resistance, and I want now to examine it in some detail.

Czechoslovakia and the Munich Principle

The defense of appeasement in 1938 sometimes involved the claim that the Sudeten Germans were, after all, entitled to self-determination. But that is a claim that might have been met through some sort of autonomy within the Czech state or through boundary changes considerably less drastic than those that Hitler demanded at Munich. In fact, Hitler's goals reached far beyond the vindication of a right, and Chamberlain and Daladier knew this, or should have known it, and surrendered anyway.[24] It was the fear of war rather than any view of justice that explains their actions. This fear was given theoretical expression in a very intelligent little book, published in 1939 by the English Catholic writer Gerald Vann. Vann's argument is the only attempt that I have come across to apply just-war theory directly to the problem of appeasement, and for that reason I shall look at it closely. He defends what might be called the "Munich principle":[25]

> If a nation finds itself called upon to defend another nation which is unjustly attacked and to which it is bound by treaty, then it is bound to fulfill its obligations . . . It may, however, be its right, and even its duty, to try to persuade the victim of aggression to avoid the ultimate evil of a general conflict by agreeing to terms less favorable than those which it can claim in justice . . . provided always that such a surrender of rights would not mean in fact a surrender once and for all to the rule of violence.

The "duty" here is simply "seek peace"—Hobbes' first law of nature and presumably near the top of Catholic lists as well, though Vann's phrase "the ultimate evil of a general conflict" suggests that it is nearer to the top than in fact it is. In just-war doctrine, as in the legalist paradigm, the triumph of aggression is a greater evil. But it is certainly a duty to avoid violence if one possibly can; this is a duty that the rulers of states owe to their own people and to others as well, and it may override obligations established by international treaties and conventions. But the argument requires the limiting clause at the end, which I would have thought applicable in September 1938. That clause is worth examining, since its purpose is obviously to tell us when to appease and when not.

Imagine a state whose government strives to press its boundaries or its sphere of influence outward, a little bit here, a little bit there, continually over a period of time—not quite Edmund Wilson's sea-slug state, something nearer to a conventional "great power." Certainly the people against whom the pressure is being brought have a right to resist; allied states and possibly other states as well ought to support their resistance. But appeasement, by the victim or the others, would not necessarily be immoral—this is Vann's argument—and there might even be a duty to seek peace at the expense of justice. Appeasement would involve a surrender to violence, but given a conventional power, it would not or might not involve absolute subjection to the "rule of violence." I take it that absolute subjection is what Vann means by "once and for all." He cannot mean "forever," for governments fall, states decay, people rebel; we know nothing about forever. "Rule of violence" is a more difficult term. Vann can hardly set the limit of appeasement at the point where it means yielding to greater physical force; that is always what it means. As a moral limit, the phrase must point to something more unusual and more frightening: the rule of men committed to the continual use of violence, to a policy of genocide, terrorism, and enslavement. Then appeasement would be, quite simply, a failure to resist evil in the world.

Now that is exactly what the Munich agreement was. Vann's argument, once we have understood its terms, undermines his own case. For there can be no doubt that Nazism represented the rule of violence, and that its true character was sufficiently known at the time. And there can be no doubt that Czechoslovakia was surrendered to Nazism in 1938; the remnants of its territory and sovereignty could not be defended—at least not by the Czechs— and that, too, was known at the time. But it remains a question whether Vann's argument might not apply to other cases. I will skip the Polish war, for the Poles were confronted again by Nazi aggression and had, no doubt, learned from the Czech experience. But the situation of Finland a few months later was different. There the "Munich principle" was urged by all of Finland's friends and by many Finns as well. It did not seem to them, despite the Czech experience, that an acceptance of Russian terms in the late fall of 1939 would have been "a surrender once and for all to the rule of violence."

Finland

Stalin's Russia was not a conventional great power, but its behavior in the months before the Finnish war was very much in the style of traditionalist power politics. It sought to expand at the expense of the Finns, but the demands it made were moderate, closely linked to questions of military security, without revolutionary implications. What was at issue, Stalin insisted, was nothing more than the defense of Leningrad, which was then within artillery range of the Finnish border (he did not fear a Finnish attack but a German attack from Finnish territory). "Since we cannot move Leningrad," he said, "we must move the border."[26] The Russians offered to yield more land (though less valuable land) than they sought to take over, and that offer gave the negotiations at least something of the character of an exchange between sovereign states. At an early point in the talks, Marshal Mannerheim, who had no illusions about Soviet policy, strongly recommended making the deal. It was more dangerous for Finland than for Russia for the Finns to be so close to Leningrad. Stalin may well have intended an eventual annexation of Finland, or its transformation into a communist state, but that was not apparent at the time. Most Finns thought the danger, though serious enough, was something less than that. They feared further encroachments and pressures of a more ordinary kind. Hence the Finnish case offers a useful test of the "Munich principle." Should Finland have agreed to terms less favorable than it could justly claim in order to avoid the carnage of war? Should its allies have pressed such terms upon it?

The first question cannot be answered flatly either way; the choice belongs to the Finns. But the rest of us have an interest, and it is important to try to understand the moral satisfaction with which their decision to fight was greeted throughout the world. I am not referring here to the excitement that always attends the beginnings of a war and that rarely lasts for long, but rather to the sense that the Finnish decision was exemplary (as the British, French, and Czech decision to surrender, greeted with an uneasy combination of relief and shame, was not). There is, of course, a natural sympathy for the underdog in any competition, including war, and a hope that he can pull off an unexpected victory. But in the case of war, this is specifically a moral sympathy and a moral hope. It has to do with the perception that underdogs are also (usually) victims or potential victims: their struggle is right. Even if national survival is not at stake—as in fact it was, for the Finns, once the war began— we hope for the defeat of the aggressor in much the same way as we hope for the defeat of a neighborhood bully, even if he is not a murderer. Our common values are confirmed and enhanced by the struggle; whereas appeasement, even when it is the better part of wisdom, diminishes those values and leaves us all impoverished.

Our values would also have been diminished, however, had Stalin quickly overwhelmed the Finns and then treated them as the Athenians did the Melians. But that suggests less the desirability of surrender than the critical importance of collective security and resistance. Had Sweden, for example, been publicly committed to send troops to fight with the Finns, there would probably never have been a Russian attack.[27] And the British and French plans to come to Finland's aid, inept and self-serving as these were, probably played a decisive part, along with the early and unexpected victories of the Finnish army, in persuading the Russians to seek a negotiated settlement. The new borders established in March 1940 were far worse than those that had been offered to Finland four months earlier; thousands of Finnish soldiers (and a greater number of Russians) were dead; hundreds of thousands of Finnish civilians were driven from their homes. But against all this must be set the vindication of Finnish independence. I don't know how one strikes the balance, still less how one might have done so in 1939 when vindication seemed an unlikely or at best a chancy prospect. Nor can its value be measured even now; it involves national pride and self-respect as much as freedom in policy-making (which no state possesses absolutely and Finland, since 1940, to a lesser degree than many). If the Finnish war is commonly thought to have been worthwhile, it is because independence is not a value that can easily be traded off.*

* It is probably less important, then, that these calculations be rightly made (since we cannot be sure what that would mean) than that they be made by the right people. One might usefully compare the decisions of the Melians and the Finns in this regard. Melos was an oligarchy, and its leaders, who wanted to fight, refused to allow the Athenian generals to address a popular assembly. Presumably they feared that the people would refuse to risk their lives and their city for the oligarchs. Finland was a democracy; its people knew the exact nature of the Russian demands; and the government's decision to fight apparently had overwhelming popular support. It would fit well with the rest of the theory of aggression if the Finns were again t.ken as exemplary: the decision to reject appeasement is best made by the men and women who will have to endure the war that follows (or by their representatives). This says nothing, of course, about the arguments one might want to make in the popular assembly: these might well be prudential and cautionary rather than defiant and heroic.

The "Munich principle" would concede the loss or erosion of independence for the sake of the survival of individual men and women. It points toward a certain sort of international society, founded not on the defense of rights but on the adjustment to power. No doubt there is realism in this view. But the Finnish example suggests that there is also realism in the alternative view, and in a twofold sense. First, the rights are real, even to the people who must die to defend them; and second, the defense is (sometimes) possible. I don't want to argue that appeasement can never be justified, only to point to the great importance we collectively attach to the values the aggressor attacks. These values are summed up in the existence of states like Finland—indeed, of many such states. The theory of aggression presupposes our commitment to a pluralist world, and that commitment is also the inner meaning of the presumption in favor of resistance. We want to live in an international society where communities of men and women freely shape their separate destinies. But that society is never fully realized; it is never safe; it must always be defended. The Finnish war is a paradigmatic example of the necessary defense. That is why, for all the complexity of the diplomatic maneuvering that preceded the war, the actual fighting has about it a great moral simplicity.

The defense of rights is a reason for fighting. I want now to stress again, and finally, that it is the only reason. The legalist paradigm rules out every other sort of war. Preventive wars, commercial wars, wars of expansion and conquest, religious crusades, revolutionary wars, military interventions—all these are barred and barred absolutely, in much the same way as their domestic equivalents are ruled out in municipal law. Or, to turn the argument around once more, all these constitute aggressive acts on the part of whoever begins them and justify forceful resistance, as their equivalents would in the homes and streets of domestic society.

But this is not yet a complete characterization of the morality of war. Though the domestic analogy is an intellectual tool of critical importance, it doesn't offer an entirely accurate picture of international society. States are not in fact like individuals (because they are collections of individuals) and the relations among states are not like the private dealings of men and women (because they are not framed in the same way by authoritative law). These differences are not unknown or obscure. I have been ignoring them only for the sake of analytical clarity. I have wanted to argue that as an account of our moral judgments, the domestic analogy and the legalist paradigm possess great explanatory power. The account is still incomplete, however, and I must look now at a series of issues and historical cases that suggest the need for revision. I cannot exhaust the range of possible revision, for our moral judgments are enormously subtle and complex. But the major points at which the argument for justice requires the amendment of the paradigm are clear enough; they have long been the focus of legal and moral debate.

5

Anticipations

The first questions asked when states go to war are also the easiest
to answer: who started the shooting? who sent troops across the
border? These are questions of fact, not of judgment, and if the
answers are disputed, it is only because of the lies that governments tell. The lies don't, in any case, detain us long; the truth
comes out soon enough. Governments lie so as to absolve themselves from the charge of aggression. But it is not on the answers
to questions such as these that our final judgments about aggression depend. There are further arguments to make, justifications
to offer, lies to tell, before the moral issue is directly confronted.
For aggression often begins without shots being fired or borders
crossed.

Both individuals and states can rightfully defend themselves
against violence that is imminent but not actual; they can fire the
first shots if they know themselves about to be attacked. This is a
right recognized in domestic law and also in the legalist paradigm
for international society. In most legal accounts, however, it is
severely restricted. Indeed, once one has stated the restrictions, it
is no longer clear whether the right has any substance at all. Thus
the argument of Secretary of State Daniel Webster in the *Caroline*
case of 1842 (the details of which need not concern us here): in
order to justify pre-emptive violence, Webster wrote, there must
be shown "a necessity of self-defense . . . instant, overwhelming,
leaving no choice of means, and no moment for deliberation."[1]
That would permit us to do little more than respond to an attack
once we had seen it coming but before we had felt its impact. Pre-

emption on this view is like a reflex action, a throwing up of one's arms at the very last minute. But it hardly requires much of a "showing" to justify a movement of that sort. Even the most presumptuous aggressor is not likely to insist, as a matter of right, that his victims stand still until he lands the first blow. Webster's formula seems to be the favored one among students of international law, but I don't believe that it addresses itself usefully to the experience of imminent war. There is often plenty of time for deliberation, agonizing hours, days, even weeks of deliberation, when one doubts that war can be avoided and wonders whether or not to strike first. The debate is couched, I suppose, in strategic more than in moral terms. But the decision is judged morally, and the expectation of that judgment, of the effects it will have in allied and neutral states and among one's own people, is itself a strategic factor. So it is important to get the terms of the judgment right, and that requires some revision of the legalist paradigm. For the paradigm is more restrictive than the judgments we actually make. We are disposed to sympathize with potential victims even before they confront an instant and overwhelming necessity.

Imagine a spectrum of anticipation: at one end is Webster's reflex, necessary and determined; at the other end is preventive war, an attack that responds to a distant danger, a matter of foresight and free choice. I want to begin at the far end of the spectrum, where danger is a matter of judgment and political decision is unconstrained, and then edge my way along to the point where we currently draw the line between justified and unjustified attacks. What is involved at that point is something very different from Webster's reflex; it is still possible to make choices, to begin the fighting or to arm oneself and wait. Hence the decision to begin at least resembles the decision to fight a preventive war, and it is important to distinguish the criteria by which it is defended from those that were once thought to justify prevention. Why not draw the line at the far end of the spectrum? The reasons are central to an understanding of the position we now hold.

Preventive War and the Balance of Power

Preventive war presupposes some standard against which danger is to be measured. That standard does not exist, as it were, on the ground; it has nothing to do with the immediate security of boundaries. It exists in the mind's eye, in the idea of a balance of power, probably the dominant idea in international politics from the seventeenth century to the present day. A preventive war is a war fought to maintain the balance, to stop what is thought to be an even distribution of power from shifting into a relation of dominance and inferiority. The balance is often talked about as if it were the key to peace among states. But it cannot be that, else it would not need to be defended so often by force of arms. "The balance of power, the pride of modern policy . . . invented to preserve the general peace as well as the freedom of Europe," wrote Edmund Burke in 1760, "has only preserved its liberty. It has been the original of innumerable and fruitless wars."[2] In fact, of course, the wars to which Burke is referring are easily numbered. Whether or not they were fruitless depends upon how one views the connection between preventive war and the preservation of liberty. Eighteenth century British statesmen and their intellectual supporters obviously thought the connection very close. A radically unbalanced system, they recognized, would more likely make for peace, but they were "alarmed by the danger of universal monarchy."* When they went to war on behalf of the balance, they thought they were defending, not national interest alone, but an international order that made liberty possible throughout Europe.

That is the classic argument for prevention. It requires of the

---

* The line is from David Hume's essay "Of the Balance of Power," where Hume describes three British wars on behalf of the balance as having been "begun with justice, and even, perhaps, from necessity." I would have considered his argument at length had I found it possible to place it within his philosophy. But in his *Enquiry Concerning the Principles of Morals* (Section III, Part I), Hume writes: "The rage and violence of public war: what is it but a suspension of justice among the warring parties, who perceive that this virtue is now no longer of any *use* or advantage to them?" Nor is it possible, according to Hume, that this suspension itself be just or unjust; it is entirely a matter of necessity, as in the (Hobbist) state of nature where individuals "consult the dictates of self-preservation alone." That standards of justice exist alongside the pressures of necessity is a discovery of the *Essays*. This is another example, perhaps, of the impossibility of carrying over certain philosophical positions into ordinary moral discourse. In any case, the three wars Hume discusses were none of them necessary to the preservation of Britain. He may have thought them just because he thought the balance generally useful.

rulers of states, as Francis Bacon had argued a century earlier, that they "keep due sentinel, that none of their neighbors do overgrow so (by increase of territory, by embracing of trade, by approaches, or the like) as they become more able to annoy them, than they were."[3] And if their neighbors do "overgrow," then they must be fought, sooner rather than later, and without waiting for the first blow. "Neither is the opinion of some of the Schoolmen to be received: that a war cannot justly be made, but upon a precedent injury or provocation. For there is no question, but a just fear of an imminent danger, though no blow be given, is a lawful cause of war." Imminence here is not a matter of hours or days. The sentinels stare into temporal as well as geographic distance as they watch the growth of their neighbor's power. They will fear that growth as soon as it tips or seems likely to tip the balance. War is justified (as in Hobbes' philosophy) by fear alone and not by anything other states actually do or any signs they give of their malign intentions. Prudent rulers assume malign intentions.

The argument is utilitarian in form; it can be summed up in two propositions: (1) that the balance of power actually does preserve the liberties of Europe (perhaps also the happiness of Europeans) and is therefore worth defending even at some cost, and (2) that to fight early, before the balance tips in any decisive way, greatly reduces the cost of the defense, while waiting doesn't mean avoiding war (unless one also gives up liberty) but only fighting on a larger scale and at worse odds. The argument is plausible enough, but it is possible to imagine a second-level utilitarian response: (3) that the acceptance of propositions (1) and (2) is dangerous (not useful) and certain to lead to "innumerable and fruitless wars" whenever shifts in power relations occur; but increments and losses of power are a constant feature of international politics, and perfect equilibrium, like perfect security, is a utopian dream; therefore it is best to fall back upon the legalist paradigm or some similar rule and wait until the overgrowth of power is put to some overbearing use. This is also plausible enough, but it is important to stress that the position to which we are asked to fall back is not a prepared position, that is, it does not itself rest on any utilitarian calculation. Given the radical uncertainties of power politics, there probably is no practical way of making out that position—deciding when to fight and when not—on utilitarian principles. Think of what one would have to know to perform the calculations, of the experiments one would have to conduct, the wars one would have to fight—and leave unfought! In any case, we mark off moral lines on the anticipation spectrum in an entirely different way.

It isn't really prudent to assume the malign intent of one's neighbors; it is merely cynical, an example of the worldly wisdom which no one lives by or could live by. We need to make judgments about our neighbor's intentions, and if such judgments are to be possible we must stipulate certain acts or sets of acts that will count as evidence of malignity. These stipulations are not arbitrary; they are generated, I think, when we reflect upon what it means *to be threatened*. Not merely *to be afraid*, though rational men and women may well respond fearfully to a genuine threat, and their subjective experience is not an unimportant part of the argument for anticipation. But we also need an objective standard, as Bacon's phrase "just fear" suggests. That standard must refer to the threatening acts of some neighboring state, for (leaving aside the dangers of natural disaster) I can only be threatened by someone who is threatening me, where "threaten" means what the dictionary says it means: "to hold out or offer (some injury) by way of a threat, to declare one's intention of inflicting injury."[4] It is with some such notion as this that we must judge the wars fought for the sake of the balance of power. Consider, then, the Spanish Succession, regarded in the eighteenth century as a paradigmatic case for preventive war, and yet, I think, a negative example of threatening behavior.

The War of the Spanish Succession

Writing in the 1750s, the Swiss jurist Vattel suggested the following criteria for legitimate prevention: "Whenever a state has given signs of injustice, rapacity, pride, ambition, or of an imperious thirst of rule, it becomes a suspicious neighbor to be guarded against: and at a juncture when it is on the point of receiving a formidable augmentation of power, securities may be asked, and on its making any difficulty to give them, its designs may be prevented by force of arms."[5] These criteria were formulated with explicit reference to the events of 1700 and 1701, when the King of Spain, last of his line, lay ill and dying. Long before those years, Louis XIV had given Europe evident signs of injustice, rapacity, pride, and so on. His foreign policy was openly expansionist and aggressive (which is not to say that justifications were not offered, ancient claims and titles uncovered, for every intended territorial acquisition). In 1700, he seemed about to receive a "formidable augmentation of power"—his grandson, the Duke of Anjou, was offered the Spanish throne. With his usual arrogance, Louis refused to provide any assurances or guarantees to his fellow monarchs. Most importantly, he refused to bar Anjou from the French succession, thus holding open the possibility of a unified and powerful Franco-Spanish state. And then, an alliance of European powers, led by Great Britain, went to war against what they assumed was Louis' "design" to dominate Europe. Having drawn his criteria so closely to his case, however, Vattel concludes on a sobering note: "it has since appeared that the policy [of the Allies] was too suspicious." That is wisdom after the fact, of course, but still wisdom, and one would expect some effort to restate the criteria in its light.

The mere augmentation of power, it seems to me, cannot be a warrant for war or even the beginning of warrant, and for much the same reason that Bacon's commercial expansion ("embracing of trade") is also and even more obviously insufficient. For both of these suggest developments that may not be politically designed at all and hence cannot be taken as evidence of intent. As Vattel says, Anjou had been invited to his throne "by the [Spanish] nation, conformably to the will of its last sovereign"—that is, though there can be no question here of democratic decision-making, he had been invited for Spanish and not for French reasons. "Have not these two Realms," asked Jonathan Swift in a pamphlet opposing the British war, "their separate maxims of Policy . . . ?"[6] Nor is Louis' refusal to make promises relating to some future time to be taken as evidence of design—only, perhaps, of hope. If Anjou's succession made immediately for a closer alliance between Spain and France, the appropriate answer would seem to have been a closer alliance between Britain and Austria. Then one could wait and judge anew the intentions of Louis.

But there is a deeper issue here. When we stipulate threatening acts, we are looking not only for indications of intent, but also for rights of response. To characterize certain acts as threats is to characterize them in a moral way, and in a way that makes a military response morally comprehensible. The utilitarian arguments for prevention don't do that, not because the wars they generate are too frequent, but because they are too common in another sense: *too ordinary*. Like Clausewitz's description of war as the continuation of policy by other means, they radically underestimate the importance of the shift from diplomacy to force. They don't recognize the problem that killing and being killed poses. Perhaps the recognition depends upon a certain way of valuing human life, which was not the way of eighteenth-century statesmen. (How many of the British soldiers who shipped to the continent with Marlborough ever returned? Did anyone bother to count?) But the point is an important one anyway, for it suggests why people have come to feel uneasy about preventive war. We don't want to fight until we are threatened, because only then can we rightly fight. It is a question of moral security. That is why Vattel's concluding remark about the War of the Spanish Succession, and Burke's general argument about the fruitlessness of such wars, is so worrying. It is inevitable, of course, that political calculations will sometimes go wrong; so will moral choices; there is no such thing as perfect security. But there is a great difference, nonetheless, between killing and being killed by soldiers who can plausibly be described as the present instruments of an aggressive intention, and killing and being killed by soldiers who may or may not represent a distant danger to our country. In the first case, we confront an army recognizably hostile, ready for war, fixed in a posture of attack. In the second, the hostility is prospective and imaginary, and it will always be a charge against us that we have made war upon soldiers who were themselves engaged in entirely legitimate (nonthreatening) activities. Hence the moral necessity of rejecting any attack that is merely preventive in character, that does not wait upon and respond to the willful acts of an adversary.

Pre-emptive Strikes

Now, what acts are to count, what acts do count as threats sufficiently serious to justify war? It is not possible to put together a list, because state action, like human action generally, takes on significance from its context. But there are some negative points worth making. The boastful ranting to which political leaders are often prone isn't in itself threatening; injury must be "offered" in some material sense as well. Nor does the kind of military preparation that is a feature of the classic arms race count as a threat, unless it violates some formally or tacitly agreed-upon limit. What the lawyers call "hostile acts short of war," even if these involve violence, are not too quickly to be taken as signs of an intent to make war; they may represent an essay in restraint, an offer to quarrel within limits. Finally, provocations are not the same as threats. "Injury and provocation" are commonly linked by Scholastic writers as the two causes of just war. But the Schoolmen were too accepting of contemporary notions about the honor of states and, more importantly, of sovereigns.[7] The moral significance of such ideas is dubious at best. Insults are not occasions for wars, any more than they are (these days) occasions for duels.

For the rest, military alliances, mobilizations, troop movements, border incursions, naval blockades—all these, with or without verbal menace, sometimes count and sometimes do not count as sufficient indications of hostile intent. But it is, at least, these sorts of actions with which we are concerned. We move along the anticipation spectrum in search, as it were, of enemies: not possible or potential enemies, not merely present ill-wishers, but states and nations that are already, to use a phrase I shall use again with reference to the distinction of combatants and noncombatants, *engaged in harming us* (and who have already harmed us, by their threats, even if they have not yet inflicted any physical injury). And this search, though it carries us beyond preventive war, clearly brings us up short of Webster's pre-emption. The line between legitimate and illegitimate first strikes is not going to be drawn at the point of imminent attack but at the point of sufficient threat. That phrase is necessarily vague. I mean it to cover three things: a manifest intent to injure, a degree of active preparation that makes that intent a positive danger, and a general situation in which waiting, or doing anything other than fighting, greatly magnifies the risk. The argument may be made more clear if I compare these criteria to Vattel's. Instead of previous signs of rapacity and ambition, current and particular signs are required; instead of an "augmentation of power," actual preparation for war; instead of the refusal of future securities, the intensification of present dangers. Preventive war looks to the past and future, Webster's reflex action to the immediate moment, while the idea of being under a threat focuses on what we had best call simply *the present*. I cannot specify a time span; it is a span within which one can still make choices, and within which it is possible to feel straitened.[8]

What such a time is like is best revealed concretely. We can study it in the three weeks that preceded the Six Day War of 1967. Here is a case as crucial for an understanding of anticipation in the twentieth century as the War of the Spanish Succession was for the eighteenth, and one suggesting that the shift from dynastic to national politics, the costs of which have so often been stressed, has also brought some moral gains. For nations, especially democratic nations, are less likely to fight preventive wars than dynasties are.

The Six Day War

Actual fighting between Israel and Egypt began on June 5, 1967, with an Israeli first strike. In the early hours of the war, the Israelis did not acknowledge that they had sought the advantages of surprise, but the deception was not maintained. In fact, they believed themselves justified in attacking first by the dramatic events of the previous weeks. So we must focus on those events and their moral significance. It would be possible, of course, to look further back still, to the whole course of the Arab-Jewish conflict in the Middle East. Wars undoubtedly have long political and moral pre-histories. But anticipation needs to be understood within a narrower frame. The Egyptians believed that the founding of Israel in 1948 had been unjust, that the state had no rightful existence, and hence that it could be attacked at any time. It follows from this that Israel had no right of anticipation since it had no right of self-defense. But self-defense seems the primary and indisputable right of any political community, merely because it is *there* and whatever the circumstances under which it achieved statehood.* Perhaps this is why the Egyptians fell back in their more formal arguments upon the claim that a state of war already existed between Egypt and Israel and that this condition justified the military moves they undertook in May 1967.[9] But the same condition would justify Israel's first strike. It is best to assume, I think, that the existing cease-fire between the two countries was at least a near-peace and that the outbreak of the war requires a moral explanation—the burden falling on the Israelis, who began the fighting.

The crisis apparently had its origins in reports, circulated by Soviet officials in mid-May, that Israel was massing its forces on the Syrian border. The falsity of these reports was almost immediately vouched for by United Nations observers on the scene. Nevertheless, on May 14, the Egyptian government put its armed forces on "maximum alert" and began a major buildup of its troops

---

* The only limitation on this right has to do with internal, not external legitimacy: a state (or government) established against the will of its own people, ruling violently, may well forfeit its right to defend itself even against a foreign invasion. I will take up some of the issues raised by this possibility in the next chapter.

in the Sinai. Four days later, Egypt expelled the United Nations Emergency Force from the Sinai and the Gaza Strip; its withdrawal began immediately, though I do not think that its title had been intended to suggest that it would depart so quickly in event of emergency. The Egyptian military buildup continued, and on May 22, President Nasser announced that the Straits of Tiran would henceforth be closed to Israeli shipping.

In the aftermath of the Suez War of 1956, the Straits had been recognized by the world community as an international waterway. That meant that their closing would constitute a *casus belli*, and the Israelis had stated at that time, and on many occasions since, that they would so regard it. The war might then be dated from May 22, and the Israeli attack of June 5 described simply as its first military incident: wars often begin before the fighting of them does. But the fact is that after May 22, the Israeli cabinet was still debating whether or not to go to war. And, in any case, the actual initiation of violence is a crucial moral event. If it can sometimes be justified by reference to previous events, it nevertheless has to be justified. In a major speech on May 29, Nasser made that justification much easier by announcing that if war came the Egyptian goal would be nothing less than the destruction of Israel. On May 30, King Hussein of Jordan flew to Cairo to sign a treaty placing the Jordanian army under Egyptian command in event of war, thus associating himself with the Egyptian purpose. Syria already had agreed to such an arrangement, and several days later Iraq joined the alliance. The Israelis struck on the day after the Iraqi annoucement.

For all the excitement and fear that their actions generated, it is unlikely that the Egyptians intended to begin the war themselves. After the fighting was over, Israel published documents, captured in its course, that included plans for an invasion of the Negev; but these were probably plans for a counter-attack, once an Israeli offensive had spent itself in the Sinai, or for a first strike at some later time. Nasser would almost certainly have regarded it as a great victory if he could have closed the Straits and maintained his army on Israel's borders without war. Indeed, it would have been a great victory, not only because of the economic blockade it would have established, but also because of the strain it would have placed on the Israeli defense system. "There was a basic assymetry in the structure of forces: the Egyptians could deploy . . . their large army of long-term regulars on the Israeli border and keep it there indefinitely; the Israelis could only counter their deployment by mobilizing reserve formations, and reservists could not be kept in uniform for very long . . . Egypt could therefore stay on the defensive while Israel would have to attack unless the crisis was defused diplomatically."[10] *Would have to attack*: the necessity cannot be called instant and overwhelming; nor, however, would an Israeli decision to allow Nasser his victory have meant nothing more than a shift in the balance of power posing possible dangers at some future time. It would have opened Israel to attack at any time. It would have represented a drastic erosion of Israeli security such as only a determined enemy would hope to bring about.

The initial Israeli response was not similarly determined but, for domestic political reasons having to do in part with the democratic character of the state, hesitant and confused. Israel's leaders sought a political resolution of the crisis—the opening of the Straits and a demobilization of forces on both sides—which they did not have the political strength or support to effect. A flurry of diplomatic activity ensued, serving only to reveal what might have been predicted in advance: the unwillingness of the Western powers to pressure or coerce the Egyptians. One always wants to see diplomacy tried before the resort to war, so that we are sure that war is the last resort. But it would be difficult in this case to make an argument for its necessity. Day by day, diplomatic efforts seemed only to intensify Israel's isolation.

Meanwhile, "an intense fear spread in the country." The extraordinary Israeli triumph, once fighting began, makes it difficult to recall the preceding weeks of anxiety. Egypt was in the grip of a war fever, familiar enough from European history, a celebration in advance of expected victories. The Israeli mood was very different, suggesting what it means to live under threat: rumors of coming disasters were endlessly repeated; frightened men and women raided food shops, buying up their entire stock, despite government announcements that there were ample reserves; thousands of graves were dug in the military cemeteries; Israel's political and military leaders lived on the edge of nervous exhaustion.[11] I have already argued that fear by itself establishes no right of anticipation. But Israeli anxiety during those weeks seems an almost classical example of "just fear"—first, because Israel really was in danger (as foreign observers readily agreed), and second, because it was Nasser's intention to put it in danger. He said this often enough, but it is also and more importantly true that his military moves served no other, more limited goal.

Anticipations

The Israeli first strike is, I think, a clear case of legitimate anticipation. To say that, however, is to suggest a major revision of the legalist paradigm. For it means that aggression can be made out not only in the absence of a military attack or invasion but in the (probable) absence of any immediate intention to launch such an attack or invasion. The general formula must go something like this: states may use military force in the face of threats of war, whenever the failure to do so would seriously risk their territorial integrity or political independence. Under such circumstances it can fairly be said that they have been forced to fight and that they are the victims of aggression. Since there are no police upon whom they can call, the moment at which states are forced to fight probably comes sooner than it would for individuals in a settled domestic society. But if we imagine an unstable society, like the "wild west" of American fiction, the analogy can be restated: a state under threat is like an individual hunted by an enemy who has announced his intention of killing or injuring him. Surely such a person may surprise his hunter, if he is able to do so.

The formula is permissive, but it implies restrictions that can usefully be unpacked only with reference to particular cases. It is obvious, for example, that measures short of war are preferable to war itself whenever they hold out the hope of similar or nearly similar effectiveness. But what those measures might be, or how long they must be tried, cannot be a matter of *a priori* stipulation. In the case of the Six Day War, the "asymmetry in the structure of forces" set a time limit on diplomatic efforts that would have no relevance to conflicts involving other sorts of states and armies. A general rule containing words like "seriously" opens a broad path for human judgment—which it is, no doubt, the purpose of the legalist paradigm to narrow or block altogether. But it is a fact of our moral life that political leaders make such judgments, and that once they are made the rest of us do not uniformly condemn them. Rather, we weigh and evaluate their actions on the basis of criteria like those I have tried to describe. When we do that we are acknowledging that there are threats with which no nation can be expected to live. And that acknowledgment is an important part of our understanding of aggression.

6

Interventions

The principle that states should never intervene in the domestic affairs of other states follows readily from the legalist paradigm and, less readily and more ambiguously, from those conceptions of life and liberty that underlie the paradigm and make it plausible. But these same conceptions seem also to require that we sometimes disregard the principle; and what might be called the rules of disregard, rather than the principle itself, have been the focus of moral interest and argument. No state can admit to fighting an aggressive war and then defend its actions. But intervention is differently understood. The word is not defined as a criminal activity, and though the practice of intervening often threatens the territorial integrity and political independence of invaded states, it can sometimes be justified. It is more important to stress at the outset, however, that it always has to be justified. The burden of proof falls on any political leader who tries to shape the domestic arrangements or alter the conditions of life in a foreign country. And when the attempt is made with armed force, the burden is especially heavy—not only because of the coercions and ravages that military intervention inevitably brings, but also because it is thought that the citizens of a sovereign state have a right, insofar as they are to be coerced and ravaged at all, to suffer only at one another's hands.

Self-Determination and Self-Help

The Argument of John Stuart Mill

These citizens are the members, it is presumed, of a single political community, entitled collectively to determine their own affairs. The precise nature of this right is nicely worked out by John Stuart Mill in a short article published in the same year as the treatise *On Liberty* (1859) and especially useful to us because the individual/community analogy was very much in Mill's mind as he wrote.[1] We are to treat states as self-determining communities, he argues, whether or not their internal political arrangements are free, whether or not the citizens choose their government and openly debate the policies carried out in their name. For self-determination and political freedom are not equivalent terms. The first is the more inclusive idea; it describes not only a particular institutional arrangement but also the process by which a community arrives at that arrangement—or does not. A state is self-determining even if its citizens struggle and fail to establish free institutions, but it has been deprived of self-determination if such institutions are established by an intrusive neighbor. The members of a political community must seek their own freedom, just as the individual must cultivate his own virtue. They cannot be set free, as he cannot be made virtuous, by any external force. Indeed, political freedom depends upon the existence of individual virtue, and this the armies of another state are most unlikely to produce—unless, perhaps, they inspire an active resistance and set in motion a self-determining politics. Self-determination is the school in which virtue is learned (or not) and liberty is won (or not). Mill recognizes that a people who have had the "misfortune" to be ruled by a tyrannical government are peculiarly disadvantaged: they have never had a chance to develop "the virtues needful for maintaining freedom." But he insists nevertheless on the stern doctrine of self-help. "It is during an arduous struggle to become free by their own efforts that these virtues have the best chance of springing up."

Though Mill's argument can be cast in utilitarian terms, the harshness of his conclusions suggests that this is not its most appropriate form. The Millian view of self-determination seems to make utilitarian calculation unnecessary, or at least subsidiary to an understanding of communal liberty. He doesn't believe that intervention fails more often than not to serve the purposes of liberty; he believes that, given what liberty is, it *necessarily* fails. The (internal) freedom of a political community can be won only by the members of that community. The argument is similar to that implied in the well-known Marxist maxim, "The liberation of the working class can come only through the workers themselves."[2] As that maxim, one would think, rules out any substitution of vanguard elitism for working class democracy, so Mill's argument rules out any substitution of foreign intervention for internal struggle.

Self-determination, then, is the right of a people "to become free by their own efforts" if they can, and nonintervention is the principle guaranteeing that their success will not be impeded or their failure prevented by the intrusions of an alien power. It has to be stressed that there is no right to be protected against the consequences of domestic failure, even against a bloody repression. Mill generally writes as if he believes that citizens get the government they deserve, or, at least, the government for which they are "fit." And "the only test . . . of a people's having become fit for popular institutions is that they, or a sufficient portion of them to prevail in the contest, are willing to brave labor and danger for their liberation." No one can, and no one should, do it for them. Mill takes a very cool view of political conflict, and if many rebellious citizens, proud and full of hope in their own efforts, have endorsed that view, many others have not. There is no shortage of revolutionaries who have sought, pleaded for, even demanded outside help. A recent American commentator, eager to be helpful, has argued that Mill's position involves "a kind of Darwinian definition [*The Origin of the Species* was also published in 1859] of self-determination as survival of the fittest within the national boundaries, even if fittest means most adept in the use of force."[3] That last phrase is unfair, for it was precisely Mill's point that force could not prevail, unless it were reinforced from the outside, over a people ready "to brave labor and danger." For the rest, the charge is probably true, but it is difficult to see what conclusions follow from it. It is possible to intervene domestically in the "Darwinian" struggle because the intervention is continuous and sustained over time. But foreign intervention, if it is a brief affair, cannot shift the domestic balance of power in any decisive way toward the forces of freedom, while if it is prolonged or intermittently resumed, it will itself pose the greatest possible threat to the success of those forces.

The case may be different when what is at issue is not intervention at all but conquest. Military defeat and governmental collapse may so shock a social system as to open the way for a radical renovation of its political arrangements. This seems to be what happened in Germany and Japan after World War II, and these examples are so important that I will have to consider later on how it is that rights of conquest and renovation might arise. But they clearly don't arise in every case of domestic tyranny. It is not true, then, that intervention is justified whenever revolution is; for revolutionary activity is an exercise in self-determination, while foreign interference denies to a people those political capacities that only such exercise can bring.

These are the truths expressed by the legal doctrine of sovereignty, which defines the liberty of states as their independence from foreign control and coercion. In fact, of course, not every independent state is free, but the recognition of sovereignty is the only way we have of establishing an arena within which freedom can be fought for and (sometimes) won. It is this arena and the activities that go on within it that we want to protect, and we protect them, much as we protect individual integrity, by marking out boundaries that cannot be crossed, rights that cannot be violated. As with individuals, so with sovereign states: there are things that we cannot do to them, even for their own ostensible good.

And yet the ban on boundary crossings is not absolute—in part because of the arbitrary and accidental character of state boundaries, in part because of the ambiguous relation of the political community or communities within those boundaries to the government that defends them. Despite Mill's very general account of self-determination, it isn't always clear when a community is in fact self-determining, when it qualifies, so to speak, for nonintervention. No doubt there are similar problems with individual persons, but these are, I think, less severe and, in any case, they are handled within the structures of domestic law.* In international

* The domestic analogy suggests that the most obvious way of not qualifying for nonintervention is to be incompetent (childish, imbecilic, and so on). Mill believed that there were incompetent peoples, barbarians, in whose interest it was to be conquered and held in subjection by foreigners. "Barbarians have no rights as a *nation* [i.e. as a political community] . . ." Hence utilitarian principles apply to them, and imperial bureaucrats legitimately work for their moral improvement. It is interesting to note a similar view among the Marxists, who also justified conquest and imperial rule at certain stages of historical development. (See Shlomo Avineri, ed , *Karl Marx on Colonialism and Modernization*, New York, 1969.) Whatever

society, the law provides no authoritative verdicts. Hence, the ban on boundary crossings is subject to unilateral suspension, specifically with reference to three sorts of cases where it does not seem to serve the purposes for which it was established:

—when a particular set of boundaries clearly contains two or more political communities, one of which is already engaged in a large-scale military struggle for independence; that is, when what is at issue is secession or "national liberation;"

—when the boundaries have already been crossed by the armies of a foreign power, even if the crossing has been called for by one of the parties in a civil war, that is, when what is at issue is counter-intervention; and

—when the violation of human rights within a set of boundaries is so terrible that it makes talk of community or self-determination or "arduous struggle" seem cynical and irrelevant, that is, in cases of enslavement or massacre.

The arguments that are made on behalf of intervention in each of these cases constitute the second, third, and fourth revisions of the legalist paradigm. They open the way for just wars that are not fought in self-defense or against aggression in the strict sense. But they need to be worked out with great care. Given the readiness of states to invade one another, revisionism is a risky business.

Mill discusses only the first two of these cases, secession and counter-intervention, though the last was not unknown even in 1859. It is worth pointing out that he does not regard them as exceptions to the nonintervention principle, but rather as negative demonstrations of its reasons. Where these reasons don't apply, the principle loses its force. It would be more exact, from Mill's standpoint, to formulate the relevant principle in this way: *always act so as to recognize and uphold communal autonomy.* Nonintervention is most often entailed by that recognition, but not always, and then we must prove our commitment to autonomy in some other way, perhaps even by sending troops across an international frontier. But the morally exact principle is also very dangerous, and Mill's account of the argument is not at this point an account of what is actually said in everyday moral discourse. We need to establish a kind of *a priori* respect for state boundaries; they are, as I have argued before, the only boundaries communities ever have. And that is why intervention is always justified as if

---

plausibility such arguments had in the nineteenth century, they have none today. International society can no longer be divided into civilized and barbarian halves; any line drawn on developmental principles leaves barbarians on both sides. I shall therefore assume that the self-help test applies equally to all peoples.

it were an exception to a general rule, made necessary by the urgency or extremity of a particular case. The second, third, and fourth revisions have something of the form of stereotyped excuses. Interventions are so often undertaken for "reasons of state" that have nothing to do with self-determination that we have become skeptical of every claim to defend the autonomy of alien communities. Hence the special burden of proof with which I began, more onerous than any we impose on individuals or governments pleading self-defense: intervening states must demonstrate that their own case is radically different from what we take to be the general run of cases, where the liberty or prospective liberty of citizens is best served if foreigners offer them only moral support. And that is how I shall characterize Mill's argument (though he characterizes it differently) that Great Britain ought to have intervened in defense of the Hungarian Revolution of 1848 and 1849.

Secession

The Hungarian Revolution

For many years before 1848, Hungary had been a part of the Hapsburg Empire. Formally an independent kingdom, with a Diet of its own, it was effectively ruled by the German authorities in Vienna. The sudden collapse of those authorities during the March Days—symbolized by the fall of Metternich—opened the way for liberal nationalists in Budapest. They formed a goverment and demanded home rule within the Empire; they were not yet secessionists. Their demand was initially accepted, but controversy developed over the issues that have always plagued federalist schemes: the control of tax revenue, the command of the army. As soon as "order" was restored in Vienna, efforts began to reassert the centralist character of the regime, and these soon took the familiar form of military repression. An imperial army invaded Hungary, and the nationalists fought back. The Hungarians were now rebels or insurgents; they quickly established what international lawyers call their belligerent rights by defeating the Austrians and taking control of much of old Hungary. In the course of the war, the new government shifted leftwards; in April 1849, a republic was proclaimed under the presidency of Lajos Kossuth.[4]

The revolution might be described, in contemporary terms, as a war of national liberation, except that the boundaries of old Hungary included a very large Slavic population, and the Hungarian revolutionaries seem to have been as hostile to Croat and Slovene nationalism as the Austrians were to their own claims for communal autonomy. But this is a difficulty that I am going to set aside, for it did not appear as such at the time; it did not enter into the moral reflections of liberal observers like Mill. The Hungarian Revolution was greeted with enthusiasm by such men, especially in France, Britain, and the United States, and its emissaries were eagerly received. Governmental response was different, in part because nonintervention was the general rule to which all three governments subscribed, in part because the first two were also committed to the European balance of power and therefore to the integrity of Austria. In London, Palmerston was formal and cold: "The British government has no knowledge of Hungary except as one of the component parts of the Austrian Empire."[5] The Hungarians sought only diplomatic recognition, not military intervention, but any British dealings with the new government would have been regarded by the Austrian regime as an interference in its internal affairs. Recognition, moreover, had commercial consequences that might have engaged the British more closely on the side of Hungary, for the revolutionaries hoped to purchase military supplies on the London market. Despite this, the establishment of formal ties, once the Hungarians had demonstrated that "a sufficient portion of them" were committed to independence and willing to fight for it, would not have been difficult to justify in Millian terms. There can be no doubt of the existence (though there was a reason to doubt the extent) of the Hungarian political community; it was one of the oldest nations in Europe, and its recognition as a sovereign state would not have violated the moral rights of the Austrian people. Military supply to insurgent armies is indeed a complex issue, and I will come back to it with reference to another case, but none of the complexities are apparent here. Soon enough, however, the Hungarians needed far more than guns and ammunition.

In the summer of 1849, the Austrian emperor asked for the help of Tsar Nicholas I, and Hungary was invaded by a Russian army. Writing ten years later, Mill argued that the British should have responded to this intervention with an intervention of their own.[6]

It might not have been right for England (even apart from the question of prudence) to have taken part with Hungary in its noble struggle against Austria; although the Austrian government in Hungary was in some sense a foreign yoke. But when, the Hungarians having shown themselves likely to prevail in this struggle, the Russian despot interposed, and joining his force to that of Austria, delivered back the Hungarians, bound hand and foot, to their exasperated oppressors, it would have been an honorable and virtuous act on the part of England to have declared that this should not be, and that if Russia gave assistance to the wrong side, England would aid the right.

The qualification "in some sense a foreign yoke" with regard to Austrian rule in Hungary is curious, for whatever its meaning, it must also qualify the nobility and rightness of the Hungarian struggle for independence. Since Mill does not intend the latter qualification, we need not take the former seriously. The clear tendency of his argument is to justify assistance to a secessionist movement at the same time as it justifies counter-intervention—indeed, to assimilate the one to the other. In both cases, the rule against interference is suspended because a foreign power, morally if not legally alien, is already interfering in the "domestic" affairs, that is, in the self-determinations of a political community.

Mill is right, however, to suggest that the issue is easier when the initial interference involves the crossing of a recognized frontier. The problem with a secessionist movement is that one cannot be sure that it in fact represents a distinct community until it has rallied its own people and made some headway in the "arduous struggle" for freedom. The mere appeal to the principle of self-determination isn't enough; evidence must be provided that a community actually exists whose members are committed to independence and ready and able to determine the conditions of their own existence.[7] * Hence the need for political or military

---

* There is a further issue here, having to do with the natural resources that are sometimes at stake in secessionist struggles. I have argued that "the land follows the people" (chapter 4). But the will and capacity of the people for self-determination may not establish a right to secede if the secession would remove not only land but also vitally needed fuel and mineral resources from some larger political community. The Katangan controversy of the early 1960s suggests the possible difficulties of such cases—and invites us to worry also about the motives of intervening states. But what was missing in Katanga was a genuine national movement capable, on its own, of "arduous struggle." (See Conor C. O'Brien, *To Katanga and Back*, New York, 1962.) Given the existence of such a movement, I would be inclined to support secession. It would then be necessary, however, to raise more general questions about distributive justice in international society.

struggle sustained over time. Mill's argument doesn't cover in-articulate and unrepresented peoples, or fledgling movements, or risings quickly suppressed. But imagine a small nation successfully mobilized to resist a colonial power but slowly being ground down in the unequal struggle: Mill would not insist, I think, that neigh-boring states stand by and watch its inevitable defeat. His argu-ment justifies military action against imperial or colonial repression as well as against foreign intervention. Only domestic tyrants are safe, for it is not our purpose in international society (nor, Mill argues, is it possible) to establish liberal or democratic commu-nities, but only independent ones. When it is required for the sake of independence, military action is "honorable and virtuous," though not always "prudent." I should add that the argument also applies to satellite regimes and great powers: designed for the first Russian intervention in Hungary (1849), it precisely fits the second (1956).

But the relation between virtue and prudence in such cases is not easy to make out. Mill's meaning is clear enough: to threaten war with Russia might have been dangerous to Britain and hence inconsistent "with the regard which every nation is bound to pay to its own safety." Now, whether or not it actually was danger-ous was surely for the British to decide, and we would judge them harshly only if the risks they declined to run were very slight indeed. Even if counter-intervention is "honorable and virtuous," it is not morally required, precisely because of the dangers it in-volves. But one can make much more of prudence than this. Palmerston was concerned with the safety of Europe, not only of England, when he decided to stand by the Austrian empire. It is perfectly possible to concede the justice of the Millian position, and yet opt for nonintervention on what are currently called "world order" principles.[8] So justice and prudence are (with a certain worldly relish) set in opposition to one another in a way that Mill never imagined they could be. He thought, naively perhaps, that the world would be more orderly if none of its political communi-ties were oppressed by foreign rule. He even hoped that Britain would one day be powerful enough, and have the necessary "spirit and courage," to insist "that not a gun [should] be fired in Europe by the soldiers of one Power against the revolted subjects of an-other," and to put itself "at the head of an alliance of free peo-ples . . ." Today, I suppose, the United States has succeeded to those old-fashioned liberal pretensions, though in 1956 its leaders, like Palmerston in 1849, thought it imprudent to enforce them.

It might also be said that the United States had (and has) no right to enforce them, given the self-serving ways in which its government defines freedom and intervention in other parts of the world. Mill's England was hardly in a better position. Had Palmerston contemplated a military move on behalf of the Hungarians, Count Schwarzenberg, Metternich's successor, was prepared to remind him of "unhappy Ireland." "Wherever revolt breaks out within the vast limits of the British Empire," Schwarzenberg wrote to the Austrian ambassador in London, "the English government always knows how to maintain the authority of the law . . . even at the price of torrents of blood. It is not for us," he went on, "to blame her."[9] He sought only reciprocity, and that kind of reciprocity among great powers is undoubtedly the very essence of prudence.

To set prudence and justice so radically at odds, however, is to misconstrue the argument for justice. A state contemplating intervention or counter-intervention will for prudential reasons weigh the dangers to itself, but it must also, *and for moral reasons*, weigh the dangers its action will impose on the people it is designed to benefit and on all other people who may be affected. An intervention is not just if it subjects third parties to terrible risks: the subjection cancels the justice. If Palmerston was right in believing that the defeat of Austria would shatter the peace of Europe, a British intervention ensuring that defeat would not have been "honorable and virtuous" (however noble the Hungarian struggle). And clearly, an American threat of atomic war in 1956 would have been morally as well as politically irresponsible. Thus far prudence can be, and has to be, accommodated within the argument for justice. But it should be said that this deference to third party rights is not at the same time a deference to the local political interests of the great powers. Nor does it involve the acceptance of a Schwarzenbergian reciprocity. Britain's recognition of Austria's imperial claims does not entitle it to a similar recognition. The prudential acceptance of a Russian sphere of influence in Eastern Europe does not entitle the United States to a free hand in its own sphere. Against national liberation and counter-intervention, there are no prescriptive rights.

Civil War

If we describe the Hungarian Revolution as Mill did, assuming that Palmerston was wrong, ignoring the claims of Croats and Slovenes, it is virtually a paradigm case for intervention. It is also, so described, an historically exceptional, indeed, it is now an hypothetical case. For these circumstances don't often arise in history: a national liberation movement unambiguously embodying the claims of a single, unified political community; capable at least initially of sustaining itself on the battlefield; challenged by an unambiguously foreign power; whose intervention can however be deterred or defeated without risking a general war. More often history presents a tangle of parties and factions, each claiming to speak for an entire community, fighting with one another, drawing outside powers into the struggle in secret, or at least unacknowledged, ways. Civil war poses hard problems, not because the Millian standard is unclear—it would require a strict stand-offishness—but because it can be and routinely is violated by degrees. Then it becomes very difficult to fix the point at which a direct and open use of force can plausibly be called a counter-intervention. And it is difficult also to calculate the effects of such a use of force on the already distressed inhabitants of the divided state and on the whole range of possible third parties.

In such cases, the lawyers commonly apply a qualified version of the self-help test.[10] They permit assistance to the established government—it is after all, the official representative of communal autonomy in international society—so long as it faces nothing more than internal dissension, rebellion, and insurgency. But as soon as the insurgents establish control over some substantial portion of the territory and population of the state, they acquire belligerent rights and an equality of status with the government. Then the lawyers enjoin a strict neutrality. Now, neutrality is conventionally regarded as an optative condition, a matter of choice, not of duty. So it is with regard to wars between states, but in civil wars there seem to be very good (Millian) reasons for making it obligatory. For once a community is effectively divided, foreign powers can hardly serve the cause of self-determination by acting militarily within its borders. The argument has been succinctly put by Montague Bernard, whose Oxford lecture "On the Principle of Non-intervention" ranks in importance with Mill's essay: "Of two things, one: the interference in the case supposed either turns the balance, or it does not. In the latter event, it misses its aim; in the former, it gives the superiority to the side which would not have been uppermost without it and establishes a sovereign, or a form of government, which the nation, if left to itself, would not have chosen."[11]

As soon as one outside power violates the norms of neutrality and nonintervention, however, the way is open for other powers to do so. Indeed, it may seem shameful not to repeat the violation —as in the case of the Spanish Civil War, where the noninterventionist policies of Britain, France, and the United States did not open the way for a local decision, but simply allowed the Germans and Italians to "turn the balance."[12] Some military response is probably required at such moments if the values of independence and community are to be sustained. But though that response upholds values shared throughout international society, it cannot accurately be described as law enforcement. Its character is not readily explicable within the terms of the legalist paradigm. For counter-intervention in civil wars does not aim at punishing or even, necessarily, at restraining the intervening states. It aims instead at holding the circle, preserving the balance, restoring some degree of integrity to the local struggle. It is as if a policeman, instead of breaking up a fight between two people, should stop anyone else from interfering or, if he cannot do that, should give proportional assistance to the disadvantaged party. He would have to have some notions about the value of the fight, and given the ordinary conditions of domestic society, those would be strange notions for him to have. But in the world of states they are entirely appropriate; they set the standards by which we judge between actual and pretended counter-interventions.

The American War in Vietnam

I doubt that it is possible to tell the story of Vietnam in a way that will command general agreement. The official American version—that the struggle began with a North Vietnamese invasion of the South, to which the United States responded in accordance with its treaty obligations—follows the legalist paradigm closely, but is on its surface unbelievable. Fortunately, it seems to be accepted by virtually no one and need not detain us here. I want to pursue a more sophisticated version of the American defense, which concedes the existence of a civil war and describes the U.S. role, first, as assistance to a legitimate government, and secondly, as counter-intervention, a response to covert military moves by the

North Vietnamese regime.[13] The crucial terms here are "legitimate" and "response." The first suggests that the government on behalf of which our counter-intervention was undertaken had a local status, a political presence independent of ourselves, and hence that it could conceivably win the civil war if no external force was brought to bear. The second suggests that our own military operations followed upon and balanced those of another power, in accordance with the argument I have put forward. Both these suggestions are false, but they point to the peculiarly confined character of counter-intervention and indicate what one has to say (at least) when one joins in the civil wars of other states.

The Geneva Agreement of 1954, ending the first Vietnamese war, established a temporary frontier between the North and the South, and two temporary governments on either side of the line, pending elections scheduled for 1956.[14] When the South Vietnamese government refused to permit these elections, it clearly lost whatever legitimacy was conferred by the agreements. But I shall not dwell on this loss, nor on the fact that some sixty states nevertheless recognized the sovereignty of the new regime in the South and opened embassies in Saigon. I doubt that foreign states, whether they act independently or collectively, sign treaties or send ambassadors, can establish or disestablish the legitimacy of a government. What is crucial is the standing of that government with its own people. Had the new regime been able to rally support at home, Vietnam today would have joined the dual states of Germany and Korea, and Geneva 1954 would be remembered only as the setting for another cold war partition. But what is the test of popular support in a country where democracy is unknown and elections are routinely managed? The test, for governments as for insurgents, is self-help. That doesn't mean that foreign states cannot provide assistance. One assumes the legitimacy of new regimes; there is, so to speak, a period of grace, a time to build support. But that time was ill-used in South Vietnam, and the continuing dependence of the new regime on the U.S. is damning evidence against it. Its urgent call for military intervention in the early 1960's is more damning evidence still. One must ask of President Diem a question first posed by Montague Bernard: "How can he impersonate [represent] his people who is begging the assistance of a foreign power in order to reduce them to obedience?"[15] Indeed, it was never a successful impersonation.

The argument might be put more narrowly: a government that receives economic and technical aid, military supply, strategic and tactical advice, and is still unable to reduce its subjects to obedience, is clearly an illegitimate government. Whether legitimacy is defined sociologically or morally, such a government fails to meet the most minimal standards. One wonders how it survives at all. It must be the case that it survives because of the outside help it receives and for no other, no local reasons. The Saigon regime was so much an American creature that the U.S. government's claim to be committed to it and obligated to ensure its survival is hard to understand. It is as if our right hand were committed to our left. There is no independent moral or political agent on the other side of the bond and hence no genuine bond at all. Obligations to one's creatures (except insofar as they pertain to the personal safety of individuals) are as insignificant politically as obligations to oneself are insignificant morally. When the U.S. did intervene militarily in Vietnam, then, it acted not to fulfill commitments to another state, but to pursue policies of its own contrivance.

Against all this, it is argued that the popular base of the South Vietnamese government was undermined by a systematic campaign of subversion, terrorism, and guerrilla war, largely directed and supplied from the North. That there was such a campaign, and that the North was involved in it, is clearly true, though the extent and timing of the involvement are very much in dispute. If one were writing a legal brief, these matters would be critically important, for the American claim is that the North Vietnamese were illegally supporting a local insurgency, with both men and material, at a time when the U.S. was still providing only economic assistance and military supply to a legitimate government. But that claim, whatever its legal force, somehow misses the moral reality of the Vietnamese case. It would be better to say that the U.S. was literally propping up a government—and shortly a series of governments—without a local political base, while the North Vietnamese were assisting an insurgent movement with deep roots in the countryside. We were far more vital to the government than they were to the insurgents. Indeed, it was the weakness of the government, its inability to help itself even against its internal enemies, that forced the steady escalation of American involvement. And that fact must raise the most serious questions about the American defense: for counter-intervention is morally possible only on behalf of a government (or a movement, party, or whatever) that has already passed the self-help test.

I can say very little here about the reasons for insurgent strength in the countryside. Why were the communists able, and the government unable, to "impersonate" Vietnamese nationalism? The character and scope of the American presence probably had a great deal to do with this. Nationalism is not easily represented by a regime as dependent as Saigon was on foreign support. It is also important that North Vietnamese moves did not similarly brand those they benefited as foreign agents. In nations divided as Vietnam was, infiltration across the dividing line is not necessarily regarded as outside interference by the men and women on the other side. The Korean War might look very different than it does if the Northerners had not marched in strength across the 38th parallel, but had made covert contact, instead, with a Southern rebellion. In contrast to Vietnam, however, there was no rebellion —and there was considerable support for the government—in South Korea.[16] These cold war dividing lines have the usual significance of an international border only insofar as they mark off, or come in time to mark off, two political communities within each of which individual citizens feel some local loyalty. Had South Vietnam taken shape in this way, American military activity, in the face of large-scale Northern connivance at terrorism and guerrilla war, might have qualified as counter-intervention. At least, the name would have been an arguable one. As it is, it is not.

It remains an issue whether the American counter-intervention, had it been such, could rightly have assumed the size and scope of the war we eventually fought. Some notion of symmetry is relevant here, though it cannot be fixed absolutely in arithmetic terms. When a state sets out to maintain or restore the integrity of a local struggle, its military activity should be roughly equivalent to that of the other intervening states. Counter-intervention is a balancing act. I have made this point before, but it is worth emphasizing, for it reflects a deep truth about the meaning of responsiveness: *the goal of counter-intervention is not to win the war.* That this is not an esoteric or obscure truth is suggested by President Kennedy's well-known description of the Vietnam War. "In the final analysis," Kennedy said, "it is their war. They are the ones who have to win it or lose it. We can help them, we can give them equipment, we can send our men out there as advisors, but they have to win it—the people of Vietnam against the Communists . . ."[17] Though this view was reiterated by later American leaders, it is not, unhappily, a definitive exposition of American policy. In fact, the United States failed in the most dramatic way to respect the character and dimensions of the Vietnamese civil war, and we failed because we could not win the war as long as it retained that character and was fought within those dimensions. Searching for a level of conflict at which our technological superiority could be brought to bear, we steadily escalated the struggle, until finally it was an American war, fought for American purposes, in someone else's country.

Humanitarian Intervention

A legitimate government is one that can fight its own internal wars. And external assistance in those wars is rightly called counterintervention only when it balances, and does no more than balance, the prior intervention of another power, making it possible once again for the local forces to win or lose on their own. The outcome of civil wars should reflect not the relative strength of the intervening states, but the local alignment of forces. There is another sort of case, however, where we don't look for outcomes of that sort, where we don't want the local balance to prevail. If the dominant forces within a state are engaged in massive violations of human rights, the appeal to self-determination in the Millian sense of self-help is not very attractive. That appeal has to do with the freedom of the community taken as a whole; it has no force when what is at stake is the bare survival or the minimal liberty of (some substantial number of) its members. Against the enslavement or massacre of political opponents, national minorities, and religious sects, there may well be no help unless help comes from outside. And when a government turns savagely upon its own people, we must doubt the very existence of a political community to which the idea of self-determination might apply.

Examples are not hard to find; it is their plenitude that is embarrassing. The list of oppressive governments, the list of massacred peoples, is frighteningly long. Though an event like the Nazi holocaust is without precedent in human history, murder on a smaller scale is so common as to be almost ordinary. On the other hand— or perhaps for this very reason—clear examples of what is called "humanitarian intervention" are very rare.[18] Indeed, I have not found any, but only mixed cases where the humanitarian motive is one among several. States don't send their soldiers into other states, it seems, only in order to save lives. The lives of foreigners don't weigh that heavily in the scales of domestic decision-making. So we shall have to consider the moral significance of mixed motives.* It is not necessarily an argument against humanitarian intervention that it is, at best, partially humanitarian, but it is a reason to be skeptical and to look closely at the other parts.

Cuba, 1898, and Bangladesh, 1971

Both these cases might be taken up under the headings of national liberation and counter-intervention. But they each have a further significance because of the atrocities committed by the Spanish and the Pakistani governments. The brutal work of the Spaniards is easier to talk about, for it fell short of systematic massacre. Fighting against a Cuban insurgent army that lived off the land and apparently had large-scale peasant support, the Spaniards first worked out the policy of forced resettlement. They called it, without euphemism, *la reconcentración*. General Weyler's proclamation required that:[19]

> All inhabitants of rural areas or areas outside the lines of fortified towns will be concentrated within the towns occupied by troops at the end of eight days. All individuals who disobey or who are found outside the prescribed areas will be considered as rebels and judged as such.

I will ask later on whether "concentration" in itself is a criminal policy. The immediate crime of the Spaniards was to enforce the policy with so little regard for the health of the people involved that thousands of them suffered and died. Their lives and deaths were widely publicized in the United States, not only in the yellow press, and undoubtedly figured in the minds of many Americans as the major justification for the war against Spain. Thus the Congressional resolution of April 20, 1898: "Whereas the abhorrent conditions which have existed for more than three years in the island of Cuba, so near our own borders, have shocked the moral sense of the people of the United States . . ."[20] But there were other reasons for going to war.

The chief of these were economic and strategic in character,

---

* The case is different, obviously, when the lives at stake are those of fellow nationals. Interventions designed to rescue citizens threatened with death in a foreign country have conventionally been called humanitarian, and there is no reason to deny them that name when life and death are really at issue. The Israeli raid on Entebbe airport in Uganda (July 4, 1976) seems likely to become a classic case. Here there is, or ought to be, no question of mixed motives: the only purpose is to rescue *these* people towards whom the intervening power has a special commitment.

having to do, first, with American investment in Cuban sugar, a matter of interest to a section of the financial community; and second, with the sea approaches to the Panamanian Isthmus where the canal would one day be, a matter of interest to the intellectuals and politicians who championed the cause of American expansion. Cuba was a minor element in the plans of men like Mahan and Adams, Roosevelt and Lodge, who were more concerned with the Pacific Ocean than the Caribbean Sea. But the canal that would connect the two gave it a certain strategic value, and the war to win it was worthwhile insofar as it accustomed Americans to imperialist adventures (and led also to the conquest of the Phillipines). By and large, the historical debate over the causes of the war has focused on the different forms of economic and political imperialism, the search for markets and investment opportunities, the pursuit of "national power for its own sake."[21] It's worth remembering, however, that the war was also supported by anti-imperialist politicians—or rather, that Cuban freedom was supported and then, in consequence of Spanish brutality, the humanitarian intervention of American military forces. The war we actually fought, however, and the intervention urged by populists and radical Democrats were two rather different things.

The Cuban insurgents made three requests of the United States: that we recognize their provisional government as the legitimate government of Cuba, that we provide their army with military supplies, and that American warships blockade the Cuban coast and cut off the supplies of the Spanish army. Given such help, it was said, the insurgent forces would grow, the Spaniards could not long hold out, and the Cubans would be left to reconstruct their country (with American help) and manage their own affairs.[22] This was also the program of American radicals. But President McKinley and his advisors did not believe the Cubans capable of managing their own affairs, or they feared a radical reconstruction. In any case, the U.S. intervened without recognizing the insurgents, invaded the island, and quickly defeated and replaced the Spanish forces. The victory undoubtedly had humane effects. Though the American military effort was remarkably inefficient, the war was short and added little to the miseries of the civilian population. Relief operations, also remarkably inefficient at first, began as soon as the battles were won. In his standard account of the war, Admiral Chadwick boasts of its relative bloodlessness: "War of itself," he writes, "cannot be the great evil; the evil is in the horrors, many of which are not necessarily concomitant . . . The war now beginning between the United States and Spain was one in which these greater horrors were largely to be absent."[23] The horrors were indeed absent; far more so, at least, than in the long years of the Cuban Insurrection. But the invasion of Cuba, the three years of military occupation, the eventual granting of a drastically limited independence (under the provisions of the Platt Amendment) go a long way toward explaining the skepticism with which America's professions of humane concern have conventionally been regarded. The entire course of action, from 1898 to 1902, might be taken as an example of benevolent imperialism, given the "piratical times," but it is not an example of humanitarian intervention.[24]

The judgments we make in cases such as this don't hang on the fact that considerations other than humanity figured in the government's plans, or even on the fact that humanity was not the chief consideration. I don't know if it ever is, and measurement is especially difficult in a liberal democracy where the mixed motives of the government reflect the pluralism of the society. Nor is it a question of benevolent outcomes. As a result of the American victory, the *reconcentrados* were able to return to their homes. But they would have been able to do that had the U.S. entered the war on the side of the Spaniards and, together with them, decisively defeated the Cuban insurgents. "Concentration" was a war policy and would have ended with the war, whatever the war's end. The crucial question is a different one. Humanitarian intervention involves military action on behalf of oppressed people, and it requires that the intervening state enter, to some degree, into the purposes of those people. It need not set itself to achieve those purposes, but it also cannot stand in the way of their achievement. The people are oppressed, presumably, because they sought some end—religious toleration, national freedom, or whatever—unacceptable to their oppressors. One cannot intervene on their behalf and against their ends. I don't want to argue that the purposes of the oppressed are necessarily just or that one need accept them in their entirety. But it does seem that a greater attention is due them than the U.S. was prepared to pay in 1898.

This regard for the purposes of the oppressed directly parallels the respect for local autonomy that is a necessary feature of counter-intervention. The two revisionist principles reflect a common commitment: that intervention be as much like nonintervention as possible. In the one case, the goal is balance; in the other, it is rescue. In neither case, and certainly not in secessions and national liberation struggles, can the intervening state rightly claim any political prerogatives for itself. And whenever it makes such claims (as the U.S. did when it occupied Cuba and again when it imposed the Platt Amendment), we suspect that political power was its purpose from the start.

The Indian invasion of East Pakistan (Bangladesh) in 1971 is a better example of humanitarian intervention—not because of the singularity or purity of the government's motives, but because its various motives converged on a single course of action that was also the course of action called for by the Bengalis. This convergence explains why the Indians were in and out of the country so quickly, defeating the Pakistani army but not replacing it, and imposing no political controls on the emergent state of Bangladesh. No doubt, strategic as well as moral interests underlay this policy: Pakistan, India's old enemy, was significantly weakened, while India itself avoided becoming responsible for a desperately poor nation whose internal politics was likely to be unstable and volatile for a long time to come. But the intervention qualifies as humanitarian because it was a *rescue*, strictly and narrowly defined. So circumstances sometimes make saints of us all.

I shall not say very much about Pakistani oppression in Bengal. The tale is a terrible one and by now fairly well documented.[25] Faced with a movement for autonomy in what was then its eastern province, the government of Pakistan, in March, 1971, literally turned an army loose on its own people—or rather, a Punjabi army loose on the Bengali people, for the unity of east and west was already a broken thing. The resulting massacre only completed the break and made it irreparable. The army was not entirely without direction; its officers carried "death lists" on which appeared the names of the political, cultural, and intellectual leaders of Bengal. There was also a systematic effort to slaughter the followers of these people: university students, political activists, and so on. Beyond these groups, the soldiers ranged freely, burning, raping, killing. Millions of Bengalis fled into India, and their arrival, destitute, hungry, and with incredible stories to tell, established the moral foundation of the later Indian attack. "It is idle to argue in such cases that the duty of the neighboring people is to look on quietly."[26] Months of diplomatic maneuvering followed, but during that time, the Indians were already assisting Bengali guerrillas and offering sanctuary not only to refugees but also to fighting men and women. The two-week war of December 1971 apparently began with a Pakistani air strike, but the Indian invasion required no such prior attack; it was justified on other grounds.

The strength of the Bengali guerrillas and their achievements between March and December are matters of some dispute; so is their role in the two-week war. Clearly, however, it was not the purpose of the Indian invasion to open the way for the Bengali struggle; nor does the strength or weakness of the guerrillas affect our view of the invasion. When a people are being massacred, we don't require that they pass the test of self-help before coming to their aid. It is their very incapacity that brings us in. The purpose of the Indian army, then, was to defeat the Pakistani forces and drive them out of Bangladesh, that is, to win the war. The purpose was different from that of a counter-intervention, and for an important moral reason. People who initiate massacres lose their right to participate in the normal (even in the normally violent) processes of domestic self-determination. Their military defeat is morally necessary.

Governments and armies engaged in massacres are readily identified as criminal governments and armies (they are guilty, under the Nuremberg code of "crimes against humanity"). Hence humanitarian intervention comes much closer than any other kind of intervention to what we commonly regard, in domestic society, as law enforcement and police work. At the same time, however, it requires the crossing of an international frontier, and such crossings are ruled out by the legalist paradigm—unless they are authorized, I suppose, by. the society of nations. In the cases I have considered, the law is unilaterally enforced; the police are self-appointed. Now, unilateralism has always prevailed in the international arena, but we worry about it more when what is involved is a response to domestic violence rather than to foreign aggression. We worry that, under the cover of humanitarianism, states will come to coerce and dominate their neighbors; once again, it is not hard to find examples. Hence many lawyers prefer to stick to the paradigm. That doesn't require them, on their view, to deny the (occasional) need for intervention. They merely deny legal recognition to that need. Humanitarian intervention "belongs in the realm not of law but of moral choice, which nations, like individuals must sometimes make . . ."[27] But that is only a plausible formulation if one doesn't stop with it, as lawyers are likely to do. For moral choices are not simply *made*; they are also judged, and so there must be criteria for judgment. If these are not provided by the law, or if legal provision runs out at some point, they are nevertheless contained in our common morality, which doesn't run out, and which still needs to be explicated after the lawyers have finished.

Morality, at least, is not a bar to unilateral action, so long as there is no immediate alternative available. There was none in the Bengali case. No doubt, the massacres were a matter of universal interest, but only India interested itself in them. The case was formally carried to the United Nations, but no action followed. Nor is it clear to me that action undertaken by the UN, or by a coalition of powers, would necessarily have had a moral quality superior to that of the Indian attack. What one looks for in numbers is detachment from particularist views and consensus on moral rules. And for that, there is at present no institutional appeal; one appeals to humanity as a whole. States don't lose their particularist character merely by acting together. If governments have mixed motives, so do coalitions of governments. Some goals, perhaps, are cancelled out by the political bargaining that constitutes the coalition, but others are super-added; and the resulting mix is as accidental with reference to the moral issue as are the political interests and ideologies of a single state.

Humanitarian intervention is justified when it is a response (with reasonable expectations of success) to acts "that shock the moral conscience of mankind." The old-fashioned language seems to me exactly right. It is not the conscience of political leaders that one refers to in such cases. They have other things to worry about and may well be required to repress their normal feelings of indignation and outrage. The reference is to the moral convictions of ordinary men and women, acquired in the course of their everyday activities. And given that one can make a persuasive argument in terms of those convictions, I don't think that there is any moral reason to adopt that posture of passivity that might be called waiting for the UN (waiting for the universal state, waiting for the messiah . . .).

> Suppose . . . that a great power decided that the only way it could continue to control a satellite state was to wipe out the satellite's entire population and recolonize the area with "reliable" people. Suppose the satellite government agreed to this measure and established the necessary mass extermination apparatus . . . Would the rest of the members of the U.N. be compelled to stand by and watch this operation merely because [the] requisite decision of U.N. organs was blocked and the operation did not involve an "armed attack" on any [member state] . . .?[28]

The question is rhetorical. Any state capable of stopping the slaughter has a right, at least, to try to do so. The legalist paradigm indeed rules out such efforts, but that only suggests that the paradigm, unrevised, cannot account for the moral realities of military intervention.

The second, third, and fourth revisions of the paradigm have this form: states can be invaded and wars justly begun to assist secessionist movements (once they have demonstrated their representative character), to balance the prior interventions of other powers, and to rescue peoples threatened with massacre. In each of these cases we permit or, after the fact, we praise or don't condemn these violations of the formal rules of sovereignty, because they uphold the values of individual life and communal liberty of which sovereignty itself is merely an expression. The formula is, once again, permissive, but I have tried in my discussion of particular cases to indicate that the actual requirements of just interventions are constraining indeed. And the revisions must be understood to include the constraints. Since the constraints are often ignored, it is sometimes argued that it would be best to insist on an absolute rule of nonintervention (as it would be best to insist on an absolute rule of a nonanticipation). But the absolute rule will also be ignored, and we will then have no standards by which to judge what happens next. In fact, we do have standards, which I have tried to map out. They reflect deep and valuable, though in their applications difficult and problematic, commitments to human rights.

7

War's Ends, and the Importance of Winning

What may be called the modernist view of war is grimly summed up in a poem by Randall Jarrell:[1]

> Profits and death grow marginal:
> Only the mourning and the mourned recall
> The wars we lose, the wars we win;
> And the world is—what it has been.

War kills; that is all it does; even its economic causes are not reflected in its outcomes; and the soldiers who die are, in the contemporary phrase, wasted. Jarrell speaks in the name of those wasted men, of comrades already dead and of others who know they will soon be killed. And theirs is an authoritative perspective: there have been so many of them. When soldiers die in small numbers, in encompassable battles, they can attribute some meaning to their deaths. Sacrifice and heroism are conceivable notions. But the slaughter of modern warfare overwhelms their capacity for moral understanding; cynicism is their last resort. It is not, however, our last resort, or the most important form of our perceptions of the war in which Jarrell fought. Indeed, most of his fellow survivors would still want to affirm that the world is different, and better, for the Allied victory and the defeat of the Nazi regime. And theirs, too, is an authoritative perspective: there are so many of them. In an age when human sensibility is finely tuned to all the nuances of despair, it still seems important to say of those who die in war *that they did not die in vain.* And when we can't say that, or think we can't, we mix our mourning with anger. We search for guilty men. We are still committed to a moral world.

What does it mean *not to have died in vain?* There must be purposes that are worth dying for, outcomes for which soldiers' lives are not too high a price. The idea of a just war requires the same assumption. A just war is one that it is morally urgent to win, and a soldier who dies in a just war does not die in vain. Critical values are at stake: political independence, communal liberty, human life. Other means failing (an important qualification), wars to defend these values are justified. The deaths that occur in their course, on both sides, are morally comprehensible—which is not to say that they are not also the products of military stupidity and bureaucratic snafu: soldiers die senselessly even in wars that are not senseless.

But if it is sometimes urgent to win, it is not always clear what winning is. On the conventional military view, the only true aim in war is "the destruction of the enemy's main forces on the battlefield."[2] Clausewitz speaks of "the overthrow of the enemy."[3] But many wars end without any such dramatic ending, and many war aims can be achieved well short of destruction and overthrow. We need to seek the legitimate ends of war, the goals that can rightly be aimed at. These will also be the limits of a just war. Once they are won, or once they are within political reach, the fighting should stop. Soldiers killed beyond that point die needlessly, and to force them to fight and possibly to die is a crime akin to that of aggression itself. It is commonly said of just war theory, however, that it does not in fact draw this line at any point short of destruction and overthrow, that the most extreme military argument and the "moralist" argument coincide in requiring that war be fought to its ultimate end. In the aftermath of World War II, a group of writers appeared who insisted that the pursuit of justice was deeply implicated in the horrors of twentieth-century war.[4] They called themselves "realists," and I shall use that name, though these were not in fact followers of Thucydides and Hobbes. Their argument was less general and ultimately less subversive of conventional morality. Just wars turn into crusades, they claimed, and then the statesmen and soldiers who fight them seek the only victory appropriate to their cause: total victory, unconditional surrender. They fight too brutally and too long. They sow justice and reap death. It is a powerful argument, though I shall want to suggest with reference both to the conduct of war and to the purposes for which it is fought that it makes no sense except as a moral argument. The remedy the realists proposed was to give up justice and aim at more modest outcomes. The remedy I want to propose instead is to understand better the justice at which we cannot help aiming.

Unconditional Surrender

Allied Policy in World War II

The realist position might be summed up in this way. It is a feature of democratic or liberal culture that peace is conceived as a normative condition. Wars can only be fought, then, if some "universal moral principle" requires it: the preservation of peace, the survival of democracy, and so on. And once war begins, this principle must be vindicated absolutely; nothing less than total victory will justify the resort to the "evil instrument" of military force. The threat to peace or democracy must be completely destroyed.[5] "Democratic cultures," as Kecskemeti has written in his well-known book on surrender, "are profoundly unwarlike: to them, war can be justified only if it is waged to eliminate war . . . This crusading ideology . . . is reflected in the conviction that hostilities cannot be brought to an end before the evil enemy system has been eradicated."[6] The *locus classicus* of this ideology is the thought of Woodrow Wilson, and its most important material expression is the Allied demand for unconditional surrender in World War II.

What is objectionable about democratic idealism, as the realists describe it, is that it sets goals that cannot possibly be reached, for which soldiers can only die in vain. This is a moral objection, and an important one if soldiers have in fact been asked to die for such purposes as "the eradication of evil." Their most heroic efforts, after all, can only bring a particular war to an end; they cannot end war. They can save democracy from a particular threat, but they cannot make the world safe for democracy. But I am inclined to think that the significance of these Wilsonian slogans has been much overestimated in the realist literature. By the time Wilson brought the United States into World War I, the fighting had already been carried well beyond the limits of justice and reason.

The worst of those "injuries . . . to the structure of human society which a century will not efface" had already been inflicted, and the men responsible were not innocent Americans but the tough-minded statesmen and soldiers of Britain, France, and Germany. Wilson's Fourteen Points made possible a German surrender on terms that fell far short of the war aims of Lloyd George and Clemenceau.[7] Indeed, it was the German charge that these terms had not been honored in the actual peace settlement (which was true) that led the Allies to insist on unconditional surrender the second time around. "No such arguments will be admitted by us as were used by Germany after the last war," Churchill told the House of Commons in February 1944.[8] "The policy of unconditional surrender," writes Kecskemeti, "represents a studied contrast with President Wilson's political conduct of the war in 1918." But if that is true, it isn't easy to see how both Wilsonian and anti-Wilsonian policies, surrender on terms and unconditional surrender, can be attributed to "the traditional moralistic all-or-nothing American approach to the problem of war and peace."[9]

For all his idealism, Wilson fought a limited war; his ideals set the limits. (Whether these were the right limits or not is another question.) Nor was World War II an unlimited war, despite the refusal of the Allies to offer terms. The demand for unconditional surrender, Churchill assured the Commons, "does not mean that [we] are entitled to behave in a barbarous manner, nor that [we] wish to blot out Germany from among the nations of Europe." What it does mean, he went on, is that "if we are bound, we are bound by our own consciences to civilization. We are not bound to the Germans as the result of a bargain struck."[10] It would have been more precise had he said that the Allies were not bound to the German *government*, for the German people, the greater number of them, at any rate, must be included under the rubric of "civilization." They were entitled to the protection of civilized norms and could never have been entirely at the mercy of their conquerors. There is really no such thing (in the moral world) as the unconditional surrender of a nation, for conditions inhere in the very idea of international relations, as they do in the idea of human relations—and they are roughly the same in each. Even domestic criminals, with whom the authorities don't usually negotiate, never surrender unconditionally. If they cannot stipulate conditions above those established in the law, it is nevertheless true that the law recognizes rights—the right not to be tortured, for example—which are theirs as human beings and as citizens, whatever their crimes.

War's Ends, and the Importance of Winning

Nations have similar rights in international society, above all the right not to be "blotted out," deprived forever of sovereignty and freedom.* Concretely, the policy of unconditional surrender involved two commitments: first, that the Allies would not negotiate with Nazi leaders, would have no dealings with them of any sort, "except to instruct them about the details of orderly capitulation;" second, that no German government would be recognized as legitimate and authoritative until the Allies had won the war, occupied Germany, and established a new regime. Given the character of the existing German government, these commitments do not seem to me to represent an excessive idealism. But they do suggest the outer limit of what can legitimately be sought in war. The outer limit is the conquest and political reconstruction of the enemy state, and only against an enemy like Nazism can it possibly be right to reach that far. In his lectures on American diplomacy, George Kennan suggests that unconditional surrender should not have been talked about, but he nevertheless agrees "that Hitler was a man with whom a compromise peace was impracticable and unthinkable . . ."[11] That is, one might say, a realistic moral judgment. It recognizes, without explicity affirming, the evil of the Nazi regime, and it rightly places Nazism outside the (moral) world of bargaining and accommodation. We can understand the right of conquest and reconstruction only with such an example. The right does not arise in every war; it did not arise, I think, in the war against Japan. It exists only in cases where the criminality of the aggressor state threatens those deep values that political independence and territorial integrity merely stand for in the international order, and when the threat is in no sense accidental or transitory but is inherent in the very nature of the regime.

One must be careful here; it is at this point that just wars come nearest to crusades. A crusade is a war fought for religious or

---

*It was once argued by jurists and philosophers that conquerors had a right to kill or enslave the citizens of a conquered state. Against this view, in the name of natural law or human rights, Montesquieu and Rousseau claimed that the conqueror's prerogatives extended only to the state, not to the individual men and women who composed it. "The state is the association of men, not the men themselves; the citizen may perish and the man remain." (*The Spirit of the Laws*, X.3) "Sometimes it is possible to kill the State without killing a single one of its members; and war gives no right which is not necessary to the gaining of its object." (*The Social Contract*, I.4) But this is still too permissive a view, for the rights of individuals include the right of political association, and if the citizen is killed or the state destroyed, something of the man dies too. Even the destruction of a particular regime is only defensible, as I will argue, in exceptional circumstances.

ideological purposes. It aims not at defense or law enforcement, but at the creation of new political orders and at mass conversions. It is the international equivalent of religious persecution and political repression, and it is obviously ruled out by the argument for justice. Yet the very existence of Nazism tempts us, as it tempted General Eisenhower, to imagine World War II as a "crusade in Europe." So we must draw the line between just wars and crusades as clearly as we can. Consider the following argument of a nineteenth-century English jurist:[12]

> The first limitation of the general right, incident to every state, of adopting whatever form of government . . . [it] may please is this:
>
> No state has a right to establish a form of government which is built upon professed principles of hostility to the government of other nations.

This is to draw the line very dangerously, for it suggests that we might make war against governments whose "professions" we have some reason to dislike or fear. But professions are not to the point. We have no clear knowledge as to when these are likely to be acted out and when they are not. No single form of government seems particularly prone to aggression. It is certainly not the case, as many nineteenth century liberals imagined, that authoritarian states are more likely to make war than democracies are: the history of democratic regimes, beginning with Athens, offers no evidence of this. Nor is hostility to governments relevant here, except insofar as these represent the self-determining activities of nations. The Nazis were at war with nations, not governments alone; they were not merely professedly but actively hostile to the very existence of entire peoples. And it is only in response to hostility of this sort that the rights of conquest and political reconstruction come into existence.

But suppose the German people had risen against Nazism, as they rose against the Kaiser in 1918, and themselves created a new regime. The Allies were apparently committed not to deal even with a revolutionary German government. "To the morally oriented Allies," writes Kecskemeti, "any abatement from the strict rules of unconditionality meant that some element of the evil past would survive after the loser's surrender and make their victory meaningless."[13] In fact, there was another, and a more realistic, motive for strictness: mutual distrust among Hitler's enemies, the needs of coalition politics. The Western powers and the Russians could agree on nothing except an absolute rule.[14] Justice points the other way, for reasons closely akin to those that mark out and drastically limit the practice of intervention. Had the Germans themselves undertaken to destroy Nazism, there would have been every reason to help them and no need for an external reconstruction of their polity. A German revolution would have made the conquest of Germany morally unnecessary. But there was no revolution and painfully little resistance to Nazi rule. Politically significant opposition developed only within the ruling cadre itself, and only in the latter days of a losing war: thus the *coup d'etat* attempted by the German generals in July 1944. In peacetime, such an attempt would count as an act of self-determination, and if it were successful, other states would have no choice but to deal with the new government. Given a war such as the Nazis fought, and in which the generals were deeply implicated, the case is harder. I am inclined to think that by 1944 the Allies had a right to expect, and to impose, a more thoroughgoing renovation of German political life. Even the generals would have had to surrender unconditionally (as some of them, at least, were ready to do).

Unconditional surrender is rightly regarded as a punitive policy. It is important to see exactly in what sense this is so. The policy would have penalized the German people only insofar as it declared their political liberty temporarily forfeit and subjected them to a military occupation. Pending the establishment of a post-Nazi and an anti-Nazi regime, the Germans were to be placed in political tutelage: it is a consequence of their failure to overthrow Hitler themselves, the chief of the ways in which they were collectively held responsible for the injuries he and his followers caused to other nations. The forfeiture of independence, however, entails no further loss of rights; the punishment was limited and temporary; it assumed, as Churchill said, the continued existence of a German nation. But the Allies also aimed at more particular and far-reaching punishments. They refused to compromise with the Nazi regime because they planned to put its leading members on trial for their lives. To wage war with such a goal in mind, Kecskemeti argues, is to succumb to "the pedagogic fallacy," that is, to try to build a peaceful post-war world "on the undying memory of a just chastisement." But that cannot be done because deterrence doesn't work in international as it does in domestic society: the number of actors is far smaller; their deeds are not stereotyped and reiterated; the lessons of punishment are interpreted very differently by those who administer and by those who receive them; and in any case, they soon become irrelevant as circumstances change.[15] Now, "just chastisement" is exactly what the legalist paradigm would require, and Kecskemeti's criticism points toward the need for further revision. But he argues only that deterrence is ineffective, and his argument, while it is plausible enough, is by no means certainly true. I want to suggest instead that the special character of international society makes the full measure of domestic law enforcement *morally* infeasible, and at the same time that the special character of Nazism in fact required the "chastisement" of the leading Nazis.

What is special about international society is the collective character of its members. Each decision-maker stands for an entire community of men and women; the impact of his aggressive and defensive wars is felt over a wide geographic and political range. War affects more people than domestic crime and punishment, and it is the rights of those people that force us to limit its purposes. We might consider a new version of the domestic analogy, oriented toward collective rather than individual action: the attack of one state upon another is more like a feudal raid than a criminal assault (even when it is, literally, a criminal assault). It resembles a feud more than a mugging, not only because there are no commonly accepted police, but also because the rituals of punishment will more probably extend than cut off the violence. Short of the most severe and extraordinary measures—extermination, exile, political dismemberment—an enemy state, like an aristocratic clan, and unlike a common criminal, cannot be entirely deprived of the power of renewed activity. But such measures can never be defended, and so enemy states must be treated, morally as well as strategically, as future partners in some sort of international order.

Stability among states, as among aristocratic factions and families, rests upon certain patterns of accommodation and restraint, which statesmen and soldiers would do well not to disrupt. But these patterns are not simply diplomatic artifacts; they have a moral dimension. They depend upon mutual understandings; they are comprehensible only within a world of shared values. Nazism was a conscious and willful challenge to the very existence of such a world: a program of extermination, exile, and political dismemberment. In a sense, aggression was the least of Hitler's crimes. It is not quite right, then, to describe the conquest and occupation of Germany and the trial of Nazi leaders as so many (unavailing) efforts to deter future aggressors. They are better understood as the expressions of a collective abhorrence, a reaffirmation of our own deepest values.[16] And it is right to say, as many people said at the time, that the war against Nazism had to end with such a reaffirmation if it was to end meaningfully at all.

Justice in Settlements

The policy of unconditional surrender, directed at the government but not the people of Germany, was an appropriate response to Nazism. But it isn't always appropriate. Doing justice, in the legalist sense, isn't always the right thing to do. (I have already argued that it cannot be the goal of counter-interventions.) The cardinal mistake of the realists is to suppose that if one fights for "universal moral principles," one must always fight in the same way, as if universal principles did not have concrete and diverse applications. We need, then, to look at a case where limited aims were set, not by the requirements of a realistic analysis—for realism imposes no moral requirements; aggressors can be realists, too—but by the argument for justice.

The Korean War

The American war in Korea was officially described as a "police action." We had come to the aid of a state defending itself against a fullscale invasion, committed ourselves to the hard work of international law enforcement. The United Nation's authorization enhanced our commitment, but its terms were in fact shaped unilaterally. Once again, we were at war with aggression itself as well as with a particular foe. Now, what were the war aims of the United States government? One would expect that American democracy, slow to anger but terrible in its righteous wrath, should have aimed at the total eradication of the North Korean regime. In fact, our initial aims were limited in character. In the Senate debate over President Truman's decision to rush American troops into battle, it was stated repeatedly that our sole purpose was to drive the North Koreans back to the partition line and to restore the *status quo ante bellum*. Senator Flanders insisted that the President "would not be within his rights in pursuing the Korean forces . . . north of the 38th parallel." Senator Lucas, a spokesman for the

Administration, "wholeheartedly agreed."[17] The debate focused on constitutional issues; there had been no declaration of war and so the President's "rights" were limited. At the same time, the Senate did not want to declare war and enlarge those rights; its members were satisfied with what might be called a conservative war. "The acquisitive state," writes Liddell Hart, "inherently unsatisfied, needs to gain victory in order to gain its object . . . The conservative state can attain its object . . . by foiling the other side's bid for victory."[18]

That was the American goal until we ourselves, in the immediate aftermath of MacArthur's triumph at Inchon, crossed the 38th parallel. The decision to cross is not at all easy to figure out, but it seems to be an example of military *hubris* far more than of democratic idealism. Its larger political and moral implications do not seem to have been thought about much at the time; the move was defended mostly in tactical terms. To halt at the old line, it was said, would have surrendered the military initiative to the enemy and allowed him to rebuild his army for a new offensive. "The aggressor's forces should not be permitted to take refuge behind an imaginary line," Ambassador Austin told the UN, "because that would recreate the threat to the peace . . ."[19] I will leave aside the odd notion that the 38th parallel was an imaginary line (how then did we recognize the initial aggression?). It is not implausible to suggest that the North Koreans had no right to a military sanctuary and that attacks across the 38th parallel with the limited purpose of preventing their regroupment might be justified. In responding to an armed invasion, one can legitimately aim not merely at a successful resistance but also at some reasonable security against future attack. But when we crossed the old line, we also took on a more radical purpose. Now it was the American goal, sanctioned, again, by the UN, to unify Korea by force of arms and create a new (democratic) government. And that required not limited attacks within the borders of North Korea, but the conquest of the entire country. The question is whether wars against aggression necessarily generate such far-reaching and exalted goals. Is this what justice requires?

If it is, we would have done well to settle for something less. But it would be strange for Americans to answer that question in the affirmative, since we had formally branded the North Korean attempt to unify the country by force a criminal aggression. Secretary of State Acheson seems to have felt the difficulty when he told the Senate (during the MacArthur hearings) that unification had never been our *military* objective. We aimed only "to round up the people that were putting on the aggression." That would have created a political vacuum in the North, he went on, and Korea would then have been unified, not through force, but "through elections and that sort of thing . . ."[20] Disingenuous as this is, it nevertheless is indicative of what the argument for justice requires. Defending the morality of American policy, Acheson is forced to insist on the limited character of our military effort and to deny that it ever was a crusade against communism. He did believe, however, that the success of our police action required something very like the conquest of North Korea.

Clearly, the analogy in his mind was with domestic law enforcement, where one doesn't simply stop the criminal activity and restore the *status quo ante*; one also "rounds up" the criminals and holds them for trial and punishment. But this feature of the domestic model (and hence of the legalist paradigm) is not easily carried over into the international arena. For the roundup of the aggressors will most often require a military conquest, and conquest has effects that reach far beyond the people who are rounded up. It prolongs a war in which large numbers of innocent men and women are virtually certain to die, and it puts a whole nation, as we have seen, under political tutelage. It does this even if its methods are democratic ("free elections and that sort of thing"), because it replaces a regime which the people of the conquered nation had not themselves sought to replace—indeed, for which they had recently fought and died. Unless the activities of that regime are a standing affront to the conscience of mankind, its destruction is not a legitimate military goal. And however grim a picture one paints, the North Korean regime was not such an affront; its policies were more like those of Bismarck's than of Hitler's Germany. Its leaders may well have been guilty of criminal aggression, but their physical capture and punishment seems at most the marginal benefit of a certain sort of military victory, not a reason for seeking such a victory.

The argument at this point might be put in terms of proportionality, a doctrine often said to fix firm limits to the length of wars and the shape of settlements. In this instance, we would have to balance the costs of continued fighting against the value of punishing the aggressors. Given our present knowledge of the Chinese invasion and its consequences, we can say that the costs were disproportionate (and the aggressors never punished). But even without such knowledge, a strong case might have been made that

Acheson's "round-up" did not warrant its likely price. On the other hand, it is characteristic of arguments of this sort that an equally strong case could have been made on the other side, simply by enlarging our conception of the purposes of the war. Proportionality is a matter of adjusting means to ends, but as the Israeli philosopher Yehuda Melzer has pointed out, there is an overwhelming tendency in wartime to adjust ends to means instead, that is, to redefine initially narrow goals in order to fit the available military forces and technologies.[21] Perhaps the conquest of North Korea could not be defended as a means of punishing aggressors; it might nonetheless have been defended as a means of doing that and simultaneously abolishing a border that could only be (in fact has been) the focus of future tension—hence, avoiding wars to come. It is necessary in such arguments to *hold ends constant*, but how does one do that? In practice, the inflation of ends is probably inevitable unless it is barred by considerations of justice itself.

Now justice in settlements is a complex notion, but it has a certain minimal content which seems to have been understood well enough by America's leaders at the beginning of the struggle. Once that minimal content has been realized, it is the rights of the people of the enemy country that rule out further fighting, whatever its added value.* These rights were no doubt badly represented by the North Korean regime, but that in itself is not, as we have seen, a sufficient reason for a war of conquest and reconstruction. It was the crime of the aggressor to challenge individual and communal rights, and states responding to aggression must not repeat the challenge once basic values have been upheld.

* Or it is the rights of one's own people. Consider the classic discussion of proportionality in war in Shakespeare's *Troilus and Cressida* (II.2). Hector and Troilus are debating the surrender of Helen:

> Hector. Brother, she is not worth what she doth cost
>   The keeping.
> Troilus. What's aught but as 'tis valued?
> Hector. But value dwells not in particular will.
>   It holds his estimate and dignity
>   As well wherein 'tis precious of itself
>   As in the prizer. 'Tis mad idolatry
>   To make the service greater than the god.

Troilus quickly switches the argument from Helen herself to the honor of the Trojan warriors, and so wins the debate, for the value of honor seems indeed to dwell in particular wills. The move is typical, and it can be countered only with a moral claim: that the Trojan warriors have no right to put a whole city at risk for the sake of their own honor. It is not that the sacrifice is greater than the god, but that the men, women, and children likely to be sacrificed are not necessarily believers in the god and don't share in the worship.

War's Ends, and the Importance of Winning

I can now restate the fifth revision of the legalist paradigm. Because of the collective character of states, the domestic conventions of capture and punishment do not readily fit the requirements of international society. They are unlikely to have significant deterrent effects; they are very likely to extend rather than restrict the number of people exposed to coercion and risk; and they require acts of conquest that can only be aimed at entire political communities. Except when they are directed against Nazi-like states, just wars are conservative in character; it cannot be their purpose, as it is the purpose of domestic police work, to stamp out illegal violence, but only to cope with particular violent acts. Hence the rights and limits fixed by the argument for justice: resistance, restoration, reasonable prevention. I am afraid that these are not as constraining as they may sound. It will often require a fairly decisive military defeat to persuade aggressor states that they cannot succeed in their conquests. They would not have begun the fighting, obviously, unless their leaders had high hopes. And further military action may be necessary before a peace settlement can be worked out that provides even minimal security for the victim: disengagement, demilitarization, arms control, external arbitration, and so on.* Some combination of these, appropriate to the circumstances of a particular case, constitutes a legitimate war aim. If this falls short of the "punishment of aggression," it has to be said that military defeat is always punishing and that the preventive measures I have listed are also penalties, indeed, collective penalties, insofar as they involve a certain derogation of state sovereignty.

"The object in war is a better state of peace."[22] And *better*, within the confines of the argument for justice, means more secure than the *status quo ante bellum*, less vulnerable to territorial expansion, safer for ordinary men and women and for their domestic

---

* The list can be extended to include the temporary occupation of enemy territory, pending a peace settlement or for some period of time stipulated in the settlement. It does not include annexation, even as a measure of security against further attack. This is so partly for reasons that Marx suggests in his "Second Address" (with reference to Alsace-Lorraine): "If limits are to be fixed by military interests, there will be no end to claims, because every military line is necessarily faulty, and may be improved by annexing some outlying territory; and moreover, they can never be fixed finally and fairly because they always must be imposed by the conqueror upon the conquered and consequently carry within them the seeds of fresh wars." It is true, however, that some lines are more "faulty" than others and that one can make out both plausible and implausible versions of the argument Marx is opposing. A stronger case against annexation, I should think, rests on the rights of the inhabitants of the annexed land.

self-determinations. The key words are all relative in character: not invulnerable, but less vulnerable; not safe, but safer. Just wars are limited wars; there are moral reasons for the statesmen and soldiers who fight them to be prudent and realistic. Overreaching is common in war, however, and has many causes; I do not want to deny that a certain characteristic distortion of the argument for justice is one among them. Democratic idealism in the debased forms of self-righteousness and zeal sometimes prolongs wars, but so does aristocratic pride, military *hubris*, religious and political intolerance. A few sentences from David Hume's essay "On the Balance of Power" suggest that we should add to the list the "obstinacy and passion" with which even sophisticated statesmen, like those of eighteenth-century Britain, defend the balance:[23]

> The same peace which was afterwards made at Ryswick in 1697 was offered so early as the year ninety-two; that concluded at Utrecht in 1712 might have been finished on as good conditions . . . in the year eight; and we might have given at Frankfurt in 1743 the same terms which we were glad to receive at Aix-la-Chappelle in the year forty-eight. Above half of our wars with France . . . are owing more to our own imprudent vehemence than to the ambition of our neighbor.

The realists have (unrealistically) looked for a single enemy; in fact, they have more than they can handle without the support of a fully developed moral doctrine.

In the heated debates over America's Korean war, those political and military figures favoring the expansion of the conflict frequently cited the maxim: *in war there is no substitute for victory*. The idea, it should be said, is more readily traceable to Clausewitz than to Woodrow Wilson; it is anyway a silly idea, since it offers no definition of victory. In the case at hand, that word was presumably meant to describe a condition in which the enemy was utterly broken, without further resources. Given that meaning, it can safely be said that the maxim is historically as well as morally false. Nor is its falsehood an esoteric doctrine; it was widely accepted among American leaders in the early 1950s, and the government was able to sustain, through a difficult time, its search for a substitute. But the maxim is right in another sense. In a just war, its goals properly limited, there is indeed nothing like winning. There are alternative outcomes, of course, but these are accepted only at some cost to basic human values. And that means that there are sometimes moral reasons for prolonging a war. Consider those long months when the Korean negotiations were stalemated over the issue of the forcible repatriation of prisoners. The American negotiators insisted on the principle of free choice, lest the peace be as coercive as war itself, and accepted the continuation of the fighting rather than yield on that point. They were probably right, though it is difficult at this distance to weigh the values involved—and here the doctrine of proportionality is surely relevant. In any case, it follows from the argument for justice that wars can end too soon. There is always a humanitarian impulse to stop the fighting, and attempts are often made by the great powers (or the United Nations) to impose a cease-fire. But it isn't always true that such cease-fires serve the purposes of humanity. Unless they create a "better state of peace," they may simply fix the conditions under which the fighting will be resumed, at a later time and with a new intensity. Or they may confirm a loss of values the avoidance of which was worth a war.

The theory of ends in war is shaped by the same rights that justify the fighting in the first place—most importantly, by the right of nations, even of enemy nations, to continued national existence and, except in extreme circumstances, to the political prerogatives of nationality. The theory incorporates arguments for prudence and realism; it is an effective bar to total war; and it is, I think, harmonious with other features of *jus ad bellum*. But the case is different with the theory of means, to which I now must turn. Here there appear to be tensions and even contradictions that are internal to the argument for justice. It is with reference to the conduct of war and not to the end for which it is fought that the urgent need to do justice seems sometimes to lead statesmen and soldiers to act unjustly, that is, to fight without restraint and with a crusading zeal.

Once we have agreed upon the character of aggression, and of those threats of war that constitute aggression, and of those acts of colonial oppression and foreign interference that justify interventions and counter-interventions, we have also made it possible to identify enemies in the world: governments and armies that can rightly be (and perhaps should be) resisted. The wars that result from this resistance are the responsibility of those governments and armies; the hell of war is their crime. And if it isn't always true that their leaders ought to be punished for their crimes, it is vitally important that they not be allowed to benefit from them. If they can rightly be resisted, they should also be successfully resisted. Hence the temptation to fight by any means—which brings us up against what I have described in Part One as the fundamental dualism of our conception of war. For the rules of encounter take no cognizance whatever of the relative guilt of governments and armies. The theory of *jus in bello*, though it, too, is founded on the rights of life and liberty, stands independently of and apart from the theory of aggression. The limits it imposes are imposed equally and indifferently on aggressors and their adversaries. And the acceptance of these limits—moderation in battle—may well make it difficut to achieve the ends of war, even if these are moderate ends. Can the rules, then, be set aside for the sake of a just cause? I shall try to answer that question, or to suggest some ways in which it might be answered, but only after examining in detail the nature and practical workings of the rules themselves.

PART THREE

THE WAR
CONVENTION

8

War's Means, and the Importance of Fighting Well

The purpose of the war convention is to establish the duties of belligerent states, of army commanders, and of individual soldiers with reference to the conduct of hostilities. I have already argued that these duties are precisely the same for states and soldiers fighting wars of aggression and wars of defense. In our judgments of the fighting, we abstract from all consideration of the justice of the cause. We do this because the moral status of individual soldiers on both sides is very much the same: they are led to fight by their loyalty to their own states and by their lawful obedience. They are most likely to believe that their wars are just, and while the basis of that belief is not necessarily rational inquiry but, more often, a kind of unquestioning acceptance of official propaganda, nevertheless they are not criminals; they face one another as moral equals.

The domestic analogy is of little help here. War as an activity (the conduct rather than the initiation of the fighting) has no equivalent in a settled civil society. It is not like an armed robbery, for example, even when its ends are similar in kind. Indeed, it is the contrast rather than the correspondence that illuminates the war convention. The contrast is readily explicated; we have only to think about the following sorts of cases. (1) In the course of a bank robbery, a thief shoots a guard reaching for his gun. The thief is guilty of murder, even if he claims that he acted in self-defense. Since he had no right to rob the bank, he also had no right to defend himself against the bank's defenders. He is no less guilty for killing the guard than he would be for killing an unarmed bystander—a customer, say, depositing his money. The thief's associates might praise him for the first killing, which was in their terms necessary, and condemn him for the second, which was wanton and dangerous. But we won't judge him in that way, because the idea of necessity doesn't apply to criminal activity: it was not necessary to rob the bank in the first place.

Now, aggression is also a criminal activity, but our view of its participants is very different: (2) In the course of an aggressive war, a soldier shoots another soldier, a member of the enemy army defending his homeland. Assuming a conventional firefight, this is not called murder; nor is the soldier regarded after the war as a murderer, even by his former enemies. The case is in fact no different from what it would be if the second soldier shot the first. Neither man is a criminal, and so both can be said to act in self-defense. We call them murderers only when they take aim at non-combatants, innocent bystanders (civilians), wounded or disarmed soldiers. If they shoot men trying to surrender or join in the massacre of the inhabitants of a captured town, we have (or ought to have) no hesitation in condemning them. But so long as they fight in accordance with the rules of war, no condemnation is possible.

The crucial point is that there are *rules* of war, though there are no rules of robbery (or of rape or murder). The moral equality of the battlefield distinguishes combat from domestic crime. If we are to judge what goes on in the course of a battle, then, "we must treat both combatants," as Henry Sidgwick has written, "on the assumption that each believes himself in the right." And we must ask "how the duties of a belligerent, fighting in the name of justice, and under the restraints of morality, are to be determined."[1] Or, more directly: without reference to the justice of their cause, how can soldiers fight justly?

War's Means, and the Importance of Fighting Well

Utility and Proportionality

The Argument of Henry Sidgwick

Sidgwick answers this question with a twofold rule that neatly sums up the most common utilitarian view of the war convention. In the conduct of hostilities, it is not permissible to do "any mischief which does not tend materially to the end [of victory], nor any mischief of which the conduciveness to the end is slight in comparison with the amount of the mischief."[2] What is being prohibited here is excessive harm. Two criteria are proposed for the determination of excess. The first is that of victory itself, or what is usually called military necessity. The second depends upon some notion of proportionality: we are to weigh "the mischief done," which presumably means not only the immediate harm to individuals but also any injury to the permanent interests of mankind, against the contribution that mischief makes to the end of victory.

The argument as stated, however, sets the interests of individuals and of mankind at a lesser value than the victory that is being sought. Any act of force that contributes in a significant way to winning the war is likely to be called permissible; any officer who asserts the "conduciveness" of the attack he is planning is likely to have his way. Once again, proportionality turns out to be a hard criterion to apply, for there is no ready way to establish an independent or stable view of the values against which the destruction of war is to be measured. Our moral judgments (if Sidgwick is right) wait upon purely military considerations and will rarely be sustained in the face of an analysis of battle conditions or campaign strategy by a qualified professional. It would be difficult to condemn soldiers for anything they did in the course of a battle or a war that they honestly believed, and had good reason to believe, was necessary, or important, or simply useful in determining the outcome. Sidgwick apparently thought this conclusion inescapable, once we agree to make no judgment as to the relative utility of different outcomes. For then we must grant that soldiers are entitled to try to win the wars they are entitled to fight. That means that they can do what they must to win; they can do their utmost, so long as what they do is actually related to winning. Indeed, they should do their utmost, so as to end the fighting as quickly as possible. The rules of war rule out only purposeless or wanton violence.

That is not, however, a small achievement. If it were made effective in practice, it would eliminate a great deal of the cruelty of war. For it has to be said of many of the people who die in the course of a war, soldiers as well as civilians, that their deaths do not "tend materially to the end [of victory]" or that the contribution they make to that end is "slight" indeed. These deaths are nothing more than the inevitable consequence of putting deadly weapons into the hands of undisciplined soldiers, and armed men into the hands of stupid or fanatical generals. Every military history is a tale of violence and destruction out of all relation to the requirements of combat: massacres on the one hand and, on the other, ill-planned and wasteful battles that are little better than massacres.

Sidgwick's twofold rule seeks to impose an economy of force. It requires discipline and calculation. Any intelligent military strategy, of course, imposes the same requirements. On Sidgwick's view, a good general is a moral man. He keeps his soldiers in check, keyed for battle, so that they don't run amuck among civilians; he sends them to fight only after having thought through a battle plan, and his plan is aimed at winning as quickly and as cheaply as possible. He is like General Roberts at the battle of Paardeberg (in the Boer War), who called off the frontal assaults on the Boer trenches ordered by Kitchener, his second in command, saying that the loss of life "did not appear . . . to be warranted by the exigencies of the situation."[3] A simple decision, though not as common in war as one might expect. I don't know if it was made out of any deep concern for human life; perhaps Roberts was thinking only of his honor as a general (who does not send his men to be slaughtered), or perhaps he was worried about the capacity of the troops to renew the fighting on the following day. It was in any case exactly the sort of decision that Sidgwick would require.

But though the limits of utility and proportionality are very important, they do not exhaust the war convention; indeed, they don't explain the most critical of the judgments we make of soldiers and their generals. If they did, moral life in wartime would be a great deal easier than it is. The war convention invites soldiers to calculate costs and benefits only up to a point, and at that point it establishes a series of clearcut rules—moral fortifications, so to speak, that can be stormed only at great moral cost. Nor can a soldier justify his violation of the rules by referring to the necessities of his combat situation or by arguing that nothing else but what he did would have contributed significantly to victory. Soldiers who reason in that way can never violate Sidgwick's limits, since all that Sidgwick requires is that soldiers . . . reason in that way. But justifications of this kind are not acceptable, or not always acceptable, either in law or morality. They have been "generally rejected," according to the U.S. Army's handbook of military law, ". . . for acts forbidden by the customary and conventional laws of war, inasmuch as [these laws] have been developed and framed with consideration for the concept of military necessity."[4] Now, what sorts of acts are these, and what are the grounds for forbidding them, if Sidgwick's criteria don't apply? I will have to explain later on how "military necessity" is taken into account in framing the prohibitions; I am concerned now with their general character.

Belligerent armies are entitled to try to win their wars, but they are not entitled to do anything that is or seems to them necessary to win. They are subject to a set of restrictions that rest in part on the agreements of states but that also have an independent foundation in moral principle. I don't think that these restrictions have ever been expounded in utilitarian fashion, though it is no doubt a good thing that they be expounded and that military conduct be shaped to their requirements. When we abstract from the utility of particular outcomes, focus exclusively on *jus in bello*, utilitarian calculations are radically constrained. It might be said that if every war in a series extending indefinitely into the future were to be fought with no other limits than those proposed by Sidgwick, the consequences for mankind would be worse than if every war in that same series were fought within limits fixed by some additional set of prohibitions.* But saying that does not suggest which prohibitions are the right ones. And any effort to figure out the right ones by calculating the likely effects over time of fighting wars in certain ways (an enormously difficult task) is sure to run up against unconstrained utilitarian arguments: that victory here and now will end the series of wars, or reduce the probability of future fighting, or avoid immediate and horrifying consequences. Hence anything should be permitted that is useful and proportionate to the

---

* The alternative utilitarian argument is that of General von Moltke: additional prohibitions merely drag out the fighting, while "the greatest kindness in war is to bring it to a speedy conclusion." But if we imagine a series of wars, this argument probably won't work. At any given level of restraint, let's say, a war will take so many months. If one of the belligerents breaks the rules, it might end more quickly, but only if the other side fails or is unable to reciprocate. If both sides fight at a lower level of restraint, the war may be shorter or longer; there isn't going to be any general rule. And if restraints have broken down in one war, they are unlikely to be maintained in the next, so any immediate benefits probably won't show up in the balance over time.

victory being sought. Utilitarianism is obviously most effective when it points to outcomes about which we have (relatively) clear ideas. For that reason, it is more likely to tell us that the rules of war should be overridden in this or that case than it is to tell us what the rules are—beyond Sidgwick's minimum injunctions which can't and don't ever have to be overridden.

Until the constraints are lifted and the substantial effects of victory and defeat are weighed in the balance, utilitarianism provides only a general endorsement of the war convention (the twofold rule and any others commonly accepted); after that, it is unlikely to specify rules at all but only particular courses of action. When to lift the constraints is one of the hardest questions in the theory of war. I will try to answer it in Part Four, and I will describe at that time the positive role of utilitarian calculation: to mark out those special cases where victory is so important or defeat so frightening that it is morally, as well as militarily, necessary to override the rules of war. But such an argument is not possible until we have recognized rules beyond Sidgwick's and understood their moral force.

Meanwhile, it is worth dwelling for a moment on the precise nature of the general endorsement. The utility of fighting limited wars is of two sorts. It has to do not only with reducing the total amount of suffering, but also with holding open the possibility of peace and the resumption of pre-war activities. For if we are (at least formally) indifferent as to which side wins, we must assume that these activities will in fact be resumed and with the same or similar actors. It is important, then, to make sure that victory is also in some sense and for some period of time a settlement among the belligerents. And if that is to be possible, the war must be fought, as Sidgwick says, so as to avoid "the danger of provoking reprisals and of causing bitterness that will long outlast" the fighting.[5] The bitterness that Sidgwick has in mind might, of course, be the consequence of an outcome thought to be unjust (like the annexation of Alsace-Lorraine in 1871), but it may also result from military conduct thought to be unnecessary, brutal or unfair, or simply "against the rules." So long as defeat follows from what are widely regarded as legitimate acts of war, it is at least possible that it will leave behind no festering resentment, no sense of scores unsettled, no deeply felt need for individual or collective revenge. (The government or officers' corps of the defeated state may have reasons of its own to encourage such feelings, but that is another matter.) An analogy might be drawn, once again, with a family feud, its origin long forgotten, its justice no longer at issue. A feud of this sort may be carried on for many years, marked by the occasional killing of a father or a grown-up son, an uncle or a nephew, first of one family, then of the other. So long as nothing more happens, the possibility of reconciliation remains open. But if someone in a fit of anger or passion, or even by accident or mistake, kills a woman or a child, the result may well be a massacre or a series of massacres, not stopping until one of the families is wiped out or driven away.[6] The case is at least similar to intermittent war among states. Some limits must be commonly accepted, and more or less consistently maintained, if there is ever to be a peace short of the complete submission of one of the belligerents.

It is probably true that any limits will be useful here, so long as they are in fact commonly accepted. But no limit is accepted simply because it is thought that it will be useful. The war convention must first be morally plausible to large numbers of men and women; it must correspond to our sense of what is right. Only then will we recognize it as a serious obstacle to this or that military decision, and only then can we debate its utility in this or that particular case. For otherwise we would not know which obstacle out of the infinite number that are conceivable, and the very large number that are historically recorded, is to be the subject of our debates. With regard to the rules of war, utilitarianism lacks creative power. Beyond the minimal limits of "conduciveness" and proportionality, it simply confirms our customs and conventions, whatever they are, or it suggests that they be overridden; but it does not provide us with customs and conventions. For that, we must turn again to a theory of rights.

Human Rights

The Rape of the Italian Women

The importance of rights may best be suggested if we look at an historical example placed, as it were, on the margin of Sidgwick's argument. Consider, then, the case of the Moroccan soldiers fighting with Free French forces in Italy in 1943. These were mercenary troops who fought on terms, and the terms included license to rape and plunder in enemy territory. (Italy was enemy territory until the Badoglio regime joined the war against Germany in October, 1943; I don't know if the license was then withdrawn; if so, the withdrawal seems to have been ineffective.) A large number of women were raped; we know the number, roughly, because the Italian government later offered them a modest pension.[7] Now, the argument for giving soldiers privileges of this sort is a utilitarian one. It was made long ago by Vitoria in the course of a discussion of the right of sack: it is not unlawful to put a city to sack, he says, if it is "necessary for the conduct of the war . . . as a spur to the courage of the troops."[8] If this argument were applied to the case at hand, Sidgwick might respond that "necessary" is probably the wrong word here and that the contribution of rape and plunder to military victory is "slight" in comparison with the harm caused to the women involved. That is not an unpersuasive response, but it is not entirely convincing either, and it hardly gets at the root of our condemnation of rape.

What is it we object to in the license given those Moroccan soldiers? Surely our judgment does not hang on the fact that rape is only a trivial or inefficient "spur" to masculine courage (if it is a spur at all: I doubt that brave men are the most likely rapists). Rape is a crime, in war as in peace, because it violates the rights of the woman who is attacked. To offer her as bait to a mercenary soldier is to treat her as if she were not a person at all but a mere object, a prize or trophy of war. It is the recognition of her personality that shapes our judgment.* And this is true even in the absence of a philosophical conception of human rights, as the following passage from the Book of Deuteronomy—the first attempt that I have found to regulate the wartime treatment of women—clearly indicates:[9]

> When thou goest forth to battle against thine enemies, and the Lord thy God deliverest them into thy hands, and thou carriest them away captive, and seest among the captives a woman of goodly form,

---

* In a powerful essay entitled "Human Personality," Simone Weil has attacked this way of talking about what we can and cannot do to other people. Rights talk, she claims, turns "what should have been a cry of protest from the depth of the the heart . . . into a shrill nagging of claims and counter-claims . . ." And she applies her argument to a case very much like ours: "if a young girl is being forced into a brothel she will not talk about her rights. In such a situation, the word would sound ludicrously inadequate." (*Selected Essays: 1934–1943*, ed. Richard Rees, London, 1962, p. 21) Weil would have us refer ourselves instead to some notion of the sacred, of the image of God in man. Perhaps some such ultimate reference is necessary, but I think she is wrong in her claim about the "sound" of rights talk. In fact, arguments about human rights have played a significant part in the struggle against oppression, including the sexual oppression of women.

and thou hast a desire unto her, and wouldst take her to thee to wife; then thou shalt bring her home to thy house . . . and she shall . . . bewail her father and mother a full month; and after that thou mayest go in unto her, and be her husband, and she shall be thy wife. And . . . if thou have no delight in her, then thou shalt let her go whither she will; but thou shalt not sell her . . . for money, thou shalt not deal with her as a slave . . .

This falls far short of contemporary views, though I expect it would be as difficult to enforce today as it was in the time of the Judean kings. Whatever theological or sociological account of the rule is appropriate, it is clear that what is at work here is a conception of the captive woman as a person who must be respected, despite her capture; hence the month of mourning before she is sexually used, the requirement of marriage, the ban on slavery. She has lost some of her rights, we might say, but not all of them. Our own war convention requires a similar understanding. Both the prohibitions that are covered by Sidgwick's twofold rule and those that lie beyond it are properly conceptualized in terms of rights. The rules of "fighting well" are simply a series of recognitions of men and women who have a moral standing independent of and resistant to the exigencies of war.

A legitimate act of war is one that does not violate the rights of the people against whom it is directed. It is, once again, life and liberty that are at issue, though we are now concerned with these two as they are individually rather than collectively possessed. I can sum up their substance in terms I have used before: no one can be forced to fight or to risk his life, no one can be threatened with war or warred against, unless through some act of his own he has surrendered or lost his rights. This fundamental principle underlies and shapes the judgments we make of wartime conduct. It is only inadequately expressed in positive international law, but the prohibitions established there have this principle as their source. Lawyers sometimes talk as if the legal rules were simply humanitarian in character, as if the ban on rape or on the deliberate killing of civilians were nothing more than a piece of kindness.[10] But when soldiers respect these bans, they are not acting kindly or gently or magnanimously; they are acting justly. If they are humanitarian soldiers, they may indeed do more than is required of them —sharing their food with civilians, for example, rather than merely not raping or killing them. But the ban on rape and murder is a matter of right. The law recognizes this right, specifies, limits, and sometimes distorts it, but doesn't establish it. And we can recognize it ourselves, and sometimes do, even in the absence of legal recognition.

States exist to defend the rights of their members, but it is a difficulty in the theory of war that the collective defense of rights renders them individually problematic. The immediate problem is that the soldiers who do the fighting, though they can rarely be said to have chosen to fight, lose the rights they are supposedly defending. They gain war rights as combatants and potential prisoners, but they can now be attacked and killed at will by their enemies. Simply by fighting, whatever their private hopes and intentions, they have lost their title to life and liberty, and they have lost it even though, unlike aggressor states, they have committed no crime. "Soldiers are made to be killed," as Napoleon once said; that is why war is hell.* But even if we take our standpoint in hell, we can still say that *no one else is made to be killed*. This distinction is the basis of the rules of war.

Everyone else retains his rights, and states remain committed, and entitled, to defend these rights whether their wars are aggressive or not. But now they do this not by fighting but by entering into agreements among themselves (which fix the details of noncombatant immunity), by observing these agreements and expecting reciprocal observance, and by threatening to punish military leaders or individual soldiers who violate them. This last point is crucial for an understanding of the war convention. Even an aggressor state can rightly punish war criminals—enemy soldiers, for example, who rape or kill civilians. The rules of war apply with equal force to aggressors and their adversaries. And we can now see that it is not merely the moral equality of soldiers that requires this mutual submission; it is also the rights of civilians. Soldiers fighting for an aggressor state are not themselves criminals: hence their war rights are the same as those of their opponents. Soldiers fighting against an aggressor state have no license to become criminals: hence they are subject to the same restraints as their opponents. The enforcement of these restraints is one of the forms of law enforcement in international society, and the law can be enforced even by criminal states against "policemen" who deliberately

---

* In quoting this sentence I do not mean to endorse the military nihilism it represents. Napoleon, especially in his later years, was given to statements of this sort, and they are not uncommon in the literature on war. One writer claims that they illustrate a quality of leadership that he calls "robustness." Napoleon's exclamation, "I do not care a fig for the lives of a million men" is, he says, an extreme example of robustness. One could think of better names. (Alfred H. Burne, *The Art of War on Land*, London, 1944, p. 8.)

kill innocent bystanders. For these bystanders do not forfeit their rights when their states wrongly go to war. An army warring against aggression can violate the territorial integrity and political sovereignty of the aggressor state, but its soldiers cannot violate the life and liberty of enemy civilians.

The war convention rests first on a certain view of combatants, which stipulates their battlefield equality. But it rests more deeply on a certain view of noncombatants, which holds that they are men and women with rights and that they cannot be used for some military purpose, even if it is a legitimate purpose. At this point, the argument is not entirely dissimilar from that which obtains in domestic society, where a man fighting in self-defense, for example, is barred from attacking or injuring innocent bystanders or third parties. He can attack only his attackers. In domestic society, however, it is relatively easy to distinguish bystanders and third parties, whereas in international society, because of the collectivist character of states and armies, the distinction is harder to make. Indeed, it is often said that it cannot be made at all, for soldiers are only coerced civilians, and civilians are willing supporters of their armies in the field. And then it cannot be what is due to the victims but only what is necessary for the battle that determines our judgments of wartime conduct. Here is the critical test, then, for anyone who argues that the rules of war are grounded in a theory of rights: to make the combatant/noncombatant distinction plausible in terms of the theory, that is, to provide a detailed account of the history of individual rights under the conditions of war and battle—how they are retained, lost, exchanged (for war rights) and recovered. That is my purpose in the chapters that follow.

9

Noncombatant Immunity
and Military Necessity

The Status of Individuals

The first principle of the war convention is that, once war has begun, soldiers are subject to attack at any time (unless they are wounded or captured). And the first criticism of the convention is that this principle is unfair; it is an example of class legislation. It does not take into account that few soldiers are wholeheartedly committed to the business of fighting. Most of them do not identify themselves as warriors; at least, that is not their only or their chief identity; nor is fighting their chosen occupation. Nor, again, do they spend most of their time fighting; they neglect war whenever they can. I want to turn now to a recurrent incident in military history in which soldiers, simply by not fighting, appear to regain their right to life. In fact, they do not regain it, but the appearance will help us understand the grounds on which the right is held, and the facts of the case will clarify the meaning of its forfeiture.

Naked Soldiers

The same tale appears again and again in war memoirs and in letters from the front. It has this general form: a soldier on patrol or on sniper duty catches an enemy soldier unaware, holds him in his gunsight, easy to kill, and then must decide whether to shoot him or let the opportunity pass. There is at such moments a great reluctance to shoot—not always for moral reasons, but for reasons that are relevant nonetheless to the moral argument I want to make. No doubt, a deep psychological uneasiness about killing plays a part in these cases. This uneasiness, in fact, has been offered as a general explanation of the reluctance of soldiers to fight at all. In the course of a study of combat behavior in World War II, S. L. A. Marshall discovered that the great majority of men on the front line never fired their guns.[1] He thought this the result above all of their civilian upbringing, of the powerful inhibitions acquired in its course against deliberately injuring another human being. But in the cases I shall list, this inhibition does not seem a critical factor. None of the five soldiers who wrote the accounts was a "non-firer," nor, so far as I can tell, were the other men who figure importantly in their stories. Moreover, they give reasons for not killing or for hesitating to kill, and this the soldiers interviewed by Marshall were rarely able to do.

1) I have taken the first case from a letter written by the poet Wilfred Owen to his brother in England on May 14, 1917.[2]

When we were marching along a sunken road, we got the wind up once. We knew we must have passed the German outposts somewhere on our left rear. All at once, the cry rang down, "Line the bank." There was a tremendous scurry of fixing bayonets, tugging of breech covers, and opening pouches, but when we peeped over, behold a solitary German, haring along toward us, with his head down and his arms stretched in front of him, as if he were going to take a high dive through the earth (which I have no doubt he would like to have done). Nobody offered to shoot him, he looked too funny . . .

Perhaps everyone was waiting for an order to shoot, but Owen's meaning is undoubtedly that no one wanted to shoot. A soldier who looks funny is not at that moment a military threat; he is not a fighting man but simply a man, and one does not kill men. In this case, indeed, it would have been superfluous to do so: the comical German was soon taken prisoner. But that is not always possible, as the remaining cases suggest, and the reluctance or re-fusal to kill has nothing to do with the existence of a military alternative. There is always a nonmilitary alternative.

2) In his autobiography *Good-bye to All That*, Robert Graves recalls the only time that he "refrained from shooting a German" who was neither wounded nor a prisoner.[3]

> While sniping from a knoll in the support line, where we had a concealed loop-hole, I saw a German, about seven hundred yards away, through my telescopic sights. He was taking a bath in the German third line. I disliked the idea of shooting a naked man, so I handed the rifle to the sergeant with me. "Here, take this. You're a better shot than I am." He got him; but I had not stayed to watch.

I hesitate to say that what is involved here is a moral feeling, certainly not a moral feeling that is conceived to extend across class lines. But even if we describe it as the disdain of an officer and a gentleman for conduct that appears to be unmanly or unheroic, Graves's "dislike" still depends upon a morally important recognition. A naked man, like a funny man, is not a soldier. And what if the obedient and presumably unfeeling sergeant had not been with him?

3) During the Spanish Civil War, George Orwell had a similar experience as a sniper working from a forward position in the republican lines. It would probably never have occurred to Orwell to hand his gun down the hierarchy of ranks; in any case, his was an anarchist battalion, and there was no hierarchy.[4]

> At this moment a man, presumably carrying a message to an officer, jumped out of the trench and ran along the top of the parapet in full view. He was half-dressed and was holding up his trousers with both hands as he ran. I refrained from shooting at him. It is true that I am a poor shot and unlikely to hit a running man at a hundred yards . . . Still, I did not shoot partly because of that detail about the trousers. I had come here to shoot at "Fascists;" but a man who is holding up his trousers isn't a "Fascist," he is visibly a fellow-creature, similar to yourself, and you don't feel like shooting at him.

Orwell says, "you don't feel like" rather than "you should not," and the difference between these two is important. But the fundamental recognition is the same as in the other cases and more fully articulated. Moreover, Orwell tells us that this "is the kind of thing that happens all the time in wars," though with what evidence he says that, and whether he means that one doesn't feel like shooting or that one doesn't shoot "all the time," I don't know.

4) Raleigh Trevelyan, a British soldier in World War II, has published a "diary of Anzio" in which he recounts the following episode.[5]

> There was a wonderfully vulgar sunrise. Everything was the color of pink geraniums, and birds were singing. We felt like Noah must have done when he saw his rainbow. Suddenly Viner pointed across the

stretch of scrubby heath. An individual, dressed in German uniform, was wandering like a sleep-walker across our line of fire. It was clear that for the moment he had forgotten war and—as we had been doing—was reveling in the promise of warmth and spring. "Shall I bump him off?" asked Viner, without a note of expression in his voice. I had to decide quickly. "No," I replied, "just scare him away."

Here, as in the Orwell passage, the crucial feature is the discovery of a man "similar to yourself," doing "as we had been doing." Of course, two soldiers shooting at one another are quite precisely similar; one is doing what the other is doing, and both are engaged in what can be called a peculiarly human activity. But the sense of being a "fellow-creature" depends for obvious reasons upon a different sort of identity, one that is entirely dissociated from anything threatening. The fellowship of spring (reveling in the sun) is a good example, though even that is not untouched by the pressures of "military necessity."

> Only Sergeant Chesteron didn't laugh. He said that we should have killed the fellow, since his friends would now be told precisely where our trenches were.

Sergeants seem to bear much of the burden of war.

5) The most reflective of the accounts I have found is by an Italian soldier who fought the Austrians in World War I: Emilio Lussu, later a socialist leader and anti-fascist exile. Lussu, then a lieutenant, together with a corporal, had moved during the night into a position overlooking the Austrian trenches. He watched the Austrians having morning coffee and felt a kind of amazement, as if he had not expected to find anything human in the enemy lines.[6]

> Those strongly defended trenches, which we had attacked so many times without success had ended by seeming to us inanimate, like desolate buildings uninhabited by men, the refuge only of mysterious and terrible beings of whom we knew nothing. Now they were showing themselves to us as they really were, men and soldiers like us, in uniform like us, moving about, talking, and drinking coffee, just as our own comrades behind us were doing at that moment.

A young officer appears and Lussu takes aim at him; then the Austrian lights a cigarette and Lussu pauses. "This cigarette formed an invisible link between us. No sooner did I see its smoke than I wanted a cigarette myself . . ." Behind perfect cover, he has time to think about his decision. He felt the war justified, "a hard necessity." He recognized that he had obligations to the men under his command. "I knew it was my duty to fire." And yet he did not. He hesitated, he writes, because the Austrian officer was so entirely oblivious to the danger that threatened him.

> I reasoned like this: To lead a hundred, even a thousand, men against another hundred, or thousand, was one thing; but to detach one man from the rest and say to him, as it were: "Don't move, I'm going to shoot you. I'm going to kill you"—that was different . . . To fight is one thing, but to kill a man is another. And to kill him like that is to murder him.

Lussu, like Graves, turned to his corporal but (perhaps because he was a socialist) with a question, not an order. "Look here—I'm not going to fire on a man alone, like that. Will you?" . . . "No, I won't either." Here the line has been clearly drawn between the member of an army who makes war together with his comrades and the individual who stands alone. Lussu objected to stalking a human prey. What else, however, does a sniper do?

It is not against the rules of war as we currently understand them to kill soldiers who look funny, who are taking a bath, holding up their pants, reveling in the sun, smoking a cigarette. The refusal of these five men, nevertheless, seems to go to the heart of the war convention. For what does it mean to say that someone has a right to life? To say that is to recognize a fellow creature, who is not threatening me, whose activities have the savor of peace and camaraderie, whose person is as valuable as my own. An enemy has to be described differently, and though the stereotypes through which he is seen are often grotesque, they have a certain truth. He alienates himself from me when he tries to kill me, and from our common humanity. But the alienation is temporary, the humanity imminent. It is restored, as it were, by the prosaic acts that break down the stereotypes in each of the five stories. Because he is funny, naked, and so on, my enemy is changed, as Lussu says, into a man. "A man!"

The case might be different if we imagine this man to be a wholehearted soldier. In his bath, smoking his morning cigarette, he is thinking only of the coming battle and of how many of his enemies he will kill. He is engaged in war-making just as I am engaged in writing this book; he thinks about it all the time or at the oddest moments. But this is an unlikely picture of an ordinary soldier. War is not in fact his enterprise, but rather surviving this battle, avoiding the next. Mostly, he hides, is frightened, doesn't fire, prays for a minor wound, a voyage home, a long rest. And when we see him at rest, we assume that he is thinking of home and peace, as we would be. If that is so, how can it be justified to kill him? Yet it is justified, as most of the soldiers in the five stories understand. Their refusals seem, even to them, to fly in the face of military duty. Rooted in a moral recognition, they are nevertheless more passionate than principled decisions. They are acts of kindness, and insofar as they entail any danger at all or lower minutely the odds for victory later, they may be likened to superogatory acts. Not that they involve doing more than is morally required; they involve doing less than is permitted.

The standards of permissibility rest on the rights of individuals, but they are not precisely defined by those rights. For definition is a complex process, historical as well as theoretical in character, and conditioned in a significant way by the pressure of military necessity. It is time now to try to see what that pressure can and cannot do, and the "naked soldier" cases provide a useful instance. In the nineteenth century, an effort was made to protect one type of "naked soldier": the man on guard duty outside his post or at the edge of his lines. The reasons given for singling out this lone figure are similar to those expressed in the five stories. "No other term than murder," wrote an English student of war, "expresses the killing of a lone sentry by a pot shot at long range. It [is] like shooting a partridge sitting."[7] The same idea is obviously at work in the code of military conduct that Francis Lieber drafted for the Union Army in the American Civil War: "Outposts, sentinels, pickets are not to be fired upon, except to drive them in . . ."[8] Now, a war is easily imaginable in which this idea was extended, so that only soldiers actually fighting, hundreds against hundreds, thousands against thousands, as Lussu says, could be attacked. Such a war would be constituted as a series of set battles, formally or informally announced in advance, and broken off in some clear fashion. The pursuit of a defeated army could be allowed, so neither side need be denied the possibility of a decisive victory. But perpetual harassment, sniping, ambush, surprise attack—all these would be ruled out. Wars have indeed been fought in this way, but the arrangements have never been stable, because they give a systematic advantage to the army that is larger and better equipped. It is the weaker side that persistently refuses to fix any limits on the vulnerability of enemy soldiers (the extreme form of this refusal is guerrilla war), pleading military necessity. What does this mean?

The Nature of Necessity (1)

The plea takes a standard form. This or that course of action, it is said, "is necessary to compel the submission of the enemy with the least possible expenditure of time, life, and money."* That is the core of what the Germans call *kriegsraison*, reason of war. The doctrine justifies not only whatever is necessary to win the war, but also whatever is necessary to reduce the risks of losing, or simply to reduce losses or the likelihood of losses in the course of the war. In fact, it is not about necessity at all; it is a way of speaking in code, or a hyperbolical way of speaking, about probability and risk. Even if one grants the right of states and armies and individual soldiers to reduce their risks, a particular course of action would be *necessary* to that end only if no other course improved the odds of battle at all. But there will always be a range of tactical and strategic options that conceivably could improve the odds. There will be choices to make, and these are moral as well as military choices. Some of them are permitted and some ruled out by the war convention. If the convention did not discriminate in this way, it would have little impact upon the actual fighting of wars and battles; it would simply be a code of expediency—which is what Sidgwick's twofold rule is likely to come to, under the pressure of actual warfare.

"Reason of war" can only justify the killing of people we already have reason to think are liable to be killed. What is involved here is not so much a calculation of probability and risk as a reflection on the status of the men and women whose lives are at stake. The case of the "naked soldier" is resolved in this way: soldiers as a class are set apart from the world of peaceful activity; they are trained to fight, provided with weapons, required to fight on command. No doubt, they do not always fight; nor is war their personal enterprise. But it is the enterprise of their class, and this fact radically distinguishes the individual soldier from the civilians he leaves behind.* If he is warned that he is always in danger, it is not so

* In his moving account of the French defeat in 1940, Marc Bloch has criticized this distinction: "Confronted by the nation's peril and by the duties that it lays on every citizen, all adults are equal and only a curiously warped mind would claim for any of them the privilege of immunity. What, after all, is a 'civilian' in time of war? He is nothing more than a man whose weight of years, whose health, whose profession . . . prevents him from bearing arms effectively . . . Why should [these factors] confer on him the right to escape from the common danger?" (*Strange*

great a disruption of his life as it would be in the case of the civilian. Indeed, to warn the civilian is in effect to force him to fight, *but the soldier has already been forced to fight.* That is, he has joined the army because he thinks his country must be defended, or he has been conscripted. It is important to stress, however, that he has not been forced to fight by a direct attack upon his person; that would repeat the crime of aggression at the level of the individual. He can be personally attacked only because he already is a fighter. He has been made into a dangerous man, and though his options may have been few, it is nevertheless accurate to say that he has allowed himself to be made into a dangerous man. For that reason, he finds himself endangered. The actual risks he lives with may be reduced or heightened: here notions of military necessity, and also of kindness and magnanimity, have free play. But the risks can be raised to their highest pitch without violating his rights.

It is harder to understand the extension of combatant status beyond the class of soldiers, though in modern war this has been common enough. The development of military technology, it might be said, has dictated it, for war today is as much an economic as a military activity. Vast numbers of workers must be mobilized before an army can even appear in the field; and once they are engaged, soldiers are radically dependent on a continuing stream of equipment, fuel, ammunition, food, and so on. It is a great temptation, then, to attack the enemy army behind its own lines, especially if the battle itself is not going well. But to attack behind the lines is to make war against people who are at least nominally civilians. How can this be justified? Here again, the judgments we make depend upon our understanding of the men and women involved. We try to draw a line between those who have lost their rights because of their warlike activities and those who have not. On the one side are a class of people, loosely called "munitions workers," who make weapons for the army or whose work directly contributes to the business of war. On the other side are all those people who, in the words of the British philosopher G. E. M. Anscombe, "are not fighting and are not engaged in supplying those who are with the means of fighting."[10]

Defeat, trans. Gerard Hopkins, New York, 1968, p. 130) But the theoretical problem is not to describe how immunity is gained, but how it is lost. We are all immune to start with; our right not to be attacked is a feature of normal human relationships. That right is lost by those who bear arms "effectively" because they pose a danger to other people. It is retained by those who don't bear arms at all.

The relevant distinction is not between those who work for the war effort and those who do not, but between those who make what soldiers need to fight and those who make what they need to live, like all the rest of us. When it is militarily necessary, workers in a tank factory can be attacked and killed, but not workers in a food processing plant. The former are assimilated to the class of soldiers—partially assimilated, I should say, because these are not armed men, ready to fight, and so they can be attacked only in their factory (not in their homes), when they are actually engaged in activities threatening and harmful to their enemies. The latter, even if they process nothing but army rations, are not similarly engaged. They are like workers manufacturing medical supplies, or clothing, or anything else that would be needed, in one form or another, in peacetime as well as war. An army, to be sure, has an enormous belly, and it must be fed if it is to fight. But it is not its belly but its arms that make it an army. Those men and women who supply its belly are doing nothing peculiarly warlike. Hence their immunity from attack: they are assimilated to the rest of the civilian population. We call them *innocent* people, a term of art which means that they have done nothing, and are doing nothing, that entails the loss of their rights.

This is a plausible line, I think, though it may be too finely drawn. What is more important is that it is drawn under pressure. We begin with the distinction between soldiers engaged in combat and soldiers at rest; then we shift to the distinction between soldiers as a class and civilians; and then we concede this or that group of civilians as the processes of economic mobilization establish its direct contribution to the business of fighting. Once the contribution has been plainly established, only "military necessity" can determine whether the civilians involved are attacked or not. They ought not to be attacked if their activities can be stopped, or their products seized or destroyed, in some other way and without significant risk. The laws of war have regularly recognized this obligation. Under the naval code, for example, merchant seamen on ships carrying military supplies were once regarded as civilians who had, despite the work they were doing, a right not to be attacked, for it was possible (and it sometimes still is) to seize their ships without shooting at them. But whenever seizure without shooting ceases to be possible, the obligation ceases also and the right lapses. It is not a retained but a war right, and rests only on the agreement of states and on the doctrine of military necessity. The history of submarine warfare nicely illustrates this process, through which groups of civilians are, as it were, incorporated into hell. It will also enable me to suggest the point at which it becomes morally necessary to resist the incorporation.

Submarine Warfare: The Laconia Affair

Naval warfare has traditionally been the most gentlemanly form of fighting, possibly because so many gentlemen went into the navy, but also and more importantly because of the nature of the sea as a battlefield. The only comparable land environment is the desert; these two have in common the absence or relative absence of civilian inhabitants. Hence battle is especially pure, a combat between combatants, with no one else involved—just what we intuitively want war to be. The purity is marred, however, by the fact that the sea is extensively used for transport. Warships encounter merchant ships. The rules governing this encounter are, or were, fairly elaborate.[11] Worked out before the invention of the submarine, they bear the marks of their technological as well as their moral assumptions. A merchant ship carrying military supplies could lawfully be stopped on the high seas, boarded, seized, and brought into port by a prize crew. If the merchant seamen resisted this process at any stage, whatever force was necessary to overcome the resistance was also lawful. If they submitted peacefully, no force could be used against them. If it was impossible to bring the ship into port, it could be sunk, "subject to the absolute duty of providing for the safety of the crew, passengers, and papers." Most often, this was done by taking all three on board the warship. The crew and passengers were then to be regarded not as prisoners of war, for their encounter with the warship was not a battle, but as civilian internees.

Now, in World War I, submarine commanders (and the state officials who commanded them) openly refused to act in accordance with this "absolute duty," pleading military necessity. They could not surface before firing their torpedoes, for their ships were lightly armed above decks and highly vulnerable to ramming; they could not provide prize crews from their own small number, unless they, too, were to return to port; nor could they take merchant seamen on board, for there was no room. Hence their policy was to "sink on sight," though they did accept some responsibility to assist survivors after the ship was down. "Sink on sight" was especially the policy of the German government. The only alternative, its defenders have argued, was not to use submarines at all, or to use them ineffectively, which would have conceded control of the sea to the British navy. After the war was over, perhaps because the Germans lost it, the traditional rules were reaffirmed. The London Naval Protocol of 1936, ratified by all the major participants in the last and the next great war (by the Germans in 1939), explicitly provided that "in their action with regard to merchant ships, submarines must conform to the rules of international law to which surface ships are subject." This is still the "binding rule," according to respected authorities on naval law, though anyone who defends the rule must do so "notwithstanding the experience of the Second World War."[12]

We can best gain access to this experience by turning immediately to the famous "*Laconia* order" issued by Admiral Doenitz of the German U-boat command in 1942. Doenitz required not only that submarines strike without warning, but also that they do nothing whatsoever to help the crew members of a sunken ship: "All attempts to rescue the crews of sunken ships should cease, including picking up men from the sea, righting capsized lifeboats, and supplying food and water."[13] This order provoked great indignation at the time, and after the war its promulgation was among the crimes with which Doenitz was charged at Nuremberg. But the judges refused to convict on this charge. I want to look closely at the reasons for their decision. Since their language is obscure, however, I shall also ask what their reasons might have been and what reasons we might have for requiring or not requiring rescue at sea.

The issue clearly was rescue and nothing else; despite the "binding rule" of international law, the policy of "sink on sight" was not challenged by the court. The judges apparently decided that the distinction between merchant ships and warships no longer made much sense.[14]

> Shortly after the outbreak of the war, the British Admiralty . . . armed its merchant vessels, in many cases convoyed them with armed escort, gave orders to send position reports upon sighting submarines, thus integrating merchant vessels into the warning system of naval intelligence. On October 1, 1939, the Admiralty announced [that] British merchant ships had been ordered to ram U-boats if possible.

At this point, the court seemed to reason, merchant seamen had been conscripted for military service; hence it was permissible to attack them by surprise exactly as if they were soldiers. But this argument, by itself, is not a very good one. For if the conscription of merchant seamen was a response to illegitimate submarine attacks (or even to the strong probability of such attacks), it cannot be invoked to justify those same attacks. It must be the case that the "sink on sight" policy was justified in the first place. The invention of the submarine had made it "necessary." The old rules were morally if not legally suspended because supply by sea—a military enterprise whose participants had always been liable to attack—had ceased now to be subject to nonviolent interdiction.

The "*Laconia* order" reached much further than this, however, for it suggested that seamen helpless in the sea, unlike wounded soldiers on land, need not be helped once the battle was over. Doenitz's argument was that the battle, in fact, was never over until the submarine was safe in its home port. The sinking of a merchant vessel was only the first blow of a long and tense struggle. Radar and the airplane had turned the wide seas into a single battlefield, and unless the submarine immediately began evasive maneuvers, it was or might be in great trouble.[15] Seamen had once been better off than soldiers, a privileged class of near-combatants treated as if they were civilians; now, suddenly, they were worse off.

Here again is the argument from military necessity, and again we can see that it is above all an argument about risk. The lives of the submarine crew would be endangered, Doenitz claimed, and the probability of detection and attack increased by this or that extent, if they attempted to rescue their victims. Now, this is clearly not always the case: in his account of the destruction of an allied convoy in the Arctic Sea, David Irving describes a number of incidents in which German submarines surfaced and offered assistance to merchant seamen in lifeboats without increasing their own risks.[16]

> Lieutenant-Commander Teichert's U-456 . . . had fired the striking torpedoes. Teichert took his submarine alongside the lifeboats and ordered the Master, Captain Strand, to come aboard; he was taken prisoner. The seamen were asked whether they had sufficient water and they were handed tinned meat and bread by the submarine officers. They were told that they would be picked up by destroyers a few days later.

This occurred only a few months before Doenitz's order prohibited such assistance, and under conditions which made it perfectly safe. Convoy PQ 17 had dispersed, abandoned by its escorts; it was no longer in any sense a fighting force; the Germans controlled the air as well as the sea. The battle was clearly over, and military necessity could hardly have justified a refusal to help. I should think that if such a refusal, under similar circumstances, could be attributed to the "*Laconia* order," Doenitz would indeed be

His armor

guilty of a war crime. But nothing like this was demonstrated at Nuremberg.

Nor, however, did the court openly adopt the argument from military necessity: that under different circumstances the refusal to help was justified by the risks it entailed. Instead, the judges reaffirmed the binding rule. "If the Commander cannot rescue," they argued, "then . . . he cannot sink a merchant vessel . . ." But they did not enforce the rule and punish Doenitz. Admiral Nimitz of the U.S. Navy, called to testify by Doenitz's attorney, had told them that "U.S. submarines [generally] did not rescue enemy survivors if by so doing the vessels were exposed to unnecessary or additional risk." British policy had been similar. In view of this, the judges declared that "the sentence of Doenitz is not assessed on the ground of his breaches of the international law of submarine warfare."[17] They did not accept the argument of the defense attorneys that the law had effectively been rewritten by informal collusion among the belligerents. But they apparently felt that this collusion did make the law unenforceable (or at least unenforceable against only one of the parties to its violation)—a proper judicial decision, but one that leaves open the moral question.

In fact, Doenitz and his allied counterparts had reasons for the policy they adopted, and these reasons fit roughly into the framework of the war convention. Wounded or helpless combatants are no longer subject to attack; in that sense they have regained their right to life. But they are not entitled to assistance so long as the battle continues and the victory of their enemies is uncertain. What is decisive here is not military necessity but the assimilation of merchant seamen to the class of combatants. Soldiers need not risk their lives for the sake of their enemies, for both they and their enemies have exposed themselves to the coerciveness of war. There are some people, however, who are safe against that coerciveness, or who ought to be safeguarded against it, and these people also have a part in the *Laconia* affair.

The *Laconia* was a liner carrying 268 British servicemen and their families, returning home from pre-war stations in the Middle East, and 1,800 Italian prisoners of war. It was torpedoed and sunk off the west coast of Africa by a U-boat whose commander did not know who its passengers were (liners were used extensively by the Allies as troopships). When Doenitz learned of the sinking, and of the identity of the people in the water, he ordered a massive rescue effort involving, initially, a number of other submarines.[18] Italian warships were also asked to hurry to the scene, and the

U-boat commander responsible for the sinking radioed in English a general call for help. But the submarines were instead attacked by several Allied planes whose pilots presumably did not know what was going on in the seas below or did not believe what they were told. The confusion is typical enough in time of war: ignorance on all sides, compounded by mutual fear and suspicion.

In fact, the planes did little damage, but Doenitz's response was harsh. He directed the German commanders to confine their rescue efforts to the Italian prisoners; the British soldiers and their families were to be set adrift. It was this spectacle of women and children abandoned at sea, and the subsequent order that seemed to require its repetition, that was widely thought to be outrageous—and rightly so, it seems to me, even though "unrestricted" submarine warfare was by then commonly accepted. For we draw a circle of rights around civilians, and soldiers are supposed to accept (some) risks in order to save civilian lives. It is not a question of going out of their way or of being, or not being, good samaritans. They are the ones who endanger civilian lives in the first place, and even if they do this in the course of legitimate military operations, they must still make some positive effort to restrict the range of the damage they do. This indeed was Doenitz's own position before the Allied attack, a position he maintained despite criticism from other members of the German High Command: "I cannot put these people into the water. I shall carry on [the rescue effort]." It is not kindness that is involved here, but duty, and it is in terms of that duty that we judge the "Laconia order". A rescue effort undertaken for the sake of noncombatants can be broken off temporarily because of an attack, but it cannot be called off in advance of any attack merely because an attack may occur (or recur). For one attack at least has already occurred and put innocent people in danger of death. Now they must be helped.

Double Effect

The second principle of the war convention is that noncombatants cannot be attacked at any time. They can never be the objects or the targets of military activity. But as the Laconia affair suggests, noncombatants are often endangered not because anyone sets out to attack them, but only because of their proximity to a battle that is being fought against someone else. I have tried to argue that what is then required is not that the battle be stopped, but that some degree of care be taken not to harm civilians— which means, very simply, that we recognize their rights as best we can within the context of war. But what degree of care should be taken? And at what cost to the individual soldiers who are involved? The laws of war say nothing about such matters; they leave the cruelest decisions to be made by the men on the spot with reference only to their ordinary moral notions or the military traditions of the army in which they serve. Occasionally one of these soldiers will write about his own decisions, and that can be like a light going on in a dark place. Here is an incident from Frank Richards' memoir of the First World War, one of the few accounts by a man from the ranks.[19]

> When bombing dug-outs or cellars, it was always wise to throw the bombs into them first and have a look around them after. But we had to be very careful in this village as there were civilians in some of the cellars. We shouted down to them to make sure. Another man and I shouted down one cellar twice and receiving no reply were just about to pull the pins out of our bombs when we heard a woman's voice and a young lady came up the cellar steps . . . She and the members of her family . . . had not left [the cellar] for some days. They guessed an attack was being made and when we first shouted down had been too frightened to answer. If the young lady had not cried out when she did, we would have innocently murdered them all.

Innocently murdered, because they had shouted first; but if they had not shouted, and then killed the French family, it would have been, Richards believed, murder simply. And yet he was accepting a certain risk in shouting, for had there been German soldiers in the cellar, they might have scrambled out, firing as they came. It would have been more prudent to throw the bombs without warning, which means that military necessity would have justified him in doing so. Indeed, he would have been justified on other grounds, too, as we shall see. And yet he shouted.

The moral doctrine most often invoked in such cases is the principle of double effect. First worked out by Catholic casuists in the Middle Ages, double effect is a complex notion, but it is at the same time closely related to our ordinary ways of thinking about moral life. I have often found it being used in military and political debates. Officers will tend to speak in its terms, knowingly or unknowingly, whenever the activity they are planning is likely to injure noncombatants. Catholic writers themselves frequently use military examples; it is one of their purposes to suggest what we ought to think when "a soldier in firing at the enemy foresees that he will shoot some civilians who are nearby."[20] Such foresight is common enough in war; soldiers could probably not fight at all, except in the desert and at sea, without endangering nearby civilians. And yet it is not proximity but only some contribution to the fighting that makes a civilian liable to attack. Double effect is a way of reconciling the absolute prohibition against attacking noncombatants with the legitimate conduct of military activity. I shall want to argue, following the example of Frank Richards, that the reconciliation comes too easily, but first we must see exactly how it is worked out.

The argument goes this way: it is permitted to perform an act likely to have evil consequences (the killing of noncombatants) provided the following four conditions hold.[21]

1) The act is good in itself or at least indifferent, which means, for our purposes, that it is a legitimate act of war.
2) The direct effect is morally acceptable—the destruction of military supplies, for example, or the killing of enemy soldiers.
3) The intention of the actor is good, that is, he aims only at the acceptable effect; the evil effect is not one of his ends, nor is it a means to his ends.
4) The good effect is sufficiently good to compensate for allowing the evil effect; it must be justifiable under Sidgwick's proportionality rule.

The burden of the argument is carried by the third clause. The "good" and evil effects that come together, the killing of soldiers and nearby civilians, are to be defended only insofar as they are the product of a single intention, directed at the first and not the second. The argument suggests the great importance of taking aim in wartime, and it correctly restricts the targets at which one can aim. But we have to worry, I think, about all those unintended but foreseeable deaths, for their number can be large; and subject only to the proportionality rule—a weak constraint—double effect provides a blanket justification. The principle for that reason invites an angry or a cynical response: what difference does it make whether civilian deaths are a direct or an indirect effect of my actions? It can hardly matter to the dead civilians, and if I know in advance that I am likely to kill so many innocent people and go ahead anyway, how can I be blameless?[22]

We can ask the question in a more concrete way. Would Frank

Richards have been blameless if he had thrown his bombs without warning? The principle of double effect would have permitted him to do so. He was engaged in a legitimate military activity, for many cellars were in fact being used by enemy soldiers. The effects of making "bomb without warning" his general policy would have been to reduce the risks of his being killed or disabled and to speed up the capture of the village, and these are "good" effects. Moreover, they were clearly the only ones he intended; civilian deaths would have served no purpose of his own. And finally, over an extended period of time, the proportions would probably have worked out favorably or at least not unfavorably; the mischief done would, let us assume, be balanced by the contribution to victory. And yet Richards was surely doing the right thing when he shouted his warning. He was acting as a moral man ought to act; his is not an example of fighting heroically, above and beyond the call of duty, but simply of fighting well. It is what we expect of soldiers. Before trying to state that expectation more precisely, however, I want to see how it works in more complex combat situations.

Bombardment in Korea

I am going to follow here a British journalist's account of the way the American army waged war in Korea. Whether it is an entirely just account I do not know, but I am more interested in the moral issues it raises than in its historical accuracy. This, then, was a "typical" encounter on the road to Pyongyang. A battalion of American troops advanced slowly, without opposition, under the shadow of low hills. "We were well into the valley now, halfway down the straight . . . strung out along the open road, when it came, the harsh stutter of automatic fire sputtering the dust around us."[23] The troops stopped and dove for cover. Three tanks moved up, "pounding their shells into the . . . hillside and shattering the air with their machine guns. It was impossible in this remarkable inferno of sound to detect the enemy, or to assess his fire." Within fifteen minutes, several fighter planes arrived, "diving down upon the hillside with their rockets." This is the new technique of warfare, writes the British journalist, "born of immense productive and material might": "the cautious advance, the enemy small arms fire, the halt, the close support air strike, artillery, the cautious advance, and so on." It is designed to save the lives of soldiers, and it may or may not have that effect. "It is certain that it kills civilian men, women, and children, indiscriminately and in great numbers, and destroys all that they have."

Now there is another way to fight, though it is only open to soldiers who have had a "soldierly" training and who are not "roadbound" in their habits. A patrol can be sent forward to outflank the enemy position. In the end, it often comes to that anyway, as it did in this case, for the tanks and planes failed to hit the North Korean machine gunners. "At last, after more than an hour . . . a platoon from Baker Company began working their way through the scrub just under the ridge of the hill." But the first reliance was always on bombardment. "Every enemy shot released a deluge of destruction." And the bombardment had, or sometimes had, its characteristic double effect: enemy soldiers were killed, and so were any civilians who happened to be nearby. It was not the intention of the officers who called in the artillery and planes to kill civilians; they were acting out of a concern for their own men. And that is a legitimate concern. No one would want to be commanded in wartime by an officer who did not value the lives of his soldiers. But he must also value civilian lives, and so must his soldiers. He cannot save them, because they cannot save themselves, by killing innocent people. It is not just that they can't kill a lot of innocent people. Even if the proportions work out favorably, in particular cases or over a period of time, we would still want to say, I think, that the patrol must be sent out, the risk accepted, before the big guns are brought to bear. The soldiers sent on patrol can plausibly argue that they never chose to make war in Korea; they are soldiers nevertheless; there are obligations that go with their war rights, and the first of these is the obligation to attend to the rights of civilians—more precisely, of those civilians whose lives they themselves endanger.

The principle of double effect, then, stands in need of correction. Double effect is defensible, I want to argue, only when the two outcomes are the product of a *double intention*: first, that the "good" be achieved; second, that the foreseeable evil be reduced as far as possible. So the third of the conditions listed above can be restated:

> 3) The intention of the actor is good, that is, he aims narrowly at the acceptable effect; the evil effect is not one of his ends, nor is it a means to his ends, and, aware of the evil involved, he seeks to minimize it, accepting costs to himself.

Simply not to intend the death of civilians is too easy; most often, under battle conditions, the intentions of soldiers are focused narrowly on the enemy. What we look for in such cases is some sign of a positive commitment to save civilian lives. Not merely to apply the proportionality rule and kill no more civilians than is militarily necessary—that rule applies to soldiers as well; no one can be killed for trivial purposes. Civilians have a right to something more. And if saving civilian lives means risking soldier's lives, the risk must be accepted. But there is a limit to the risks that we require. These are, after all, unintended deaths and legitimate military operations, and the absolute rule against attacking civilians does not apply. War necessarily places civilians in danger; that is another aspect of its hellishness. We can only ask soldiers to minimize the dangers they impose.

Exactly how far they must go in doing that is hard to say, and for that reason it may seem odd to claim that civilians have rights in such matters. What can this mean? Do civilians have a right not only not to be attacked but also not to be put at risk to such and such a degree, so that imposing a one-in-ten chance of death on them is justified, while imposing a three-in-ten chance is unjustified? In fact, the degree of risk that is permissible is going to vary with the nature of the target, the urgency of the moment, the available technology, and so on. It is best, I think, to say simply that civilians have a right that "due care" be taken.[24] * The case is the same in domestic society: when the gas company works on the lines that run under my street, I have a right that its workmen observe very strict safety standards. But if the work is urgently required by the imminent danger of an explosion on a neighboring street, the standards may be relaxed and my rights not violated. Now, military necessity works exactly like civil emergency, except that in war the standards with which we are familiar in domestic society are always relaxed. That is not to say, however, that there are no standards at all, and no rights involved. Whenever there is likely to be a second effect, a second intention is morally required. We can move some way toward defining the limits of that second intention if we consider two more wartime examples.

---

* Since judgments of "due care" involve calculations of relative value, urgency, and so on, it has to be said that utilitarian arguments and rights arguments (relative at least to indirect effects) are not wholly distinct. Nevertheless, the calculations required by the proportionality principle and those required by "due care" are not the same. Even after the highest possible standards of care have been accepted, the probable civilian losses may still be disproportionate to the value of the target; then the attack must be called off. Or, more often, military planners may decide that the losses entailed by the attack, even if it is carried out at minimal risk to the attackers, are not disproportionate to the value of the target: then "due care" is an additional requirement.

The Bombing of Occupied France and the Vemork Raid

During World War II, the Free French air force carried out bombing raids against military targets in occupied France. Inevitably, their bombs killed Frenchmen working (under coercion) for the German war effort; inevitably too, they killed Frenchmen who simply happened to live in the vicinity of the factories under attack. This posed a cruel dilemma for the pilots, which they resolved not by giving up the raids or asking someone else to carry them out, but by accepting greater risks for themselves. "It was . . . this persistent question of bombing France itself," says Pierre Mendes-France, who served in the air force after his escape from a German prison, "which led us to specialize more and more in precision bombing—that is, flying at a very low altitude. It was more risky, but it also permitted greater precision . . ."[25] The same factories, of course, could have been (perhaps should have been) attacked by squads of partisans or commandos carrying explosives; their aim would have been perfect, not merely more precise, and no civilians except those working in the factories would have been endangered. But such raids would have been extremely dangerous and the chances of success, and especially of reiterated success, very slim. Risks of that sort were more than the French expected, even of their own soldiers. The limits of risk are fixed, then, roughly at that point where any further risk-taking would almost certainly doom the military venture or make it so costly that it could not be repeated.

There is obviously leeway for military judgment here: strategists and planners will for reasons of their own weigh the importance of their target against the importance of their soldiers' lives. But even if the target is very important, and the number of innocent people threatened relatively small, they must risk soldiers before they kill civilians. Consider, for example, the one case I have found from the Second World War where a commando raid was tried instead of an air attack. In 1943, the heavy water plant at Vemork in occupied Norway was destroyed by Norwegian commandos operating on behalf of the British S.O.E. (Special Operations Executive). It was vitally important to stop the production of heavy water so as to delay the development of an atomic bomb by German scientists. British and Norwegian officials debated whether to make the attempt from the air or on the ground and chose the latter approach because it was less likely to injure civilians.[26] But it was very dangerous for the commandos. The first attempt failed, and thirty-four men were killed in its course; the second attempt, by a smaller number of men, succeeded without casualties—to the surprise of everyone involved, including the commandos. It was possible to accept such risks for a single operation that would not, it was thought, have to be repeated. For a "battle" that extended over time, consisting of many separate incidents, it would not have been possible.

Later in the war, after production was resumed at Vemork and security considerably tightened, the plant was bombed from the air by American planes. The bombing was successful, but it resulted in the deaths of twenty-two Norwegian civilians. At this point, double effect seems to work, justifying the air attack. Indeed, in its unrevised form it would have worked sooner. The importance of the military aim and the actual casualty figures (foreseeable in advance, let us assume) would have justified a bombing raid in the first place. But the special value we attach to civilian lives precluded it.

Now, the same value attaches to the lives of German as to those of French or Norwegian civilians. There are, of course, additional moral as well as emotional reasons for paying that respect and accepting its costs in the case of one's own people or one's allies (and it is no accident that my two examples involve attacks on occupied territory). Soldiers have direct obligations to the civilians they leave behind, which have to do with the very purpose of soldiering and with their own political allegiance. But the structure of rights stands independently of political allegiance; it establishes obligations that are owed, so to speak, to humanity itself and to particular human beings and not merely to one's fellow citizens. The rights of German civilians—who did no fighting and were not engaged in supplying the armed forces with the means of fighting— were no different from those of their French counterparts, just as the war rights of German soldiers were no different from those of French soldiers, whatever we think of their war.

The case of occupied France (or Norway) is, however, complex in another way. Even if the French pilots had reduced their risks and flown at high altitudes, we would not hold them solely responsible for the additional civilian deaths they caused. They would have shared that responsibility with the Germans—in part because the Germans had attacked and conquered France, but also (and more importantly for our immediate purposes) because they had mobilized the French economy for their own strategic ends, forcing French workers to serve the German war machine, turning

French factories into legitimate military targets, and putting the adjacent residential areas in danger. The question of direct and indirect effect is complicated by the question of coercion. When we judge the unintended killing of civilians, we need to know how those civilians came to be in a battle zone in the first place. This is, perhaps, only another way of asking who put them at risk and what positive efforts were made to save them. But it raises issues that I have not yet addressed and that are most dramatically visible when we turn to another, and a much older, kind of warfare.

10

War Against Civilians: Sieges and Blockades

Siege is the oldest form of total war. Its long history suggests that neither technological advance nor democratic revolution are the crucial factors pushing warfare beyond the combatant population. Civilians have been attacked along with soldiers, or in order to get at soldiers, as often in ancient as in modern times. Such attacks are likely whenever an army seeks what might be called civilian shelter and fights from behind the battlements or from within the buildings of a city, or whenever the inhabitants of a threatened city seek the most immediate form of military protection and agree to be garrisoned. Then, locked into the narrow circle of the walls, civilians and soldiers are exposed to the same risks. Proximity and scarcity make them equally vulnerable. Or perhaps not equally so: in this kind of war, once combat begins, noncombatants are more likely to be killed. The soldiers fight from protected positions, and the civilians, who don't fight at all, are quickly made over (in a phrase I have taken from the military literature) into "useless mouths." Fed last, and only with the army's surplus, they die first. More civilians died in the siege of Leningrad than in the modernist infernos of Hamburg, Dresden, Tokyo, Hiroshima, and Nagasaki, taken together. They probably died more painfully, too, even if in old-fashioned ways. Diaries and memoirs of twentieth-century sieges are entirely familiar to anyone who has read, for example, Josephus' harrowing history of the Roman siege of Jerusalem. And the moral issues raised by Josephus are familiar to anyone who has thought about twentieth-century war.

Coercion and Responsibility

The Siege of Jerusalem 72 A.D.

Collective starvation is a bitter fate: parents and children, friends and lovers must watch one another die, and the dying is terribly drawn out, physically and morally destructive long before it is over. Though it sounds like the end of the world, the following passage from Josephus refers to a time relatively early in the Roman siege.[1]

> The restraint of liberty to pass in and out of the city took from the Jews all hope of safety, and the famine now increasing consumed whole households and families; and the houses were full of dead women and infants; and the streets filled with the dead bodies of old men. And the young men, swollen like dead men's shadows, walked in the market place and fell down dead where it happened. And now the multitude of dead bodies was so great that they that were alive could not bury them; nor cared they for burying them, being now uncertain what should betide themselves. And many endeavoring to bury others fell down themselves dead upon them . . . And many being yet alive went unto their graves and there died. Yet for all this calamity was there no weeping nor lamentation, for famine overcame all affections. And they who were yet living, without tears beheld those who being dead were now at rest before them. There was no noise heard within the city . . .

This is not a firsthand account; Josephus was outside the walls, with the Roman army. According to other writers, it is the women who last longest in sieges, the young men who soonest fall into that deadly lethargy that precedes actual death.[2] But the account is accurate enough: that is what a siege is like. Moreover, *that is what it is meant to be like.* When a city is encircled and deprived of food, it is not the expectation of the attackers that the garrison will hold out until individual soldiers, like Josephus' old men, drop dead in the streets. The death of the ordinary inhabitants of the city is expected to force the hand of the civilian or military leadership. The goal is surrender; the means is not the defeat of the enemy army, but the fearful spectacle of the civilian dead.

The principle of double effect, however it is expounded, provides no justification here. These are intentional deaths. And yet siege warfare is not ruled out by the laws of war. "The propriety of attempting to reduce [a city] by starvation is not questioned."[3] If there is a general rule that civilian deaths must not be aimed at, the siege is a great exception—and the sort of exception that seems, if it is morally warranted, to shatter the rule itself. We must consider why it has been made. How can it be thought right to lock civilians up in the death trap of an encircled city?

The obvious answer is simply that the capture of cities is often an important military objective—in the age of the city-state, it was the ultimate objective—and, frontal assault failing, the siege is the only remaining means to success. In fact, however, it is not even necessary that a frontal assault fail before a siege is thought justifiable. Sitting and waiting is far less costly to the besieging army than attacking, and such calculations are permitted (as we have seen) by the principle of military necessity. But this argument is not the most interesting defense of siege warfare and not the one, I think, with which commanders themselves have assuaged their consciences. Josephus suggests the alternative. Titus, he tells us, lamented the deaths of so many Jerusalemites, "and, lifting up his hands to heaven . . . called God to witness, that it was not his doing."[4] Whose doing was it?

After Titus himself, there are only two candidates: the political or military leaders of the city, who have refused to surrender on terms and forced the inhabitants to fight; or the inhabitants themselves, who have acquiesced in that refusal and agreed, as it were, to run the risks of war. Titus implicitly, and Josephus explicitly, opts for the first of these possibilities. Jerusalem, they argue, has been seized by the fanatical Zealots, who have imposed the war upon the mass of moderate Jews, ready otherwise to surrender. There is perhaps a measure of truth in this view, but it is not a satisfactory argument. It makes Titus himself into an impersonal agent of destruction, set off by the obstinacy of others, without plans and purposes of his own. And it suggests that cities (and why not countries?) that do not surrender are justly exposed to total war. Neither of these is a plausible proposition. Even if we reject them both, however, the attribution of responsibility in siege warfare is a complex business. This complexity helps explain though I shall argue that it does not justify the peculiar status of sieges in the laws of war. It also leads us to see that there are moral questions that must be answered before the principle of double effect comes into play. How did those civilians come to be so near the battlefield, where they are now (intentionally or incidentally) killed? Are they there by choice? Or have they been forced into their encounter with war and death?

A city can indeed be defended against the will of its citizens—by an army, beaten in the field, that retreats within its walls; by an alien garrison, serving the strategic interests of a distant commander; by militant, politically powerful minorities of one or another sort. If they were competent casuists, the leaders of any of these groups might reason in the following way: "We know that civilians will die as a result of our decision to fight here rather than somewhere else. But we will not do the killing, and the deaths will not in any way benefit us. They are not our purpose, nor a part of our purpose, nor a means to our purpose. By collecting and rationing food, we will do all we can to save civilian lives. Those who die are not our responsibility." Clearly, such leaders cannot be condemned under the principle of double effect. But they can be condemned nevertheless—so long as the inhabitants of the city decline to be defended. There are many examples of this sort of thing in medieval history: burghers eager to surrender, aristocratic warriors committed (not to the burghers) to continue the fight.[5] In such cases, the warriors surely bear some responsibility for burgher deaths. They are agents of coercion within the city, as the besieging army is without, and the civilians are trapped between the two. But such cases are rare today, as they were in classical times. Political integration and civic discipline make for cities whose inhabitants expect to be defended and are prepared, morally if not always materially, to endure the burdens of a siege. Consent clears the defenders, and only consent can do so.

What of the attackers? I assume that they offer surrender on terms; that is simply the collective equivalent of quarter and should always be available. But surrender is refused. There are then two military options. First, the strongholds of the city can be bombarded and the walls stormed. No doubt, civilians will die, but for these deaths the attacking soldiers can rightly say that they are not to blame. Though they do the killing, these deaths are, in an important sense, not their "doing." The attackers are cleared by the refusal of surrender, which is an acceptance of the risks of war (or, moral responsibility is shifted onto the defending army, which has made surrender impossible). But this argument applies only to those deaths that are in fact incidental to legitimate military operations. The refusal of surrender does not turn the civilians into direct objects of attack. They have not thereby joined the war, though some of them may subsequently be mobilized for warlike activities within the city. They are simply in their "proper and permanent abode," and their status as citizens of a besieged city is no different from their status as citizens of a country at war. If they can be killed, who cannot be? But then it would appear that the second military option is ruled out: the city cannot be surrounded, cut off, its people systematically starved.

The lawyers have drawn the line differently, though they, too, acknowledge that questions of coercion and consent precede questions of direct and indirect effect. Consider the following case from Machiavelli's Art of War:[6]

> Alexander the Great, anxious to conquer Leucadia, first made himself master of the neighboring towns and turned all the inhabitants into Leucadia; at last the town was so full of people that he immediately reduced it by famine.

Machiavelli was enthusiastic about this strategy, but it never became accepted military practice. Moreover, it is not accepted even if the purpose of the forced evacuation is more benign than Alexander's: simply to clear the suburbs for military operations, say, or to drive away people whom the besieging army cannot afford to feed. Had Alexander acted from such motives, and then taken Leucadia by storm, the incidental death of any of the evacuees would still be his special responsibility, since he had forcibly exposed them to the risks of war.

The legal norm is the *status quo*.[7] The commander of the besieging army is not conceived to be, and does not think himself to be, responsible for those people who have always lived in the city —who are there, so to speak, naturally—nor for those who are there voluntarily, who sought the protection of city walls, driven only by the general fear of war. He is in the clear with regard to these people, however horribly they die, however much to his purpose it is that they die horribly, because he did not force them into their death place. He did not push them through the gates of the city before he locked them in. This is, I suppose, an understandable way of drawing the line, but it does not seem to me the right way. The hard question is whether the line can be drawn differently without ruling out sieges altogether. In the long history of siege warfare, this question has a specific form: should civilians be allowed to leave the city, saving themselves from starvation and relieving pressure on the collective food supply, after it has been invested? More generally, isn't locking them into the besieged city morally the same as driving them in? And if it is, shouldn't they be let out, so that those that remain, to fight and starve, can really be said to have chosen to remain? During the siege of Jerusalem, Titus ordered that any Jews who fled the city were to be crucified. It is the one point in his narrative where Josephus feels the need to apologize for his new master.[8] But I want to turn now to a modern example, for these questions were directly addressed by the Nuremberg courts after World War II.

The Right to Leave

The Siege of Leningrad

When its last road and rail links to the east were cut by advancing German forces, on September 8, 1941, Leningrad held over three million people, of whom about 200,000 were soldiers.[9] This was roughly the peacetime population of the city. About half a million people had been evacuated before the siege began, but the number had been made up by refugees from the Baltic states, the Karelian Isthmus, and Leningrad's western and southern suburbs. These people ought to have been moved on, and the evacuation of the city itself speeded up; the Soviet authorities were frighteningly inefficient. But evacuation is always a difficult political issue. To organize it early and on a large scale seems defeatist; it is a way of acknowledging that the army won't be able to hold a line in front of the city. Moreover, it requires a massive effort at a time, it is usually said, when resources and manpower should be concentrated on military defense. And even when the danger is imminent, it is likely to encounter civilian resistance. Politics makes for two sorts of resistance: from those who hope to welcome the enemy and profit from his victory, and from those who are unwilling to "desert" the patriotic struggle. Inevitably, the very authorities organizing the evacuation are also conducting a propaganda campaign that makes desertion seem dishonorable. But the greater resistance is nonpolitical in character, deeply rooted in feelings of place and kin: the unwillingness to leave one's home, to separate from friends and family, to become a refugee.

For all these reasons, the large proportion of Leningraders trapped in the city after September 8 is not unusual in the history of sieges. Nor were they trapped absolutely. The Germans were never able to link up with Finnish forces either on the western or eastern shores of Lake Lagoda, and so there remained an evacuation route to the interior of Russia, at first by boat across the lake, and then as the waters froze, progressively by foot, sled, and truck. Until large-scale convoys could be organized (in January 1942), however, only a slow trickle of people were able to escape. A more immediate escape route was available—through the German lines. For the siege was maintained along a wide arc south of the city, many miles long and in places thinly held. It was possible for civilians on foot to filter through the lines and, as desperation grew within the city, thousands attempted to do so. The German command responded to these attempts with an order, first announced on September 18, and then repeated two months later, to stop the escapes at all costs. Artillery was to be used "to prevent any such attempt at the greatest possible distance from our own lines by opening fire as early as possible, so that the infantry is spared . . . shooting at civilians."[10] I have not been able to find any account of how many civilians died as a direct or indirect result of this order; nor do I know whether or not infantrymen actually opened fire. But if we assume that the German effort was at least partially successful, many would-be escapees, hearing of the shelling or the shooting, must have remained in the city. And there many of them died. Before the siege ended in 1943, more than a million civilians were dead of starvation and disease.

At Nuremberg, Field Marshal von Leeb, who commanded Army Group North from June to December 1941, and who was therefore responsible for the first months of siege operations, was formally charged with war crimes because of the order of September 18. Von Leeb claimed in defense that what he had done was customary practice in wartime, and the judges, after consulting the legal handbooks, were led to agree. They cited Professor Hyde, an American authority on international law: "It is said that if the commander of a besieged place expels the non-combatants, in order to lessen the number of those who consume his stock of provisions, it is lawful, though an extreme measure, to drive them back so as to hasten the surrender."[11] No effort was made to distinguish "expelled" civilians from those leaving voluntarily, and probably the distinction is not relevant to the guilt or innocence of von Leeb. The benefit to the besieged army would be the same in either case.

The laws of war permit the attackers to bar the benefit if they can. "We might wish the law were otherwise," said the judges, "but we must administer it as we find it." Von Leeb was acquitted.

The judges could have found cases in which civilians were allowed to leave besieged cities. During the Franco-Prussian War, the Swiss managed to arrange for a limited evacuation of civilians from Strasbourg. The American commander permitted civilians to leave Santiago before ordering the bombardment of that city in 1898. The Japanese offered free exit for noncombatants trapped in Port Arthur in 1905, but the offer was declined by the Russian authorities.[12] These were all cases, however, in which the attacking army expected to carry the city by storm, and its commanders were willing to make a humanitarian gesture—they would not have said that they were recognizing noncombatant rights—that would cost them nothing. But when the defenders are to be waited out, subjected to slow starvation, the precedents are different. The siege of Plevna in the Russo-Turkish war of 1877 is more typical.[13]

> When Osman Pasha's food supplies began to fail, he turned out the old men and women who were in the town and demanded free passage for them to Sofia or Rakhovo. General Gourko [the Russian commander] refused and sent them back.

And the student of international law who cites this case, then comments: "He could not do otherwise without detriment to his plans." Field Marshal von Leeb might have recalled the shining example of General Gourko.

The argument that needs to be made against both Gourko and von Leeb is suggested by the terms of the German order of September 18. Suppose that large numbers of Russian civilians, convinced that they would die if they returned to Leningrad, had persisted in the face of artillery fire and advanced on the German lines. Would the infantry have shot them down? Its officers were apparently uncertain. That sort of thing was the work of special "death squads," not of ordinary soldiers, even in Hitler's army. Surely there would have been some reluctance, and even some refusals; and surely it would have been right to refuse. Or, suppose that these same refugees were not killed, but rounded up and imprisoned. Would it have been acceptable under the laws of war to inform the commander of the besieged city that they would be held without food, systematically starved, until he surrendered? No doubt, the judges would have found this unacceptable, (even though they sometimes recognized the right to kill hostages). They would not have questioned the responsibility of von Leeb for these people whom he had, in my alternative case, actually locked up. But how is the siege of a city different?

The inhabitants of a city, though they have freely chosen to live within its walls, have not chosen to live under siege. The siege itself is an act of coercion, a violation of the *status quo*, and I cannot see how the commander of the besieging army can escape responsibility for its effects. He has no right to wage total war, even if civilians and soldiers within the city are politically united in refusing surrender. The systematic starvation of civilians under siege is one of those military acts which "though permissible by custom, is a glaring violation of the principle by which custom professes to be governed."[14]

The only justifiable practice, I think, is indicated in the Talmudic law of sieges, summed up by the philosopher Maimonides in the twelfth century (whose version is cited by Grotius in the seventeenth): "When siege is laid to a city for the purpose of capture, it may not be surrounded on all four sides, but only on three, in order to give an opportunity for escape to those who would flee to save their lives . . ."[15] But this seems hopelessly naive. How is it possible to "surround" a city on three sides? Such a sentence, it might be said, could only appear in the literature of a people who had neither a state nor an army of their own. It is an argument offered not from any military perspective, but from a refugee perspective. It makes, however, the crucial point: that in the direness of a siege, people have a right to be refugees. And then it has to be said that the besieging army has a responsibility to open, if it possibly can, a path for their flight.

In practice, many men and women will refuse to leave. Though I have described civilians under siege as people in a trap, hostage-like, life in the city is not like life in a prison camp; it is both much worse and much better. There is, for one thing, important work to do, and there are shared reasons for doing it. Besieged cities are arenas for a collective heroism, and even after ordinary love of place gives out, the emotional life of the threatened city makes departure difficult, at least for some of the citizens.[16] Civilians performing essential services for the army will not, of course, be permitted to leave; they are in effect conscripted. Along with the civilian heroes of the siege, they are henceforth legitimate objects of military attack. The offer of free exit turns all those people who choose to remain in the city, or who are forced to remain, even if they are still in their "proper and permanent abode," into something like a garrison: they have yielded their civilian rights. It is another example of the coerciveness of war that men and women must, in this case, leave their homes to maintain their immunity. But that is not a judgment on the siege commander. When he opens his lines to civilian refugees, he is reducing the immediate coerciveness of his own activity, and having done that he probably has a right to carry on that activity (assuming that it has some significant military purpose). The offer of free exit clears him of responsibility for civilian deaths.

At this point, the argument needs to be made more general. I have been suggesting that when we judge those forms of warfare that closely involve the civilian population, like sieges (and, as we shall see, guerrilla war), the issue of coercion and consent takes precedence over the issue of direction and indirection. We want to know how civilians came to be in militarily exposed positions: what force was used against them, what choices they freely made. There are a wide range of possibilities:

1) that they are coerced by their ostensible defenders, who must then share responsibility for the resulting deaths, even though they do no killing themselves;

2) that they consent to be defended, and so clear the military commander of the defending army;

3) that they are coerced by their attackers, driven into an exposed position and killed, in which case it doesn't matter whether the killing is a direct effect or a side effect of the attack, for it is a crime either way;

4) that they are attacked but not coerced, attacked in their "natural" place, and then the principle of double effect comes into play and siege by starvation is morally unacceptable; and

5) that they are offered free exit by their attackers, after which those that remain can justifiably be killed, directly or indirectly.

The last two of these are the most important, though I will want to qualify them later on. They require a clearcut reversal of contemporary law as stated or restated at Nuremberg, so as to establish and give substance to a principle that is, I think, commonly accepted: that soldiers are under an obligation to help civilians leave the scene of a battle. In the case of a siege, I want to say, it is only when they fulfill this obligation that the battle itself is morally possible.

But is it still militarily possible? Once free exit has been offered, and been accepted by significant numbers of people, the besieging army is placed under a certain handicap. The city's food supply will now last so much longer. It is precisely this handicap that siege

commanders have in the past refused to accept. I don't see, however, that it is different in kind from other handicaps imposed by
the war convention. It doesn't make siege operations entirely im-
practical, only somewhat more difficult—given the ruthlessness of
the modern state, one has to say, marginally more difficult; for the
presence of large numbers of civilians in a besieged city is unlikely
to be allowed to interfere with the provisioning of the army; and,
as the Leningrad example suggests, the death of large numbers of
civilians is unlikely to be allowed to interfere with the defense of
the city. In Leningrad, soldiers did not starve, though civilians
died of hunger. On the other hand, civilians were evacuated from
Leningrad, once Lake Lagoda had frozen solid, and food supplies
were brought in. In different circumstances, free exit might make a
greater military difference, forcing a frontal assault on the city (because the besieging army may also have supply problems) or a major
prolongation of the siege. But these are acceptable consequences,
and they are only "detrimental" to the plans of the siege commander if he has not planned for them in advance. In any case,
if he wants (as he probably will want) to lift his hands to heaven
and say of the civilians he kills, "It's not my doing," he has no
choice but to offer them the chance to leave.

Taking Aim and the Doctrine of Double Effect

The issue is more difficult, however, when a whole country is subjected to siege conditions, when an invading army sets about systematically to destroy crops and food supplies, for example, or when
a naval blockade cuts off vitally needed imports. Here free exit is
not a plausible possibility (mass migration would be necessary),
and the question of responsibility takes on a somewhat different
form. Once again, it should be stressed that the struggle to secure
and deny supplies is a common feature of ancient as well as modern
warfare. It was the subject of legislation long before the modern
laws of war were worked out. The Deuteronomic code, for example, explicitly bans the cutting down of fruit trees: "Only the trees
of which thou knowest that they are not trees for food, them thou
mayest destroy and cut down, that thou mayest build bulwarks

against the city . . ."[17] But few armies seem ever to have respected the ban. It was apparently unknown in Greece; during the Peloponnesian War, the destruction of olive groves was virtually the first act of an invading army; judging from Caesar's *Gallic Wars*, the Romans fought in the same way.[18] In early modern times, long before the scientific destruction of crops became possible, the doctrine of strategic devastation was a kind of conventional wisdom among military commanders. "The Palatinate was wasted [in the Thirty Years War] in order that the imperial armies should be denied the military produce of the country; Marlborough destroyed the farms and crops of Bavaria for a similar purpose [in The War of the Spanish Succession] . . ."[19] The Shenandoah Valley was laid waste in the American Civil War; and the burning of farms on Sherman's march through Georgia had, among other purposes, the strategic goal of starving the Confederate army. In our own time, and with a more advanced technology, vast sections of Vietnam were subjected to a similar destruction.

The contemporary laws of war require that such efforts be directed, whatever their indirect effects, only against the armed forces of the enemy. Civilians in a city have been thought a legitimate target, civilians at large not so: they are, though in vast numbers, only the incidental victims of strategic devastation. The allowable military purpose here is to make the provisioning of the enemy army impossible, and when generals have exceeded that purpose—attempting, like General Sherman, to end the war by "punishing" the civilian population—they have been commonly condemned. Why this is so I am not sure, though why it should be so is easier to make out. The impossibility of free exit rules out any direct attack on the civilian population.

This is not, however, much protection for civilians, since military supplies cannot be destroyed without first destroying civilian supplies. The morally desirable rule is stated by Spaight: "If under such peculiar conditions as existed in the Confederate States and in South Africa [during the Boer War] . . . the enemy depends for his supplies on the surplus of cereals, etc., held by the non-combatant population, then a commander is justified by the necessity of war in destroying or seizing that *surplus*."[20] But it is not the case that the army lives off the civilian surplus; more likely, civilians are forced to make do with what is left after the army has been fed. Hence, strategic devastation is not aimed, and cannot be, at "military produce," but at food supplies generally. And civilians suffer long before soldiers feel the pinch. But who is it who inflicts this suffering, the army that destroys food stocks or the army that seizes what remains for itself? This question is taken up in the British government's official history of World War I.

The British Blockade of Germany

In its origins, a blockade was simply a naval siege, an "investment by sea," barring all ships from entering or leaving the blockaded area (usually a major port) and cutting off, so far as possible, all supplies. It was not thought legally or morally justifiable, however, to extend this interdiction to the trade of an entire country. Most nineteenth century commentators shared the view that the economic life of an enemy country could never be a legitimate military objective. The denial of military supplies was, of course, permissible, and given the possibility of stopping and searching ships on the high seas, elaborate rules were developed for the regulation of wartime trade. Lists of goods qualified as "contraband" and liable to confiscation were regularly published by belligerent powers. Though these lists tended to get longer and more inclusive, the laws of naval warfare stipulated the existence of a category of "conditional contraband" (commonly thought to include foodstuffs and medical supplies) that could not be seized unless it was known to be destined for military use. The relevant principle here was an extension of the combatant/noncombatant distinction. "The seizure of articles of commerce becomes illegitimate so soon as it ceases to aim at enfeebling the naval and military resources of the [enemy] country and puts immediate pressure on the civilian population."[21]

In the course of the First World War, these rules were undermined in two ways; first, by extending the notion of blockade, and then by assuming the military utility of all conditional contraband. The result was full-scale economic warfare, a struggle over supply analogous in its purposes and effects to strategic devastation. The Germans fought this war with the submarine; the British, who controlled at least the surface of the sea, used conventional naval forces, blockading the entire German coast. In this case, conventional forces won the day. The convoy system eventually overcame the submarine threat, whereas the blockade, according to Liddell Hart, was a decisive factor in Germany's defeat. "The spectre of slow enfeeblement ending in eventual collapse," he argues, drove the High Command to undertake its disastrous offensive of 1918.[22] More immediate, and less military consequences can also be traced to the blockade. The "slow enfeeblement" of a country unhappily entails the actual deaths of individual citizens. Though civilians did not starve to death in Germany during the last years of the war, mass malnutrition greatly heightened the normal effects of disease. Statistical studies carried out after the war indicate that some half million civilian deaths, directly attributable to diseases such as influenza and typhus, in fact resulted from the deprivations imposed by the British blockade.[23]

British officials defended the blockade in legal terms by calling it a reprisal for German submarine warfare. More important for our purposes, however, is their consistent denial that the interdiction of supply was aimed at German civilians. The Cabinet had planned only a "limited economic war," directed, as the official history has it, "against the armed forces of the enemy." But the German government maintained its resistance "by interposing the German people between the armies and the economic weapons that had been leveled against them and by making the civil populace bear the suffering inflicted."[24] The sentence invites ridicule, and yet it is hard to imagine any other defense of the naval blockade (or of strategic devastation in land warfare). The passive form of the verb "inflicted" carries the argument. Who did the inflicting? Not the British, though they stopped ships and confiscated cargoes; they took aim at the German army and sought only military ends. And then, the official historian suggests, the Germans themselves pushed civilians into the front line of the economic war—it is as if they had driven them into the forward trenches at the Battle of the Somme—where the British could not help but kill them in the course of legitimate military operations.

If we are to pursue this argument, we will have to assume what seems unlikely: that the British did not in fact aim at the benefits they won from the slow starvation of German civilians. Given that fortunate blindness, the claim that Britain be acquitted of those civilian deaths is at least interesting, though finally unacceptable. It is interesting, first of all, that the official British historian makes the claim in this complex form rather than simply asserting a war right (as in the siege cases) to starve civilians. And it is interesting, secondly, because the acquittal of the British depends so radically on the indictment of the Germans. Without "interposition," the British have no case, for the revised principle of double effect bars the strategy they adopted.

It is, of course, false to say that the German government "interposed" the civilian population between the blockade and the army.

The civilians were where they had always been. If they stood behind the army in the national food line, that is where they had always stood. The army's prior claim to resources was not invented in order to cope with the exigencies of the blockade. Moreover, that claim was probably accepted by the great majority of the German people, at least until the very last months of the war. When the British took aim at the enemy army, therefore, they were aiming *through* the civilian population, knowing that the civilians were there and that they were in their normal place, "their proper and permanent abode." In relation to the German army, they were placed in exactly the same way as British civilians in relation to their own army. It may be that the British did not intend to kill them; killing them wasn't (if we take the official history seriously) a means to the end set by the Cabinet. But if the success of the British strategy did not depend upon civilian deaths, it nevertheless required that nothing at all be done to avoid those deaths. Civilians had to be hit before soldiers could be hit, and this kind of attack is morally unacceptable. A soldier must take careful aim *at* his military target and *away from* nonmilitary targets. He can only shoot if he has a reasonably clear shot; he can only attack if a direct attack is possible. He can risk incidental deaths, but he cannot kill civilians simply because he finds them between himself and his enemies.*

This principle rules out the extended form of the naval blockade and every sort of strategic devastation, except in cases where adequate provision can be made, and is made, for noncombatants. It is not a principle that has been commonly accepted in war, at least not by the combatants. But it is consistent, I think, with other parts of the war convention, and it has gradually won acceptance, for political as much as moral reasons, with reference to a very important form of contemporary warfare. The systematic destruction of crops and food supplies is a frequent strategy in antiguerrilla struggles, and since the governments engaged in such

---

* It remains true, however, that the issue of "interposition" (or coercion) has to be resolved first. Consider an example from the Franco-Prussian War of 1870: during the siege of Paris, the French used irregular forces behind enemy lines to attack trains carrying military supplies to the German army. The Germans responded by placing civilian hostages on the trains. Now it was no longer possible to get a "clear shot" at what was still a legitimate military target. But the civilians on the trains were not in their normal place; they had been radically coerced; and responsibility for their deaths, even if these deaths were actually inflicted by the French, lay with the German commanders. On this point, see Robert Nozick's discussion of "innocent shields of threats" in *Anarchy, State and Utopia*, p. 35.

struggles generally claim sovereignty over the territory and population involved, they have been inclined to accept responsibility for feeding civilians (which is not to say that civilians have always been fed). Just what this involves I will consider in the next chapter. I have been arguing here that even enemy civilians, over whom sovereignty is not claimed, are the responsibility of attacking armies, whenever those armies adopt strategies that put civilians at risk.

11

Guerrilla War

Resistance to Military Occupation

A Partisan Attack

Surprise is the essential feature of guerrilla war; thus the ambush is the classic guerrilla tactic. It is also, of course, a tactic in conventional war; the concealment and camouflage that it involves, though they were once repugnant to officers and gentlemen, have long been regarded as legitimate forms of combat. But there is one kind of ambush that is not legitimate in conventional war and that places in sharp focus the moral difficulties guerrillas and their enemies regularly encounter. This is the ambush prepared behind political or moral rather than natural cover. An example is provided by Captain Helmut Tausend, of the German Army, in Marcel Ophuls' documentary film *The Sorrow and the Pity*. Tausend tells of a platoon of soldiers on a march through the French countryside during the years of the German occupation. They passed a group of young men, French peasants, or so it seemed, digging potatoes. But these were not in fact peasants; they were members of the Resistance. As the Germans marched by, the "peasants" dropped their shovels, picked up guns hidden in the field, and opened fire. Fourteen of the soldiers were hit. Years later, their captain was still indignant. "You call that 'partisan' resistance? I don't. Partisans for me are men that can be identified, men who wear a special armband or a cap, something with which to recognize them. What happened in that potato field was murder."[1]

Guerrilla War

The captain's argument about armbands and caps is simply a citation from the international law of war, from the Hague and Geneva conventions, and I shall have more to say about it later on. It is important to stress first that the partisans had here taken on a double disguise. They were disguised as peaceful peasants and also as Frenchmen, that is, citizens of a state that had surrendered, for whom the war was over (just as guerrillas in a revolutionary struggle disguise themselves as unarmed civilians and also as loyal citizens of a state that is not at war at all). It was because of this second disguise that the ambush was so perfect. The Germans thought they were in a rear area, not at the front, and so they were not battle-ready; they were not preceded by a scouting party; they were not suspicious of the young men in the field. The surprise achieved by the partisans was of a kind virtually impossible in actual combat. It derived from what might be called the protective coloration of national surrender, and its effect was obviously to erode the moral and legal understandings upon which surrender rests.

Surrender is an explicit agreement and exchange: the individual soldier promises to stop fighting in exchange for benevolent quarantine for the duration of the war; a government promises that its citizens will stop fighting in exchange for the restoration of ordinary public life. The precise conditions of "benevolent quarantine" and "public life" are specified in the law books; I need not go into them here.[2] The obligations of individuals are also specified: they may try to escape from the prison camp or to flee occupied territory, and if they succeed in their escape or flight, they are free to fight again; they have regained their war rights. But they may not resist their quarantine or occupation. If a prisoner kills a guard in the course of his escape, the act is murder; if the citizens of a defeated country attack the occupation authorities, the act has, or once had, an even grimmer name: it is, or was, "war treason" (or "war rebellion"), a breaking of political faith, punishable, like the ordinary treason of rebels and spies, by death.

But "traitor" does not seem the right name for those French partisans. Indeed, it is precisely their experience, and that of other guerrilla fighters in World War II, that has led to the virtual disappearance of "war treason" from the law books and of the idea of breaking faith from our moral discussions of wartime resistance (and of peacetime rebellion also, when it is directed against alien or colonial rule). We tend to deny, today, that individuals are automatically subsumed by the decisions of their government or the fate of its armies. We have come to understand the moral commitment they may feel to defend their homeland and their political community, even after the war is officially over.[3] A prisoner of war, after all, knows that the fighting will go on despite his own capture; his government is in place, his country is still being defended. But after national surrender the case is different, and if there are still values worth defending, no one can defend them except ordinary men and women, citizens with no political or legal standing. I suppose it is some general sense that there are such values, or often are, that leads us to grant these men and women a kind of moral authority.

But though this grant reflects new and valuable democratic sensibilities, it also raises serious questions. For if citizens of a defeated state still have a right to fight, what is the meaning of surrender? And what obligations can be imposed on conquering armies? There can be no ordinary public life in occupied territory if the occupation authorities are subject to attack at any time and at the hands of any citizen. And ordinary life is a value, too. It is what most of the citizens of a defeated country most ardently hope for. The heroes of the resistance put it in jeopardy, and we must weigh the risks they impose on others in order to understand the risks they must accept themselves. Moreover, if the authorities actually do aim at the restoration of everyday peacefulness, they seem entitled to enjoy the security they provide; and then they must also be entitled to regard armed resistance as a criminal activity. So the story with which I began might end this way (in the film it has no end): the surviving soldiers rally and fight back; some of the partisans are captured, tried as murderers, condemned, and executed. We would not, I think, add those executions to the list of Nazi war crimes. At the same time, we would not join in the condemnation.

So the situation can be summed up: resistance is legitimate, and the punishment of resistance is legitimate. That may seem like a simple standoff and an abdication of ethical judgment. It is actually a precise reflection of the moral realities of military defeat. I want to stress again that our understanding of these realities has nothing to do with our view of the two sides. We can deplore the resistance, without calling the partisans traitors; we can hate the occupation, without calling the execution of the partisans a crime. If we alter the story or add to it, of course, the case is changed. If the occupation authorities do not live up to their obligations under the surrender agreement, they lose their entitlements. And once the guerrilla struggle has reached a certain point of seriousness and intensity, we may decide that the war has effectively been renewed, notice has been given, the front has been re-established (even if it is not a *line*), and soldiers no longer have a right to be surprised even by a surprise attack. Then guerrillas captured by the authorities must be treated as prisoners of war—provided, that is, they have themselves fought in accordance with the war convention.

But guerrillas don't fight that way. Their struggle is subversive not merely with reference to the occupation or to their own government, but with reference to the war convention itself. Wearing peasant clothes and hiding among the civilian population, they challenge the most fundamental principle of the rules of war. For it is the purpose of those rules to specify for each individual a single identity; he must be either a soldier or a civilian. The British *Manual of Military Law* makes the point with special clarity: "Both these classes have distinct privileges, duties, and disabilities . . . an individual must definitely choose to belong to one class or the other, and shall not be permitted to enjoy the privileges of both; in particular . . . an individual [shall] not be allowed to kill or wound members of the army of the opposed nation and subsequently, if captured or in danger of life, pretend to be a peaceful citizen."[4] That is what guerrillas do, however, or sometimes do. So we can imagine another conclusion to the story of the partisan attack. The partisans successfully disengage, disperse to their homes, and go about their ordinary business. When German troops come to the village that night, they cannot distinguish the guerrilla fighters from any other of the villagers. What do they do then? If, through searches and interrogations—police, not soldier's work— they seize one of the partisans, should they treat him as a captured criminal or a prisoner of war (leaving aside now the problems of surrender and resistance)? And if they seize no one, can they punish the whole village? If the partisans don't maintain the distinction of soldiers and civilians, why should they?

The Rights of Guerrilla Fighters

As this example suggests, the guerrillas don't subvert the war convention by themselves attacking civilians; at least, it is not a necessary feature of their struggle that they do that. Instead, they invite their enemies to do it. By refusing to accept a single identity, they seek to make it impossible for their enemies to accord to combatants and noncombatants their "distinct privileges . . . and disabilities." The political creed of the guerrillas is essentially a defense of this refusal. The people, they say, are no longer being defended by an army; the only army in the field is the army of the oppressors; the people are defending themselves. Guerrilla war is "people's war," a special form of the *levée en masse*, authorized from below. "The war of liberation," according to a pamphlet of the Vietnamese National Liberation Front, "is fought by the people themselves; the entire people . . . are the driving force . . . Not only the peasants in the rural areas, but the workers and laborers in the city, along with intellectuals, students, and businessmen have gone to. fight the enemy."[5] And the NLF drove the point home by naming its paramilitary forces *Dan Quan*, literally, civilian soldiers. The guerrilla's self-image is not of a solitary fighter hiding among the people, but of a whole people mobilized for war, himself a loyal member, one among many. If you want to fight against us, the guerrillas say, you are going to have to fight civilians, for you are not at war with an army but with a nation. Therefore, you should not fight at all, and if you do, you are the barbarians, killing women and children.

In fact, the guerrillas mobilize only a small part of the nation—a very small part, when they first begin their attacks. They depend upon the counter-attacks of their enemies to mobilize the rest. Their strategy is framed in terms of the war convention: they seek to place the onus of indiscriminate warfare on the opposing army. The guerrillas themselves have to discriminate, if only to prove that they are really soldiers (and not enemies) of the people. It is also and perhaps more importantly true that it is relatively easy for them to make the relevant discriminations. I don't mean that guerrillas never engage in terrorist campaigns (even against their fellow countrymen) or that they never take hostages or burn villages. They do all those things, though they generally do less of them than the anti-guerrilla forces. For the guerrillas know who their enemies are, and they know where they are. They fight in small groups, with small arms, at close quarters—and the soldiers they fight against wear uniforms. Even when they kill civilians, they are able to make distinctions: they aim at well-known officials, notorious collaborators, and so on. If the "entire people" are not really the "driving force," they are also not the objects of guerrilla attack.

For this reason, guerrilla leaders and publicists are able to stress the moral quality not only of the goals they seek but also of the means they employ. Consider for a moment Mao Tse-tung's famous "Eight Points for Attention." Mao is by no means committed to the notion of noncombatant immunity (as we shall see), but he writes as if, in the China of the warlords and the Kuomintang, only the communists respect the lives and property of the people. The "Eight Points" are meant to mark off the guerrillas first of all from their predecessors, the bandits of traditional China, and then from their present enemies, who ravage the countryside. They suggest how the military virtues can be radically simplified for a democratic age.[6]

1. Speak politely.
2. Pay fairly for what you buy.
3. Return everything you borrow.
4. Pay for anything you damage.
5. Do not hit or swear at people.
6. Do not damage crops.
7. Do not take liberties with women.
8. Do not ill-treat captives.

The last of these is particularly problematic, for in the conditions of guerrilla war it must often involve releasing prisoners, something most guerrillas are no doubt loath to do. Yet it is at least sometimes done, as an account of the Cuban revolution, originally published in the *Marine Corps Gazette*, suggests:[7]

> That same evening, I watched the surrender of hundreds of *Batistianos* from a small-town garrison. They were gathered within a hollow square of rebel Tommy-gunners and harangued by Raul Castro:
> "We hope that you will stay with us and fight against the master who so ill-used you. If you decide to refuse this invitation—and I am not going to repeat it—you will be delivered to the custody of the Cuban Red Cross tomorrow. Once you are under Batista's orders again, we hope that you will not take arms against us. But, if you do, remember this:
> "We took you this time. We can take you again. And when we do, we will not frighten or torture or kill you . . . If you are captured a second time or even a third . . . we will again return you exactly as we are doing now."

Even when guerrillas behave this way, however, it is not clear that they are themselves entitled to prisoner of war status when captured, or that they have any war rights at all. For if they don't make war on noncombatants, it also appears that they don't make *war* on soldiers: "What happened in that potato field was murder."

They attack stealthily, deviously, without warning, and in disguise. They violate the implicit trust upon which the war convention rests: soldiers must feel safe among civilians if civilians are ever to be safe from soldiers. It is not the case, as Mao once suggested, that guerrillas are to civilians as fish to the ocean. The actual relation is rather of fish to other fish, and the guerrillas are as likely to appear among the minnows as among the sharks.

That, at least, is the paradigmatic form of guerrilla war. I should add that it is not the form such war always or necessarily takes. The discipline and mobility required of guerrilla fighters often preclude a domestic retreat. Their main forces commonly operate out of base camps located in remote areas of the country. And, curiously enough, as the guerrilla units grow larger and more stable, their members are likely to put on uniforms. Tito's partisans in Yugoslavia, for example, wore distinctive dress, and this was apparently no disadvantage in the kind of war they fought.[8] All the evidence suggests that quite apart from the rules of war guerrillas, like other soldiers, prefer to wear uniforms; it enhances their sense of membership and solidarity. In any case, soldiers attacked by a guerrilla main force know who their enemies are as soon as the attack begins; ambushed by uniformed men, they would know no sooner. When the guerrillas "melt away" after such an attack, they more often disappear into jungles or mountains than into villages, a retreat that raises no moral problems. Battles of this sort can readily be assimilated to the irregular combat of army units like Wingate's "Chindits" or "Merrill's Marauders" in World War II.[9] But this is not what most people have in mind when they talk about guerrilla war. The paradigm worked out by guerrilla publicists (together with their enemies) focuses precisely on what is morally difficult about guerrilla war—and also, as we shall see, about anti-guerrilla war. In order to deal with these difficulties, I shall simply accept the paradigm and treat guerrillas as they ask to be treated, as fish among the ocean's fish. What then are their war rights?

The legal rules are simple and clear-cut, though not without their own problems. To be eligible for the war rights of soldiers, guerrilla fighters must wear "a fixed distinctive sign visible at a distance" and must "carry their arms openly."[10] It is possible to worry at length about the precise meaning of distinctiveness, fixity, and openness, but I do not think we would learn a great deal by doing so. In fact, these requirements are often suspended, particularly in the interesting case of a popular rising to repel invasion or resist foreign tyranny. When the people rise *en masse,* they are not required to put on uniforms. Nor will they carry arms openly, if they fight, as they usually do, from ambush: hiding themselves, they can hardly be expected to display their weapons. Francis Lieber, in one of the earliest legal studies of guerrilla war, cites the case of the Greek rebellion against Turkey, where the Turkish government killed or enslaved all prisoners: "But I take it," he writes, "that a civilized government would not have allowed the fact that the Greeks . . . carried on mountain guerilla [war] to influence its conduct toward prisoners."[11]

The key moral issue, which the law gets at only imperfectly, does not have to do with distinctive dress or visible weapons, but with the use of civilian clothing as a ruse and a disguise.* The French partisan attack perfectly illustrates this, and it has to be said, I think, that the killing of those German soldiers was more like assassination than war. That is not because of the surprise, simply, but because of the kind and degree of deceit involved: the same sort of deceit that is involved when a public official or party leader is shot down by some political enemy who has taken on the appearance of a friend and supporter or of a harmless passer-by. Now it may be the case—I am more than open to this suggestion —that the German army in France had attacked civilians in ways that justified the assassination of individual soldiers, just as it may be the case that the public official or party leader is a brutal tyrant who deserves to die. But assassins cannot claim the protection of the rules of war; they are engaged in a different activity. Most of the other enterprises for which guerrillas require civilian disguise are also "different." These include all the possible varieties of espionage and sabotage; they can best be understood by comparing them to acts carried out behind enemy lines by the secret agents of conventional armies. It is widely agreed that such agents possess no war rights, even if their cause is just. They know the risks their efforts entail, and I see no reason to describe the risks

---

* The case is the same with the wearing of civilian clothing as with the wearing of enemy uniforms. In his memoir of the Boer War, Deneys Reitz reports that Boer guerrillas sometimes wore uniforms taken from British soldiers. Lord Kitchener, the British commander, warned that anyone captured in khaki would be shot, and a considerable number of prisoners were later executed. While he insists that "none of us ever wore captured uniforms with the deliberate intention of decoying the enemy, but only out of sheer necessity," Reitz nevertheless justifies Kitchener's order by telling of an incident in which two British soldiers were killed when they hesitated to shoot at guerrillas dressed in khaki. (*Commando,* London, 1932, p. 247)

of guerrillas engaged in similar projects any differently. Guerrilla leaders claim war rights for all their followers, but it makes sense to distinguish, if this is possible, between those guerrillas who use civilian dress as a ruse and those who depend upon camouflage, the cover of darkness, tactical surprise, and so on.

The issues posed by the guerrilla war paradigm, however, are not resolved by this distinction. For guerrillas don't merely fight *as* civilians; they fight *among* civilians, and this in two senses. First, their day-to-day existence is much more closely connected with the day-to-day existence of the people around them than is ever the case with conventional armies. They live with the people they claim to defend, whereas conventional troops are usually billeted with civilians only after the war or the battle is over. And second, they fight where they live; their military positions are not bases, posts, camps, forts, or strongholds, but villages. Hence they are radically dependent on the villagers, even when they don't succeed in mobilizing them for "people's war." Now, every army depends upon the civilian population of its home country for supplies, recruits, and political support. But this dependence is usually indirect, mediated by the bureaucratic apparatus of the state or the exchange system of the economy. So food is passed from the farmer to the marketing co-op, to the food processing plant, to the trucking company, to the army commissary. But in guerrilla war, the dependence is immediate: the farmer hands the food to the guerrilla, and whether it is received as a tax or paid for in accordance with Mao's Second Point for Attention, the relation between the two men is face-to-face. Similarly, an ordinary citizen may vote for a political party that in turn supports the war effort and whose leaders are called in for military briefings. But in guerrilla war, the support a civilian provides is far more direct. He doesn't need to be briefed; he already knows the most important military secret; he knows who the guerrillas are. If he doesn't keep this information to himself, the guerrillas are lost.

Their enemies say that the guerrillas rely on terror to win the support or at least the silence of the villagers. But it seems more likely that when they have significant popular support (which they don't always have), they have it for other reasons. "Violence may explain the cooperation of a few individuals," writes an American student of the Vietnamese war, "but it cannot explain the cooperation of a whole social class [the peasantry]."[12] If the killing of civilians were sufficient to win civilian support, the guerrillas would always be at a disadvantage, for their enemies possess far more fire power than they do. But killing will work against the killer "unless he has already pre-empted a large part of the population and then limits his acts of violence to a sharply defined minority." When the guerrillas succeed, then, in fighting among the people, it is best to assume that they have some serious political support among the people. The people, or some of them, are complicitous in guerrilla war, and the war would be impossible without their complicity. That doesn't mean that they seek out opportunities to help. Even when he sympathizes with the goal of the guerrillas, we can assume that the average civilian would rather vote for them than hide them in his house. But guerrilla war makes for enforced intimacies, and the people are drawn into it in a new way even though the services they provide are nothing more than functional equivalents of the services civilians have always provided for soldiers. For the intimacy is itself an additional service, which has no functional equivalent. Whereas soldiers are supposed to protect the civilians who stand behind them, guerrillas are protected by the civilians among whom they stand.

But the fact that they accept this protection, and depend upon it, doesn't seem to me to deprive the guerrillas of their war rights. Indeed, it is more plausible to make exactly the opposite argument: that the war rights the people would have were they to rise *en masse* are passed on to the irregular fighters they support and protect—assuming that the support, at least, is voluntary. For soldiers acquire war rights not as individual warriors but as political instruments, servants of a community that in turn provides services for its soldiers. Guerrillas take on a similar identity whenever they stand in a similar or equivalent relationship, that is, whenever the people are helpful and complicitous in the ways I have described. When the people do not provide this recognition and support, guerrillas acquire no war rights, and their enemies may rightly treat them when captured as "bandits" or criminals. But any significant degree of popular support entitles the guerrillas to the benevolent quarantine customarily offered prisoners of war (unless they are guilty of specific acts of assassination or sabotage, for which soldiers, too, can be punished.) *

---

* The argument I am making here parallels that made by lawyers with reference to "belligerent recognition." At what point, they have asked, should a group of rebels (or secessionists) be recognized as a belligerent power and granted those war rights which customarily belong only to established governments? The answer has usually been that the recognition follows upon the establishment of a secure territorial base by the rebels. For then they actually function like a government, taking

This argument clearly establishes the rights of the guerrillas; it raises the most serious questions, however, about the rights of the people; and these are the crucial questions of guerrilla war. The intimacies of the struggle expose the people in a new way to the risks of combat. In practice, the nature of this exposure, and its degree, are going to be determined by the government and its allies. So the burdens of decision are shifted by the guerrillas onto their enemies. It is their enemies who must weigh (as we must) the moral significance of the popular support the guerrillas both enjoy and exploit. One can hardly fight against men and women who themselves fight among civilians without endangering civilian lives. Have these civilians forfeited their immunity? Or do they, despite their wartime complicity, still have rights vis-a-vis the anti-guerrilla forces?

The Rights of Civilian Supporters

If civilians had no rights at all, or were thought to have none, it would be a small benefit to hide among them. In a sense, then, the advantages the guerrillas seek depend upon the scruples of their enemies—though there are other advantages to be had if their enemies are unscrupulous: that is why anti-guerrilla warfare is so difficult. I shall want to argue that these scruples in fact have a moral basis, but it is worth suggesting first that they also have a strategic basis. It is always in the interest of the anti-guerrilla forces to insist upon the soldier/civilian distinction, even when the guerrillas act (as they always will if they can) so as to blur the line. All the handbooks on "counter-insurgency" make the same argument: what is necessary is to isolate the guerrillas from the civilian population, to cut them off from their protection and at the same time to shield civilians from the fighting.[13] The last point is more important in guerrilla than in conventional war, for in conventional war one assumes the hostility of "enemy civilians,"

---

on responsibility for the people who live on the land they control. But this assumes a conventional or near-conventional war. In the case of a guerrilla struggle, we may have to describe the appropriate relation between the rebels and the people differently: it is not when the guerrillas look after the people that they acquire war rights, but when the people "look after" the guerrillas.

while in a guerrilla struggle one must seek their sympathy and support. Guerrilla war is a political, even an ideological conflict. "Our kingdoms lay in each man's mind," wrote T. E. Lawrence of the Arab guerrillas he led in World War I. "A province would be won when we had taught the civilians in it to die for our ideal of freedom."[14] And it can be won back only if those same civilians are taught to live for some counter-ideal (or in the case of a military occupation, to acquiesce in the re-establishment of order and ordinary life). That is what is meant when it is said that the battle is for the "hearts and minds" of the people. And one cannot triumph in such a battle by treating the people as so many enemies to be attacked and killed along with the guerrillas who live among them.

But what if the guerrillas cannot be isolated from the people? What if the *levée en masse* is a reality and not merely a piece of propaganda? Characteristically, the military handbooks neither pose nor answer such questions. There is, however, a moral argument to be made if this point is reached: the anti-guerrilla war can then no longer be fought—and not just because, from a strategic point of view, it can no longer be won. It cannot be fought because it is no longer an anti-guerrilla but an anti-social war, a war against an entire people, in which no distinctions would be possible in the actual fighting. But this is the limiting case of guerrilla war. In fact, the rights of the people come into play earlier on, and I must try now to give them some plausible definition.

Consider again the case of the partisan attack in occupied France. If, after the ambush, the partisans hide in a nearby peasant village, what are the rights of the peasants among whom they hide? German soldiers arrive that night, let's say, seeking the men and women directly involved or implicated in the ambush and looking also for some way of preventing future attacks. The civilians they encounter are hostile, but that doesn't make them *enemies* in the sense of the war convention, for they don't actually resist the efforts of the soldiers. They behave exactly as citizens sometimes do in the face of police interrogations: they are passive, blank, evasive. We must imagine a domestic state of emergency and ask how the police might legitimately respond to such hostility. Soldiers can do no more when what they are doing is police work; for the status of the hostile civilians is no different. Interrogations, searches, seizures of property, curfews—all these seem to be commonly accepted (I will not try to explain why); but not the torture of suspects or the taking of hostages or the internment of men and women who are or might be innocent.[15] Civilians still have rights in such circumstances. If their liberty can be temporarily abridged in a variety of ways, it is not entirely forfeit; nor are their lives at risk. The argument would be much harder, however, had the troops been ambushed as they marched through the village itself, shot at from the cover of peasant homes and barns. To understand what happens then, we must look at another historical example.

The American "Rules of Engagement" in Vietnam

Here is a typical incident of the Vietnam war. "An American unit moving along Route 18 [in Long An province] received small arms fire from a village, and in reply the tactical commander called for artillery and air strikes on the village itself, resulting in heavy civilian casualties and extensive physical destruction."[16] Something like this must have happened hundreds, even thousands of times. The bombing and strafing of peasant villages was a common tactic of the American forces. It is a matter of special interest to us that it was permitted by the U.S. Army's "rules of engagement," worked out, so it was said, to isolate the guerrillas and minimize civilian casualties.

The attack on the village near Route 18 looks as if it was intended to minimize only army casualties. It looks like another instance of a practice I have already examined: the indiscriminate use of modern fire power to save soldiers from trouble and risk. But in this case, the trouble and risk are of a sort very different from anything encountered on the front line of a conventional war. It is most unlikely that an army patrol moving into the village would have been able to locate and destroy an enemy position. The soldiers would have found . . . a village, its population sullen and silent, the guerrilla fighters hiding, the guerrilla "fortifications" indistinguishable from the homes and shelters of the villagers. They might have drawn hostile fire; more likely, they would have lost men to mines and booby traps, the exact location of which everyone in the village knew and no one would reveal. Under such circumstances, it was not difficult for soldiers to convince themselves that the village was a military stronghold and a legitimate target. And if it was known to be a stronghold, surely it could be attacked, like any other enemy position, even before hostile fire was encountered. In fact, this became American policy quite early in the war: villages from which hostile fire might reasonably be expected were shelled and bombed before soldiers moved in and even if no movement was planned. But then how does one minimize civilian casualties, let alone win over the civilian population? It was to answer this question that the rules of engagement were developed.

The crucial point of the rules, as they are described by the journalist Jonathan Schell, was that civilians were to be given warning in advance of the destruction of their villages, so that they could break with the guerrillas, expel them, or leave themselves.[17] The goal was to force the separation of combatants and noncombatants, and the means was terror. Enormous risk was attached to complicity in guerrilla war, but this was a risk that could only be imposed on whole villages; no further differentiation was possible. It is not the case that civilians were held hostage for the activities of the guerrillas. Rather, they were held responsible for their own activity, even when this activity was not overtly military. The fact that the activity sometimes was overtly military, that ten-year-old children threw hand grenades at American soldiers (the incidence of such attacks was probably exaggerated by the soldiers, in part to justify their own conduct toward civilians) blurs the nature of this responsibility. But it has to be stressed that a village was regarded as hostile not because its women and children were prepared to fight, but because they were not prepared to deny material support to the guerrillas or to reveal their whereabouts or the location of their mines and booby traps.

These were the rules of engagement: (1) A village could be bombed or shelled without warning if American troops had received fire from within it. The villagers were presumed able to prevent the use of their village as a fire base, and whether or not they actually were able, they certainly knew in advance whether it would be so used. In any case, the shooting itself was a warning, since return fire was to be expected—though it is unlikely that the villagers expected the response to be as disproportionate as it usually was, until the pattern had become familiar. (2) Any village known to be hostile could be bombed or shelled if its inhabitants were warned in advance, either by the dropping of leaflets or by helicopter loudspeaker. These warnings were of two sorts: sometimes they were specific in character, delivered immediately before an attack, so that the villagers only just had time to leave (and then the guerrillas could leave with them), or they were general, describing the attack that might come if the villagers did not expel the guerrillas.

The U.S. Marines will not hesitate to destroy immediately any village or hamlet harboring the Vietcong . . . The choice is yours. If you refuse to let the Vietcong use your villages and hamlets as their battlefield, your homes and your lives will be saved.

And if not, not. Despite the emphasis on choice, this is not quite a liberal pronouncement, for the choice in question is very much a collective one. Exodus, of course, remained an individual option: people could move out of villages where the Vietcong had established itself, taking refuge with relatives in other villages, or in the cities, or in government-run camps. Most often, however, they did this only after the bombing had begun, either because they did not understand the warnings, or did not believe them, or simply hoped desperately that their own homes would somehow be spared. Hence it was sometimes thought humane to dispense with choice altogther and forcibly to deport villagers from areas that were considered under enemy control. Then the third rule of engagement went into effect. (3) Once the civilian population had been moved out, the village and surrounding country might be declared a "free fire zone" that could be bombed and shelled at will. It was assumed that anyone still living in the area was a guerrilla or a "hardened" guerrilla supporter. Deportation had stripped away civilian cover as defoliation stripped away natural cover, and left the enemy exposed.[18]

In considering these rules, the first thing to note is that they were radically ineffective. "My investigation disclosed," writes Schell, "that the procedures for applying these restraints were modified or twisted or ignored to such an extent that in practice the restraints evaporated entirely . . ."[19] Often, in fact, no warning was given, or the leaflets were of little help to villagers who could not read, or the forcible evacuation left large numbers of civilians behind, or no adequate provision was made for the deported families and they drifted back to their homes and farms. None of this, of course, would reflect on the value of the rules themselves, unless the ineffectiveness were somehow intrinsic to them or to the situation in which they were applied. This was clearly the case in Vietnam. For where the guerrillas have significant popular support and have established a political apparatus in the villages, it is unrealistic to think that the villagers will or can expel them. This has nothing to do with the virtues of guerrilla rule: it would have been equally unrealistic to think that German workers, though their homes were bombed and their families killed, would overthrow the Nazis. Hence the only protection the rules provide is in advising or enforcing the departure not of guerrillas from peaceful villages but of civilians from what is likely to become a battlefield.

Guerrilla War

Now, in a conventional war, removing civilians from a battlefield is clearly a good thing to do; positive international law requires it wherever possible. Similarly in the case of a besieged city: civilians must be allowed to leave; and if they refuse (so I have argued), they can be attacked along with the defending soldiers. But a battlefield and a city are determinate areas, and a battle and a siege are, usually, of limited duration. Civilians move out; then they move back. Guerrilla war is likely to be very different. The battlefield extends over much of the country and the struggle is, as Mao has written, "protracted." Here the proper analogy is not to the siege of a city but to the blockade or strategic devastation of a much wider area. The policy underlying the American rules of engagement actually envisaged the uprooting and resettlement of a very substantial part of the rural population of Vietnam: millions of men, women, and children. But that is an incredible task, and, leaving aside for the moment the likely criminality of the project, there was never more than a pretense that sufficient resources would be made available to accomplish it. It was inevitable then, and it was known to be inevitable, that civilians would be living in the villages that were shelled and bombed.

What happened is quickly described:[20]

> In August 1967, during Operation Benton, the "pacification" camps became so full that Army units were ordered not to "generate" any more refugees. The Army complied. But search and destroy operations continued. Only now the peasants were not warned before an air-strike was called on their village. They were killed in their villages because there was no room for them in the swamped pacification camps.

I should add that this sort of thing doesn't always happen, even in anti-guerrilla war—though the policy of forced resettlement or "concentration," from its origins in the Cuban Insurgency and the Boer War, has rarely been carried out in a humane manner or with adequate resources.[21] But one can find counter-examples. In Malaya, in the early 1950s, where the guerrillas had the support of only a relatively small part of the rural population, a limited resettlement (to new villages, not concentration camps) seems to have worked. At any rate, it has been said that after the fighting was over, few of the resettled villagers wanted to return to their former homes.[22] That is not a sufficient criterion of moral success, but it is one sign of a permissible program. Since governments are generally thought to be entitled to resettle (relatively small numbers of) their own citizens for the sake of some commonly accepted social purpose, the policy cannot be ruled out altogether in time of guerrilla war. But unless the numbers are restricted, it will be difficult to make the case for common acceptance. And here, as in peacetime, there is some requirement to provide adequate economic support and comparable living space. In Vietnam, that was never possible. The scope of the war was too wide; new villages could not be built; the camps were dismal; and hundreds of thousands of displaced peasants crowded into the cities, forming there a new *lumpen* proletariat, miserable, sick, jobless, or quickly exploited in ill-paid and menial jobs or as servants, prostitutes, and so on.

Even had all this worked, in the limited sense that civilian deaths had been avoided, the rules of engagement and the policy they embodied could hardly be defended. It seems to violate even the principle of proportionality—which is by no means easy to do, as we have seen again and again, since the values against which destruction and suffering are to be measured are so readily inflated. But in this case, the argument is clear, for the defense of resettlement comes down finally to a claim something like that made by an American officer with reference to the town of Ben Tre: we had to destroy the town in order to save it.[23] In order to save Vietnam, we had to destroy the rural culture and the village society of the Vietnamese. Surely the equation does not work and the policy cannot be approved, at least in the context of the Vietnamese struggle itself. (One can always shift, I suppose, to the higher mathematics of international statecraft.)

But the rules of engagement raise a more interesting question. Suppose that civilians, duly warned, not only refuse to expel the guerrillas but also refuse to leave themselves. Can they be attacked and killed, as the rules imply? What are their rights? They can certainly be exposed to risks, for battles are likely to be fought in their villages. And the risks they must live with will be considerably greater than those of conventional combat. The increased risk results from the intimacies I have already described; I would suggest now that it is the only result of those intimacies, at least in the moral realm. It is serious enough. Anti-guerrilla war is a terrible strain on conventional troops, and even if they are both disciplined and careful, as they should be, civilians are certain to die at their hands. A soldier who, once he is engaged, simply fires at every male villager between the ages of fifteen and fifty (say) is probably justified in doing so, as he would not be in an ordinary firefight. The innocent deaths that result from this kind of fighting are the responsibility of the guerrillas and their civilian supporters; the soldiers are cleared by the doctrine of double effect. It has to be stressed, however, that the supporters themselves, so long as they give only political support, are not legitimate targets, either as a group or as distinguishable individuals. Conceivably, some of them can be charged with complicity (not in guerrilla war generally but) in particular acts of assassination and sabotage. But charges of that sort must be proved before some sort of judicial tribunal. So far as combat goes, these people cannot be shot on sight, when no fire-fight is in progress; nor can their villages be attacked merely because they might be used as firebases or because it is expected that they will be used; nor can they be randomly bombed and shelled, even after warning has been given.

The American rules have only the appearance of recognizing and attending to the combatant/noncombatant distinction. In fact, they set up a new distinction: between loyal and disloyal, or friendly and hostile noncombatants. The same dichotomy can be seen at work in the claims American soldiers made about the villages they attacked: "This place is almost entirely V.C. controlled, or pro-V.C." "We consider just about everyone here to be a hard-core V.C., or at least some kind of supporter."[24] It is not the military activities of the villagers that are being stressed in statements of this sort, but their political allegiance. Even with reference to that, the statements are palpably false, since at least some of the villagers are children who cannot be said to have any allegiance at all. In any case, as I have already argued in the example of the villagers of occupied France, political hostility does not make people enemies in the sense of the war convention. (If it did, there would be no civilian immunity at all, except when wars were fought in neutral countries.) They have done nothing to forfeit their right to life, and that right must be respected as best it can be in the course of attacks against the irregular fighters the villagers both resemble and harbor.

It is important to say something now about the possible shape of those attacks, though I cannot talk about them like a military strategist; I can only report on some of the things that strategists say. Bombing and shelling from a distance have undoubtedly been defended in terms of military necessity. But that is as bad an argument strategically as it is morally. For there are other and more effective ways of fighting. Thus a British expert on counter-insurgency writes that the use of "heavily armed helicopters" against peasant villages "can only be justified if the campaign has deteriorated to the extent where it is virtually indistinguishable from conventional war."[25] I doubt that it can be justified even then, but I want to stress again what this expert has grasped: that counter-insurgency requires a strategy and tactics of discrimination. Guerrillas can be defeated (and, similarly, they can win) only at close quarters. With regard to peasant villages, this suggests two different sorts of campaigns, both of which have been extensively discussed in the literature. In areas of "low intensity operations," the villages must be occupied by small units specially trained for the political and police work necessary to seek out guerrilla supporters and informants. In areas where the guerrillas are effectively in control and the fighting intense, the villages must be encircled and entered in force. Bernard Fall has reported in some detail on a French attack of this sort in Vietnam in the 1950's.[26] What is involved here is an effort to bring numbers, expertise, and technology directly to bear, forcing the guerrillas to give battle in a situation where fire can be relatively precise, or driving them into a surrounding net of soldiers. If the soldiers are properly prepared and equipped, they need not accept unbearable risks in fighting of this sort, and they need not inflict indiscriminate destruction. As Fall points out, a very considerable number of men are required for this strategy: "No sealing off of an enemy force could be successful unless the proportion of attackers to defenders was 15 to 1 or even 20 to 1, for the enemy had in its favor an intimate knowledge of the terrain, the advantages of defensive organization, and the sympathy of the population." But these proportions are frequently achieved in guerrilla war, and the "surround and storm" strategy would be eminently feasible were it not for a second and more serious difficulty.

Since the villages are not (or should nʊʈ be) destroyed when they are stormed, and since the villagers are not resettled, it is always possible for the guerrillas to return once the specially assembled task force has moved on. Success requires that the military operation be followed by a political campaign—and this neither the French in Vietnam nor the Americans who followed them were able to mount in any serious fashion. The decision to destroy villages from a distance was a consequence of this failure, which is not at all the same thing as the "deterioration" of guerrilla into conventional war.

At some point in the military progress of the rebellion, or in the decline of the political capacity of the government that opposes it, it may well become impossible to fight the guerrillas at close quarters. There aren't enough men or, more likely, the government, though it can win particular battles, has no staying power. As soon as the fighting is over, the villagers welcome back the insurgent forces. Now the government (and its foreign allies) face what is in effect, or rather what has become, a people's war. This honorific name can be applied, however, only after the guerrilla movement has won very substantial popular support. It is by no means true all the time. One need only study Che Guevara's abortive campaign in the jungles of Bolivia to realize how easy it is to destroy a guerrilla band that has no popular support at all.[27] From there, one might trace a continuum of increasing difficulty: at some point along that continuum, guerrilla fighters acquire war rights, and at some further point, the right of the government to continue the struggle must be called into question.

This last is not a point which soldiers are likely to recognize or acknowledge. For it is an axiom of the war convention (and a qualification on the rules of war) that if attack is morally possible, counter-attack cannot be ruled out. It cannot be the case that guerrillas can hug the civilian population and make themselves invulnerable. But if it is always morally possible to fight, it is not always possible to do whatever is required to win. In any struggle, conventional or unconventional, the rules of war may at some point become a hindrance to the victory of one side or another. If they could then be set aside, however, they would have no value at all. It is precisely then that the restraints they impose are most important. We can see this clearly in the Vietnam case. The alternative strategies I have briefly outlined were conceivably a way of winning (as the British won in Malaya) until the guerrillas consolidated their political base in the villages. That victory effectively ended the war. It is not, I suppose, a victory that can be distinguished in any definitive fashion from the political and military struggle that preceded it. But one can say with some assurance that it has occurred whenever ordinary soldiers (who are not moral monsters and would fight by the rules if they could) become convinced that old men and women and children are their enemies. For after that, it is unlikely that the war can be fought except by setting out systematically to kill civilians or to destroy their society and culture.

I am inclined to say more than this. In the theory of war, as we have seen, considerations of *jus ad bellum* and *jus in bello* are logically independent, and the judgments we make in terms of one and the other are not necessarily the same. But here they come together. The war cannot be won, and it should not be won. It cannot be won, because the only available strategy involves a war against civilians; and it should not be won, because the degree of civilian support that rules out alternative strategies also makes the guerrillas the legitimate rulers of the country. The struggle against them is an unjust struggle as well as one that can only be carried on unjustly. Fought by foreigners, it is a war of aggression; if by a local regime alone, it is an act of tyranny. The position of the anti-guerrilla forces has become doubly untenable.

12

Terrorism

The Political Code

The word "terrorism" is used most often to describe revolutionary violence. That is a small victory for the champions of order, among whom the uses of terror are by no means unknown. The systematic terrorizing of whole populations is a strategy of both conventional and guerrilla war, and of established governments as well as radical movements. Its purpose is to destroy the morale of a nation or a class, to undercut its solidarity; its method is the random murder of innocent people. Randomness is the crucial feature of terrorist activity. If one wishes fear to spread and intensify over time, it is not desirable to kill specific people identified in some particular way with a regime, a party, or a policy. Death must come by chance to individual Frenchmen, or Germans, to Irish Protestants, or Jews, simply because they are Frenchmen or Germans, Protestants or Jews, until they feel themselves fatally exposed and demand that their governments negotiate for their safety.

In war, terrorism is a way of avoiding engagement with the enemy army. It represents an extreme form of the strategy of the "indirect approach."[1] It is so indirect that many soldiers have refused to call it war at all. This is a matter as much of professional pride as of moral judgment. Consider the statement of a British admiral in World War II, protesting the terror bombing of German cities: "We are a hopelessly unmilitary nation to imagine that we [can] win the war by bombing German women and children instead of defeating their army and navy."² The key word here is unmilitary. The admiral rightly sees terrorism as a civilian strategy. One might say that it represents the continuation of war by political means. Terrorizing ordinary men and women is first of all the work of domestic tyranny, as Aristotle wrote: "The first aim and end [of tyrants] is to break the spirit of their subjects."³ The British described the "aim and end" of terror bombing in the same way: what they sought was the destruction of civilian morale.

Tyrants taught the method to soldiers, and soldiers to modern revolutionaries. That is a crude history; I offer it only in order to make a more precise historical point: that terrorism in the strict sense, the random murder of innocent people, emerged as a strategy of revolutionary struggle only in the period after World War II, that is, only after it had become a feature of conventional war. In both cases, in war and revolution, a kind of warrior honor stood in the way of this development, especially among professional officers and "professional revolutionaries." The increasing use of terror by far left and ultranationalist movements represents the breakdown of a political code first worked out in the second half of the nineteenth century and roughly analogous to the laws of war worked out at the same time. Adherence to this code did not prevent revolutionary militants from being called terrorists, but in fact the violence they committed bore little resemblance to contemporary terrorism. It was not random murder but assassination, and it involved the drawing of a line that we will have little difficulty recognizing as the political parallel of the line that marks off combatants from noncombatants.

The Russian Populists, the IRA, and the Stern Gang

I can best describe the revolutionary "code of honor" by giving some examples of so-called terrorists who acted or tried to act in accordance with its norms. It have chosen three historical cases. The first will be readily recognizable, for Albert Camus made it the basis of his play The Just Assassins.

1) In the early twentieth century, a group of Russian revolutionaries decided to kill a Tsarist official, the Grand Duke Sergei, a man personally involved in the repression of radical activity. They planned to blow him up in his carriage, and on the appointed day one of their number was in place along the Grand Duke's usual route. As the carriage drew near, the young revolutionary, a bomb hidden under his coat, noticed that his victim was not alone; on

his lap he held two small children. The would-be assassin looked, hesitated, then walked quickly away. He would wait for another occasion. Camus has one of his comrades say, accepting this decision: "Even in destruction, there's a right way and a wrong way—and there are limits."[4]

2) During the years 1938-39, the Irish Republican Army waged a bombing campaign in Britain. In the course of this campaign, a republican militant was ordered to carry a pre-set time bomb to a Coventry power station. He traveled by bicycle, the bomb in his basket, took a wrong turn, and got lost in a maze of streets. As the time for the explosion drew near, he panicked, dropped his bike, and ran off. The bomb exploded, killing five passers-by. No one in the IRA (as it was then) thought this a victory for the cause; the men immediately involved were horrified. The campaign had been carefully planned, according to a recent historian, so as to avoid the killing of innocent bystanders.[5]

3) In November 1944, Lord Moyne, British Minister of State in the Middle East, was assassinated in Cairo by two members of the Stern Gang, a right-wing Zionist group. The two assassins were caught, minutes later, by an Egyptian policeman. One of them described the capture at his trial: "We were being followed by the constable on his motorcycle. My comrade was behind me. I saw the constable approach him . . . I would have been able to kill the constable easily, but I contented myself with . . . shooting several times into the air. I saw my comrade fall off his bicycle. The constable was almost upon him. Again, I could have eliminated the constable with a single bullet, but I did not. Then I was caught."[6]

What is common to these cases is a moral distinction, drawn by the "terrorists," between people who can and people who cannot be killed. The first category is not composed of men and women bearing arms, immediately threatening by virtue of their military training and commitment. It is composed instead of officials, the political agents of regimes thought to be oppressive. Such people, of course, are protected by the war convention and by positive international law. Characteristically (and not foolishly), lawyers have frowned on assassination, and political officials have been assigned to the class of nonmilitary persons, who are never the legitimate objects of attack.[7] But this assignment only partially represents our common moral judgments. For we judge the assassin by his victim, and when the victim is Hitler-like in character, we are likely to praise the assassin's work, though we still do not call him a soldier. The second category is less problematic: ordinary citizens, not engaged in political harming—that is, in administering or enforcing laws thought to be unjust—are immune from attack whether or not they support those laws. Thus the aristocratic children, the Coventry pedestrians, even the Egyptian policeman (who had nothing to do with British imperialism in Palestine)—these people are like civilians in wartime. They are innocent politically as civilians are innocent militarily. It is precisely these people, however, that contemporary terrorists try to kill.

The war convention and the political code are structurally˙similar, and the distinction between officials and citizens parallels that between soldiers and civilians (though the two are not the same). What lies behind them both, I think, and lends them plausibility, is the moral difference between aiming and not aiming—or, more accurately, between aiming at particular people because of things they have done or are doing, and aiming at whole groups of people, indiscriminately, because of who they are. The first kind of aiming is appropriate to a limited struggle directed against regimes and policies. The second reaches beyond all limits; it is infinitely threatening to whole peoples, whose individual members are systematically exposed to violent death at any and every moment in the course of their (largely innocuous) lives. A bomb planted on a streetcorner, hidden in a bus station, thrown into a cafe or pub—this is aimless killing, except that the victims are likely to share what they cannot avoid, a collective identity. Since some of these victims must be immune from attack (unless liability follows from original sin), any code that directs and controls the fire of political militants is going to be at least minimally appealing. It is so much of an advance over the willful randomness of terrorist attacks. One might even feel easier about killing officials than about killing soldiers, since the state rarely conscripts its political, as it does its military agents; they have chosen officialdom as a career.

Soldiers and officials are, however, different in another respect. The threatening character of the soldier's activities is a matter of fact; the unjust or oppressive character of the official's activities is a matter of political judgment. For this reason, the political code has never attained to the same status as the war convention. Nor can assassins claim any rights, even on the basis of the strictest adherence to its principles. In the eyes of those of us whose judgments of oppression and injustice differ from their own, political assassins are simply murderers, exactly like the killers of ordinary citizens. The case is not the same with soldiers, who are not judged politically at all and who are called murderers only when they kill noncombatants. Political killing imposes risks quite unlike those of combat, risks whose character is best revealed by the fact that there is no such thing as benevolent quarantine for the duration of the political struggle. Thus the young Russian revolutionary, who eventually killed the Grand Duke, was tried and executed for murder, as were the Stern Gang assassins of Lord Moyne. All three were treated exactly like the IRA militants, also captured, who were held responsible for the deaths of ordinary citizens. That treatment seems to me appropriate, even if we share the political judgments of the men involved and defend their resort to violence. On the other hand, even if we do not share their judgments, these men are entitled to a kind of moral respect not due to terrorists, because they set limits to their actions.

The Vietcong Assassination Campaign

The precise limits are hard to define, as in the case of noncombatant immunity. But we can perhaps move toward a definition by looking at a guerrilla war in which officials were attacked on a large scale. Beginning at some point in the late 1950's, the NLF waged a campaign aimed at destroying the governmental structure of the South Vietnamese countryside. Between 1960 and 1965, some 7,500 village and district officials were assassinated by Vietcong militants. An American student of the Vietcong, describing these officials as the "natural leaders" of Vietnamese society, argues that "by any definition this NLF action . . . amounts to genocide."[8] This assumes that all Vietnam's natural leaders were government officials (but then, who was leading the NLF?) and hence that government officials were literally indispensable to national existence. Since these assumptions are not remotely plausible, it has to be said that "by any definition" the killing of leaders is not the same as the destruction of entire peoples. Terrorism may foreshadow genocide, but assassination does not.

On the other hand, the NLF campaign did press against the limits of the notion of officialdom as I have been using it. The Front tended to include among officials anyone who was paid by the government, even if the work he was doing—as a public health officer, for example—had nothing to do with the particular policies the NLF opposed.[9] And it tended to assimilate into officialdom people like priests and landowners who used their nongovernmental authority in specific ways on behalf of the government. They did not kill anyone, apparently, just because he was a priest or a landowner; the assassination campaign was planned with considerable attention to the details of individual action, and a concerted effort was made "to ensure that there were no unexplained killings."[10] Still, the range of vulnerability was widened in disturbing ways.

One might argue, I suppose, that any official is by definition engaged in the political efforts of the (putatively) unjust regime, just as any soldier, whether he is actually fighting or not, is engaged in the war effort. But the variety of activities sponsored and paid for by the modern state is extraordinary, and it seems intemperate and extravagant to make all such activities into occasions for assassination. Assuming that the regime is in fact oppressive, one should look for agents of oppression and not simply for government agents. As for private persons, they seem to me immune entirely. They are subject, of course, to the conventional forms of social and political pressure (which are conventionally intensified in guerrilla wars) but not to political violence. Here the case is the same with citizens as with civilians: if their support for the government or the war were allowable as a reason for killing them, the line that marks off immune from vulnerable persons would quickly disappear. It is worth stressing that political assassins generally don't want that line to disappear; they have reasons for taking careful aim and avoiding indiscriminate murder. "We were told," a Vietcong guerrilla reported to his American captors, "that in Singapore the rebels on certain days would dynamite every 67th streetcar . . . the next day it might be every 30th, and so on; but that this hardened the hearts of the people against the rebels because so many people died needlessly."[11]

I have avoided noticing until now that most political militants don't regard themselves as assassins at all but rather as executioners. They are engaged, or so they regularly claim, in a revolutionary version of vigilante justice. This suggests another reason for killing only some officials and not others, but it is entirely a self-description. Vigilantes in the usual sense apply conventional conceptions of criminality, though in a rough and ready way. Revolutionaries champion a new conception, about which there is unlikely to be wide agreement. They hold that officials are vulnerable because or insofar as they are actually guilty of "crimes against the people." The more impersonal truth is that they are vulnerable, or more vulnerable than ordinary citizens, simply because their activities are open to such descriptions. The exercise of political power is a dangerous business. Saying this, I do not mean to defend assassination. It is most often a vile politics, as vigilante justice is most often a bad kind of law enforcement; its agents are usually gangsters, and sometimes madmen, in political dress. And yet "just assassinations" are at least possible, and men and women who aim at that kind of killing and renounce every other kind need to be marked off from those who kill at random—not as doers of justice, necessarily, for one can disagree about that, but as revolutionaries with honor. They do not want the revolution, as one of Camus' characters says, "to be loathed by the whole human race."

However the political code is specified, terrorism is the deliberate violation of its norms. For ordinary citizens are killed and no defense is offered—none could be offered—in terms of their individual activities. The names and occupations of the dead are not known in advance; they are killed simply to deliver a message of fear to others like themselves. What is the content of the message? I suppose it could be anything at all; but in practice terrorism, because it is directed against entire peoples or classes, tends to communicate the most extreme and brutal intentions—above all, the tyrannical repression, removal, or mass murder of the population under attack. Hence contemporary terrorist campaigns are most often focused on people whose national existence has been radically devalued: the Protestants of Northern Ireland, the Jews of Israel, and so on. The campaign announces the devaluation. That is why the people under attack are so unlikely to believe that compromise is possible with their enemies. In war, terrorism is associated with the demand for unconditional surrender and, in similar fashion, tends to rule out any sort of compromise settlement.

In its modern manifestations, terror is the totalitarian form of war and politics. It shatters the war convention and the political code. It breaks across moral limits beyond which no further limitation seems possible, for within the categories of civilian and citizen, there isn't any smaller group for which immunity might be claimed (except children; but I don't think children can be called "immune" if their parents are attacked and killed). Terrorists anyway make no such claim; they kill anybody. Despite this, terrorism has been defended, not only by the terrorists themselves, but also by philosophical apologists writing on their behalf. The political defenses mostly parallel those that are offered whenever soldiers attack civilians. They represent one or another version of the argument from military necessity.* It is said, for example, that there is no alternative to terrorist activity if oppressed peoples are to be liberated. And it is said, further, that this has always been so: terrorism is the only means and so it is the ordinary means of destroying oppressive regimes and founding new nations.[12] The cases I have already worked through suggest the falsity of these assertions. Those who make them, I think, have lost their grip on the historical past; they suffer from a malign forgetfulness, erasing all moral distinctions along with the men and women who painfully worked them out.

Violence and Liberation

Jean-Paul Sartre and the Battle of Algiers

But there is another argument which, because of the currency it has gained, must be taken up here, even though it has no immediate analogue in wartime debates. It has been put forward in its starkest form by Sartre in a justification of FLN terrorism in Algeria, published as a preface to Franz Fanon's *The Wretched of the Earth*. The summary lines of Sartre's argument are these:[13]

> To shoot down a European is to kill two birds with one stone, to destroy an oppressor and the man he oppresses at the same time: there remains a dead man and a free man.

In his usual fashion, with a certain zest for Hegelian melodrama, Sartre is here describing what he takes to be an act of psychological liberation. Only when the slave turns on his master, physically confronts him and kills him, does he create himself as a free human being. The master dies; the slave is reborn. Even if this were a believable picture of the terrorist act, the argument is not persua-

---

* Among revolutionaries as among government officials, this argument often slides from an analysis of particular cases of duress and necessity (which are rarely convincing) to the general claim that war is hell and anything goes. General Sherman's view is upheld, for example, by the Italian leftist Franco Solinas, who wrote the screenplay for Pontecorvo's *The Battle of Algiers* and defended the terrorism of the Algerian FLN: "For centuries they've tried to prove that war is fair play, like duels, but war isn't and therefore any method used to fight it is good . . . It's not a question of ethics or fair play. What we must attack is war itself and the situations that lead to it." (*The Battle of Algiers*, edited and translated by PierNico Solinas, New York, 1973, pp. 195–96.) Compare the same argument made by American officials in defense of the bombing of Hiroshima, chapter 16.

sive; it is open to two obvious and crippling questions. First, is the one-to-one relation necessary? Did it take one dead European to make one free Algerian? If so, there were not enough Europeans living in Algeria; more would have had to be brought over if the Algerian people were to free themselves by Sartrean means. If not, it must follow that some one else besides the man-who-kills can be liberated. . . . How? By watching? By reading about the murder in the newspaper? It is hard to see how vicarious experience can play an important part in a process of personal liberation (as described by an existentialist philosopher).

The second question raises more familiar issues: will any European do? Unless Sartre thinks all Europeans, including children, are oppressors, he cannot believe that. But if it is only liberating to attack and kill an agent of oppression, we are back with the political code. From Sartre's perspective, that cannot be right, since the men and women he is defending had explicitly rejected that code. They killed Europeans at random, as in the well-known scene from the (historically accurate) film *The Battle of Algiers*, in which a bomb is set off in a milk bar where French teenagers are drinking and dancing.[14]

MILK BAR. EXPLOSION. OUTSIDE. DAY.
The jukebox is flung into the middle of the street. There is blood, strips of flesh, material . . . the white smoke and shouts, weeping, hysterical girls' screams. One of them no longer has an arm and runs around howling despairingly; it is impossible to control her . . . The sounds of sirens is heard . . . The ambulances arrive . . .

Such an event is not easily reconstructed as an existentialist encounter between masters and slaves.

Certainly, there are historical moments when armed struggle is necessary for the sake of human freedom. But if dignity and self-respect are to be the outcomes of that struggle, it cannot consist of terrorist attacks upon children. One can argue that such attacks are the inevitable products of oppression, and in a sense, I suppose, that is right. Hatred, fear, and the lust for domination are the psychological marks of oppressed and oppressor alike, and their acting out, on either side, can be said to be radically determined. The mark of a revolutionary struggle against oppression, however, is not this incapacitating rage and random violence, but restraint and self-control. The revolutionary reveals his freedom in the same way as he earns it, by directly confronting his enemies and refraining from attacks on anyone else. It was not only to save the innocent that revolutionary militants worked out the distinction between officials and ordinary citizens, but also to save themselves from killing the innocent. Whatever its strategic value, the political code is intrinsically connected to psychological liberation. Among men and women trapped in a bloody struggle, it is the key to self-respect. The same thing can be said of the war convention: in the context of a terrible coerciveness, soldiers most clearly assert their freedom when they obey the moral law.

13

Reprisals

Deterrence Without Retribution

When the British imposed their blockade of Germany in 1916,
they called it a reprisal; when the Germans began the systematic
bombing of London in 1940, they defended themselves in the
same way. No part of the war convention is so open to abuse, is
so openly abused, as the doctrine of reprisals. For the doctrine
is, or once was thought to be, permissive with regard to all the
rest of the convention. It legitimates actions otherwise criminal,
if these actions are undertaken in response to crimes previously
committed by the enemy. "Reprisals," writes a pacifist critic of
the rules of war, "mean doing what you think wrong on the plea
that someone else did it first."[1] And, he goes on, someone else will
always do it first. Hence reprisals create a chain of wrongdoing at
the end of which every responsible actor can point to some other
actor and say "*tu quoque.*"

It is the explicit purpose of reprisals, however, to break off the
chain, to stop the wrongdoing *here*, with this final act. Sometimes
—though it has to be said, not often—that purpose is realized. I
want to begin with a case in which it was realized, so that we can at
least make sense of what was for many years the conventional opinion—as stated, for example, by a nineteenth-century French lawyer:
"Reprisals are a means of preventing war from becoming entirely
barbarous."[2]

The FFI Prisoners at Annecy

In the summer of 1944, much of France was a battleground. Allied armies were fighting in Normandy; partisan groups, organized now into the French Forces of the Interior and in touch with both the Allies and the Gaullist Provisional Government in Algeria, operated on a large scale in many parts of the country. They wore insignias of battle; they bore their arms openly. It is clear that the 1940 armistice had effectively been voided, and the military struggle resumed. Nevertheless, the German authorities continued to treat captured partisans as war traitors or war rebels, subject to summary execution. On the day after the Allied landings, for example, fifteen partisans captured at Caen were immediately shot.[3] And the executions continued, as the pace of the fighting increased, during the next months. The FFI complained of these executions to the Provisional Government, which in turn sent a formal protest to the Germans. Since they did not recognize the Government, the Germans refused to accept the protest. In their note, the French had threatened reprisals against German prisoners. The continued killing did not, however, elicit any such response—perhaps because troops directly subject to the Provisional Government, recruited outside occupied France, were regularly accorded prisoner-of-war status by the Germans.

In August 1944, large numbers of German soldiers in Southern France began surrendering to partisan groups, and the FFI leadership was suddenly in a position to carry out the Government's threat. "When . . . it became known that the Germans . . . had executed 80 French prisoners, and that further executions were imminent, the FFI command at Annecy decided that 80 of the prisoners in [its] hands would in turn be shot."[4] At this point, the Red Cross intervened, won a postponement of the executions, and sought from the Germans an agreement henceforth to treat captured partisans as prisoners of war. The partisans waited six days and then, the Germans not replying, the 80 prisoners were shot.* The effects of the reprisal are not easy to make out, for the German army was hard-pressed, and many other factors must have figured

---

* I have never understood why, in cases like this one, the men are not simply hidden away when their deaths are announced. Why must they actually be killed? Since deceit of various sorts is accepted under the war convention, it certainly should not be ruled out here. But I have been unable to find any case in which such a ruse was tried.

in its decisions. It is apparently true, however, that no partisans were executed after the Annecy shootings.

Now in one sense, this case is easy to judge: the Geneva Convention of 1929, which the French had signed and the FFI itself reaffirmed, explicitly barred reprisals against prisoners of war.[5] No other group of innocent men and women was granted a similar immunity; prisoners were singled out because of the contract implied by surrender, in which they are promised life and benevolent quarantine. Killing them would be a breach of faith as well as a violation of the positive laws of war. But I shall not focus on this exception to the general rule of reprisals, for it does not open up the larger question, whether the deliberate killing of innocent men and women should ever be declared lawful or morally justified. And I doubt very much that we will want to say, in answer to that question, that some innocent people can be killed and others not. The case of the FFI prisoners is useful because it provides a classic example of reprisal, and one in which our sympathies are likely to be engaged, at least initially, on the side of the "reprisers."

Reprisals of this sort have as their purpose the enforcement of the war convention. In international society, as in Locke's state of nature, every individual member (every belligerent power) claims the right to enforce the law. The content of this right is the same as it is in domestic society: it is first of all a right of retribution, to punish guilty men and women; it is secondly a right of deterrence, to protect oneself and others against criminal activity. In domestic society, these two most often go together. Criminal activity is deterred by punishing or threatening to punish guilty individuals. That, at least, is the commonly accepted doctrine. In international society, however, and especially in wartime, the two rights are not equally enforceable. It is often impossible to get at guilty individuals, but it's always possible to prevent or try to prevent further criminal activity by responding in kind as the French partisans did, that is, by "punishing" innocent people. The result might be described as a one-sided sort of law enforcement: deterrence without retribution.

It might also be described as a prime example of radical utilitarianism—indeed, of a ultilitarianism so radical that utilitarian philosophers have been concerned to deny its existence. Yet it is common enough in the theory as well as in the practice of war. One of the criticisms most frequently leveled against utilitarianism is that its calculations would under certain circumstances require the authorities to "punish" an innocent person (to kill or imprison him, under cover of punishment). The usual response has been to adjust the calculations so that they yield different and more conventionally acceptable results.[6] But in the history of international law and in debates over wartime behavior, the effort at adjustment has mostly been foregone. Reprisals have been defended, with admirable directness, on strictly utilitarian grounds. Under the special conditions of combat, at least, utilitarian calculations have indeed required the "punishing" of innocent people. The political or military leaders of belligerent powers have commonly invoked the requirement, claiming that no other means were available to check the criminal excesses of their opponents. And detached observers, students of the law, venerable doctors have generally accepted this as a possible argument "in extreme cases" (the cases, of course, are often disputed). Hence it is a "principle of war law," according to a leading authority: "For every offense punish someone; the guilty, if possible, but someone."[7]

This is not an attractive principle, and it would not be accurate to explain the traditional acceptance of reprisals by reference to it alone. In wartime, after all, innocent people are often attacked and killed in the name of utility, in order, it is said, to shorten the war, save lives, and so on. But such attacks don't have the same status as reprisals. It is not their utility, assuming now that they are in fact useful, that makes reprisals different, but some other quality. This quality is misunderstood, I think, by those writers who describe reprisal as the most primitive feature of the war convention, a survival of the ancient *lex talionis*.[8] For the talion is a return of evil for evil, and what is crucial about reprisal is precisely that evil, though it may be repeated, is not returned. The new crime has a new victim, who is not the original criminal, though he probably has the same nationality. The particular choice is (so far as utility goes) quite impersonal; in this sense, reprisal is chillingly modern. Something, however, of the talion survives: not the idea of return, but the idea of response. Reprisal is characterized by a certain posture of looking back, acting after, which implies a willingness not to act at all, to abide by some set of restraints. "They did it first." This sentence carries a moral argument. I do not believe that it is a very strong argument or one that will take us far. But it serves to mark off reprisal from other, equally useful violations of the war convention. There is no right to commit crimes in order to shorten a war, but there is a right, so it was once thought, to commit crimes (or rather, acts that would otherwise be called crimes) in order to cope with the previous criminal activity of one's enemies.

The backward-looking character of reprisals is confirmed by the rule of proportionality that restrains them. The rule is quite different and far more precise than that which figures, for example, in the doctrine of double effect. The partisan commanders at Annecy acted in strict accordance with its provisions when they decided to kill 80 Germans in response to the killing of 80 Frenchmen. Reprisals are limited with reference to previous crimes, not with reference to the crimes they are designed to deter (not with reference to their effects or their hoped-for effects). This point has sometimes been disputed by writers committed to utilitarian modes of thought. Thus McDougal and Feliciano argue, in characteristic style, "that the kind and amount of permissible . . . violence is that which is reasonably designed so to affect the enemy's expectations about the costs and gains of reiteration or continuation of his initial criminal act as to induce the termination of and future abstention from such act."[9] They admit that the amount of violence, so determined, may be greater than that originally inflicted by the enemy. In the Annecy case, it might well have been less: the shooting of 40 Germans, or 20, or 10, might have had the same effect as the shooting of 80. But however the calculations work out, this kind of forward-looking proportionality has never been accepted either by the general run of theorists writing about war or by ordinary practitioners. During World War II, to be sure, the Germans often responded to partisan activity in the occupied states of Europe by shooting ten hostages for every German killed.[10] This proportion may have reflected a peculiar notion about the relative value of German lives, or it may have been "reasonably designed so to affect the enemy's expectations, etc." In any case, the practice was universally condemned.

It was condemned, of course, not only because of the actual disproportion involved, but also because the previous partisan activity was in many cases not thought to violate the war convention. Hence the German response was simply utilitarian deterrence, not law enforcement. It is another feature of the backward-looking character of reprisals that the acts to which they respond must be crimes, violations of the recognized rules of war. Moreover, the rules must be commonly recognized, on both sides of the battle-line, if the special character of reprisals is to be maintained. When the British army resorted to reprisals during the War of 1812, an opposition member of the House of Commons, who thought such conduct barbarous, asked why His Majesty's soldiers didn't scalp their captives when they fought with the American Indians or enslave them in their wars with the Barbary corsairs.[11] I suppose the answer is that scalping and enslavement were not thought illegitimate by the Indians and the corsairs. And so the imitation of these practices by the British would not have been understood as law enforcement (nor would it have had any deterrent effect); it would only have confirmed their enemies' notions of appropriate wartime behavior. Reprisals may involve deterrence without retribution, but this must nevertheless be a reactive deterrence, and what it reacts to is a violation of the war *convention*. If there is no convention, there can be no reprisal.

At the same time, we are uneasy about reprisals precisely because there is a convention, and one that categorically rules out the acts that reprisal usually requires. If it is wrong, and for the deepest reasons, to kill innocent people, how can it be right to kill them? In treatises on international law, the defense of reprisal is always qualified, first by a great show of reluctance and anxiety, and secondly by some words about the extremity of the case.[12] It is not easy to know what this last qualification means, however, and it appears in fact that any violation of the rules is sufficiently "extreme" to justify a proportionate response. Backward-looking proportionality is a genuine limit: it would have barred, for example, the two so-called reprisals with which I began this chapter. But extremity is not a limit at all. It is certainly not true that reprisals are undertaken only when the enemy's crimes pose a drastic danger to the war effort as a whole or to the cause for which the war is being fought. For the purpose of reprisal is not to win the war or prevent the defeat of the cause, but simply to enforce the rules. Perhaps the meaning of the appeal to extremity is like that of the show of reluctance: both suggest a view of reprisal as a last resort. In practice, again, the only action required before one reaches this last resort is a formal protest, such as the French delivered to the Germans in 1944, and a threat to respond in kind if this or that criminal activity is continued. But one might require much more than that, both in the way of law enforcement and in the way of military action. The FFI might, for example, have announced that they would treat German soldiers involved in the execution of captured partisans as war criminals; they might even have begun to publish the names of those who would be accused. Given the military situation of the German army in 1944, such an announcement could well have had a significant effect. Or the partisans might have attempted to raid the prisons or camps where their comrades were being held. Such raids were not impossible, though they would have involved risks entirely absent when one shoots down captured soldiers.

If the notion of last resort were taken seriously, it would limit reprisal in a radical way. But suppose that the partisans had issued the announcement and undertaken the raids without stopping the German executions. Would they then have been justified in shooting their prisoners? "A reckless enemy often leaves his opponent *no other means* of securing himself against the repetition of barbarous outrage."[18] But the truth is that there are always other means, more or less dangerous, more or less effective. To argue against the executions isn't to deny the partisans a last resort. It is only to say, for example, that military raids are their last resort. If the raids fail, they can only be tried again; there is nothing more to be done. (Reprisals might fail, too—they usually do—and what comes after that?) This is the conclusion that I want to defend, and I will defend it, once again, by reflecting on the status and character of the German prisoners.

Who are these men? Once they were soldiers; now they are disarmed and helpless. Perhaps some of them are war criminals; perhaps some of them were involved in the murder of captured partisans. Then, surely, they should be put on trial, not shot out of hand. We will want to hear the evidence against them and make sure that we punish the right ones. Only a trial can signal our own commitment to the rules of war. But here, let us assume, are ordinary prisoners who neither made nor carried out criminal decisions. Their day-to-day activities were very much like those of their enemies. How can they be shot out of hand, treated more cruelly than we would treat suspected criminals? It seems incredible that some number of them should be arbitrarily separated from the rest and then killed, simply so that we can announce their deaths, and all this for the sake of justice! Killing them would be murder: the name is exact, no matter what crimes we hope to avoid by becoming murderers. For these men are not mere material out of whose lives we can fashion a deterrent strategy. Even as prisoners, or precisely as prisoners, they have rights against us.

The current thrust of international law is to condemn reprisals against innocent people, and for essentially the reasons that I have suggested: the helplessness of the victims rules them out as objects of military attack, and their noninvolvement in criminal activity rules them out as objects of retributive violence. The Geneva Convention of 1929, as we have seen, declared prisoners immune; the 1949 Conventions did the same for wounded, sick, and shipwrecked members of the armed forces and for civilian persons in occupied territory.[14] This last provision effectively bars the killing of hostages, the paradigm case of using innocent people for one's own military purposes. The only class of disengaged men and women against whom reprisals are still legally defensible is the civilian population of the enemy country. Its members can still be held hostage, though only at a distance, for the good behavior of their government and army. It has been argued that this way of judging reprisals is a logical extension of the general principle "that persons whose usefulness as bases of enemy power is precluded . . . by belligerent control or capture cease to be legitimate objects of violence."[15] But this is to misstate the general principle. It would allow not only reprisals but also first strikes against enemy civilians. However peaceful their pursuits, after all, these civilians remain a "significant base of enemy power," providing political and economic support to the armed forces. Even children are not "precluded" from serving that power: they will grow up to be soldiers, munitions workers, and so on. Yet such people are protected by the war convention; they are admitted, along with prisoners and wounded soldiers, to the class of the innocent. The underlying purpose of recent developments in the law is not to extend a general principle, which is already (in principle) fully extended, but to prohibit its violation in the special circumstances once thought to justify reprisals. And if there are good reasons for doing that, there would seem to be no good reasons for drawing the line as it has currently been drawn.*

---

* It is not difficult, however, to account for the present legal situation. The threat to take reprisals against enemy civilians is a crucial feature of the contemporary system of nuclear deterrence, and statesmen and soldiers are not prepared solemnly to denounce that system. Moreover, though nuclear deterrence rests only on threats, and the acts threatened are of such a nature that moral men and women might well refuse at the final moment to carry them out, no one is prepared in advance to admit to inhibitions. "Any act of cruelty to the innocent," wrote an American jurist of the pre-atomic age, "any act, especially, by which noncombatants are made to feel the stress of war, is what brave men shrink from, although they may feel obliged to threaten it." (T. D. Woolsey, Introduction to the Study of International Law, New York, 1908, p. 211.) But can they threaten it effectively if it is known in advance that they will shrink from acting? I will take up the problems of nuclear deterrence in chapter 17.

Reprisals

So the necessary judgment is readily summed up: we must condemn all reprisals against innocent people, whether these people are "subject to belligerent control" or not. This is to set radical limits to a practice that once was commonly defended, and not with casual or inconsequential arguments. But I don't want to claim that those old arguments have no force at all. They correctly point to a certain moral difference between the initial crime and the reprisal-response. From a position of great detachment, these two may seem to constitute a vicious circle—and a circle fully accounted for by the pious maxim that "violence breeds violence." The maxim, however, is sometimes wrong and, what is more important, it fails to distinguish violence that is responsive and restrained from violence that is neither. Stand beside the French commanders at Annecy and the circle looks different. German guilt in this case is greater than that of the French, because the Germans acted first, breaking the conventional rules for some military advantage; the French reacted, repeating the violations for the declared purpose of re-establishing the rules. I don't know how to measure the difference between them; perhaps it isn't great; but it is worth stressing that there is a difference, even as we give their crimes a common name.

With regard to the most important of the rules of war, the violation of the rules for the sake of law enforcement is ruled out. The doctrine of reprisal, then, refers only to the lesser parts of the war convention, where the rights of the innocent are not at stake. Consider, for example, the ban on the use of poison gas. Winston Churchill was entirely justified when he warned the German government, early in World War II, that the use of gas by its armies would bring an immediate Allied reprisal.[16] For soldiers have only a war right, and no more basic right, to be attacked with certain weapons and not with others. The rule about poison gas is legally established, but it is not morally required. Hence, when it is violated, parallel and proportionate violations, narrowly aimed at re-establishing the rule and at no larger military purpose, are morally permissible. They are permissible because the people against whom they are directed are already the legitimate objects of military attack. The case is the same with all those informal agreements and reciprocal arrangements that limit the extent and intensity of warfare. Here the threat of reprisal is the major means of enforcement, and there is no reason to hesitate about making the threat or carrying it out. It might be argued that when restraints of this sort are violated, they simply disappear, and then there is no reason to limit one's own violations by attending to the proportionality rule. But that is true only if reprisal fails to restore the old limits. One must aim first at restoration: in that sense, we still use reprisals as a bar to the barbarism of war.

The Problem of Peacetime Reprisals

But all this assumes that warfare of the ordinary sort is already in progress. What is at issue is the mode or means of attack. In the case of peacetime reprisals, what is at issue is the attack itself. It has come from across the border: a raid of one sort or another. The victim state responds with a second raid, which isn't aimed at re-affirming the rules of war but at re-establishing the broken peace. The crime that is repeated is the act of force, the violation of sovereignty. It will be called aggression and justified as self-defense —talked about, that is, in the language of *jus ad bellum*—but it remains a "military measure short of war" as long as the restraints appropriate to reprisals, established by the theory of *jus in bello*, are maintained. And so it is best discussed here, with reference to those restraints.[17]

The Attack on Khibye and the Beirut Raid

The term "peacetime reprisals" is not entirely accurate. The legal handbooks divide their subject into "war" and "peace," but much of history is a *demi-monde* that neither word adequately describes. It is to this *demi-monde* that reprisals most commonly pertain; they are a form of action appropriate to periods of insurgency, border strife, cease-fire, and armistice. Now it is a feature of such periods that acts of force are not always acts of state in any simple sense. They are not the work of recognized officials and of soldiers acting on official orders, but (often) of guerrilla bands and terrorist organizations—tolerated, perhaps patronized by the officials, but not directly subject to their control. Thus Israel, since its founding in 1948, has repeatedly been attacked by Palestinian guerrillas and terrorists operating out of the neighboring Arab states but not formally affiliated with their armies. In response to these attacks, the Israeli authorities have tried over the years virtually every conceivable form of counter-attack—testing out, as it were, the politics and morality of reprisal. It is a grim and unusual history, providing the theorist with all the examples he could want (and more). And if it doesn't suggest that peacetime reprisals make for peace, it also doesn't point to any alternative response to illegitimate attacks.

Most of the Palestinian raids have been the work of terrorists, not guerrillas; that is, following the argument of the last two chapters, they have been directed randomly against civilian targets: against farmers working near the border, buses on country roads, village schools and houses, and so on. Hence there is no question about their illegitimacy, whatever one thinks of the larger Arab-Israeli conflict. Nor can there be any question that the Israelis have a right to respond in some way. The right exists in the case of any across-the-border raid, but it is especially clear when the raid is aimed at civilians, who can offer no immediate resistance. Nevertheless, particular Israeli responses have indeed been questionable, for it is a hard matter to know what to do in such cases. Terrorists harbored by neighboring states with which one is not openly at war do not provide an easy target. Any military response will be marked by a kind of asymmetry characteristic of peacetime reprisal: the initial foray is unofficial; the counter-attack is the act of a sovereign state, challenging the sovereignty of another state. How do we judge such challenges? What are the rules that govern peacetime reprisals?

The first rule is a familiar one. Though the terrorist raid is aimed at civilians, the reprisal must not be so aimed. Moreover, the "reprisers" must take care that civilians are not the incidental victims of their attack. With regard to its conduct, peacetime reprisal is exactly like war itself, and so certain of our judgments are obvious enough. Consider, for example, the Israeli raid on Khibye:[18]

> Following the killing of a woman and her two children in a village near Lod Airport, the Israelis launched a night attack against the Jordanian village of Khibye on 14 October 1953 . . . [They] fought their way into the village, rounded up the inhabitants, and blew up forty-five houses. Not all the houses were cleared beforehand, and more than forty villagers were buried under the rubble . . . The brutality of the raid led to sharp protests in Israel and abroad . . .

These killings probably cannot be called "unintended," and it certainly cannot be said that due care was taken to avoid them; so the protests were justified; the killings were criminal. But what if no civilians had died, or, as in most on-the-ground Israeli reprisals, only a small number, killed in the course of a firefight with

Jordanian regulars? What are we to say of the raid itself, of the Jordanian soldiers killed in its course (who had no part in the murder of Israeli civilians), of the houses destroyed? This is not a standard military operation, though it is the most common form of peacetime reprisal. Its purpose is coercive: to force the officials of a neighboring state to keep the peace and to repress guerrillas and terrorists on their own side of the border. But it is not directly or continuously coercive; otherwise it would require a full-scale invasion. Reprisals have the form of a warning: if our villages are attacked, yours will also be attacked. Hence they must always respond to previous raids. And they are governed, after the rule of noncombatant immunity, by the rule of backward-looking proportionality. Though life cannot be balanced against life, the second raid must be similar in character and scope to the first.

I am inclined to defend counter-attacks of this sort, when these two restraints are accepted. The defense, I should stress, doesn't depend in any way upon the notions of extremity or last resort. In peacetime, war is the last resort (and a long series of terrorist raids might justify a war, if no other means seemed likely to end the series). Reprisal is a first resort to force, once diplomacy has proven ineffective. It is, again, a "military measure short of war," an alternative to war, and that description is an important argument in its favor. But the general argument remains a difficult one, as we can see if we turn to another historical example, where (in contrast to Khibye) the rules of immunity and proportionality were scrupulously respected.

In 1968, the focus of Palestinian terrorism shifted from Israel itself to the Israeli national airline and its passengers. On December 26 of that year, two terrorists attacked an Israeli plane preparing for takeoff at Athens Airport.[19] Some 50 people were aboard at the time and, although only one was killed, it was clearly the purpose of the terrorists to kill as many as possible. They aimed their guns at the windows of the plane, at seat level. The two men were captured by Athenian police, and it was discovered that they were members of the Popular Front for the Liberation of Palestine, an organization with headquarters in Beirut. They were traveling on Lebanese documents. Repeatedly over the previous months, Israel had warned the Lebanese government that it could not "escape responsibility" for its support of groups like the PFLP. Now the Israelis undertook a dramatic reprisal.

Two days after the Athens attack, Israeli commandos landed by helicopter at Beirut Airport and destroyed 13 planes belonging to civilian airlines licensed in Lebanon. According to an Israeli news release, the commandos "at great risk to themselves . . . exercised the strictest precautions to prevent civilian casualties. The planes were emptied of passengers and ground crews, and people in the vicinity were led away to safety." Whatever the extent of the risks involved, no one was killed; Lebanese authorities later claimed that two Israeli soldiers were wounded during the attack. From a military point of view, the raid was a spectacular success— and, I think, from a moral point of view too. It was clearly responsive to the incident at Athens; it was parallel and proportionate in its means (for one can destroy a great deal of property in answer to the destruction of human life); and it was carried out so as to avoid civilian deaths.

Despite all this, the Beirut raid was much criticized at the time (and condemned at the UN)—above all, because of the seriousness of the attack upon Lebanese sovereignty. It is the attack upon Jordanian sovereignty that would stand out in the Khibye case, too, had civilian lives been spared. The killing of civilians is an affront to humanity, but attacks on military installations and the destruction of civilian property pose a more narrow and direct challenge to the state. Indeed, that is the purpose of the attacks; and the vulnerability of soldiers, on the one hand, and of airplanes, boats, buildings, and so on, on the other, hangs on the vulnerability of the sovereign state. Soldiers are vulnerable, if the state is, because they are the visible symbols and the active agents of its authority. And civilian property is vulnerable because the innocence of its owners extends only to their persons, not (or not necessarily) to their possessions. The value we attach to human life is such that rights to life are forfeit only when particular men and women are actually engaged in war-making or national defense. But the lesser value of property is such that property rights are forfeit whenever the state that protects property, and taxes it, is itself subject to attack. Individuals can be taxed without becoming legitimate targets, but property, or certain sorts of property, may be a legitimate target even if its owners are not.* But this argument hangs on the liability of the state, and that remains a matter of dispute.

The Israeli argument followed the pattern of positive law (or

---

* This is probably what the lawyers have in mind when they argue that, in cases of reprisal, the private citizen "is held to be identified with his state." The identification is by no means total; it does not obliterate personal rights. Nor, I think, does the effect extend to private homes, which seem to share in the innocence of their inhabitants (unless they have been used as terrorist bases).

at least of positive law before the era of the UN). Israel insisted that the Lebanese government had an obligation to prevent the use of its territory as a base for terrorist raids. No one seems to deny the reality of the obligation, but it was argued on behalf of the Lebanese (though not by them) that the government in Beirut was in fact incapable of honoring it. Events since 1968 may seem to have borne out that claim, and if it is right, the Israeli attack would be difficult to defend. It is surely wrong to destroy the property of innocent people so as to bring pressure on other people who are in any case unable to act differently from the way they are acting. But one should never be too quick to deny the competence of an established government, for a certain loss of sovereignty is the legal and moral result of political powerlessness. If a government literally cannot control the inhabitants of the territory over which it supposedly presides, or police its borders, and if other countries suffer because of this incapacity, then surrogate controlling and policing are clearly permissible. And these may well go beyond the limits commonly accepted for reprisal raids. At this point, reprisal is like retributive punishment in domestic society: as punishment assumes moral agency, so reprisal assumes political responsibility. Both assumptions are worth holding onto, for as long as possible.

The critical question is whether one sovereign state can be forced by another to fulfill its obligations. It is the official position of the UN that this kind of law enforcement, even when it is restrained by the rules of war, is illegal.[20] This position rests not only on the general claim of the UN to declare the (positive) law, but also on its readiness and ability, at least some of the time, to enforce the law itself. But the world organization was clearly not ready or able to enforce the law in 1968; nor has it been ready or able to do so at any time since. Nor is there any evidence that individual members of the UN, however they vote on ritual occasions, are prepared to renounce reprisals when the lives of their own citizens are at stake. Reprisals are clearly sanctioned by the practice of nations, and the (moral) reason behind the practice seems as strong as ever. Nothing the UN has actually done, no effects it can presently have, suggest a centralization of legal or moral authority in international life.*

* With regard to the routine UN condemnations of Israeli reprisals, Richard Falk has written: "One may argue against the fairness of such constraints upon Israel's discretion in these circumstances, but it is essentially an extra-legal appeal as the organs of the UN have the procedural capacity to authorize or prohibit spe-

But the sheer unreality of the UN position doesn't by itself establish the legitimacy of peacetime reprisals. In his edition of Kelsen's *Principles of International Law*, Robert Tucker has insisted that anyone defending reprisals must show "that more often than not the independent use of force by states has served the purposes of law . . ."[21] This is to shift the ground from the effectiveness of the UN to the utility of reprisal itself and to invite a historical examination the results of which are not likely to favor the "reprisers" in any decisive way. But the ground of reprisal is not its overall effectiveness. It is the right, in the difficult conditions of the *demi-monde*, to seek certain effects. So long as the conditions exist, the right must also exist, even if those same conditions (as in Locke's state of nature) make it unlikely that rightful action will have entirely satisfactory consequences. If, in a particular case, reprisal is certain to fail, then obviously it should not be tried. But whenever there is some substantial chance of success, it is the legitimate resort of a victim state; for no state can be required passively to endure attacks upon its citizens.

Reprisal is a practice carried over from the war convention to the world of "peacetime," because it provides an appropriately limited form of military action. It is better, I think, to defend the limits than to try to abolish the practice. Soldiers engaged in a reprisal raid will cross over an international boundary, but they will quickly cross back; they will act destructively, but only up to a point; they will violate sovereignty, but they will also respect it. And finally, they will attend to the rights of innocent people. Reprisals are always limited responses to particular transgressions: crimes against the rules of war, small-scale breaches of the peace. Though they have often been used, they cannot rightly be used, as a cover for invasions or interventions or assaults upon innocent life. It may be that there are moments of extremity and crisis when state's rights and human rights have to be violated; but such moments are not generated by the particular crimes of our enemies, and the violations are not usefully called reprisals. None of the

cific uses of force, and it is the exercise of this capacity that most clearly distinguishes what is 'legal' from what is 'illegal' . . . in international society." I am not sure that any legislative body, domestic or international, can abolish self-help unless it provides alternative means of help, but I will leave such matters to the lawyers. Assuming Falk is right, it must be said that the extra-legal appeal is a moral appeal the success of which probably will and certainly should undermine the newly enacted "law." See "International Law and the US Role in Vietnam: A Response," in Falk, ed., *The Vietnam War and International Law*, Princeton, 1968, p. 493.

cases of reprisal that I have come across in the lawbooks and the military histories are extreme cases in any meaningful sense of that term. Nor does the war convention provide for extreme cases. Extremity lies, so to speak, beyond the reach of conventional provision. I will consider its character and provenance in Part Four of this book. The analysis of reprisals concludes the discussion of the ordinary means of war. I must turn now to those extraordinary means that the moral urgency of our ends seems sometimes to require.

PART FOUR

DILEMMAS OF

WAR

14

Winning and Fighting Well

"Asinine Ethics"

Chairman Mao and the Battle of the River Hung

In the year 638 B.C., during the period of China's history known as the Spring and Autumn Era, the two feudal states of Sung and Ch'u fought a battle at the Hung River in central China.[1] The army of Sung, led by its ruler Duke Hsiang, was drawn up in battle formation on the river's northern bank; the Ch'u army had to ford the stream. When its soldiers were halfway across, one of Hsiang's ministers came to him and said, "They are many, and we are few. Pray let us attack them before they are all crossed over." The Duke refused. When the enemy army had reached the northern bank but had not yet re-formed its lines, the minister again asked leave to begin the fight; again the Duke refused. Only after the Ch'u soldiers were properly marshaled did he signal the attack. And then, in the ensuing battle, the Duke himself was wounded and his army put to flight. According to the chronicles, the people of Sung blamed their ruler for the defeat, but he said, "The superior man does not inflict a second wound, and does not take prisoner anyone of grey hairs. When the ancients had their armies in the field, they would not attack an enemy when he was in a defile; and though I am but the poor representative of a fallen dynasty, I will not sound my drums to attack an unformed host."

This is the code of a feudal warrior, an obscure warrior in this case until Mao Tse-tung drew his story out of the chronicles in order to make a modern point. "We are not the Duke of Sung," he declared in one of his lectures On Protracted War (1938), "and we have no use for his asinine ethics."[2] Mao's lecture was an innovative discussion of guerrilla tactics. His argument against the Duke of Sung, however, was familiar enough, and to Chinese as well as Western readers. It is an argument common among practical men, like Hsiang's minister, to whom winning is always more important than aristocratic honor. But it enters significantly into the theory of war only when winning is seen to be *morally* important, that is, only when the outcome of the struggle is conceived in terms of justice. Some 200 years after the battle at the River Hung, more than two millennia before the communist revolution, the philosopher Mo Tzu perfectly described Mao's case, as he himself must understand it.[3]

> Suppose there is a country which is being persecuted and oppressed by its rulers, and a Sage . . . in order to rid the world of this pest raises an army and sets out to punish the evil-doers. If, when he has won a victory, he conforms to the doctrine of the Confucians, he will issue an order to his troops saying, "Fugitives are not to be pursued, an enemy who has lost his helmet is not to be shot at; if a chariot overturns, you are to help the occupants to right it"—if this is done, the violent and the disorderly will escape with their lives and the world will not be rid of its pest.

Mo Tzu believed in the doctrine of Righteous War. Mao Tse-tung has introduced into China the western theory of the just war. No doubt, there are fine points of difference between these two ideas, which I cannot pursue here. But they are not different in any major way. They set up the tension between winning and fighting well in similar fashion, and for Mo Tzu and Chairman Mao they point to the same resolution: the feudal rules for fighting well are simply cast aside. The tension is overcome as soon as it is recognized. That doesn't mean that there are no rules of engagement at all; I have already cited Mao's "Eight Points for Attention," which recapitulate in democratic style the old chivalric code. But for Mao himself the "Eight Points" apparently reflect only the utilitarian requirements of guerrilla war, and they cannot stand against the higher utility of winning—which he is likely to describe in extravagant terms, a combination of Wilsonian idealism and Marxist apocalypse: "The aim of war is to eliminate war . . . Mankind's era of wars will be brought to an end by our own efforts, and beyond doubt the war we wage is part of the final battle."[4] And in the final battle, no one will insist upon the "Eight Points." Exceptions will readily be made whenever the conflict seems critical. Consider, for example, the last of the Eight: "Do not ill-treat captives." Mao has also argued that guerrilla bands on the move cannot take prisoners. "It is best first to require the prisoners to hand over their weapons and then to disperse them or execute them."[5] Since prisoners are not conceived as men-with-rights, the choice between dispersal and execution is purely tactical, and to insist in all cases upon the rule against ill treatment would presumably be an example of "asinine ethics."

Nor were rights thought to be at stake in the old warrior codes. Duke Hsiang believed it unworthy and demeaning to strike a wounded soldier or attack an unformed host. Combat was only possible between peers; otherwise war would not be an occasion for the display of aristocratic virtue. It is not hard to understand why anyone convinced of the moral urgency of victory would be impatient with such notions. Of what use is the (undoubted) virtue of the Duke of Sung if the world is ruled by violence and aggression? Indeed, a war in which the Duke's virtue was more important than a military triumph would seem to be a very unimportant war. Thus the argument of Hsiang's minister after the defeat of the Sung army: "If we grudge a second wound, it would be better not to wound at all. If we would spare the grey-haired, we had better submit to the enemy."[6] Either fight all-out or not at all. This argument is often said to be typical of American thought, but in fact it is universal in the history of war. Once soldiers are actually engaged, and especially if they are engaged in a Righteous War or a just war, a steady pressure builds up against the war convention and in favor of particular violations of its rules. And then, more often than the belligerent powers are prepared to admit—itself a matter of interest—the rules are broken. They are not broken for the sake of military necessity alone. That argument justifies too much, and it does so without reference to the cause for which the war is being fought. The rules are broken for the sake of the cause. It is with some version of the argument for justice that the violations are defended.

On this view, the rules have no standing in any war that is worth fighting. They are at most "rules of thumb," general precepts of honor (or utility) to be observed only until observing them comes into conflict with the requirements of victory. But this is to misunderstand the status of the war convention. If we consider noncombatant immunity rather than warrior honor, and the protection of human rights rather than the expediencies of guerrilla war—that is, if we attend to what is really fundamental in the rules of war— the conflict between winning and fighting well is not so easily resolved. If we recognize, for example, that the protection afforded by the "Eight Points" is morally required, and that men and women are rightly indignant if they are robbed and ravaged by guerrilla bands, then Mao's rules take on a greater significance than their author attributes to them. They cannot simply be set aside; nor can they be balanced, in utilitarian fashion, against this or that desirable outcome. For the rights of innocent people have the same moral effectiveness in the face of just as in the face of unjust soldiers.

And yet the case for breaking the rules and violating those rights is made sufficiently often, and by soldiers and statesmen who cannot always be called wicked, so that we have to assume that it isn't pointless. Anyway, we know its point all too well. We know how high the stakes sometimes are in war and how urgent victory can be. "For there are peoples," as Simone Weil has written, "[who] have never recovered after having once been conquered."[7] The very existence of a community may be at stake, and then how can we fail to consider possible outcomes in judging the course of the fighting? At this point if at no other, the restraint on utilitarian calculation must be lifted. Even if we are inclined to lift it, however, we cannot forget that the rights violated for the sake of victory are genuine rights, deeply founded and in principle inviolable. And there is nothing asinine about this principle: the very lives of men and women are at stake. So the theory of war, when it is fully understood, poses a dilemma, which every theorist (though not, fortunately, every soldier) must resolve as best he can. And no resolution is serious unless it recognizes the force of both *jus ad bellum* and *jus in bello*.

The Sliding Scale and the Argument from Extremity

The immediate issue is whether we should discriminate between soldiers fighting a just war and soldiers fighting an unjust war. It is, of course, those who claim membership in the first group who raise the issue, making what might be called an appeal against combatant equality. Though such appeals are particular in character, they have a general form. They all involve the claim that the equality I have been defending is merely conventional and that the truth about war rights is best expressed in terms of a sliding scale: *the more justice, the more right.* Something like this appears to be what the philosopher John Rawls has in mind when he says, "Even in a just war, certain forms of violence are strictly inadmissible; and when a country's right to war is questionable and uncertain, the constraints on the means it can use are all the more severe. Acts permissible in a war of legitimate self-defense, when these are necessary, may be flatly excluded in a more doubtful situation."[8] The greater the justice of my cause, the more rules I can violate for the sake of the cause—though some rules are always inviolable. The same argument can be put in terms of outcomes: the greater the injustice likely to result from my defeat, the more rules I can violate in order to avoid defeat—though some rules, and so on. The value of this position is that it grants the existence of rights (of some sort) while still opening the way for soldiers resisting aggression to do (some of) the things they believe necessary for victory. It allows the justice of one's cause to make a difference in the way one fights. Exactly how much of a difference is allowed, however, is radically unclear, and so is the status of the men and women who are now drawn into the hell of war so that justice can triumph. The practical effects of the argument are probably more far-reaching than its proponents would like, but I will say nothing about these effects until I can look at a number of historical cases. First, however, something more must be said about the structure of the argument.

According to the war convention as I have described it, there is no range of actions, over which the sliding scale might move, between legitimate combat and inadmissible violence. There is only a line, not entirely distinct but meant simply to mark off the one from the other. Given this view, the argument quoted from Rawls might be taken to mean that borderline cases should be decided systematically against that country whose "right to war is questionable" or even that the military and political leaders of that country should keep some distance away from the border, never doubling the doubtfulness of their cause with the doubtfulness of their methods. This last would simply be a plea for scrupulousness, which is always a good thing. But there is another meaning that can be drawn out of Rawls' argument (though I don't think it is his own meaning): that the class of "strictly inadmissible" acts should be kept very small, and space should be opened up within the rules of war where the sliding scale might be applied. The effect of sliding the scale to point x within this space, it should be said, is not to remove all restraints on military action up to that point, but rather to leave only the restraints of usefulness and proportionality. The sliding scale makes way for those utilitarian calculations that rules and rights are intended to bar. It creates a new class of generally inadmissible acts and of quasi-rights, subject to piecemeal erosion by soldiers whose cause is just—or by soldiers who believe that their cause is just. And so it enables those soldiers to do terrible things and to defend in their own consciences and among their associates and followers the terrible things they do.

Now, the extreme form of the sliding-scale argument is the claim that soldiers fighting a just war can do anything at all that is useful in the fighting. This effectively annuls the war convention and denies or suspends the rights that the convention was designed to protect. The war rights of the just are total, and any blame their actions entail falls upon the leaders of the other side. General Sherman took this view of war, as we have seen, and I have called it the "war is hell" doctrine. It is not so much a resolution of the tension between winning and fighting well as a denial of its moral significance. The only kind of justice that matters is *jus ad bellum*. Beyond that there are only such considerations as rational men will always attend to: they will not waste their substance in useless killing of the innocent, though they will kill them readily enough if victory seems to require it. It may be that this is what the sliding scale comes to in any case, but its advocates at least claim to recognize the existence of rules and rights, and so their argument requires a separate analysis.

The only alternative to the sliding scale, it is often said, is a position of moral absolutism. To resist the slide, one must hold that the rules of war are a series of categorical and unqualified prohibitions, and that they can never rightly be violated even in order to defeat aggression.[9] But that is a hard line to take, and especially so in the modern age, when aggression has assumed such frightening forms. Perhaps the Duke of Sung was right not to break the warrior code for the sake of his dynasty. But if what is being defended is the state itself and the political community it protects and the lives and liberties of the members of that community. . . . *Fiat justicia ruat coelum*, do justice even if the heavens fall, is not for most people a plausible moral doctrine.

There is an alternative doctrine that stops just short of absolutism and that I shall try to defend in the chapters that follow. It might be summed up in the maxim: do justice unless the heavens are (really) about to fall. This is the utilitarianism of extremity, for it concedes that in certain very special cases, though never as a matter of course even in just wars, the only restraints upon military action are those of usefulness and proportionality. Throughout my discussion of the rules of war, I have been resisting this view and denying its force. I have argued, for example, against the notion that civilians can be locked into a besieged city or reprisals taken against innocent people "in extreme cases." For the idea of extremity has no place in the making of the war convention—or if it is said that combat is always extreme, then the idea is naturalized within the convention. The rules are adjusted to the everyday extremities of war; no further adjustment is possible if we are to have any rules at all, and if we are to attend to the rights of the innocent. But now the question is not one of rule-making, but of rule-breaking. We know the form and substance of the moral code; we must decide, at a moment of desperation and looming disaster, whether to live (and perhaps to die) by its rules.

The sliding scale erodes the convention bit by bit, and so it eases the way for the decision-maker who believes himself "forced" to violate human rights. The argument from extremity permits (or requires) a more sudden breach of the convention, but only after holding out for a long time against the process of erosion. The reasons for holding out have to do with the nature of the rights at issue and the status of the men and women who hold them. These rights, I shall argue, cannot be eroded or undercut; nothing diminishes them; they are still standing at the very moment they are overridden: that is why they have to be *overridden*.[10] Hence breaking the rules is always a hard matter, and the soldier or statesman who does so must be prepared to accept the moral consequences and the burden of guilt that his action entails. At the same time, it may well be that he has no choice but to break the rules: he confronts at last what can meaningfully be called necessity.

The tension between the rules of war and the theory of aggression, between *jus in bello* and *jus ad bellum*, can be dealt with in four different ways:

1) the war convention is simply set aside (derided as "asinine ethics") under the pressure of utilitarian argument;

2) the convention yields slowly to the moral urgency of the

cause: the rights of the righteous are enhanced, and those of their enemies devalued;

3) the convention holds and rights are strictly respected, whatever the consequences; and

4) the convention is overridden, but only in the face of an imminent catastrophe.

The second and fourth of these are the most interesting and the most important. They explain how it is that morally serious men and women, who have some sense of what rights are, come nevertheless to violate the rules of war, escalate its brutality and extend its tyranny. The fourth seems to me the right argument. It provides the best account of the two kinds of justice and most fully recognizes the force of each. I shall focus on it in the chapters that follow, but try at the same time to suggest the inadequacies and dangers of the sliding scale. I will look first at a number of cases involving the practice of neutrality, perhaps the most disputed feature of the war convention. Since neutral rights constitute a kind of noncombatant immunity, they might have been taken up earlier on. The disputes they have generated, however, raise questions less about the content than about the force and endurance of rights in war. How long must one wait before breaking the rules? The answer I want to defend is best expressed by reversing Chairman Mao's dictum: with reference to our own conventions, and until the very last minute, *we are all the Duke of Sung.*

15

Aggression and Neutrality

The doctrine of neutrality has a twofold form, which is best expressed (and which is conventionally expressed) in the language of rights. States possess, first, a *right to be neutral*, which is simply an aspect of their sovereignty. In any prospective or on-going conflict between two other states, they are free to opt for what might be called the condition of "thirdness." And if they do that, they then possess *neutral rights*, specified at great length in positive international law. As with the war convention generally, the initial right and the subsequent rights exist without reference to the moral character of the belligerent powers or to the probable outcome of the war. The more convinced we are, however, that one of the belligerents is an aggressor or that the outcome is going to be disastrous, the more likely we are to deny the very possibility of non-involvement. How can any state stand and watch the destruction of a neighbor? How can the rest of us respect its right to stand and watch if, by violating that right, we might avert the destruction?

These questions have been posed with a special insistence in the years since World War II, but in fact the argument implicit in them is an old one. Consider, for example, a British proclamation issued in 1793: the political and military policies of the revolutionary government of France, it was said, involved "all the surrounding powers in one common danger . . . giving them the right . . . *imposing on them the duty,* to stop the progress of an evil which exists only by the successive violation of all law and property . . ."[1] The practical consequence of this sort of thing is obvious. If states don't do their duty, they can be forced to do it. One asserts the urgency of the struggle, and one erodes or denies the right to be neutral, in order to pave the way for the violation of neutral rights. The history of neutrality provides many examples of such violations, defended with some version of the argument from extremity or with the sliding scale, and I shall refer to that history in order to analyze those defenses. But first I must say something about the nature of neutrality itself and its place in the war convention.

The Right to Be Neutral

Neutrality is a collective and voluntary form of noncombatancy. It is collective in that its benefits obtain for all the members of a political community without reference to the status of individuals. Soldiers and civilians are alike protected, so long as their state is "not engaged in war-making." The rights of disengagement distribute equally to all citizens. Neutrality is voluntaristic in that it can be assumed at will by any state with regard to a war or a prospective war between any other states. Individuals can be conscripted, but states cannot. They may ask that other powers formally acknowledge their neutrality, but the condition is unilaterally assumed and the acknowledgment unnecessary. The "scrap of paper" that Germany brushed aside when it invaded Belgium in 1914 did not establish Belgian neutrality; the Belgians themselves did that. And had the Germans formally renounced their guarantee or waited for its expiration, their invasion would still have been the crime it was said to be at the time. It would have been a crime, that is, as long as the Belgians not only claimed the rights but also observed the duties of a neutral state.

These duties can be summed up very simply, although international law on this subject is elaborate and detailed: they require a strict impartiality toward the belligerents, without reference to the justice of their cause or to any sentiments of neighborliness, cultural affinity, or ideological agreement.[2] It is not only fighting on one or another side that is prohibited, but every sort of official discrimination. This rule is very strict; if it is violated, neutral rights are forfeit, and the neutral state is subject to reprisals from whichever belligerent is injured by the violations. The rule applies, however, only to state action. Private citizens remain free to choose sides in a variety of ways, to campaign politically, raise money, even raise volunteers (though they cannot launch forays across the border). What is more important, normal patterns of trade may be maintained with both belligerents. Hence the neutrality of any given state is likely to be more helpful to one side than to the other. So far as the warring powers are concerned, neutrality is rarely a matter of equal benefit, for neither the balance of private sympathy and effort nor the balance of trade is likely to be even between them.* But neither can complain of the unofficial help the other receives. This is a help that cannot be helped; it derives from the very existence of the neutral state, its geography, economy, language, religion, and so on, and could only be interdicted by the most rigorous coercion of its citizens. But the neutral state is not required to coerce its own citizens. So long as it takes no positive action to help one side or the other, it has fulfilled its duty not to get involved, and then it is automatically entitled to the full enjoyment of its right not to get involved.

The moral basis of the right is not entirely clear, however, in large part because its domestic analogue is so unappealing. In both political and moral life, the "neuter" is not a person one instinctively likes. Perhaps he has a right to avoid if he can the quarrels of his neighbors, but what about their troubles? We have to ask again: can he stand and watch a neighbor being assaulted on the street? Might not the neighbor say at such a time, "You're either for me or against me"? As a revolutionary slogan, that sentence suggests, perhaps, an unwarranted pressure and a threat of retaliations to come. But in the case at hand, its message is simpler and less objectionable. Surely a strict neutrality here, a refusal to discriminate in any way in favor of the victim, would be disquieting and strange. Neighbors are not mere spectators, studying one another's misfortunes from some great distance. The social life they

---

* Neutral states have sometimes sought a more perfect neutrality by embargoing all trade with belligerent powers. But this does not seem a plausible course. For if the normal balance of trade favors one belligerent, a total embargo is likely to favor the other. There is no zero point; the *status quo ante bellum* seems the only reasonable norm.

share entails a degree of mutual concern. On the other hand, if I am obligated to be "for" my neighbor, I am not obligated to rush to his rescue—first, because that may not be an effective way of being for him; and second, because it may be disastrous for me. I have a right to weigh the risks of joining the battle. But let's assume that the risks are minor: there are a large number of us watching, and I can count on the support of the others if I take the lead; or there is a policeman around the corner, and I can count on him to take the lead. Then I have no right to be neutral, and any efforts on my part to escape, make excuses, bury my head in the sand, are sure to be thought reprehensible.

But the right of a state is different, and not only because there is no policeman around the corner. For there may well be a majority of states and an overwhelming predominance of force at least potentially available on behalf of a state under attack, thought to be the victim of aggression. All that stands in the way of mobilizing this force, it may be, is the war convention and the right of neutrality. Even in such a case, the right holds, because risk in war is very different from what it is in domestic fighting. Years ago, John Westlake argued that "neutrality is not morally justifiable unless intervention in the war is unlikely to promote justice or could do so only at a ruinous cost to the neutral."[8] Ruination is to be avoided, but is this only the ruination of states? When a state joins a war, it risks its survival to this or that degree, depending on the nature of the conflict, the power of its allies, and the readiness and fighting capacity of its army; and these risks may be acceptable or not. But at the same time, it condemns an indefinite number of its citizens to certain death. It does this, to be sure, without knowing which citizens those are. But the decision itself is irrevocable: once fighting begins, it is certain that soldiers (and probably civilians, too) will die. The right of neutrality follows from this fact. Like other provisions of the war convention, it represents a limit on the coerciveness of war. At least this group of men and women, citizens of the neutral state, who do not choose to risk their lives, will be protected from having to do so.

But why should these men and women be immune and free when so many others are driven into battle? In what possible way are they entitled to their neutrality? The question is especially important if we imagine a situation where a particular state's decision to be neutral means that more people will be killed than would be killed if it joined the war, for the participation of its armies might turn the tide and shorten the fighting by so many weeks or months. But the leaders of such a state are not required to calculate as if every human life carried the same moral weight for every decision-maker at every moment in time. Their people's lives are not international resources to be distributed in war so as to balance the risks or reduce the losses of other people. These are innocent lives. With reference to the soldiers of the neutral state, that means only that they have not yet been attacked and forced to fight. Still, they are disengaged, and no one has a right to challenge their disengagement. Perhaps that disengagement is a matter of luck; it is often, in cases of successful neutrality, a matter of geography. But people are entitled to their good fortune in such matters, as states are, or are presumed to be, entitled to their geographic locations.*

So neutral citizens are immune from attack; the coerciveness of war can never willfully be extended beyond the limits fixed by the material causes of the conflict and the military organization of the states involved. The leaders of a neutral state are entitled to maintain that immunity; indeed, they may be bound to do so, given the consequences of its loss for their fellow citizens. The same solidarity that makes noninvolvement at home morally questionable may well make it obligatory in the international arena: this group of men and women must save one another's lives first. They cannot do this by killing other people, unless those others are attacking them. The rules of neutrality suggest, however, that they can do it by allowing other people to die rather than dying themselves. If they have incurred obligations towards some of those people—for the sake, perhaps, of collective security—then, of course, they cannot allow them to die; otherwise, the right holds, even if its assertion seems ignoble.

But there is one sort of case in which this right might be denied. Imagine (what is easily imaginable) that some great power launches a campaign of conquest, aimed not merely at this or that

* But this argument doesn't seem to work with reference to the property and prosperity (rather than the lives) of the citizens. If a state can discriminate economically against an aggressor, even if the costs to itself are considerable, it seems bound to do so, unless the discrimination is likely to involve it in the fighting. Aggressor states, of course, have a right to respond to discriminatory measures, by force if necessary. But they won't always be in a position to respond, and if they are not, the measures may be morally required. When the League of Nations invoked economic sanctions against Italy in the Ethiopian War of 1936, it made the requirement legal as well. But I should think that the moral obligation would have held had there been only an Ethiopian appeal and no League resolution. In any case, the example suggests the relative status of property rights in the theory of war.

state but at some larger ideological or imperial goal. Why should such a campaign be resisted only by its first victims, when in fact many other states will be threatened if the initial resistance fails? Or consider the common argument that aggression anywhere threatens everyone. Aggression is like crime: if one does not stamp it out, it will spread. Then again, there is no reason for the immediate victims to fight alone. They are fighting on behalf of future victims, that is, of all other states, and the others will reap the benefits of their fighting and dying. How can they stand aside? President Wilson took this position in his war message of April 2, 1917: "Neutrality is no longer feasible or desirable when the peace of the world is involved and the freedom of its peoples."[4] He presumably meant *morally* feasible, since a practical alternative to war, namely continued neutrality, clearly existed. The argument against that alternative must go something like this. If one imagines a particular aggressor moving on from one triumph to another, or if one imagines a radical increase in the incidence of aggression as a result of this particular triumph, then it has to be said that peace and freedom are in general danger. And then continued neutrality is not morally feasible; for while a neutral state has or may have a right to let others die in quarrels of their own, it cannot let them die on its behalf. Any danger that is shared by all the members of international society is morally coercive, even if it is not yet materially present, for all of them.

This argument, however, rests uneasily on "imaginings" about which there is no general agreement and which often look painfully implausible after the fact. It seems very strange today, for example, that any conceivable outcome of World War I could have been thought to pose a universal threat to peace and freedom (or a greater threat than was posed by the actual outcome). And this is so even if one grants that the war began with an act or a series of acts of aggression. The mere recognition of a criminal attack, without some profoundly pessimistic or, as in this case, highly extravagant view of its likely consequences, does not require the leaders of a neutral state to draw President Wilson's conclusions. They can always refuse to do so, imagining in their turn that their own country and the whole world are in no real danger. That is a unilateral view of the situation, to be sure, and one can argue (as I would often be inclined to do) with the leaders who put it forward. But they and their people are entitled to act on it. That is the real right of neutrality.

The Nature of Necessity (2)

At this point, however, the crucial moral decision may not lie with the neutral state. The belligerents also have a choice: to respect neutral rights or not. Violations of those rights are usually thought to be an especially bad kind of aggression—on the principle, I suppose, that it is worse to strike out at uninvolved states than at states with which one has been quarreling. Unless we take a rather permissive view of the initial resort to violence, this seems a dubious principle. On the other hand, attacks on neutrals are usually an especially clear kind of aggression, whereas responsibility for the war itself may be difficult to assess. When armies move across the frontier of a state that has maintained a strict impartiality, we have little difficulty in recognizing the move as a criminal act. Violations short of armed attack are harder to recognize but almost equally reprehensible, for they invite and justify military responses from the other side. If neutrality collapses and the war is extended to new territory and people, the crime is that of the first violator (assuming a proportionate response from the second).

But what if neutrality is violated for a good cause: for the sake of national survival and the defeat of aggression; or, more largely, for the sake of "civilization as we know it" or the "peace and freedom" of the whole world? Here is the paradigmatic form of the collision between *jus ad bellum* and *jus in bello*. The belligerent power believes itself pressed by the exigencies of a just war. The neutral state is firm in its rights: its citizens are not bound to sacrifice themselves to someone else's exigencies. The belligerent power talks of the vital importance of the ends for which it is fighting; the neutral state invokes the rules of war. Neither side is entirely convincing, though in particular cases we must choose between them. I have tried to make the strongest possible case for neutral rights. Their violation almost certainly entails the killing (or the causing to be killed) of innocent people, and so it is not a casual matter even when the end in view is very important. Indeed, we are likely to recognize good men fighting for important ends by their reluctance to invade neutral states and force their citizens to fight. The value of that reluctance will be apparent if we look at two cases in which neutral rights were wrongly violated: first, on the plea of necessity, and second, with the argument *more justice, more right.* The first is the most famous violation of neutrality since the Athenian attack on Melos, and I have given it the name originally assigned in wartime propaganda.

The Rape of Belgium

The German attack on Belgium in August 1914 is unusual in that it was openly and honestly described by the Germans themselves as a violation of neutral rights. The speech of Chancellor von Bethmann Hollweg to the Reichstag on August 4 deserves to be remembered.[5]

> Gentlemen, we are now in a state of necessity, and necessity knows no law. Our troops have already entered Belgian territory.
>
> Gentlemen, that is a breach of international law. It is true that the French government declared at Brussels that France would respect Belgian neutrality as long as her adversary respected it. We know, however, that France stood ready for an invasion. France could wait, we could not. A French attack on our flank on the lower Rhine might have been disastrous. Thus we were forced to ignore the rightful protests of the Government of Belgium. The wrong—I speak openly—the wrong we thereby commit we will try to make good as soon as our military aims have been attained.
>
> He who is menaced as we are and is fighting for his highest possession can only consider how he is to hack his way through (*durchhauen*).

This is frank talk, though it is not quite like the "frankness" of the Athenian generals at Melos. For the chancellor does not step outside the moral world when he defends the German invasion. He grants that a wrong has been done, and he promises to make it good after the fighting is over. That promise was not taken seriously by the Belgians. Their neutrality having been violated and their borders crossed, they had no reason to expect anything good from the invaders; nor did they believe that their independence would be respected. They chose to resist the invasion, and once their soldiers were fighting and dying, it is hard to see how the wrong the Germans had done could ever be made good.

The force of von Bethmann Hollweg's argument lies not in the promise of reparation, but in the plea of necessity. This will be a useful occasion to consider again what that plea might mean—and to suggest that here, as in military history generally, it means a great deal less than it appears to do. We can see clearly in the chancellor's speech the two levels at which the concept works. First, there is the instrumental or strategic level: the attack on Belgium was necessary, it is being argued, if German defeat was to be avoided. But that is an improbable argument. The attack had long seemed to the General Staff the most expedient way of striking a hard blow against the French and winning a quick victory in the west (before Germany was fully engaged with the Russians on the eastern front).[6] By no means, however, was it the only way of defending German territory. A French invasion along the lower Rhine, after all, could only outflank the German army if the Germans were mobilized for action further north (along the Belgium frontier). The chancellor's actual claim was that the odds of victory would be improved and German lives saved if the Belgians were sacrificed. But that expectation, which turned out to be wrong, had nothing to do with necessity.

The second level of the argument is moral: not only is the attack necessary to win, but winning itself is necessary, since Germany is fighting for its "highest possession." I don't know what von Bethmann Hollweg thought Germany's highest possession was. Perhaps he had in mind some notion of honor or military glory, which could only be upheld by victory over the nation's enemies. But honor and glory belong to the realm of freedom, not necessity. We are likely to think that Germany's victory was morally necessary (essential, required) only if its survival as an independent nation or the very lives of its people were at stake. And on the best construction of the German cause, that was certainly not the case; what was at stake was Alsace-Lorraine, Germany's African colonies, and so on. So the argument fails on both levels. It would have to succeed on both, I think, before the violation of Belgian neutrality could be defended.

The German chancellor puts forward exactly the sort of argument that would be appropriate at a time of genuine extremity. He rejects every kind of deceitfulness. He does not pretend that the Belgians have failed in their duty of impartiality. He does not claim that the French have already violated Belgian neutrality or even that they are threatening to do so. He does not argue that Belgium cannot rightly stand aside in the presence of (French) aggression. He recognizes the force of the war convention and hence of the right of neutrality, and he makes the case for overriding that right. He wants to override it, however, not at the last minute but at the very first, and not when Germany's survival is in danger but when the dangers are of a more ordinary kind. So his is not a plausible case; its structure is right, but not its content. Nor was it thought plausible at the time. The German invasion was almost universally condemned (by many Germans, too). It was an important reason for the determination and high morale with which Britain entered the war and for the sympathy with which the Allied cause was viewed in other neutral countries—the United States, above all.[7] Even Lenin, who led the leftist opposition to the war, thought the defense of Belgium a reason to fight: "Let us suppose that all the states interested in the observation of international treaties declared war on Germany, with the demand for the liberation and indemnification of Belgium. In such a case, the sympathies of Socialists would, of course, be on the side of Germany's enemies."[8] But, he went on, that is not what the war is really about. He was right; the war as a whole does not lend itself to an easy description in terms of justice and injustice. But the attack on Belgium does. We must turn now, and at much greater length, to a harder case.

The Sliding Scale

Winston Churchill and Norwegian Neutrality

The day after Britain and France declared war on Germany in 1939, King Haakon VII formally proclaimed Norway's neutrality. The policy of the king and his government was not founded on political or ideological indifference. "We never had neutrality of thought in Norway," the Foreign Minister wrote, "and I never wanted it." Norway's political and cultural ties were with the Allies, and there seems no reason to doubt what historians of the period tell us: "The Norwegians firmly believed in the high ideals of democracy, individual freedom, and international justice."[9] They were not, however, prepared to fight for those ideals. The war was a struggle among the great powers of Europe, and Norway was very much a small power, traditionally disengaged from European *machtpolitik*, and now virtually disarmed. Whatever the moral importance of the issues over which the war was being fought, the Norwegian government could hardly intervene in any decisive way. Nor could it intervene at all without accepting great risks. Its first task was to make sure that Norway was still intact and its citizens alive at the end.

With this purpose in mind, the government adopted a strict policy of "neutrality in deed." On balance, this policy favored the

Germans, even though most of Norway's normal trade was with the Allied powers, especially Britain. For the Germans depended on Norway for a very large part of their iron ore supply. The ore was mined at Gallivare in northern Sweden, and during the summer months it was shipped out of the Swedish town of Lulea on the Baltic Sea. But in the winter, the Baltic froze; then the ore was moved by rail to Narvik on the Norwegian coast, the nearest warm-water port. There German ships picked it up and carried it down the coast, keeping within Norwegian territorial waters so as to avoid the British navy. The German ore supply was thus protected by Norwegian (and Swedish) neutrality, and for this reason the invasion of Norway was no part of Hitler's original strategic plan. Instead, "[he] emphasized repeatedly that in his opinion the most desirable attitude for Norway as well as for the rest of Scandinavia would be one of complete neutrality."[10]

The British view was very different. During the long months of the "phony war," Scandinavian neutrality was a constant topic of Cabinet discussion. Winston Churchill, then First Lord of the Admiralty, proposed one plan after another to interdict the shipments of iron ore. Here was a chance, he argued, here was the only chance, to strike a quick blow against Germany. Instead of waiting for a German attack in France and the Low Countries, the Allies could force Hitler to disperse his armies and to fight—Churchill never doubted that the Germans would fight for their ore supply—in a part of the world where the strength of the British navy could most effectively be brought to bear.[11] The French were also disinclined to wait for an attack on their own soil. Sir Edward Spears writes of Prime Minister Daladier that "his views on military matters were confined to keeping warlike operations as remote from France as possible."[12] The Norwegian prime minister no doubt had a parallel idea in mind. But there is this difference: the war which the Norwegians wished to see fought in France, and which the French were ready to fight in Norway, was France's and not Norway's war. Churchill confronted the same difficulty; Norwegian neutrality was a bar to each of his plans. It was only a moral and legal bar, perhaps, for he did not expect the Norwegians to fight very hard for their neutrality, but it was an important bar nonetheless, since the British were inclined to distinguish themselves from their enemies by their respect for international law and justice. "All the cards are against us in playing with these neutrals," General Ironside, Chief of the Imperial General Staff, confided to his diary. "Germany does not mean to respect them if it so suits her and we must respect them."[13] The case was especially difficult because it did in fact suit the Germans, but not the British, to respect Norway's neutral rights.

The Russo-Finnish war opened a new possibility for Allied strategists (and moralists). The League of Nations, which had said nothing about the German attack on Poland, now condemned the Russians for waging an aggressive war. Churchill, who "sympathized ardently with the Finns," proposed to send troops to Finland in fulfillment of Britain's obligations under the Covenant —and to send them via Narvik, Gallivare, and Lulea. Under the plan drawn up by the General Staff, only a battalion of soldiers would actually have reached Finland, while three divisions would have guarded the "lines of communication" across Norway and Sweden, not only stopping the shipments of iron ore, but seizing it at its source and digging in for an expected German response in the spring.[14] It was a bold plan which would almost certainly have led to a German invasion of Sweden and Norway and to large-scale military operations in the two countries. "We have more to gain than to lose," Churchill argued, "by a German attack on Norway." One immediately wants to ask whether the Norwegians had more to gain than to lose. Apparently they did not think so, for they rejected repeated requests that they permit the free passage of British troops. The Cabinet decided in favor of the expedition anyway, but the instructions prepared for its commander would have allowed him to proceed only in the face of "token opposition." General Ironside worried that the political will necessary for success did not exist. "We must . . . remain quite cynical about anything except stopping the iron ore."[15] The Cabinet seems to have been cynical enough about its Finnish cover. As it turned out, however, the members were unwilling to do without it, and when the Finns sued for peace in March 1940, the plan was shelved.

Churchill now pressed a more modest proposal. He urged the mining of Norwegian territorial waters, so as to force German merchant ships out into the Atlantic where the British navy could capture or sink them. It was a proposal he had made immediately after the war began and that he brought forward whenever his larger plans seemed in danger. Even this "genteel little act of bellicosity," however, encountered opposition. Though the Cabinet seemed favorable to Churchill's original presentation (in September 1939), "the Foreign Office arguments about neutrality were weighty, and I could not prevail. I continued . . . to press my point by every means and on all occasions." It is interesting to note, as Liddell Hart does, that a similar project had been brought forward in 1918 and rejected by the Commander-in-Chief, Lord Beatty. "[He] said it would be most repugnant to the officers and men in the Grand Fleet to steam in overwhelming strength into the waters of a small but high-spirited people and coerce them. If the Norwegians resisted, as they probably would, blood would be shed; this, said the Commander-in-Chief, 'would constitute a crime as bad as any that the Germans had committed elsewhere.' "[16] The words have a somewhat archaic ring (and it should be said that Beatty's last line, repeated in 1939-40, would not have been true), but many Englishmen still felt a similar repugnance. These were more likely to be professional diplomats and soldiers than civilian politicians. General Ironside, for example, not always the cynic he pretended to be, wrote in his diary that the mining of Norwegian waters, though it could be described as "a reprisal for the way Germany had treated neutral ships . . . may well start off some form of totalitarian war."[17]

Churchill presumably believed that Britain was in for that kind of war anyway, given the political character of its enemy. He defended his proposal with a moral argument focusing on the nature and long-term goals of the Nazi regime. It is not merely that he did not sympthasize with Beatty's repugnance; he told the Cabinet that such feelings courted disaster, not for Britain alone but for all Europe.[18]

> We are fighting to re-establish the reign of law and to protect the liberties of small countries. Our defeat would mean an age of barbaric violence, and would be fatal, not only to ourselves, but to the independent life of every small country in Europe. Acting in the name of the Covenant, and as virtual mandatories of the League and all it stands for, we have a right, indeed are bound in duty, to abrogate for a space some of the conventions of the very laws we seek to consolidate and reaffirm. Small nations must not tie our hands when we are fighting for their rights and freedom. The letter of the law must not in supreme emergency obstruct those who are charged with its protection and enforcement. It would not be right or rational that the aggressive Power should gain one set of advantages by tearing up all laws, and another set by sheltering behind the innate respect for law of its opponents. Humanity, rather than legality, must be our guide.

This is a powerful argument, though its rhetoric is sometimes misleading; it requires close examination. I want to begin by accepting Churchill's description of the British as defenders of the rule of law. (Indeed, they vindicated their claim to that title by refusing for months to adopt his proposals.) It may even be accurate to talk of Britain as the "virtual mandatory" of the League of Nations, so long as one understands that phrase to mean that it was not the actual mandatory; the British decision to invade Norwegian waters was as unilateral as was Norway's decision to stay out of the war. The problem lies in the consequences Churchill believes to follow from the justice of Britain's cause.

He puts forward a version of what I have called the sliding scale argument: the greater the justice of one's cause, the more rights one has in battle.* But Churchill pretends that these are rights against the Germans. The British, he says, are entitled to violate those legal conventions behind which Germany is sheltering. Legal conventions, however, have (or sometimes have) their moral reasons. The purpose of the laws of neutrality is not primarily to protect belligerent powers but to save the lives of neutral citizens. It was in fact the Norwegians who were sheltered by the "letter of the law"; the Germans were only its secondary beneficiaries. This ordering suggests the crucial difficulty with the sliding scale. However much the rights of the British are enhanced by the justice of their cause, they can hardly acquire a title to kill *Norwegians* or to put their lives at risk unless Norwegian rights are somehow simultaneously diminished. The sliding scale argument presupposes and requires some such symmetry, but I do not see how it can be generated. It is not enough to argue that the just side can do more. Something must be said about the objects as well as the subjects of this military doing. Who is being done to? In this case, the objects are Norwegian citizens, who are in no sense responsible for the war into which they are to be dragged. They have not challenged the rule of law or the peace of Europe. How have they become liable to attack?

There is an implicit answer to this question in Churchill's Cabinet memorandum. He obviously believes that the Norwegians ought to be involved in the struggle against Germany, not only because their involvement would be good for Britain, but also be-

* Hugo Grotius, who generally favors the sliding scale, is particularly clear on the question of neutrality: "From what has been said we can understand how it is permissible for one who is waging a just war to take possession of a place situated in a country free from hostilities." He sets three conditions, the first of which does not quite fit the Norwegian case: "that there is not an imaginary but a real danger that the enemy will seize the place and cause irreparable damage." But Churchill might have argued that the Germans enjoyed all the benefits of seizure without the effort. See *Of the Law of War and Peace*, Book II, Chapter ii, Section x.

cause, if Britain and France were forced into a "shameful peace," they would certainly be among the "next victims." Neutral rights fade away, he argues, when brought up against aggression and illegal violence on the one hand and legitimate resistance on the other. Or at least, they fade away whenever the aggressor poses a general threat: to the rule of law, the independence of small nations, and so on. Britain is fighting on behalf of Germany's future victims, and they must sacrifice their rights rather than hinder the struggle. Taken as moral exhortation, this seems to me, in the circumstances of 1939-40, entirely justified. But it remains a question whether the sacrifice is to be required because the Norwegians recognize the German threat or because the British do. Churchill is repeating Wilson's argument of 1917: neutrality is not morally feasible. But this is a dangerous argument when made not by the leader of a neutral state but by a leader of one of the belligerents. It is not a question now of the voluntary surrender of neutral rights, but of their "abrogation for a time." And even that phrase is a euphemism. Since human life is at stake, the abrogation is not temporary, unless Churchill plans to raise the dead after the war is over.

In most wars, it can plausibly be said that one side fights justly, or probably does, or fights with greater justice than the other, and in all these cases the enemy against which it fights may well pose a general threat. The right of third parties to be neutral is a moral entitlement to ignore those distinctions and to recognize or not to recognize that threat. It may well be that they have to fight if they do recognize a danger to themselves, but they cannot rightly be forced to fight if they do not. They may be morally blind, or obtuse, or selfish, but these faults do not turn them into the resources of the righteous. This is, however, exactly the effect of Churchill's argument: the sliding scale is a way of transferring the rights of third parties to the citizens and soldiers of a state whose war is, or is said to be, just.

But there is another argument in Churchill's memorandum which does not require the application of the sliding scale; it is most clearly suggested by the phrase "supreme emergency." In an emergency, neutral rights can be overridden, and when we override them we make no claim that they have been diminished, weakened, or lost. They have to be overridden, as I have already said, precisely because they are still there, in full force, obstacles to some great (necessary) triumph for mankind. To British strategists, Norwegian neutrality was an obstacle of just this sort. It appears now that they greatly exaggerated the effects they could have had on Germany's war effort by cutting off the ore shipments. But their estimates were honestly made, and they were shared by Hitler himself. "We can under no circumstances afford to lose the Swedish ore," he told General Falkenhurst in February 1940. "If we do, we will soon have to wage war with wooden sticks."[19] That attractive prospect must have weighed heavily with the British Cabinet. They had available to them a simple utilitarian argument, backed up by a theory of justice, for violating Norway's neutral rights: the violations were militarily necessary to defeat Nazism, and it was morally essential that Nazism be defeated.

Here again is the two-level argument, and in this case the argument works on the second level: the moral necessity is clear (I will try to explain why this is so in the next chapter). That is why we are likely to be far more sympathetic to Churchill's than to von Bethmann Hollweg's position. But the instrumental or strategic claim is as questionable in the Norwegian as in the Belgian example. The Allied armies had not yet fought a single battle; the force of the German *blitzkrieg* had not yet been felt in the West; the military significance of the airplane was not yet understood. The British still had full confidence in the Royal Navy. The First Lord of the Admiralty certainly had such confidence: all his Norwegian plans depended upon naval power. Only a Churchill, having called the situation at the beginning of 1940 a "supreme emergency," could still find words to describe Britain's danger six months later. The truth is that when the British finally decided "to sail in overwhelming strength into the waters of a small but high-spirited people and coerce them," they were not thinking of avoiding defeat but (like the Germans in 1914) of winning a quick victory.

So the British move is another example of overriding at the first minute rather than the last. We judge it less harshly than the German attack on Belgium, not only because of what we know of the character of the Nazi regime, but also because we look back on the events of the next months which so quickly brought Britain to the brink of national disaster. But it has to be stressed again that Churchill had no foresight of that disaster. To understand and weigh the actions he advocated, we must stand beside him in those early months of the war and try to think as he did. Then the question is simply this: can one do *anything*, violating the rights of the innocent, in order to defeat Nazism? I am going to argue that one can indeed do what is necessary, but the violation of Norwegian neutrality was not necessary in April 1940; it was only a piece of expediency. Can one then reduce the risks of fighting Nazism, at the expense of the innocent? Surely one cannot do that, however just the struggle. Churchill's argument hangs on the reality and the extremity of the crisis, but here (in his own view) there was no crisis. The "phony war" was not yet a supreme emergency. The emergency came on unexpectedly, as emergencies are likely to do, its dangers first revealed by the fighting in Norway.

The final British decision was made late in March, and the Leads were mined on April 8. The next day, the Germans invaded Norway. Eluding the British navy, they landed troops all along the coast, even as far north as Narvik. It was a response not so much to the actual laying of the mines as to the months of plans, arguments, and hesitations, none of which were concealed from Hitler's agents and strategic analysts. It was also the response Churchill had expected and hoped for, though it came too soon and with complete surprise. The Norwegians fought bravely and briefly; the British were tragically unready to defend the country they had made vulnerable to attack. There were a number of counter-landings by British troops; Narvik was captured and held for a short time; but the navy was ineffective against the German airforce, and Churchill, still First Lord of the Admiralty, presided over a series of humiliating evacuations.[20] Germany's ore supply was safe for the duration of the war, as it would have been had Norway's neutrality been respected. Norway was an occupied country, with a fascist government; many of its soldiers were dead; the "phony war" was over.

At Nuremberg in 1945, German leaders were charged with having planned and carried out an aggressive war against Norway. Liddell Hart finds it "hard to understand how the British and French governments had the face to approve . . . this charge."[21] His indignation derives from his belief that neutral rights are equally invulnerable to the claims of just and unjust belligerents. So they are, and it would have been better if after the war the British had acknowledged that the mining of the Leads had been a breach of international law and that the Germans were entitled, if not to invade and conquer Norway, at least to respond in some military way. I do not want to deny the anomaly of the argument that Hitler's Germany could have any rights at all in its wars of conquest. German entitlements, however, came by way of Norwegian rights, and so long as one recognizes the practice of neutrality, there is no way around them. In a supreme emergency, indeed, it may be necessary "to hack one's way through," but it is no virtue to be too eager to do that or to do it too soon, for it is not the opposing army that is hacked through in such a case, but innocent men and women, whose rights are intact, whose lives are at stake.

16

Supreme Emergency

The Nature of Necessity (3)

Everyone's troubles make a crisis. "Emergency" and "crisis" are
cant words, used to prepare our minds for acts of brutality. And
yet there are such things as critical moments in the lives of men
and women and in the history of states. Certainly, war is such a
time: every war is an emergency, every battle a possible turning
point. Fear and hysteria are always latent in combat, often real,
and they press us toward fearful measures and criminal behavior.
The war convention is a bar to such measures, not always effective,
but there nevertheless. In principle at least, as we have seen, it
resists the ordinary crises of military life. Churchill's description of
Britain's predicament in 1939 as a "supreme emergency" was a
piece of rhetorical heightening designed to overcome that resistance. But the phrase also contains an argument: that there is a
fear beyond the ordinary fearfulness (and the frantic opportunism)
of war, and a danger to which that fear corresponds, and that this
fear and danger may well require exactly those measures that the
war convention bars. Now, a great deal is at stake here, both for the
men and women driven to adopt such measures and for their victims, so we must attend carefully to the implicit argument of
"supreme emergency."

Though its use is often ideological, the meaning of the phrase is a matter of common sense. It is defined by two criteria, which correspond to the two levels on which the concept of necessity works: the first has to do with the imminence of the danger and the second with its nature. The two criteria must both be applied. Neither one by itself is sufficient as an account of extremity or as a defense of the extraordinary measures extremity is thought to require. Close but not serious, serious but not close—neither one makes for a supreme emergency. But since people at war can rarely agree on the seriousness of the dangers they face (or pose for one another), the idea of closeness is sometimes made to do the job alone. Then we are offered what might best be called the back-to-the-wall argument: that when conventional means of resistance are hopeless or worn out, anything goes (anything that is "necessary" to win). Thus British Prime Minister Stanley Baldwin, writing in 1932 about the dangers of terror bombing:[1]

> Will any form of prohibition of bombing, whether by convention, treaty, agreement, or anything you like, be effective in war? Frankly, I doubt it, and in doubting it, I make no reflection on the good faith of either ourselves or any other country. If a man has a potential weapon and has his back to the wall and is going to be killed, he will use that weapon, whatever it is and whatever undertaking he has given about it.

The first thing that has to be said about this statement is that Baldwin does not mean his domestic analogy to be applied literally. Soldiers and statesmen commonly say that their backs are to the wall whenever military defeat seems imminent, and Baldwin is endorsing this view of extremity. The analogy is from survival at home to victory in the international sphere. Baldwin claims that people will necessarily (inevitably) adopt extreme measures if such measures are necessary (essential) either to escape death or to avoid military defeat. But the argument is wrong at both ends. It is simply not the case that individuals will always strike out at innocent men and women rather than accept risks for themselves. We even say, very often, that it is their duty to accept risks (and perhaps to die); and here as in moral life generally, "ought" implies "can." We make the demand knowing that it is possible for people to live up to it. Can we make the same demand on political leaders, acting not for themselves but for their countrymen? That will depend upon the dangers their countrymen face. What is it that defeat entails? Is it some minor territorial adjustment, a loss of face (for the leaders), the payment of heavy indemnities, political reconstruction of this or that sort, the surrender of national independence, the exile or murder of millions of people? In such cases, one's back is always to the wall, but the dangers one confronts take very different forms, and the different forms make a difference.

If we are to adopt or defend the adoption of extreme measures, the danger must be of an unusual and horrifying kind. Such descriptions, I suppose, are common enough in time of war. One's enemies are often thought to be—at least they are often said to be—unusual and horrifying.[2] Soldiers are encouraged to fight fiercely if they believe that they are fighting for the survival of their country and their families, that freedom, justice, civilization itself are at risk. But this sort of thing is only sometimes plausible to the detached observer, and one suspects that its propagandistic character is also understood by many of the participants. War is not always a struggle over ultimate values, where the victory of one side would be a human disaster for the other. It is necessary to be skeptical about such matters, to cultivate a wary disbelief of wartime rhetoric, and then to search for some touchstone against which arguments about extremity might be judged. We need to make a map of human crises and to mark off the regions of desperation and disaster. These and only these constitute the realm of necessity, truly understood. Once again, I am going to use the experience of World War II in Europe to suggest at least the rough contours of the map. For Nazism lies at the outer limits of exigency, at a point where we are likely to find ourselves united in fear and abhorrence.

That is what I am going to assume, at any rate, on behalf of all those people who believed at the time and still believe a third of a century later that Nazism was an ultimate threat to everything decent in our lives, an ideology and a practice of domination so murderous, so degrading even to those who might survive, that the consequences of its final victory were literally beyond calculation, immeasurably awful. We see it—and I don't use the phrase lightly—as evil objectified in the world, and in a form so potent and apparent that there could never have been anything to do but fight against it. I obviously cannot offer an account of Nazism in these pages. But such an account is hardly necessary. It is enough to point to the historical experience of Nazi rule. Here was a threat to human values so radical that its imminence would surely constitute a supreme emergency; and this example can help us understand why lesser threats might not do so.

In order to get the map right, however, we must imagine a Nazi-like danger somewhat different from the one the Nazis actually posed. When Churchill said that a German victory in World War II "would be fatal, not only to ourselves, but to the independent life of every small country in Europe," he was speaking the exact truth. The danger was a general one. But suppose it had existed for Britain alone. Can a supreme emergency be constituted by a particular threat—by a threat of enslavement or extermination directed against a single nation? Can soldiers and statesmen override the rights of innocent people for the sake of their own political community? I am inclined to answer this question affirmatively, though not without hesitation and worry. What choice do they have? They might sacrifice themselves in order to uphold the moral law, but they cannot sacrifice their countrymen. Faced with some ultimate horror, their options exhausted, they will do what they must to save their own people. That is not to say that their decision is inevitable (I have no way of knowing that), but the sense of obligation and of moral urgency they are likely to feel at such a time is so overwhelming that a different outcome is hard to imagine.

Still, the question is difficult, as its domestic analogue suggests. Despite Baldwin, it is not usually said of individuals in domestic society that they necessarily will or that they morally can strike out at innocent people, even in the supreme emergency of self-defense.[3] They can only attack their attackers. But communities, in emergencies, seem to have different and larger prerogatives. I am not sure that I can account for the difference, without ascribing to communal life a kind of transcendence that I don't believe it to have. Perhaps it is only a matter of arithmetic: individuals cannot kill other individuals to save themselves, but to save a nation we can violate the rights of a determinate but smaller number of people. But then large nations and small ones would have different entitlements in such cases, and I doubt very much that that is true. We might better say that it is possible to live in a world where individuals are sometimes murdered, but a world where entire peoples are enslaved or massacred is literally unbearable. For the survival and freedom of political communities—whose members share a way of life, developed by their ancestors, to be passed on to their children—are the highest values of international society. Nazism challenged these values on a grand scale, but challenges more narrowly conceived, *if they are of the same kind*, have similar moral consequences. They bring us under the rule of necessity (and necessity knows no rules).

I want to stress again, however, that the mere recognition of such a threat is not itself coercive; it neither compels nor permits attacks on the innocent, so long as other means of fighting and winning are available. Danger makes only half the argument; imminence makes the other half. Now let us consider a time when the two halves came together: the terrible two years that followed the defeat of France, from the summer of 1940 to the summer of 1942, when Hitler's armies were everywhere triumphant.

Overriding the Rules of War

The Decision to Bomb German Cities

There have been few decisions more important than this one in the history of warfare. As a direct result of the adoption of a policy of terror bombing by the leaders of Britain, some 300,000 Germans, most of them civilians, were killed and another 780,000 seriously injured. No doubt, these figures are low when compared to the results of Nazi genocide; but they were, after all, the work of men and women at war with Nazism, who hated everything it stood for and who were not supposed to imitate its effects, even at lagging rates. And the British policy had further consequences: it was the crucial precedent for the fire-bombing of Tokyo and other Japanese cities and then for Harry Truman's decision to drop atomic bombs on Hiroshima and Nagasaki. The civilian death toll from Allied terrorism in World War II must have exceeded half a million men, women, and children. How could the initial choice of this ultimate weapon ever have been defended?

The history is a complex one, and it has already been the subject of several monographic analyses.[4] I can review it only briefly, attending especially to the arguments put forward at the time by Churchill and other British leaders, and always remembering what sort of a time it was. The decision to bomb cities was made late in 1940. A directive issued in June of that year had "specifically laid down that targets had to be identified and aimed at. Indiscriminate bombing was forbidden." In November, after the German raid on Coventry, "Bomber Command was instructed simply to aim at the center of a city." What had once been called indiscriminate bombing (and commonly condemned) was now required, and by early 1942, aiming at military or industrial targets was barred: "the aiming points are to be the built-up areas, *not*, for instance, the dockyards or aircraft factories."[5] The purpose of the raids was explicitly declared to be the destruction of civilian morale. Following the famous minute of Lord Cherwell in 1942, the means to this demoralization were specified: working-class residential areas were the prime targets. Cherwell thought it possible to render a third of the German population homeless by 1943.[6]

Before Cherwell provided his "scientific" rationale for the bombing, a number of reasons had already been offered for the British decision. From the beginning, the attacks were defended as reprisals for the German blitz. This is a very problematic defense, even if we leave aside the difficulties of the doctrine of reprisals (which I have already canvassed). First of all, it appears possible, as one scholar has recently argued, that Churchill deliberately provoked the German attacks on London—by bombing Berlin—in order to relieve pressure on R.A.F. installations, until then the major *Luftwaffe* target.[7] Nor was it Churchill's purpose, once the blitz began, to deter the German attacks or to establish a policy of mutual restraint.[8]

> We ask no favor of the enemy. We seek from them no compunction. On the contrary, if tonight the people of London were asked to cast their votes whether a convention should be entered into to stop the bombing of all cities, the overwhelming majority would cry, "No, we will mete out to the Germans the measure, and more than the measure, that they have meted out to us."

Needless to say, the people of London were not in fact asked to vote on such a convention. Churchill assumed that the bombing of German cities was necessary to their morale and that they wanted to hear (what he told them in a radio broadcast of 1941) that the British air force was making "the German people taste and gulp each month a sharper dose of the miseries they have showered upon mankind."[9] This argument has been accepted by many historians: there was "a popular clamor" for revenge, one of them writes, which Churchill had to satisfy if he was to maintain a fighting spirit among his own people. It is especially interesting to note, then, that a 1941 opinion poll showed that "the most determined demand for [reprisal raids] came from Cumberland, Westmoreland, and the North Riding of Yorkshire, rural areas barely touched by bombing, where some three-quarters of the population wanted them. In central London, conversely, the proportion was only 45 percent."[10] Men and women who had experienced terror bombing were less likely to support Churchill's policy than those who had not—a heartening statistic, and one which suggests that the morale of the British people (or perhaps better, their conventional morality) allowed for political leadership of a different sort than Churchill provided. The news that Germany was being bombed was certainly glad tidings in Britain; but as late as 1944, according to other opinion surveys, the overwhelming majority of Britishers still believed that the raids were directed solely against military targets. Presumably, that is what they wanted to believe; there was by then quite a bit of evidence to the contrary. But that says something, again, about the character of British morale. (It should also be said that the campaign against terror bombing, run largely by pacifists, attracted very little popular support.)

Reprisal was a bad argument; revenge was a worse one. We must concentrate now on the military justifications for terror bombing, which were presumably paramount in Churchill's mind, whatever he said on the radio. I can discuss these only in a general way. There was a great deal of dispute at the time, some of it technical, some of it moral in character. The calculations of the Cherwell minute, for example, were sharply attacked by a group of scientists whose opposition to terrorism may well have had moral grounds, but whose position, to the best of my knowledge, was never stated in moral terms.[11] Explicit moral disagreement developed most importantly among the professional soldiers involved in the decision-making process. These disagreements are described, in characteristic fashion, by a strategic analyst and historian who has studied the British escalation: "The . . . debate had been beclouded by emotion on one side of the argument, on the part of those who as a matter of moral principle objected to making war on civilians."[12] The focus of these objections seems to have been some version of the doctrine of double effect. (The arguments had, to the mind of the strategic analyst, "a curiously scholastic flavor.") At the height of the blitz, many British officers still felt strongly that their own air attacks should be aimed only at military targets and that positive efforts should be made to minimize civilian casualties. They did not want to imitate Hitler, but to differentiate themselves from him. Even officers who accepted the desirability of killing civilians still sought to maintain their professional honor: such deaths, they insisted, were desirable "only insofar as [they] remained a by-product of the primary intention to hit a military target . . ."[13] A tendentious argument, no doubt, yet one that would drastically have limited the British offensive against cities. But all such proposals ran up against the operational limits of the bomber technology then available.

Early in the war, it became clear that British bombers could fly effectively only at night and, given the navigational devices with which they were equipped, that they could reasonably aim at no target smaller than a fairly large city. A study made in 1941 indicated that of those planes that actually succeeded in attacking their target (about two-thirds of the attacking force), only one-third dropped their bombs within five miles of the point aimed at.[14] Once this was known, it would seem dishonest to claim that the intended target was, say, this aircraft factory and that the indiscriminate destruction around it was only an unintended, if foreseeable, consequence of the justified attempt to stop the production of planes. What was really unintended but foreseeable was that the factory itself would probably escape harm. If any sort of strategic bombing offensive was to be maintained, one would have to plan for the destruction that one could and did cause. Lord Cherwell's minute was an effort at such planning. In fact, of course, navigational devices were rapidly improved as the war went on, and the bombing of specific military targets was an important part of Britain's total air offensive, receiving top priority at times (before the June 1944 invasion of France, for example) and cutting into the resources allowed for attacks on cities. Today many experts believe that the war might have ended sooner had there been a greater concentration of air power against targets such as the German oil refineries.[15] But the decision to bomb cities was made at a time when victory was not in sight and the specter of defeat ever present. And it was made when no other decision seemed possible if there was to be any sort of military offensive against Nazi Germany.

Bomber Command was the only offensive weapon available to the British in those frightening years, and I expect there is some truth to the notion that it was used simply because it was there. "It was the only force in the West," writes Arthur Harris, chief of Bomber Command from early 1942 until the end of the war, "which could take offensive action . . . against Germany, our only means of getting at the enemy in a way that would hurt at all."[16] Offensive action could have been postponed until (or in hope of) some more favorable time. That is what the war convention would require, and there was also considerable military pressure for postponement. Harris was hard-pressed to keep his Command together in the face of repeated calls for tactical air support—which would have been coordinated with ground action largely defensive in character, since the German armies were still advancing everywhere. Sometimes, in his memoirs, he sounds like a bureaucrat defending his function and his office, but obviously he was also defending a certain conception of how the war might best be fought. He did not believe that the weapons he commanded should be used because he commanded them. He believed that the tactical use of bombers could not stop Hitler and that the destruction of cities could. Later in the war, he argued that only the destruction of cities could bring the fighting to a quick conclusion. The first of these arguments, at least, deserves a careful examination. It was apparently accepted by the Prime Minister. "The bombers alone," Churchill had said as early as September 1940, "provide the means of victory."[17]

The bombers alone—that poses the issue very starkly, and perhaps wrongly, given the disputes over strategy to which I have already referred. Churchill's statement suggested a certainty to which neither he nor anyone else had any right. But the issue can be put so as to accommodate a degree of skepticism and to permit even the most sophisticated among us to indulge in a common and a morally important fantasy: suppose that I sat in the seat of power and had to decide whether to use Bomber Command (in the only way that it could be used systematically and effectively) against cities. Suppose further that unless the bombers were used in this way, the probability that Germany would eventually be defeated would be radically reduced. It makes no sense at this point to quantify the probabilities; I have no clear notion what they actually were or even how they might be calculated given our present knowledge; nor am I sure how different figures, unless they were very different, would affect the moral argument. But it does seem to me that the more certain a German victory appeared to be in the absence of a bomber offensive, the more justifiable was the decision to launch the offensive. It is not just that such a victory was frightening, but also that it seemed in those years very close; it is not just that it was close, but also that it was so frightening. Here was a supreme emergency, where one might well be required to override the rights of innocent people and shatter the war convention.

Given the view of Nazism that I am assuming, the issue takes this form: should I wager this determinate crime (the killing of innocent people) against that immeasurable evil (a Nazi triumph)?

Obviously, if there is some other way of avoiding the evil or even a reasonable chance of another way, I must wager differently or elsewhere. But I can never hope to be sure; a wager is not an experiment. Even if I wager and win, it is still possible that I was wrong, that my crime was unnecessary to victory. But I can argue that I studied the case as closely as I was able, took the best advice I could find, sought out available alternatives. And if all this is true, and my perception of evil and imminent danger not hysterical or self-serving, then surely I must wager. There is no option; the risk otherwise is too great. My own action is determinate, of course, only as to its direct consequences, while the rule that bars such acts is founded on a conception of rights that transcends all immediate considerations. It arises out of our common history; it holds the key to our common future. But I dare to say that our history will be nullified and our future condemned unless I accept the burdens of criminality here and now.

This is not an easy argument to make, and yet we must resist every effort to make it easier. Many people undoubtedly found some comfort in the fact that the cities being bombed were German and some of the victims Nazis. In effect, they applied the sliding scale and denied or diminished the rights of German civilians so as to deny or diminish the horror of their deaths. This is a tempting procedure, as we can see most clearly if we consider again the bombing of occupied France. Allied fliers killed many Frenchmen, but they did so while bombing what were (or were thought to be) military targets. They did not deliberately aim at the "built-up areas" of French cities. Suppose such a policy had been proposed. I am sure that we would all find the wager more difficult to undertake and defend if, through some strange combination of circumstances, it required the deliberate slaughter of Frenchmen. For we had special commitments to the French; we were fighting on their behalf (and sometimes the bombers were flown by French pilots). But the status of the civilians in the two cases is no different. The theory that distinguishes combatants from noncombatants does not distinguish Allied from enemy noncombatants, at least not with regard to the question of their murder. I suppose it makes sense to say that there were more people in German than in French cities who were responsible (in some fashion) for the evil of Nazism, and we may well be reluctant to extend to them the full range of civilian rights. But even if that reluctance is justified, there is no way for the bombers to search out the right people. And for all the others, terrorism only reiterates the tyranny that the Nazis had already established. It assimilates ordinary men and women to their government as if the two really made a totality, and it judges them in a totalitarian way. If one is forced to bomb cities, it seems to me, it is best to acknowledge that one has also been forced to kill the innocent.

Once again, however, I want to set radical limits to the notion of necessity even as I have myself been using it. For the truth is that the supreme emergency passed long before the British bombing reached its crescendo. The greater number by far of the German civilians killed by terror bombing were killed without moral (and probably also without military) reason. The decisive point was made by Churchill in July of 1942:[18]

> In the days when we were fighting alone, we answered the question: "How are you going to win the war?" by saying: "We will shatter Germany by bombing." Since then the enormous injuries inflicted on the German Army and manpower by the Russians, and the accession of the manpower and munitions of the United States, have rendered other possibilities open.

Surely, then, it was time to stop the bombing of cities and to aim, tactically and strategically, only at legitimate military targets. But that was not Churchill's view: "All the same, it would be a mistake to cast aside our original thought . . . that the severe, ruthless bombing of Germany on an ever-increasing scale will not only cripple her war effort . . . but will create conditions intolerable to the mass of the German population." So the raids continued, culminating in the spring of 1945—when the war was virtually won —in a savage attack on the city of Dresden in which something like 100,000 people were killed.[19] Only then did Churchill have second thoughts. "It seems to me that the moment has come when the question of bombing German cities simply for the sake of increasing the terror, though under other pretexts, should be reviewed . . . The destruction of Dresden remains a serious query against the conduct of Allied bombing."[20] Indeed it does, but so does the destruction of Hamburg and Berlin and all the other cities attacked simply for the sake of terror.

The argument used between 1942 and 1945 in defense of terror bombing was utilitarian in character, its emphasis not on victory itself but on the time and price of victory. The city raids, it was claimed by men such as Harris, would end the war sooner than it would otherwise end and, despite the large number of civilian casualties they inflicted, at a lower cost in human life. Assuming this claim to be true (I have already indicated that precisely opposite claims are made by some historians and strategists), it is nevertheless not sufficient to justify the bombing. It is not sufficient, I think, even if we do nothing more than calculate utilities. For such calculations need not be concerned only with the preservation of life. There is much else that we might plausibly want to preserve: the quality of our lives, for example, our civilization and morality, our collective abhorrence of murder, even when it seems, as it always does, to serve some purpose. Then the deliberate slaughter of innocent men and women cannot be justified simply because it saves the lives of other men and women. I suppose it is possible to imagine situations where that last assertion might prove problematic, from a utilitarian perspective, where the number of people involved is small, the proportions are right, the events hidden from the public eye, and so on. Philosophers delight in inventing such cases in order to test out our moral doctrines. But their inventions are somehow put out of our minds by the sheer scale of the calculations necessary in World War II. To kill 278,966 civilians (the number is made up) in order to avoid the deaths of an unknown but probably larger number of civilians and soldiers is surely a fantastic, godlike, frightening, and horrendous act.*

I have said that such acts can probably be ruled out on utilitarian grounds, but it is also true that utilitarianism as it is commonly understood, indeed, as Sidgwick himself understands it, encourages the bizarre accounting that makes them (morally) possible. We can recognize their horror only when we have acknowledged the personality and value of the men and women we destroy in committing them. It is the acknowledgment of rights that puts a stop to such calculations and forces us to realize that the destruction of the innocent, whatever its purposes, is a kind of blasphemy against our deepest moral commitments. (This is true even in a supreme emergency, when we cannot do anything else.) But I want to look at one more case before concluding my argument—a case

---

* George Orwell has suggested an alternative utilitarian rationale for the bombing of German cities. In a column written for the leftist journal *Tribune* in 1944, he argued that the bombing brought the true character of contemporary combat home to all those people who supported the war, even enjoyed it, only because they never felt its effects. It shattered "the immunity of civilians, one of the things that have made war possible," and so it made war less likely in the future. See *The Collected Essays, Journalism and Letters of George Orwell*, ed. Sonia Orwell and Ian Angus, New York, 1968, Vol. 3, pp. 151–152. Orwell assumes that civilians had really been immune in the past, which is false. In any case, I doubt that his argument would lead anyone to begin bombing cities. It is an apology after the fact, and not a convincing one.

where the utilitarian accounting, however bizarre, seemed so radically clear-cut to the decision-makers as to leave them, they thought, no choice but to attack the innocent.

The Limits of Calculation

Hiroshima

"They all accepted the 'assignment' and produced The Bomb," Dwight Macdonald wrote in August 1945 of the atomic scientists. "Why?" It is an important question, but Macdonald poses it badly and then gives the wrong answer. "Because they thought of themselves as specialists, technicians, and not as complete men."[21] In fact, they did not accept the assignment; they sought it out, taking the initiative, urging upon President Roosevelt the critical importance of an American effort to match the work being done in Nazi Germany. And they did this precisely because they were "complete men," many of them European refugees, with an acute sense of what a Nazi victory would mean for their native lands and for all mankind. They were driven by a deep moral anxiety, not (or not most crucially) by any kind of scientific fascination; they were certainly not servile technicians. On the other hand, they were men and women without political power or following, and once their own work was done, they could not control its use. The discovery in November 1944 that German scientists had made little progress ended their own supreme emergency, but it did not end the program they had helped to launch. "If I had known that the Germans would not succeed in constructing the atom bomb," Albert Einstein said, "I would never have lifted a finger."[22] By the time he found that out, however, the scientists had largely finished their work; now indeed technicians were in charge, and the politicians in charge of them. And in the event, the bomb was not used against Germany (or to deter its use by Hitler, which is what men like Einstein had in mind), but against the Japanese, who had never posed such a threat to peace and freedom as the Nazis had.*

* In his novel *The New Men*, C. P. Snow describes the discussions among atomic scientists as to whether or not the bomb should be used. Some of them, his narrator says, answered that question with "an absolute no," feeling that if the weapon were used to kill hundreds of thousands of innocent people, "neither science nor

Still, it was an important feature of the American decision that the President and his advisors believed the Japanese to be fighting an aggressive war and, moreover, to be fighting it unjustly. Thus Truman's address to the American people on August 12, 1945:

> We have used [the bomb] against those who attacked us without warning at Pearl Harbor, against those who have starved and beaten and executed American prisoners of war, against those who have abandoned all pretense of obeying international laws of warfare. We have used it in order to shorten the agony of war . . .

Here again, the sliding scale is being used to open the way for utilitarian calculations. The Japanese have forfeited (some of) their rights, and so they cannot complain about Hiroshima so long as the destruction of the city actually does, or could reasonably be expected to, shorten the agony of war. But had the Japanese exploded an atomic bomb over an American city, killing tens of thousands of civilians and thereby shortening the agony of war, the action would clearly have been a crime, one more for Truman's list. This distinction is only plausible, however, if one renders a judgment not only against the leaders of Japan but also against the ordinary people of Hiroshima and insists at the same time that no similar judgment is possible against the people of San Francisco, say, or Denver. I can find, as I have said before, no way of defending such a procedure. How did the people of Hiroshima forfeit their rights? Perhaps their taxes paid for some of the ships and planes used in the attack on Pearl Harbor; perhaps they sent their sons into the navy and air force with prayers for their success; perhaps they celebrated the actual event, after being told that their country had won a great victory in the face of an imminent American threat. Surely there is nothing here that makes these people liable to direct attack. (It is worth noting, though the fact is not relevant in judging the Hiroshima decision, that the raid on Pearl Harbor was directed entirely against naval and army installations: only a few stray bombs fell on the city of Honolulu.)[23]

But if Truman's argument on August 12 was weak, there was a worse one underlying it. He did not intend to apply the sliding scale with any precision, for he seems to have believed that, given

---

the civilization of which science is bone and fibre, would be free from guilt again." But the more common view was the one I have been defending: "Many, probably the majority, gave a conditional no with much the same feeling behind it; but if there were *no other way* of saving the war against Hitler, they would be prepared to drop the bomb." *The New Men*, New York, 1954, p. 177 (Snow's emphasis).

Japanese aggression, the Americans could do anything at all to win (and shorten the agony of war). Along with most of his advisors, he accepted the "war is hell" doctrine; it is a constant allusion in defenses of the Hiroshima decision. Thus Henry Stimson:[24]

> As I look back over the five years of my service as Secretary of War, I see too many stern and heartrending decisions to be willing to pretend that war is anything else but what it is. The face of war is the face of death; death is an inevitable part of every order that a wartime leader gives.

And James Byrnes, Truman's friend and his Secretary of State:[25]

> . . . war remains what General Sherman said it was.

And Arthur Compton, chief scientific advisor to the government:[26]

> When one thinks of the mounted archers of Ghengiz Khan . . . the Thirty Years War . . . the millions of Chinese who died during the Japanese invasion . . . the mass destruction of western Russia . . . one realizes that in whatever manner it is fought, war is precisely what General Sherman called it.

And Truman himself:[27]

> Let us not become so preoccupied with weapons that we lose sight of the fact that war itself is the real villain.

War itself is to blame, but also the men who begin it . . . while those who fight justly merely participate in the hell of war, choicelessly, and there are no moral decisions for which they can be called to account. This is not, or not necessarily, an immoral doctrine, but it is radically one-sided; it evades the tension between *jus ad bellum* and *jus in bello*; it undercuts the need for hard judgments; it relaxes our sense of moral restraint. When he was choosing a target for the first bomb, Truman reports, he asked Stimson which Japanese cities were "devoted exclusively to war production."[28] The question was reflexive; Truman did not want to violate the "laws of war." But it wasn't serious. Which American cities were devoted exclusively to war production? It is possible to ask such questions only when the answer doesn't matter. If war is hell however it is fought, then what difference can it make how we fight it? And if war itself is the villain, then what risks do we run (aside from the strategic risks) when we make decisions? The Japanese, who began the war, can also end it; only they can end it, and all we can do is fight it, enduring what Truman called "the daily tragedy of bitter war." I don't doubt that that was really Truman's view; it was not a matter of convenience but of conviction. But it is a distorted view. It mistakes the actual hellishness of war, which is particular in character and open to precise definition, for the limitless pains of religious mythology. The pains of war are limitless only if we make them so —only if we move, as Truman did, beyond the limits that we and others have established. Sometimes, I think, we have to do that, but not all the time. Now we must ask whether it was necessary to do it in 1945.

The only possible defense of the Hiroshima attack is a utilitarian calculation made without the sliding scale, a calculation made, then, where there was no room for it, a claim to override the rules of war and the rights of Japanese civilians. I want to state this argument as strongly as I can. In 1945, American policy was fixed on the demand for the unconditional surrender of Japan. The Japanese had by that time lost the war, but they were by no means ready to accept this demand. The leaders of their armed forces expected an invasion of the Japanese main islands and were preparing for a last-ditch resistance. They had over two million soldiers available for the fighting, and they believed that they could make the invasion so costly that the Americans would agree to a negotiated peace. Truman's military advisors also believed that the costs would be high, though the public record does not show that they ever recommended negotiations. They thought that the war might continue late into 1946 and that there would be as many as a million additional American casualties. Japanese losses would be much higher. The capture of Okinawa in a battle lasting from April to June of 1945 had cost almost 80,000 American casualties, while virtually the entire Japanese garrison of 120,000 men had been killed (only 10,600 prisoners were taken).[29] If the main islands were defended with a similar ferocity, hundreds of thousands, perhaps millions, of Japanese soldiers would die. Meanwhile, the fighting would continue in China and in Manchuria, where a Russian attack was soon due. And the bombing of Japan would also continue, and perhaps intensify, with casualty rates no different from those anticipated from the atomic attack. For the Americans had adopted in Japan the British policy of terrorism: a massive incendiary raid on Tokyo early in March 1945 had set off a firestorm and killed an estimated 100,000 people. Against all this was set, in the minds of American decision-makers, the impact of the atomic bomb—not materially more damaging but psychologically more frightening, and holding out the promise, perhaps, of a quick end to the war. "To avert a vast, indefinite butchery . . . at the cost of a few explosions," wrote Churchill in support of Truman's decision, "seemed, after all our toils and perils, a miracle of deliverance."[30]

"A vast indefinite butchery" involving quite probably the deaths of several million people: surely this is a great evil, and if it was imminent, one could reasonably argue that extreme measures might be warranted to avert it. Secretary of War Stimson thought it was the sort of case I have already described, where one had to wager; there was no option. "No man, in our position and subject to our responsibilities, holding in his hand a weapon of such possibilities for . . . saving those lives, could have failed to use it."[31] This is by no means an incomprehensible or, on the surface at least, an outrageous argument. But it is not the same as the argument I suggested in the case of Britain in 1940. It does not have the form: if we don't do x (bomb cities), they will do y (win the war, establish tyrannical rule, slaughter their opponents). What Stimson argued is very different. Given the actual policy of the U.S. government, it amounts to this: if we don't do x, we will do y. The two atomic bombs caused "many casualties," James Byrnes admitted, "but not nearly so many as there would have been had our air force continued to drop incendiary bombs on Japan's cities."[32] Our purpose, then, was not to avert a "butchery" that someone else was threatening, but one that we were threatening, and had already begun to carry out. Now, what great evil, what supreme emergency, justified the incendiary attacks on Japanese cities?

Even if we had been fighting in strict accordance with the war convention, the continuation of the struggle was not something forced upon us. It had to do with our war aims. The military estimate of casualties was based not only on the belief that the Japanese would fight almost to the last man, but also on the assumption that the Americans would accept nothing less than unconditional surrender. The war aims of the American government required either an invasion of the main islands, with enormous losses of American and Japanese soldiers and of Japanese civilians trapped in the war zones, or the use of the atomic bomb. Given that choice, one might well reconsider those aims. Even if we assume that unconditional surrender was morally desirable because of the character of Japanese militarism, it might still be morally undesirable because of the human costs it entailed. But I would suggest a stronger argument than this. The Japanese case is sufficiently different from the German so that unconditional surrender should never have been asked. Japan's rulers were engaged in a more ordinary sort of military expansion, and all that was morally required was that they be defeated, not that they be conquered and totally overthrown. Some restraint upon their war-making power might be justified, but their domestic authority was a matter of concern only to the Japanese people. In any case, if killing millions (or many thousands) of men and women was militarily necessary for their conquest and overthrow, then it was morally necessary—in order not to kill those people—to settle for something less. I have made this argument before (in chapter 7); here is a further example of its practical application. If people have a right not to be forced to fight, they also have a right not to be forced to continue fighting beyond the point when the war might justly be concluded. Beyond that point, there can be no supreme emergencies, no arguments about military necessity, no cost-accounting in human lives. To press the war further than that is to re-commit the crime of aggression. In the summer of 1945, the victorious Americans owed the Japanese people an experiment in negotiation. To use the atomic bomb, to kill and terrorize civilians, without even attempting such an experiment, was a double crime.[33]

These, then are the limits of the realm of necessity. Utilitarian calculation can force us to violate the rules of war only when we are face-to-face not merely with defeat but with a defeat likely to bring disaster to a political community. But these calculations have no similar effects when what is at stake is only the speed or the scope of victory. They are relevant only to the conflict between winning and fighting well, not to the internal problems of combat itself. Whenever that conflict is absent, calculation is stopped short by the rules of war and the rights they are designed to protect. Confronted by those rights, we are not to calculate consequences, or figure relative risks, or compute probable casualties, but simply to stop short and turn aside.

17

Nuclear Deterrence

The Problem of Immoral Threats

Truman used the atomic bomb to end a war that seemed to him limitless in its horrors. And then, for a few minutes or hours in August 1945, the people of Hiroshima endured a war that actually was limitless in its horrors. "In this last great action of the Second World War," wrote Stimson, "we were given final proof that war is death."[1] *Final proof* is exactly the wrong phrase, for war had never been like that before. A new kind of war was born at Hiroshima, and what we were given was a first glimpse of its deadliness. Though fewer people were killed than in the fire-bombing of Tokyo, they were killed with monstrous ease. One plane, one bomb: with such a weapon the 350 planes that raided Tokyo would virtually have wiped out human life on the Japanese islands. Atomic war was death indeed, indiscriminate and total, and after Hiroshima, the first task of political leaders everywhere was to prevent its recurrence.

The means they adopted is the promise of reprisal in kind. Against the threat of an immoral attack, they have put the threat of an immoral response. This is the basic form of nuclear deterrence. In international as in domestic society, deterrence works by calling up dramatic images of human pain. "In the groves of *their* academy," wrote Edmund Burke of the liberal theorists of crime and punishment, "at the end of every vista, you see nothing but the gallows."[2] The description is uncomplimentary, for Burke believed that domestic peace must rest upon some other foundation. But

269

there is this much to be said for the gallows: in principle, at least, only guilty men need fear the death it brings. About the theorists of deterrence, however, it must be said, "In the groves of *their* academy, at the end of every vista, you see nothing but the mushroom cloud"—and the cloud symbolizes indiscriminate slaughter, the killing of the innocent (as in Hiroshima) on a massive scale. No doubt, the threat of such slaughter, if it is believed, makes nuclear attack a radically undesirable policy. Doubled by a potential enemy, the threat produces a "balance of terror." Both sides are so terrified that no further terrorism is necessary. But is the threat itself morally permissible?

The question is a difficult one. It has generated in the years since Hiroshima a significant body of literature exploring the relation between nuclear deterrence and just war.[3] This has been the work mostly of theologians and philosophers, but some of the strategists of deterrence have also been involved; they worry about the act of terrorizing much as conventional soldiers worry about the act of killing. I cannot review this literature here, though I shall draw upon it freely. The argument against deterrence is familiar enough. Anyone committed to the distinction between combatants and noncombatants is bound to be appalled by the specter of destruction evoked, and purposely evoked, in deterrence theory. "How can a nation live with its conscience," John Bennett has asked, "and know that it is preparing to kill twenty million children in another nation if the worst should come to the worst?"[4] And yet, we have lived with that knowledge, and with our consciences too, for several decades now. How have we managed? The reason for our acceptance of deterrent strategy, most people would say, is that preparing to kill, even threatening to kill, is not at all the same thing as killing. Indeed it is not, but it is frighteningly close—else deterrence wouldn't "work"—and it is in the nature of that closeness that the moral problem lies.

The problem is often misdescribed—as in the following analogy for nuclear deterrence first suggested by Paul Ramsey and frequently repeated since:[5]

> Suppose that one Labor Day weekend no one was killed or maimed on the highways; and that the reason for the remarkable restraint placed on the recklessness of automobile drivers was that suddenly everyone of them discovered he was driving with a baby tied to his front bumper! That would be no way to regulate traffic *even if it succeeds* in regulating it perfectly, since such a system makes innocent human lives the *direct object* of attack and uses them as a mere means for restraining the drivers of automobiles.

No one, of course, has ever proposed regulating traffic in this ingenious way, while the strategy of deterrence was adopted with virtually no opposition at all. That contrast should alert us to what is wrong with Ramsey's analogy. Though deterrence turns American and Russian civilians into mere means for the prevention of war, it does so without restraining any of us in any way. Ramsey reproduces the strategy of the German officers during the Franco-Prussian War who forced civilians to ride on military trains in order to deter saboteurs. By contrast with those civilians, however, we are hostages who lead normal lives. It is in the nature of the new technology that we can be threatened without being held captive. That is why deterrence, while in principle so frightening, is so easy to live with. It cannot be condemned for anything it does to its hostages. It is so far from killing them that it does not even injure or confine them; it involves no direct or physical violation of their rights. Those critics of deterrence who are also committed consequentialists have had to imagine psychic injuries. Thus Erich Fromm, writing in 1960: "To live for any length of time under the constant threat of destruction creates certain psychological effects in most human beings—fright, hostility, callousness . . . and a resulting indifference to all the values we cherish. Such conditions will transform us into barbarians . . ."[6] But I don't know of any evidence that bears out either the assertion or the prediction; surely we are no more barbarians now than we were in 1945. In fact, for most people, the threat of destruction, though constant, is invisible and unnoticed. We have come to live with it casually—as Ramsey's babies, traumatized for life in all probability, could never do, and as hostages in conventional wars have never done.

If deterrence were more painful, we might have found other means of avoiding nuclear war—or we might not have avoided it. If we had to keep millions of people under restraint in order to maintain the balance of terror, or if we had to kill millions of people (periodically) in order to convince our adversaries of our credibility, deterrence would not be accepted for long.[7] The strategy works because it is easy. Indeed, it is easy in a double sense: not only don't we do anything to other people, we also don't believe that we will ever have to do anything. The secret of nuclear deterrence is that it is a kind of bluff. Perhaps we are only bluffing ourselves, refusing to acknowledge the real terrors of a precarious and temporary balance. But no account of our experience is accurate which fails to recognize that, for all its ghastly potential, deterrence has so far been a bloodless strategy.

So far as consequences go, then, deterrence and mass murder are very far apart. Their closeness is a matter of moral posture and intention. Once again, Ramsey's analogy misses the point. His babies are not really the "direct object of attack," for whatever happens on that Labor Day weekend, no one will deliberately set out to kill them. But deterrence depends upon a readiness to do exactly that. It is as if the state should seek to prevent murder by threatening to kill the family and friends of every murderer—a domestic version of the policy of "massive retaliation." Surely that would be a repugnant policy. We would not admire the police officials who designed it or those pledged to carry it out, even if they never actually killed anybody. I don't want to say that such people would necessarily be transformed into barbarians; they might well have a heightened sense of how awful murder is and a heightened desire to avoid it; they might loathe the work they were pledged to do and fervently hope that they never had to do it. Nevertheless, the enterprise is immoral. The immorality lies in the threat itself, not in its present or even its likely consequences. Similarly with nuclear deterrence: it is our own intentions that we have to worry about and the potential (since there are no actual) victims of those intentions. Here Ramsey has put the case very well: "Whatever is wrong to do is wrong to threaten, if the latter means 'mean to do' . . . If counter-population warfare is murder, then counter-population deterrent threats are murderous."[8] No doubt, killing millions of innocent people is worse than threatening to kill them. It is also true that no one wants to kill them, and it may well be true that no one expects to do so. Nevertheless, we intend the killings under certain circumstances. That is the stated policy of our government; and thousands of men, trained in the techniques of mass destruction and drilled in instant obedience, stand ready to carry it out. And from the perspective of morality, the readiness is all. We can translate it into degrees of danger, high and low, and worry about the risks we are imposing on innocent people, but the risks depend on the readiness. What we condemn in our own government, as in the police in my domestic analogy, is the commitment to murder.*

---

* Would it make any difference if this commitment were mechanically fixed? Suppose we set up a computer which would automatically respond to any enemy attack by releasing our missiles. Then we informed our potential enemies that if they attacked our cities, theirs would be attacked. And they would be responsible for both attacks, we might say, since in the interval between the two, no political decision, no act of the will, would be possible on our side. I don't want to comment

But this analogy, too, can be questioned. We don't prevent murder any more than we control traffic in these bizarre and inhuman ways. But we do deter or seek to deter our nuclear adversaries. Perhaps deterrence is different because of the danger its advocates claim to avoid. Traffic deaths and occasional murders, however much we deplore them, do not threaten our common liberties or our collective survival. Deterrence, so we have been told, guards us against a double danger: first, of atomic blackmail and foreign domination; and second, of nuclear destruction. The two go together, since if we did not fear the blackmail, we might adopt a policy of appeasement or surrender and so avoid the destruction. Deterrence theory was worked out at the height of the cold war between the United States and the Soviet Union, and those who worked it out were concerned above all with the political uses of violence—which are not relevant in either the traffic or police analogies. Underlying the American doctrine, there seemed to lurk some version of the slogan "Better dead than Red" (I don't know the Russian parallel). Now that is not really a believable slogan; it is hard to imagine that a nuclear holocaust was really thought preferable to the expansion of Soviet power. What made deterrence attractive was that it seemed capable of avoiding both.

We need not dwell on the nature of the Soviet regime in order to understand the virtues of this argument. Deterrence theory doesn't depend upon a view of Stalinism as a great evil (though that is a highly plausible view) in the same way that my argument about terror bombing depended upon an assertion about the evils of Nazism. It requires only that we see appeasement or surrender to involve a loss of values central to our existence as an independent nation-state. For it is not tolerable that advances in technology should put our nation, or any nation, at the mercy of a great power willing to menace the world or to press its authority outwards in the shadow of an implicit threat. The case here is very different from that which arises commonly in war, where *our* adherence to the war convention puts us, or would put us, at a disadvantage vis-à-vis *them*. For disadvantages of that sort are partial and relative; various counter-measures and compensating steps are always available. But in the nuclear case, the disadvantage is absolute.

---

on the possible effectiveness (or the dangers) of such an arrangement. But it is worth insisting that it would not solve the moral problem. The men and women who designed the computer program or the political leaders who ordered them to do so would be responsible for the second attack, for they would have planned it and organized it and intended that it should occur (under certain conditions).

Against an enemy actually willing to use the bomb, self-defense is impossible, and it makes sense to say that the only compensating step is the (immoral) threat to respond in kind. No country capable of making such a threat is likely to refuse to make it. What is not tolerable won't be tolerated. Hence any state confronted by a nuclear adversary (it makes little difference what the adversary relationship is like or what ideological forms it assumes), and capable of developing its own bomb, is likely to do so, seeking safety in a balance of terror.* Mutual disarmament would clearly be a preferable alternative, but it is an alternative available only to the two countries working closely together, whereas deterrence is the likely choice of either one of them alone. They will worry about one another's readiness to attack; they will each assume their own commitment to resist; and they will realize that the greatest danger of such a confrontation would not be the defeat of one side or the other but the total destruction of both—and possibly of everyone else too. This in fact is the danger that has faced mankind since 1945, and our understanding of nuclear deterrence must be worked out with reference to its scope and imminence. Supreme emergency has become a permanent condition. Deterrence is a way of coping with that condition, and though it is a bad way, there may well be no other that is practical in a world of sovereign and suspicious states. We threaten evil in order not to do it, and the doing of it would be so terrible that the threat seems in comparison to be morally defensible.

Limited Nuclear War

If the bomb were ever used, deterrence would have failed. It is a feature of massive retaliation that while there is or may be some rational purpose in threatening it, there could be none in carrying it out. Were our "bluff" ever to be called and our population centers suddenly attacked, the resulting war could not (in any usual

---

* This is obviously the grim logic of nuclear proliferation. So far as the moral question goes, each new balance of terror created by proliferation is exactly like the first one, justified (or not) in the same way. But the creation of regional balances may well have general effects upon the stability of the great power equilibrium, thereby introducing new moral considerations that I cannot take up here.

sense of the word) be *won*. We could only drag our enemies after us into the abyss. The use of our deterrent capacity would be an act of pure destructiveness. For this reason, massive retaliation, if not literally unthinkable, has always seemed undo-able, and this is a source of considerable anxiety for military strategists. Deterrence only works, they argue, if each side believes that the other might actually carry out its threat. But would we carry it out? George Kennan has recently given what must be the moral response:[9]

> Let us suppose there were to be a nuclear attack of some sort on this country and millions of people were killed and injured. Let us further suppose that we had the ability to retaliate against the urban centers of the country that had attacked us. Would you want to do that? I wouldn't . . . I have no sympathy with the man who demands an eye for an eye in a nuclear attack.

A humane position—though one that should probably be whispered, rather than published, if the balance of terror is to be sustained. But the argument might look very different if the original attack or the planned response avoided cities and people. If a limited nuclear war were possible, wouldn't it also be do-able? And might not the balance of terror then be re-established on the basis of threats that were neither immoral nor unconvincing?

Over a brief timespan, in the late 1950s and the early 1960s, these questions were answered with an extraordinary outpouring of strategic arguments and speculations, overlapping in important ways with the moralizing literature I described earlier.[10] For the debate among the strategists focused on the attempt (though this was rarely made explicit) to fit nuclear war into the structure of the war convention, to apply the argument for justice as if this sort of conflict were like any other sort. The attempt involved, first, a defense of the use of tactical nuclear weapons in deterring and, if that failed, in resisting conventional or small-scale nuclear attacks; and it involved, secondly, the development of a "counter-force" strategy directed at the enemy's military installations and also at major economic targets (but not at entire cities). These two had a similar purpose. By holding out the promise of a limited nuclear war, they made it possible to imagine actually fighting such a war —they made it possible to imagine *winning* it—and so they strengthened the intention that lay behind the deterrent threat. They transformed the "bluff" into a plausible option.

Until the late 1950s, the tendency of most people was to regard the atomic bomb and its thermonuclear successors as forbidden weapons. They were treated on analogy with poison gas, though the prohibition on their use was never legally established. "Ban the bomb" was everyone's policy, and deterrence was simply a practical way of enforcing the ban. But now the strategists suggested (rightly) that the crucial distinction in the theory and practice of war was not between prohibited and acceptable weapons but between prohibited and acceptable targets. Massive retaliation was painful and difficult to contemplate because it was modeled on Hiroshima; the people we were planning to kill were innocent, militarily uninvolved, as removed from and ignorant of the weapons with which their leaders threatened us as we were of the weapons with which our leaders threatened them. But this objection would disappear if we could deter our adversaries by threatening a limited and morally acceptable destruction. Indeed, it might disappear so entirely that we would be tempted to give up deterrence and initiate the destruction ourselves whenever it seemed to our advantage to do so. This was certainly the tendency of much strategic argument, and several writers painted rather attractive pictures of limited nuclear war. Henry Kissinger likened it to war at sea—the very best kind of war, since no one lives in the sea. "The proper analogy . . . is not traditional land warfare, but naval strategy, in which self-contained, [highly mobile] units with great fire power gradually gain the upper hand by destroying their enemy counterparts without physically occupying territory or establishing a front line."[11] The only difficulty is that Kissinger imagined fighting a war like that in Europe.*

Tactical and counter-force warfare meets the formal requirements of *jus in bello*, and it was seized upon eagerly by certain moral theorists. That is not to say, however, that it makes moral sense. There remains the possibility that the new technology of war simply doesn't fit and cannot be made to fit within the old limits. This proposition can be defended in two different ways. The first is to argue that the collateral damage likely to be caused even by a "legitimate" use of nuclear weapons is so great that it would violate both of the proportionality limits fixed by the theory of war: the number of people killed in the war as a whole would not be warranted by the goals of the war—particularly since the dead

---

* Kissinger later moved away from these views, and they have pretty much dropped out of the strategic debates. But this picture of limited nuclear war is worked out in graphic detail in a novel by Joe Haldeman (*The Forever War*, New York, 1974), where the fighting goes on not at sea but in outer space. Many of the strategic speculations of the 1950s and 1960s have ended up as science fiction. Does this mean that the strategists had too much imagination or that the authors of science fiction have too little?

would include many if not most of the people for whose defense the war was being fought; and the number of people killed in individual actions would be disproportionate (under the doctrine of double effect) to the value of the military targets directly attacked. "The disproportion between the cost of such hostilities and the results they could achieve," wrote Raymond Aron, thinking of a limited nuclear war in Europe, "would be colossal."[12] It would be colossal even if the formal limits on targeting were in fact observed. But the second argument against limited nuclear war is that these limits would almost certainly not be observed.

At this point, of course, one can only guess at the possible shape and course of the battles; there is no history to study. Neither moralists nor strategists can refer to cases; instead they design scenarios. The scene is empty; one can fill it in very different ways, and it is not impossible to imagine that limits might be maintained even after nuclear weapons had been used in battle. The prospect that they would be maintained and the war extended over time is so frightening to those countries on whose soil such wars are likely to be fought that they have generally opposed the new strategies and insisted upon the threat of massive retaliation. Thus, as André Beaufre has written, "Europeans would prefer to risk general war in an attempt to avoid war altogether rather than have Europe become the theater of operations for limited war."[13] In fact, however, the risks of escalation will be great whatever limits are adopted, simply because of the immense destructive power of the weapons involved. Or rather, there are two possibilities: either nuclear weapons will be held at such low levels that they won't be significantly different from or of greater military utility than conventional explosives, in which case there is no reason to use them at all; or their very use will obliterate the distinction between targets. Once a bomb has been aimed at a military target but has, as a side effect, destroyed a city, the logic of deterrence will require the other side to aim at a city (for the sake of its seriousness and credibility). It is not necessarily the case that every war would become a total war, but the danger of escalation is so great as to preclude the first use of nuclear weapons—except by someone willing to face their final use. "Who would even launch such hostilities," Aron has asked, "unless he was determined to persist to the bitter end?"[14] But such a determination is not imaginable in a sane human being, let alone in a political leader responsible for the safety of his own people; it would involve nothing less than national suicide.

These two factors, the extent even of limited destruction and the dangers of escalation, seem to rule out any sort of nuclear war between the great powers. They probably rule out large-scale conventional war, too, including the particular conventional war about which the strategists of the 1950's and 1960's were most concerned: a Russian invasion of western Europe. "The spectacle of a large Soviet field army crashing across the line into western Europe in the hope *and expectation* that nuclear weapons would not be used against it—thereby putting itself and the USSR totally at risk while leaving the choice of weapons to us—would seem to be hardly worth a second thought . . ."[15] It is important to stress that the bar lies in the totality of the risk: not in the possibility of what the strategists called a "flexible response," finely adjusted to the scope of the attack, but in the stark reality of ultimate horror should the adjustments fail. It may well be that "flexible response" enhanced the value of a counter-population deterrent by making it possible to reach that final point in "easy" stages, but it is also and more importantly true that we have never begun the staged escalation and are never likely to begin it, because of what lies at the end. Hence the persistence of counter-population deterrence, and hence also the virtual end of the strategic debate, which petered out in the middle 1960s. At that point, I think, it became clear that given the existence of large numbers of nuclear weapons and their relative invulnerability, and barring major technological breakthroughs, *any imaginable strategy* is likely to deter a "central war" between the great powers. The strategists helped us to understand this, but once it was understood it became unnecessary to adopt any of their strategies—or at least, any particular one of them. We continue to live, then, with the paradox that pre-existed the debate: nuclear weapons are politically and militarily unusable only because and insofar as we can plausibly threaten to use them in some ultimate way. And it is immoral to make threats of that kind.

The Argument of Paul Ramsey

Before deciding (or refusing) to live with this paradox, I want to consider in some detail the work of the Protestant theologian Paul Ramsey, who has over a period of years argued that there exists a justifiable deterrent strategy. From the beginning of the moral and strategic debates, Ramsey has been a sharp opponent of the advocates of counter-city deterrence and also of those of its critics who think that it is the only form of deterrence and therefore opt for nuclear disarmament. He has condemned both these groups for the all-or-nothing character of their thinking: either total and immoral destruction or a kind of "pacifistic" inertia. He argues that these twin perspectives conform to the traditional American view of war as an all-out conflict, which must therefore be avoided whenever possible. Ramsey himself, I think, is a Protestant soldier in a different tradition; he would have Americans gird themselves for a long, continuous struggle with the forces of evil.[16]

Now if there is to be a justified deterrent strategy, there must be a justified form of nuclear war, and Ramsey has conscientiously argued "the case for making just war possible" in the modern age. He takes a lively and well-informed interest in the strategic debates and has at various times defended the use of tactical nuclear weapons against invading armies and of strategic weapons against nuclear installations, conventional military bases, and isolated economic objectives. Even these targets are only "conditionally" permissible, since the proportionality rule would have to be applied in each case, and Ramsey does not believe that its standards will always be met. Like everyone (or almost everyone) who writes about these matters, he has no zest for nuclear combat; his main interest is in deterrence. But he needs at least the possibility of legitimate warfare if he is to maintain a deterrent posture without making immoral threats. That is his central purpose, and the effort to achieve it involves him in a highly sophisticated application of just war theory to the problems of nuclear strategy. In the best sense of the word, Ramsey is engaged with the realities of his world. But the realities in this case are intractable, and his way around them is finally too complex and too devious to provide a plausible account of our moral judgments. He multiplies distinctions like a Ptolemaic astronomer with his epicycles and comes very close at the end to what G. E. M. Anscombe has called "double-think about double effect."[17] But his work is important; it suggests the outer limits of the just war and the dangers of trying to extend those limits.

Ramsey's central claim is that it is possible to prevent nuclear attack without threatening to bomb cities in response. He believes that "the collateral civilian damage that would result from counter-force warfare in its maximum form" would be sufficient to deter potential aggressors.[18] Since the civilians likely to die in such a war would be the incidental victims of legitimate military strikes, the threat of counter-force warfare plus collateral damage is also morally superior to deterrence in its present form. These are not hostages whom we intend to murder (under certain circumstances). Nor are we planning their deaths; we are only pointing out to our possible enemies the unavoidable consequences even of a war justly fought—which is, we could honestly say were we to adopt Ramsey's proposal, the only sort of war we were preparing to fight. Collateral damage is simply a fortunate feature of nuclear warfare; it serves no military purpose, and we would avoid it if we could, though it is clearly a good thing that we cannot. And since the damage is justifiable in prospect, it is also justifiable here and now to call that prospect to mind for the sake of its deterrent effects.

But there are two problems with this argument. First, the danger of collateral damage is unlikely to work as a deterrent unless the damage expected is radically disproportionate to the ends of the war or the value of this or that military target. Hence Ramsey is driven to argue that "the threat of something disproportionate is not always a disproportionate threat."[19] What that means is this: proportionality in combat is measured, let's say, against the value of a particular missile base, while proportionality in deterrence is measured against the value of world peace. So the damage may not be justifiable in prospect (under the doctrine of double effect), and yet the threat of such damage may still be morally permitted. Perhaps that argument is right, but I should stress that its result is to void the proportionality rule. Now there is no limit on the number of people whose deaths we can threaten, so long as those deaths are to be caused "collaterally" and not by taking direct aim. As we have seen before, the idea of proportionality, once it is worked on a bit, tends to fade away. And then the entire burden of Ramsey's argument falls on the idea of death by indirection. That is indeed an important idea, central to the permissions and restraints of conventional war. But its standing is undermined here by the fact that Ramsey relies so heavily on the deaths he supposedly doesn't intend. He wants, like other deterrent theorists, to prevent nuclear attack by threatening to kill very large numbers of innocent civilians, but unlike other deterrent theorists, he expects to kill these people without aiming at them. That may be a matter of some moral significance, but it does not seem significant enough to serve as the cornerstone of a justified deterrent. If counter-force warfare had no collateral effects, or had minor and controllable effects, then it could play no part in Ramsey's strategy. Given the effects it does have and the central part it is assigned, the word "collateral" seems to have lost much of its meaning. Surely anyone designing such a strategy must accept moral responsibility for the effects on which he is so radically dependent.

But we have not yet seen the whole of Ramsey's design, for he doesn't pull back from the hardest questions. What if the likely collateral damage of a just nuclear war isn't great enough to deter a would-be aggressor? What if the aggressor threatens a counter-city strike? Surrender would be intolerable, and yet we cannot ourselves threaten mass murder in response. Fortunately (again), we don't have to. "We do not need . . . to threaten that we will use [nuclear weapons] in case of attack," Bernard Brodie has written. "We do not need to threaten anything. Their being there is quite enough."[20] So it is, too, according to Ramsey, with counter-city strikes: the mere possession of nuclear weapons constitutes an implicit threat which no one actually has to make. If the immorality lies in uttering the threat, then it may in practice be avoided—though one may wonder at the ease of this solution. Nuclear weapons, Ramsey writes, have a certain inherent ambiguity: "they may be used either against strategic forces or against centers of population," and that means that "*apart from intention,* their capacity to deter cannot be removed from them . . . No matter how often we declare, and quite sincerely declare, that our targets are an enemy's forces, he can never be quite *certain* that in the fury or the fog of war his cities may not be destroyed."[21] Now, the possession of conventional weapons is both innocent and ambiguous in exactly the way Ramsey suggests. The fact that I am holding a sword or a rifle doesn't mean that I am going to use it against innocent people, though it is quite effective against them; it has the same "dual use" that Ramsey has discovered in nuclear weapons. But the bomb is different. In a sense, as Beaufre has said, it isn't designed for war at all.[22] It is designed to kill whole populations, and its deterrent value depends upon that fact (whether the killing is direct or indirect). It serves the purpose of preventing war only by virtue of the implicit threat it poses, and we possess it for the sake of that purpose. And men and women are responsible for the threats they live by, even if they don't speak them out loud.

Ramsey presses on. Perhaps the mere possession of nuclear weapons won't be enough to deter some reckless aggressor. Then, he suggests, we must distinguish "between the appearance and the actuality of being . . . committed to go to city exchanges . . . In that case, only the appearance should be cultivated."[23] I am not sure exactly what that means, and Ramsey (for once) seems reluctant to say, but presumably it would allow us to hint at the possibility of massive retaliation without actually planning for it or intending to carry it out. Thus we are offered a continuum of increasing moral danger along which four points are marked out:

the articulated prospect of collateral (and disproportionate) civilian deaths; the implicit threat of counter-city strikes; the "cultivated" appearance of a commitment to counter-city strikes; and the actual commitment. These may well be distinct points, in the sense that one can imagine policies focused around each of them, and these would be different policies. But I am inclined to doubt that the differences make a difference. To rule out the last for moral reasons, while permitting the first three, can only make people cynical about one's moral reasons. Ramsey aims to clear our intentions without prohibiting those policies that he believes necessary (and that probably are necessary under present conditions) for the dual prevention of war and conquest. But the unavoidable truth is that all these policies rest ultimately on immoral threats. Unless we give up nuclear deterrence, we cannot give up such threats, and it is best if we straightforwardly acknowledge what it is we are doing.

The real ambiguity of nuclear deterrence lies in the fact that no one, including ourselves, can be sure that we will ever carry out the threats we make. In a sense, all we ever do is to "cultivate the appearance." We strain for credibility, but what we are putatively planning and intending remains incredible. As I have already suggested, that helps make deterrence psychologically bearable, and perhaps also it makes a deterrent posture marginally better from a moral standpoint. But at the same time, the reason for our hesitancy and self-doubt is the monstrous immorality that our policy contemplates, an immorality we can never hope to square with our understanding of justice in war. Nuclear weapons explode the theory of just war. They are the first of mankind's technological innovations that are simply not encompassable within the familiar moral world. Or rather, our familiar notions about *jus in bello* require us to condemn even the threat to use them. And yet there are other notions, also familiar, having to do with aggression and the right of self-defense, that seem to require exactly that threat. So we move uneasily beyond the limits of justice for the sake of justice (and of peace).

According to Ramsey, this is a dangerous move. For if we "become convinced," he writes, "that in the matter of deterrence a number of things are wicked which are not," then, seeing no way of avoiding wickedness, we will "set no limits on it."[24] Once again, this argument is precisely right with reference to conventional warfare; it catches the central error of what I have called the "war is hell" doctrine. But it is persuasive in the case of nuclear warfare only if one can describe plausible and morally significant limits, and that Ramsey has not done; nor have the strategists of "flexible response" been able to do it. All their arguments depend upon the ultimate wickedness of counter-city strikes. The pretense that this is not so carries with it dangers of its own. To draw insignificant lines, to maintain the formal categories of double effect, collateral damage, noncombatant immunity, and so on, when so little moral content remains is to corrupt the argument for justice as a whole and to render it suspect even in those areas of military life to which it properly pertains. And those areas are wide. Nuclear deterrence marks their outer limits, forcing us to contemplate wars that can never be fought. Within those limits there are wars that can and will and perhaps even should be fought, and to which the old rules apply with all their force. The specter of a nuclear holocaust does not invite us to act wickedly in conventional wars. Indeed, it probably is a deterrent there, too; it is hard to imagine a repetition of Dresden or Tokyo in a conventional war between nuclear powers. For destruction on such a scale would invite a nuclear response and a drastic and unacceptable escalation of the struggle.

Nuclear war is and will remain morally unacceptable, and there is no case for its rehabilitation. Because it is unacceptable, we must seek out ways to prevent it, and because deterrence is a bad way, we must seek out others. It is not my purpose here to suggest what the alternatives might look like. I have been more concerned to acknowledge that deterrence itself, for all its criminality, falls or may fall for the moment under the standard of necessity. But as with terror bombing, so here with the threat of terrorism: supreme emergency is never a stable position. The realm of necessity is subject to historical change. And, what is more important, we are under an obligation to seize upon opportunities of escape, even to take risks for the sake of such opportunities. So the readiness to murder is balanced, or should be, by the readiness not to murder, not to threaten murder, as soon as alternative ways to peace can be found.

PART FIVE

THE QUESTION OF
RESPONSIBILITY

18

The Crime of Aggression: Political Leaders and Citizens

The assignment of responsibility is the critical test of the argument for justice. For if war is fought not under the aegis of necessity but, most often, of freedom, then soldiers and statesmen have to make choices that are sometimes moral choices. And if they do that, it must be possible to single them out for praise and blame. If there are recognizable war crimes, there must be recognizable criminals. If there is such a thing as aggression, there must be aggressors. It is not the case that for every violation of human rights in wartime we can name a guilty person or group of persons. The conditions of war supply a plethora of excuses: fear, coercion, ignorance, even madness. But the theory of justice should point us to the men and women from whom we can rightly demand an accounting, and it should shape and control the judgments we make of the excuses they offer (or that are offered on their behalf). It does not point to people by their proper names, of course, but by their offices and circumstances. We learn the names (sometimes) only as we work our way through cases, attending to the details of moral and military action. Insofar as we name the right names, or at least insofar as our assignments and judgments are in accordance with the actual experience of war, sensitive to all its painfulness, the argument for justice is greatly strengthened. There can be no justice in war if there are not, ultimately, responsible men and women.

The question here is of moral responsibility; we are concerned with the blameworthiness of individuals, not their legal guilt or innocence. Much of the debate about aggression and war crimes, however, has focused on the latter issue, not the former. And as we read through these arguments, or listen to them, it often seems that what is being said is this: that if an individual is not legally liable for some particular act or omission but, as it were, merely immoral, not much can usefully be said about his guilt. For legal liability is a matter of definite rules, well-known procedures, and authoritative judges, while morality is nothing more than endless talk, where every talker has an equal right to his opinions. Consider, for example, the view of a contemporary law professor who believes that the "essentials" of "the question of war crimes" can be set forth "with tolerable clarity and brevity," so long as one caveat is accepted: "I shall make no attempt to say what is immoral— not because I believe morality unimportant, but because my views on it are entitled to no more weight than Jane Fonda's or Richard M. Nixon's, or yours."[1] Of course, morality *is* unimportant if all opinions are equal, because then no particular opinion has any force. Moral authority is no doubt different from legal authority; it is earned in different ways; but Professor Bishop is wrong to think that it doesn't exist. It has to do with the capacity to evoke commonly accepted principles in persuasive ways and to apply them to particular cases. No one can argue about justice and war, as I have been doing, without striving for an authoritative voice and laying claim to a certain "weightiness."

Moral argument is especially important in wartime because— as I have said before, and as Bishop's "brevity" makes clear—the laws of war are radically incomplete. Authoritative judges are rarely called to the business of judging. Indeed, there are often prudential reasons for not calling them, for even well-wrought judicial decisions are likely at certain moments in the history of international society to be understood only as acts of cruelty and vengeance. Trials like those that took place at Nuremberg after World War II seem to me both defensible and necessary; the law must provide some recourse when our deepest moral values are savagely attacked. But such trials by no means exhaust the field of judgment. We have more to do in these matters, and it is my purpose to do it here: to point at criminals and possible criminals across the whole range of wartime activity, though not to suggest, except tangentially, how we should deal with such people.[2] What is crucial is that they can be pointed at; we know where to look for them, if we are ready to look.

The World of Officials

I will begin with the assignments and judgments that are required by the crime of war itself. That is to begin with politics rather than combat, civilians rather than soldiers, for aggression is first of all the work of political leaders. We must (naively) imagine them sitting around the elegant table of an old-fashioned chancellery or in the electronic fastness of a modern command room plotting illegitimate attacks, conquests, interventions. No doubt it is not always like that, though recent history provides ample evidence of direct and open criminal planning. "Statesmen" are more devious, aiming at war only indirectly, like Bismarck in 1870, and taking a very complicated view of their own efforts. Then it is not easy, perhaps, to mark out aggressors, though I think we should start with the assumption that it is always possible. The men and women who lead their people into war owe them and us an accounting. For every person who is killed, every drop of blood that falls is

.... a sore complaint
Gainst him whose wrongs gives edge unto the swords.

Listening to the excuses and lies, and also to the true accounts, of political leaders, we search for the "wrongs" that lie behind the fighting and are its moral cause.

The lawyers have not always encouraged this search. Until very recently, at least, they have held that "acts of state" cannot be the crimes of individual persons. The legal reasons for this denial lie in the theory of sovereignty, as it was once understood. Sovereign states by definition know no superiors, it was argued, and accept no external judgments: hence there is no way to prove the criminality of acts imputed to the state, that is, carried out by recognized authorities in the course of their official duties (unless domestic law provides procedures for bringing such proof to bear).[3] This argument is without moral effect, however, for in this regard states were never morally but only legally sovereign. All of us are capable of judging the acts of political leaders, and we commonly do so. Nor does legal sovereignty any longer provide protection against external judgments. Here Nuremberg is the decisive precedent.

But there is another, more informal version of the "act of state" doctrine, which refers not to the sovereignty of the political community but to the representativeness of its leaders. We are often urged not to condemn the acts of statesmen, or not to be too quick to condemn them, since, after all, these people are not acting selfishly or for private reasons. They are, as Townsend Hoopes wrote of America's leaders during the Vietnam war, "struggling in good conscience . . . to serve the broad national interest according to their lights."[4] They are acting for the sake of other people and in their name. The same assertion can be made on behalf of military officers, except when the crimes they commit are passionate or selfish. It might be made, too, on behalf of revolutionary militants who kill innocent people for the sake of the cause (not because of any personal grudge), even though the cause has no official but only a putative connection to the national interest. These are leaders, too; they may have risen to their "offices" by means not all that different from those adopted by more conventional officials, and they can sometimes say that acts of the movement or the revolution are as representative as acts of state. If this argument is acceptable in the case of statesmen and officers, I can see no reason to reject it in the case of revolutionaries. But it is a bad argument in all these cases, for it is false to suggest that representative functions are morally risk-free. They are instead peculiarly risky, precisely because statesmen, officers, and revolutionaries act for other people and with wide-ranging effects. They act sometimes so as to endanger the people they represent, sometimes so as to endanger the rest of us; they can hardly complain if we hold them subject to moral judgment.

Political power is a good that people seek. They aspire to office, connive at control and leadership, compete for positions from which they can do evil as well as good. If they hope to be praised for the good they do, they cannot escape blame for the evil. Still, blame is always resented, even when we may think it well-deserved, and it is important to try to say why this is so. Moral criticism goes very deep; it calls into question a leader's good faith and his personal rectitude. Since political leaders are rarely cynical about their work, and can never afford to appear to be cynical, they take such criticism seriously and dislike it intensely. Disagreement they can accept (if they are democratic leaders), but not accusations of criminality. Indeed, they are likely to treat all moral criticism as an illegitimate displacement of political controversy. I suppose they are right to recognize that morality is often a mask for politics. The case is the same with the law. Legal accusation can be a very powerful form of political attack, but though it is often used in that way, and often degraded in the use, it remains true nevertheless that political leaders are bound by the legal code and can rightly be charged and punished for criminal acts. Similarly with the moral code: though the terms of praise and blame are universally available and often misused, the code is still binding, and praise and blame are at least sometimes appropriate. The misuse of law and morality is common in wartime, and so we have to be careful not only in punishing political leaders for the wars they wage but also in stigmatizing them. They have no *a priori* claim to escape the stigma of aggression, however, when they violate the rights of another people and force its soldiers to fight.

Acts of state are also acts of particular persons, and when they take the form of aggressive war, particular persons are criminally responsible. Just who those persons are, and how many they are, is not always apparent. But it makes sense to begin with the head of state (or the effective head) and the men and women immediately around him, who actually control the government and make key decisions. Their accountability is clear, like that of the commanders of a military campaign for the strategy and tactics they adopt, for they are the source rather than the recipients of superior orders. When they defend themselves, they don't look up the political hierarchy, but across the battleline: they blame their opponents for forcing *them* to fight. They point to the intricate complexity of the pre-war maneuvering and to the extravagant demands and harassing actions of their adversaries. They have long stories to tell:[5]

> Who first attacked? Who turned the other cheek?
> Aggression perpetrated is as soon
> Denied, and insult rubbed into the injury
> By cunning agents trained in these affairs,
> With whom it's touch-and-go, don't tread-on-me,
> I-dare-you-to, keep-off, and kiss-my-hand.
> Tempers could sharpen knives, and do; we live
> In states provocative.

In order to work our way through the claims and counter-claims, we need a theory such as I have attempted to set forth in Part Two of this book. Often enough, despite the cunning agents, the theory is readily applied. It is worth setting down some of the cases about which we have, I think, no doubts: the German attack on Belgium in 1914, the Italian conquest of Ethiopia, the Japanese attack on China, the German and Italian interventions in Spain, the Russian invasion of Finland, the Nazi conquests of Czechoslovakia, Poland, Denmark, Belgium, and Holland, the Russian invasions of Hungary and Czechoslovakia, the Egyptian challenge to Israel in 1967, and so on—the twentieth century makes for easy listing. I have argued that the American war in Vietnam belongs to the same series. Sometimes, no doubt, the going is more muddy; political leaders are not always in control of their own provocations, and wars do break out without anyone planning or intending to violate anyone else's rights. But insofar as we can recognize aggression, there should be little difficulty in blaming heads of state. The hard and interesting problems arise when we ask how responsibility for aggression is diffused though a political system.

At Nuremberg, the crime of aggression ("crime against peace") was said to involve "the planning, preparation, initiation, and waging of [aggressive] war." These four activities were distinguished from the planning and prepartion of particular military campaigns and from the actual fighting of the war, which were (rightly) held to be noncriminal in character. Now, "planning, preparation, initiation, and waging" would appear to be the work of a fairly large number of people. But in fact the courts restricted the range of accountability so that convictions were obtained only against those officials who were part of "Hitler's inner circle of advisors" or who played such a major role in the making or execution of policy that their protests and refusals would have had a significant impact.[6] Persons lower down the bureaucratic hierarchy, though their contribution was cumulatively significant, were not held individually responsible. It is not at all clear, however, just where we should draw that line; nor is it clear that we ought to assign blame in the same way as we assign legal culpability. The best way to deal with these issues is to turn immediately to a critical case.

Nuremberg: "The Ministries Case"

In an important article on responsibility for crimes of war, Sanford Levinson has analyzed the Nuremberg verdicts, focusing especially on the trial of Ernst von Weizsaecker, who was State

Secretary of the German Foreign Ministry from 1938 to 1943, second only to von Ribbentrop (one of the "inner circle") in the foreign policy hierarchy. I want to follow Levinson's account, and then draw some conclusions from it. Von Weizsaecker was charged with crimes against the peace and initially convicted, but the conviction was reversed upon review. His defense emphasized two points: first, that he took no part in actual policy planning, and secondly, that within the Foreign Ministry he opposed Nazi aggression; he was also involved, at least marginally, in underground opposition to Hitler's regime. The review court accepted this defense, emphasizing its second part: von Weizsaecker's diplomatic activity, which "aided and abetted" German war plans, was so important that it would have been held against him had he not criticized Hitler's policies within his ministry and passed information to more active opponents outside. Thus the line of criminal responsibility was drawn so as to include officials like von Weizsaecker, while he himself was acquitted because, though he clearly played a part in "preparing" an aggressive war, he also "opposed and objected to" that war.

The prosecution argued the insufficiency of this opposition: since he knew of plans for aggression, it was said, he had a positive duty to reveal those plans to the potential victims. But the court rejected this argument because of the risks such action would have entailed and also because it might have led to greater German losses on the battlefield.[7]

> One may quarrel with, and oppose to the point of violence and assassination, a tyrant whose programs mean the ruin of one's country. But the time has not yet arrived when any man would view with satisfaction the ruin of his own people and the loss of its young manhood. To apply any other standard of conduct is to set up a test that has never yet been suggested as proper and which, assuredly, we are not prepared to accept as either wise or good.

This is too strong, I think, for it is obviously not a question of "viewing with satisfaction" the battle losses of one's own side. One might be greatly saddened by them and still feel it morally right to protect the innocent people of the victim state. And surely we would think it both wise and good, indeed heroic, had some German opponent of Hitler warned the Danes or the Belgians or the Russians of the coming attacks. But there is probably no legal or moral obligation to act in this way. Not only the risk but also the inner pain that a man might feel at such a time is more than we require. On the other hand, von Weizsaecker's alternative actions, though they satisfied the judges, may have amounted to less than we require. For he continued to serve the regime whose policies he disapproved; he did not resign.

The issue of resignation came up more directly in connection with charges that von Weizsaecker was guilty of war crimes and crimes against humanity, the latter relating to the extermination of the Jews. Here, too, he argued "that minimal participation should be negated by the fact that he opposed what was being done." But in this case, intra-office opposition was not deemed sufficient. The SS had formally requested the Foreign Ministry's opinions in regard to its policy on the Jewish question. And von Weizsaecker, though he knew what that policy was, had voiced no objections. Apparently he thought his silence the price of his office, and he wanted to retain his office so that he "might be in a position to initiate or aid in attempts to negotiate peace" and so that he might continue to pass on information to Hitler's underground opponents. But the court held that "One cannot give consent to . . . the commission of murder because by so doing he hopes eventually to be able to rid society of the chief murderer. The first is a crime of imminent actuality while the second is but a future hope." The court did not believe that failure to resign was itself a matter of criminal liability. While it might be true that no "decent man could continue to hold office under a regime which carried out . . . wholesale barbarities of this kind," indecency is not a crime. But to hold office and keep silent was a punishable offense, and von Weizsaecker was sentenced to seven years in prison.[8]

Now, the criteria of "significant contribution" or the possibility of "significant protest" seem entirely appropriate in deciding upon trial and punishment. The standards of blame, however, are much more strict: we need to say more about indecency. If von Weizsaecker was bound to resign in protest, I don't see why lesser officials with similar knowledge were not similarly bound. In the United States during the Vietnam years, only a very small number of foreign policy officials resigned, most of them holding low-level positions, but those resignations were morally heartening (to those of us, at least, who knew their reasons) in a way which suggests that they should have been imitated.[9] The courage required to resign in Germany in the late 1930s or early 1940s was far greater than that required in the U.S. three decades later, where opposition to the war was public and vociferous. But it was not a death-defying courage that was necessary even in Germany, but something less, well within the reach of ordinary people. Many officials who failed to resign offered excuses for not doing so, which suggests that they recognized the imperative, however dimly. These excuses were mostly like von Weizsaecker's, focused on distant goods. But there were also men who remained in office in order to engage, often at great personal risk, in concrete and immediate acts of benevolence or sabotage. The most extraordinary of these was the SS lieutenant Kurt Gerstein, whose case has been carefully documented by Saul Friedlander.[10]

> Gerstein represented the type of man who, by virtue of his deepest convictions, disavowed the Nazi regime, even hated it inwardly, but collaborated with it in order to combat it from within and to prevent worse things from happening.

I cannot retell Gerstein's story here; it is enough to say that it demonstrates that it was possible to live a moral life even in the SS, though at a cost in personal agony (Gerstein eventually committed suicide) which we can expect few people to pay. Resignation is much easier, and sometimes, I think, we must take it as the minimal sign of moral decency.

Von Weizsaecker's case invites us to reflect on one further problem. The State Secretary was a diplomat who carried out negotiations with foreign countries under instructions from his superiors. But he was also an advisor to those superiors; his own views were frequently requested. Now advisors are in a curious position with regard to both legal and moral judgment. Their most important advice is often given orally, whispered in the ruler's ear. What is written down may be incomplete, tailored to the requirements of bureaucratic correspondence. We miss the nuances and qualifications, the subtle signs of doubt, the private emphases and hesitations. If sufficient documentation is available, we may go ahead and make judgments anyway. It's certainly not the case that only "line" and never "staff" officals can be held responsible for decisions made. But whispering in the ruler's ear is problematic; it is easier to suggest what should be said than what we should do if we suspect that it hasn't been said.

What von Weizsaecker said was probably insufficient, for according to his own account he urged nothing more than the likelihood of German defeat; his opposition to Hitler's policies were always expressed in expediential terms.[11] Perhaps those were the only terms likely to be effective in Germany during those years. That is probably true in other cases, too, even with governments less openly committed to a program of conquest. But it is often important to use the language of morality, if only to break through the forms of euphemism and silence with which officials conceal even from themselves the extent and nature of the crimes they are committing. Sometimes the best way for an advisor to say no is simply to give an accurate name to the policy he is being asked to approve. This point is beautifully made in a speech in Shakespeare's *King John*. With hints and indirection, John had ordered the murder of his nephew Arthur, Duke of Brittany. Later he came to regret the murder and turned on his courtier, Hubert de Burgh, who had carried it out.[12]

> Hadst thou but shook thy head or made a pause
> When I spoke darkly what I purposed,
> Or turned an eye of doubt upon my face,
> As bid me tell my tale in express words,
> Deep shame had struck me dumb, made me break off . . .
> But thou didst understand me by my signs,
> And didst in signs again parley with sin;
> Yea, without stop, didst let thy heart consent,
> And consequently thy rude hand to act,
> The deed which both our tongues held vile to name.

The speech is hypocritical, but it captures the common quality of bureaucratic acquiescence, and it suggests very forcefully that advisors and agents, when they have the opportunity, must speak out "in express words," using the moral language that we all know. They may be judged insufficiently tough or hard-headed if they talk that way. But to be "tough" enough to carry out policies that are literally unmentionable is either to be very cowardly or very wicked.

Democratic Responsibilities

What about the rest of us—citizens, let's say, of a state engaged in an aggressive war? Collective responsibility is a hard notion, though it is worth stressing at once that we have fewer problems with collective punishment. Resistance to aggression is itself "punishing" to the aggressor state and is often described in those terms. With reference to the actual fighting, as I have already argued, civilians on both sides are innocent, equally innocent, and never legitimate military targets. They are, however, political and economic targets once the war is over; that is, they are the victims of military occupation, political reconstruction, and the exaction of reparative payments. We may take the last of these as the clearest and simplest case of collective punishment. Reparations are surely due the victims of aggressive war, and they can hardly be collected only from those members of the defeated state who were active supporters of the aggression. Instead, the costs are distributed through the tax system, and through the economic system generally, among all the citizens, often over a period of time extending to generations that had nothing to do with the war at all.[13] In this sense, citizenship is a common destiny, and no one, not even its opponents (unless they become political refugees, which has its costs, too) can escape the effects of a bad regime, an ambitious or fanatic leadership, or an overreaching nationalism. But if men and women must accept this destiny, they can sometimes do so with a good conscience, for the acceptance says nothing about their individual responsibility. The distribution of costs is not the distribution of guilt.

At least one writer has tried to argue that political destiny is a kind of guilt: existential, unavoidable, frightening. For the soldier or citizen of a state at war, writes J. Glenn Gray in his philosophical memoir of World War II, is the member of a "coarse, vulgar, heedless, and violent" community and, willy-nilly, a participant in an enterprise "whose spirit is to win at any cost." He cannot cut himself loose.[14]

> He is bound to reflect that his nation has given him refuge and sustenance, provided him with whatever education and property he calls his own. He belongs and will always belong to it in some sense no matter where he goes or how hard he seeks to alter his inheritance. The crimes, therefore, that his nation or one of its units commits cannot be indifferent to him. He shares the guilt as he shares the satisfaction in the generous deeds and worthy products of nation or army. Even if he did not consciously will them and was unable to prevent them, he cannot wholly escape responsibility for collective deeds.

Maybe; but it is not an easy move from "the ache of guilt," which Gray almost lovingly describes, to hard talk about responsibility. It might be better to say of loyal citizens who watch their government or army (or their comrades in battle) doing terrible things that they feel or should feel ashamed rather than responsible—unless they actually are responsible by virtue of their particular participation or acquiescence. Shame is the tribute we pay to the inheritance that Gray describes. "A burning sense of shame at the deeds of his government and the acts of horror committed by German soldiers and police was the mark of a conscientious German at the close of the war." That is exactly right, but we won't ourselves blame that conscientious German or call him responsible; nor need he blame himself unless there was something he should have done, and could do, in the face of the horror.

Perhaps it can always be said of such a person that he could have done more than he did do. Certainly conscientious men and women are likely to believe that of themselves; it is a sign of their conscientiousness.[15]

> On this or that occasion he has been silent when he should have spoken out. In his own smaller or larger circle of influence he has not made his whole weight felt. Had he brought forth the civil courage to protest in time, some particular act of injustice might have been avoided.

Such reflections are endless and endlessly dispiriting; they lead Gray to argue that behind collective responsibility there lies "metaphysical guilt," which derives from "our failure as human beings to live in accordance with our potentialities and our vision of the good." But some of us, surely, fail more dismally than others; and it is necessary, with all due caution and humility, to mark out standards by which we can measure the respective failures. Gray suggests the right standard, though he goes on very quickly to insist that we can never apply it to anyone but ourselves. But that kind of self-regard is not possible in politics and morality. Judging ourselves, we necessarily judge other people, with whom we share a common life. And how is it possible to criticize and blame our leaders, as we sometimes must do, without involving their enthusiastic followers (our fellow citizens)? Though responsibility is always personal and particular, moral life is always collective in character.

This is Gray's principle, which I mean to adopt and expound: *"The greater the possibility of free action in the communal sphere, the greater the degree of guilt for evil deeds done in the name of everyone."*[16] The principle invites us to focus our attention on democratic rather than authoritarian regimes. Not that free action is impossible even in the worst of authoritarian regimes; at the very least, people can resign, withdraw, flee. But in democracies there are opportunities for positive response, and we need to ask to what extent these opportunities fix our obligations, when evil deeds are committed in our name.

The Crime of Aggression: Political Leaders and Citizens

The American People and the War in Vietnam

If the argument in chapters 6 and 11 is right, the American war in Vietnam was, first of all, an unjustified intervention, and it was, secondly, carried on in so brutal a manner that even had it initially been defensible, it would have to be condemned, not in this or that aspect but generally. I am not going to re-argue that description, but assume it, so that we can look closely at the responsibility of democratic citizens—and at a particular set of democratic citizens, namely, ourselves.[17]

Democracy is a way of distributing responsibility (just as monarchy is a way of refusing to distribute it). But that doesn't mean that all adult citizens share equally in the blame we assign for aggressive war. Our actual assignments will vary a great deal, depending on the precise nature of the democratic order, the place of a particular person in that order, and the pattern of his own political activities. Even in a perfect democracy, it cannot be said that every citizen is the author of every state policy, though every one of them can rightly be called to account. Imagine, for example, a small community where all the citizens are fully and accurately informed about public business, where all of them participate, argue, vote on matters of communal interest, and where they all take turns holding public office. Now this community, let us say, initiates and wages an unjust war against its neighbors—for the sake of some economic advantage, perhaps, or out of zeal to spread its (admirable) political system. There is no question of self-defense; no one has attacked it or is planning to do so. Who is responsible for this war? Surely all those men and women who voted for it and who cooperated in planning, initiating, and waging it. The soldiers who do the actual fighting are not responsible as soldiers; but as citizens, they are, assuming that they were old enough to have shared in the decision to fight.* All of them are

---

* Why aren't they responsible as soldiers? If they are morally bound to vote against the war, why aren't they also bound to refuse to fight? The answer is that they vote as individuals, each one deciding for himself, but they fight as members of the political community, the collective decision having already been made, subject to all the moral and material pressures that I described in chapter 3. They act very well if they refuse to fight, and we should honor those—they are likely to be few—who have the self-certainty and courage to stand against their fellows. I have argued elsewhere that democracies ought to respect such people and ought certainly to tolerate their refusals. (See the essay on "Conscientious Objection" in *Obligations*.) That doesn't mean, however, that the others can be called criminals. Patri-

guilty of the crime of aggressive war and of no lesser charge, and we would not hesitate in such a case to blame them publicly. Nor would it make any difference whether their motive was economic selfishness or a political zeal that appeared to them entirely disinterested. Either way, the blood of their victims would complain against them.

Those who voted against the war or who refused to cooperate in the waging of it could not be blamed. But what would we think of a group of citizens that didn't vote? Had they voted, let's say, the war might have been avoided, but they were lazy, didn't care, or were afraid to come down on one side or the other of a hotly disputed issue. The day of the crucial decision was a day off from work; they spent it in their gardens. I am inclined to say that they are blameworthy, though they are not guilty of aggressive war. Surely those of their fellow citizens who went to the assembly and opposed the war can blame them for their indifference and inaction. This seems a clear counter-example to Gray's assertion that "No citizen of a free land can justly accuse his neighbor . . . of not having done as much as he should to prevent the state of war or the commission of this or that state crime. But each can . . . accuse himself . . ."[18] In a perfect democracy, we would know a great deal about one another's duties, and just accusations would not be impossible.

Imagine now that the minority of citizens that was defeated could have won (and prevented the war) if instead of merely voting, they had held meetings outside the assembly, marched and demonstrated, organized for a second vote. Let's assume that none of this would have been terribly dangerous to them, but they chose not to take these measures because their opposition to the war wasn't all that strong; they thought it unjust but were not horrified by the prospect; they hoped for a quick victory; and so on. Then they are blameworthy, too, though to a lesser degree than those slothful citizens who did not even bother to go to the assembly.

These last two examples resemble the good samaritan cases in domestic society, where we commonly say that if it is possible to do good, without risk or great cost, one ought to do good.

___

otism may be the last refuge of scoundrels, but it is also the ordinary refuge of ordinary men and women, and it requires of us another sort of toleration. But we should expect opponents of the war to refuse to become officers or officials, even if they feel bound to share combat risks with their countrymen.

The Crime of Aggression: Political Leaders and Citizens

But when the issue is war, the obligation is stronger, for it is not a question of doing good, but of preventing serious harm, and harm that will be done in the name of my own political community—hence, in some sense, in my own name. Here, assuming still that the community is a perfect democracy, it looks as if a citizen is blameless only if he takes back his name. I don't think this means that he must become a revolutionary or an exile, actually renouncing his citizenship or loyalty. But he must do all he can, short of accepting frightening risks, to prevent or stop the war. He must withdraw his name from this act (the war policy) though not necessarily from every communal action, for he may still value, as he probably should, the democracy he and his fellow citizens have achieved. This, then, is the meaning of Gray's maxim: the more one can do, the more one has to do.

We can now drop the myth of perfection and paint a more realistic picture. The state that goes to war is, like our own, an enormous state, governed at a great distance from its ordinary citizens by powerful and often arrogant officials. These officials, or at least the leading among them, are chosen through democratic elections, but at the time of the choice very little is known about their programs and commitments. Political participation is occasional, intermittent, limited in its effects, and it is mediated by a system for the distribution of news which is partially controlled by those distant officials and which in any case allows for considerable distortions. It may be that a politics of this sort is the best we can hope for (though I don't believe that) once the political community reaches a certain size. Anyway, it is no longer as easy to impose responsibility as it is in a perfect democracy. One doesn't want to regard those distant officials as if they were kings, but for certain sorts of state action, secretly prepared or suddenly launched, they bear a kind of regal responsibility.

When a state like this commits itself to a campaign of aggression, its citizens (or many of them) are likely to go along, as Americans did during the Vietnam war, arguing that the war may after all be just; that it is not possible for them to be sure whether it is just or not; that their leaders know best and tell them this or that, which sounds plausible enough; and that nothing they can do will make much difference anyway. These are not immoral arguments, though they reflect badly on the society within which they are made. And they can, no doubt, be made too quickly by citizens seeking to avoid the difficulties that might follow if they thought about the war for themselves. These people are or may be blameworthy, not for aggressive war, but for bad faith as citizens. But that is a hard charge to make, for citizenship plays such a small part in their everyday lives. "Free action in the communal sphere" is a possibility for men and women in such a state only in the formal sense that serious governmental restraint, actual repression, doesn't exist. Perhaps it should also be said that the "communal sphere" doesn't exist, for it is only the day-by-day assumption of responsibility that creates that sphere and gives it meaning. Even patriotic excitement, war fever, among such people is probably best understood as a reflex of distance, a desperate identification, stimulated, it may be, by a false account of what is going on. One might say of them what one says of soldiers in combat, that they are not to blame for the war, since it is not their war.*

But as an account of all the citizens, even in such a state, this is certainly exaggerated. For there exists a group of more knowledgeable men and women, members of what political scientists call the foreign policy elites, who are not so radically distanced from the national leadership; and some subset of these people, together with others in touch with them, is likely to form an "opposition" or perhaps even a movement of opposition to the war. It would seem possible to regard the entire group of knowledgeable people as at least potentially blameworthy if that war is aggressive and unless they join the opposition.[19] To say that is to presume upon the knowledge they have and their private sense of political possibility. But if we turn to an actual case of imperfect democracy, like the United States in the late 1960s and early 1970s, the presumption doesn't seem unwarranted. Surely there was knowledge and opportunity enough among the country's elites, the national and local leaders of its political parties, its religious establishments, its corporate hierarchies, and perhaps above all its intellectual teachers and spokesmen—the men and women whom Noam Chomsky has named, in tribute to the role they play in contemporary government, "the new mandarins."[20] Surely many of these people were morally complicitous in our Vietnam aggression. I

---

* But see the note in Anne Frank's *Diary*: "I don't believe that only governments and capitalists are guilty of aggression. Oh no, the little man is just as keen on it, for otherwise the people of the world would have risen in revolt long ago." I'm sure she is right about the keenness, and I don't want to excuse it. But we don't, for all that, call the little men war criminals, and I am trying to explain why we don't. (*The Diary of a Young Girl*, trans. B. M. Mooyaart-Doubleday, New York, 1953, p. 201.)

suppose one can also say of them what many of them have said of themselves: that they were simply mistaken in their judgments of the war, failed to realize this or that, thought that was true when it was not, or hoped for this result which never came about. In moral life generally, one makes allowances for false beliefs, misinformation, and honest mistakes. But there comes a time in any tale of aggression and atrocity when such allowances can no longer be made. I cannot mark out that time here; nor am I interested in pointing at particular people or certain that I can do so. I only want to insist that there are responsible people even when, under the conditions of imperfect democracy, moral accounting is difficult and imprecise.

The real moral burden of the American war fell on that subset of men and women whose knowledge and sense of possibility was made manifest by their oppositional activity. They were the ones most likely to reproach themselves and one another, continually asking whether they were doing enough to stop the fighting, devoting enough time and energy, working hard enough, working as effectively as they could. For most of their fellow citizens, anxious, apathetic, and alienated, the war was merely an ugly or an exciting spectacle (until they were forced to join it). For the dissidents, it was a kind of moral torture—self-torture, as Gray describes it, though they also tortured one another, wastefully, in savage internecine conflicts over what was to be done. And this self-torture bred a kind of self-righteousness vis-a-vis the others, an endemic failing on the Left, though understandable enough under conditions of aggressive war and mass acquiescence. The expression of that self-righteousness, however, is not a useful way to get one's fellow citizens to think seriously about the war or to join the opposition: nor was it useful in this case. It is not easy to know what course of action might serve these purposes. Politics is difficult at such a time. But there is intellectual work to do that is less difficult: one must describe as graphically as one can the moral reality of war, talk about what it means to force people to fight, analyze the nature of democratic responsibilities. These, at least, are encompassable tasks, and they are morally required of the men and women who are trained to perform them. Nor is it dangerous to perform them, in a democratic state, waging war in a distant country. And the citizens of such a state have time to listen and reflect; they, too, are in no immediate danger. War imposes harsher burdens than any these people have to bear—as we shall see when we consider, finally, the moral life of men at arms.

19

War Crimes: Soldiers and Their Officers

We are concerned now with the conduct of war and not its overall justice. For soldiers, as I have already argued, are not responsible for the overall justice of the wars they fight; their responsibility is limited by the range of their own activity and authority. Within that range, however, it is real enough, and it frequently comes into question. "There wasn't a single soldier," says an Israeli officer who fought in the Six Day War, "who didn't at some stage have to decide, to choose, to make a moral decision . . . quick and modern though [the war] was, the soldier was not turned into a mere technician. He had to make decisions that were of real significance."[1] And when faced with decisions of that sort, soldiers have clear obligations. They are bound to apply the criteria of usefulness and proportionality until they come up against the basic rights of the people they are threatening to kill or injure, and then they are bound not to kill or injure them. But judgments about usefulness and proportionality are very difficult for soldiers in the field. It is the doctrine of rights that makes the most effective limit on military activity, and it does so precisely because it rules out calculation and establishes hard and fast standards. Hence in my initial cases I will focus on specific violations of rights and on the defenses that soldiers commonly offer for these violations. The defenses are basically of two sorts. The first refers to the heatedness of battle and the passion or frenzy it engenders. The second refers to the disciplinary system of the army and the obedience it requires. These are serious defenses; they suggest the loss of self that is involved in warfare, and they remind us that most soldiers most of the time have not chosen the combat and discipline they endure. Where is their freedom and responsibility?

But there is a related issue that I must consider before trying to mark out the realm of freedom from the coercions and hysteria of war. The war convention requires soldiers to accept personal risks rather than kill innocent people. This requirement takes different forms in different combat situations, and I have already discussed these in considerable detail; my concern now is with the requirement itself. The rule is absolute: self-preservation in the face of the enemy is not an excuse for violations of the rules of war. Soldiers, it might be said, stand to civilians like the crew of a liner to its passengers. They must risk their own lives for the sake of the others. No doubt this is easy to say, less easy to do. But if the rule is absolute, the risks are not; it is a question of degree; the crucial point is that soldiers cannot enhance their own security at the expense of innocent men and women.* This might be called an obligation of soldiering as an office, but it is a hard question whether one can rightly be said to assume such obligations when one comes into the office as unwillingly as most soldiers do. Imagine a liner manned by kidnapped sailors: would the members of such

---

* Telford Taylor suggests a possible exception to this rule, citing a hypothetical case which has often been discussed in the legal literature. A small detachment of troops on a special mission or cut off from its main force takes prisoners "under such circumstances that men cannot be spared to guard them . . . and that to take them along would greatly endanger the success of the mission or the safety of the unit." The prisoners are likely to be killed, Taylor says, in accordance with the principle of military necessity. (*Nuremberg and Vietnam*, New York, 1970, p. 36.) But if it is only the safety of the unit that is in question (its mission may already have been accomplished), the proper appeal would be to self-preservation. The argument from necessity has not, despite Taylor, been accepted by legal writers; the argument from self-preservation has won greater support. In his military code for the Union Army, for example, Francis Lieber writes that "a commander is permitted to direct his troops to give no quarter . . . when his own salvation makes it impossible to cumber himself with prisoners." (Taylor, p. 36n.) But surely in such a case the prisoners should be disarmed and then released. Even if it is "impossible" to take them along, it is not impossible to set them free. There may be risks in doing that, but these are exactly the sorts of risks soldiers must accept. The risks involved in leaving wounded men behind are of the same sort, but that is not a satisfactory reason for killing them. For a useful discussion of these issues, see Marshall Cohen, "Morality and the Laws of War," in Held, Morgenbesser, and Nagel, eds., *Philosophy, Morality, and International Affairs*, New York, 1974, pp. 76–78.

a crew be bound, as the ship was sinking, to see to the safety of the passengers before seeing to their own?

I am not sure how to answer that question, but there is a crucial difference between the work of coerced crew members and that of military conscripts: the first group is not in the business of sinking ships, the second is. Conscripts impose risks on innocent people; they are themselves the immediate source of the danger and they are its effective cause. And so it is not a question of saving themselves, letting others die, but of killing others in order to improve their own odds. Now that they cannot do, because that no man can do. Their obligation isn't in practice mediated by the office of soldiering. It arises directly from the activity in which they are engaged, whether that activity is voluntary or not, or at least it arises so long as we regard soldiers as moral agents and even if we regard them as coerced moral agents.[2] They are not mere instruments; they do not stand to the army as their weapons do to them. It is precisely because they do (sometimes) choose to kill or not, to impose risks or accept them, that we require them to choose in a certain way. That requirement shapes the whole pattern of their rights and duties in combat. And when they break out of that pattern, it is a matter of some significance that they don't by and large deny the requirement. They claim, instead, that they literally were not able to fulfill it; that they were not at the moment of their "crime," moral agents at all.

In the Heat of Battle

Two Accounts of Killing Prisoners

In his fine memoir of World War I, Guy Chapman tells the following story. After a minor but bloody advance from one line of trenches to the next, he encountered one of his fellow officers, his face "slack and haggard, but not from weariness." Chapman asked him what was wrong.[3]

"Oh, I don't know. Nothing . . . At least . . . Look here, we took a lot of prisoners in those trenches yesterday morning. Just as we got into their line, an officer came out of a dugout. He'd got one hand above his head, and a pair of fieldglasses in the other. He held the glasses out to S_____, . . . and said, 'Here you are, sergeant, I surrender.' S_____ said, 'Thank you, sir,' and took the glasses with his left hand. At the same moment, he tucked the butt of his rifle under his arm and shot the officer straight through his head. What the hell ought I to do?"

"I don't see that you can do anything," I answered slowly. "What can you do? Besides I don't see that S_____'s really to blame. He must have been half mad with excitement by the time he got into that trench. I don't suppose he ever thought what he was doing. If you start a man killing, you can't turn him off like an engine. After all, he is a good man. He was probably half off his head."

"It wasn't only him. Another did exactly the same thing."

"Anyhow, it's too late to do anything now. I suppose you ought to have shot both on the spot. The best thing now is to forget it."

That sort of thing happens often in war, and it is commonly excused. Chapman's argument makes some sense: it is, in effect, a plea of temporary insanity. It suggests a kind of killing frenzy that begins in combat and ends in murder, the line between the two being lost to the mind of the individual soldier. Or it suggests a frenzy of fear such that the soldier cannot recognize the moment when he is no longer in danger. He is not, indeed, a machine that can just be turned off, and it would be inhumanly righteous not to look with sympathy on his plight. And yet, if it is true that enemy soldiers are often killed trying to surrender, it is also true that a relatively small number of men do the "extra" killing. The rest seem ready enough to stop as soon as they can, whatever the state of mind they had worked themselves into during the battle itself. This fact is morally decisive, for it suggests a common acknowledgment of the right to quarter, and it proves that the right can in fact be recognized, since it often is, even in the chaos of combat. It is simply not true of soldiers, as one philosopher has recently written, that "war . . . in some important ways makes psychopaths of them all."[4] The argument has to be more particular than that. When we make allowances for what individual soldiers do "in the heat of battle," it must be because of some knowledge we have that distinguishes these soldiers from the others or their circumstances from the usual ones. Perhaps they have encountered enemy troops who feigned surrender in order to kill their captors: then the war rights of other troops are made problematic in a new way, for one cannot be sure when killing is "extra." Or perhaps they have been under some special strain or have been fighting too long and are near to nervous exhaustion. But there is no general rule that requires us to make allowances, and sometimes, at least, soldiers should be censured or punished for killings that take place after the battle is over (though summary execution is probably not the best form of punishment). They should certainly never be encouraged to believe that a total lack of restraint can be excused merely by reference to the passions that cause it.

There are officers, however, who encourage exactly that belief, not out of compassion but calculation, not because of the heat of the battle but in order to raise the temperature of men in combat. In his novel *The Thin Red Line*, one of the best accounts of jungle fighting in World War II, James Jones tells of another incident of "extra" killing.⁵ He describes a new army unit, its members unblooded and without confidence in their ability to fight. After a hard march through the jungle, they come upon a Japanese position from the rear. There is a brief and savage fight. At a certain point, Japaneses soldiers start trying to surrender, but some of the Americans cannot or will not stop the killing.⁶ Even after the firefight is definitely over, those Japanese who have succeeded in surrendering are brutally treated—by men, so Jones wants to suggest, who are caught up in a kind of intoxication, their inhibitions suddenly gone. The commanding officer watches all this and does nothing. "He did not want to jeopardize the new toughness of spirit that had come over the men after achieving success here. That spirit was more important than whether or not a few Jap soldiers got kicked around or killed."

I suppose that soldiers must be "men of spirit," like Plato's guardians, but Jones' colonel has mistaken the nature of their spiritedness. It is almost certainly true that they fight best when they are most disciplined, when they are most in control of themselves and committed to the restraints appropriate to their trade. "Extra" killing is less a sign of toughness than of hysteria, and hysteria is the wrong kind of spiritedness. But even if the colonel's calculations were correct, he would still be bound to stop the killing if he could, for he cannot train and toughen his men at the expense of Japanese prisoners. He is also bound to act so as to prevent such killings in the future. This is a crucial aspect of what is called "command responsibility," and I will take it up in detail later on. It is important to stress now that it is a large responsibility; for the general policy of the army, expressed through its officers, the climate they create by their day-to-day actions, has far more to do with the incidence of "extra" killing than does the intensity of the actual fighting. But this doesn't mean that individual soldiers must be excused; indeed, it suggests once again that heatedness isn't the issue, but murderousness; and for their own murderousness individuals are always responsible, even when under the conditions of military discipline they are not exclusively so.

War Crimes: Soldiers and Their Officers

It is a feature of criminal responsibility that it can be distributed without being divided. We can, that is, blame more than one person for a particular act without splitting up the blame we assign.[7] When soldiers are shot trying to surrender, the men who do the actual shooting are fully responsible for what they do, unless we recognize particular extenuating circumstances; at the same time, the officer who tolerates and encourages the murders is also fully responsible, if it lay within his power to prevent them. Perhaps we blame the officer more, for his coolness, but I have tried to suggest that combat soldiers, too, should be held to high standards in such matters (and they will surely want their enemies held to high standards). The case looks very different, however, when combatants are actually ordered to take no prisoners or to kill the ones they take or to turn their guns on enemy civilians. Then it is not their own murderousness that is at issue but that of their officers; they can act morally only by disobeying their orders. In such a case, we are likely to divide as well as distribute responsibility: we regard soldiers under orders as men whose acts are not entirely their own and whose liability for what they do is somehow diminished.

Superior Orders

The My Lai Massacre

The incident is infamous and hardly needs retelling. A company of American soldiers entered a Vietnamese village where they expected to encounter enemy combatants, found only civilians, old men, women, and children, and began to kill them, shooting them singly or collecting them in groups, ignoring their obvious helplessness and their pleas for mercy, not stopping until they had murdered between four and five hundred people. Now, it has been argued on behalf of these soldiers that they acted, not in the heat of battle (since there was no battle) but in the context of a brutal and brutalizing war which was in fact, if only unofficially, a war against the Vietnamese people as a whole. In this war, the argument goes on, they had been encouraged to kill without making careful discriminations—encouraged to do so by their own officers and driven to do so by their enemies, who fought and hid among the civilian population.[8] These statements are true, or partly true; and yet massacre is radically different from guerrilla war, even from a guerrilla war brutally fought, and there is considerable evidence that the soldiers at My Lai knew the difference. For while some of them joined in the murders readily enough, as if eager to kill without risk, there were a few who refused to fire their guns and others who had to be ordered to fire two or three times before they could bring themselves to do so. Others simply ran away; one man shot himself in the foot so as to escape the scene; a junior officer tried heroically to stop the massacre, standing between the Vietnamese villagers and his fellow Americans. Many of his fellows, we know, were sick and guilt-ridden in the days that followed. This was not a fearful and frenzied extension of combat, but "free" and systematic slaughter, and those men that participated in it can hardly say that they were caught in the grip of war. They can say, however, that they were following orders, caught in the grip of the United States Army.

The orders of Captain Medina, the company commander, had in fact been ambiguous; at least, the men who heard them could not agree afterwards as to whether or not they had been told to "waste" the inhabitants of My Lai. He is quoted as having told his company to leave nothing living behind them and to take no prisoners: "They're all V.C.'s, now go and get them." But he is also said to have ordered only the killing of "enemies," and when asked, "Who is the enemy?" to have offered the following definition (in the words of one of the soldiers): "anybody that was running from us, hiding from us, or who appeared to us to be the enemy. If a man was running, shoot him; sometimes even if a woman with a rifle was running, shoot her."[9] That is a very bad definition, but it isn't morally insane; barring a loose interpretation of the "appearance" of enmity, it would have excluded most of the people killed at My Lai. Lieutenant Calley, who actually led the unit that entered the village, gave far more specific orders, commanding his men to kill helpless civilians who were neither running nor hiding, let alone carrying rifles, and repeating the command again and again when they hesitated to obey.* The

---

* It may be useful to suggest the sorts of commands that should be issued at such a time. Here is an account of an Israeli unit entering Nablus during the Six Day War: "The battalion CO got on the field telephone to my company and said, 'Don't touch the civilians . . . don't fire until you're fired at and don't touch the civilians. Look, you've been warned. Their blood be on your heads.' In just those words. The boys in the company kept talking about it afterwards . . . They kept repeating the words . . . 'Their blood be on your heads.' " *The Seventh Day: Soldiers Talk About the Six Day War*, London, 1970, p. 132.

army's judicial system singled him out for blame and punishment, though he claimed he was only doing what Medina had ordered him to do. The enlisted men who did what Calley ordered them to do were never charged.

It must be a great relief to follow orders. "Becoming a soldier," writes J. Glenn Gray, "was like escaping from one's own shadow." The world of war is frightening; decisions are difficult; and it is comforting to slough off responsibility and simply do what one is told. Gray reports soldiers insisting on this special kind of freedom: "When I raised my right hand and took the [army oath], I freed myself of the consequences for what I do. I'll do what they tell me and nobody can blame me."[10] Army training encourages this view, even though soldiers are also informed that they must refuse "unlawful" orders. No military force can function effectively without routine obedience, and it is the routine that is stressed. Soldiers are taught to obey even petty and foolish commands. The teaching process has the form of an endless drill, aimed at breaking down their individual thoughtfulness, resistance, hostility, and waywardness. But there is some ultimate humanity that cannot be broken down, the disappearance of which we will not accept. In his play *The Measures Taken*, Bertolt Brecht describes militant communists as "blank pages on which the Revolution writes its instructions."[11] I suppose there are many drill sergeants who dream of a similar blankness. But the description is a false one and the dream a fantasy. It is not that soldiers don't sometimes obey as if they were morally blank. What is crucial is that the rest of us hold them responsible for what they do. Despite their oath, we blame them for the crimes that follow from "unlawful" or immoral obedience.

Soldiers can never be transformed into mere instruments of war. The trigger is always part of the gun, not part of the man. If they are not machines that can just be turned off, they are also not machines that can just be turned on. Trained to obey "without hesitation," they remain nevertheless capable of hesitating. I have already cited examples of refusal, delay, doubt, and anguish at My Lai. These are internal confirmations of our external judgments. No doubt we can make these judgments too quickly, without hesitations and doubts of our own, paying too little attention to the harshness of battle and the discipline of the army. But it is a mistake to treat soldiers as if they were automatons who make no judgments at all. Instead, we must look closely at the particular features of their situation and try to understand what it might mean, in *these* circumstances, at *this* moment, to accept or defy a military command.

The defense of superior orders breaks down into two more specific arguments: the claim of ignorance and the claim of duress. These two are standard legal and moral claims, and they seem to function in war very much as they do in domestic society.[12] It is not the case, then, as has often been argued, that when we judge soldiers we must balance the necessities of military discipline (that obedience be quick and unquestioning) against the requirements of humanity (that innocent people be protected).[13] Rather, we view discipline as one of the conditions of wartime activity, and we take its particular features into account in determining individual responsibility. We do not excuse individuals in order to maintain or strengthen the disciplinary system. The army may cover up the crimes of soldiers or seek to limit liability for them with that end (or that pretended end) in view, but such efforts do not represent the delicate working out of a conception of justice. What justice requires is, first of all, that we commit ourselves to the defense of rights and, second, that we attend carefully to the particular defenses of men who are charged with violating rights.

Ignorance is the common lot of the common soldier, and it makes an easy defense, especially when calculations of usefulness and proportionality are called for. The soldier can plausibly say that he does not know and cannot know whether the campaign in which he is engaged is really required for the sake of victory, or whether it has been designed so as to hold unintended civilian deaths within acceptable limits. From his narrow and confined vantage point, even direct violations of human rights—as in the conduct of a siege, for example, or in the strategy of an anti-guerrilla campaign—may be unseen and unseeable. Nor is he bound to seek out information; the moral life of a combat soldier is not a research assignment. We might say that he stands to his campaigns as to his wars: he is not responsible for their overall justice. When war is fought at a distance, he may not be responsible even for the innocent people he himself kills. Artillery men and pilots are often kept in ignorance of the targets at which their fire is directed. If they ask questions, they are routinely assured that the targets are "legitimate military objectives." Perhaps they should always be skeptical, but I don't think we blame them if they accept the assurances of their commanders. We blame instead the far-seeing commanders. As the example of My Lai suggests, however, the ignorance of common soldiers has its limits. The soldiers in the Vietnamese village could hardly have doubted the innocence of the people they were ordered to kill. It is in such a situation that we want them to disobey: when they receive orders which, as the army judge said at the Calley trial, "a man of ordinary sense and understanding would, under the circumstances, know to be unlawful."[14]

Now, this implies an understanding not only of the circumstances but also of the law, and it was argued at Nuremberg and has been argued since that the laws of war are so vague, uncertain, and incoherent that they can never require disobedience.[15] Indeed, the state of the positive law is not very good, especially where it relates to the exigencies of combat. But the prohibition against massacre is plain enough, and I think it is fair to say that common soldiers have been charged and convicted only for the knowing murder of innocent people: shipwrecked survivors struggling in the water, for example, or prisoners of war, or helpless civilians. Nor is it a question here only of the law, for these are acts that not only "violate unchallenged rules of warfare," as the British field manual of 1944 states, but that also "outrage the general sentiments of humanity."[16] Ordinary *moral* sense and understanding rule out killings like those at My Lai. One of the soldiers there remembers thinking to himself that the slaughter was "just like a Nazi-type thing." That judgment is precisely right, and there is nothing in our conventional morality that renders it doubtful.

But the excuse of duress may hold even in a case like this, if the order to kill is backed up by a threat of execution. I have argued that soldiers in combat cannot plead self-preservation when they violate the rules of war. For the dangers of enemy fire are simply the risks of the activity in which they are engaged, and they have no right to reduce those risks at the expense of other people who are not engaged. But a threat of death directed not at soldiers in general but at a particular soldier—a threat, as the lawyers say, "imminent, real, and inevitable"—alters the case, lifting it out of the context of combat and war risk. Now it becomes like those domestic crimes in which one man forces another, under threat of immediate death, to kill a third. The act is clearly murder, but we are likely to think that the man in the middle is not the murderer. Or, if we do think him a murderer, we are likely to accept the excuse of duress. Surely someone who refuses to kill at such

313

a time, and dies instead, is not just doing his duty; he is acting heroically. Gray provides a paradigmatic example:[17]

> In the Netherlands, the Dutch tell of a German soldier who was a member of an execution squad ordered to shoot innocent hostages. Suddenly he stepped out of rank and refused to participate in the execution. On the spot he was charged with treason by the officer in charge and was placed with the hostages, where he was promptly executed by his comrades.

Here is a man of extraordinary nobility, but what are we to say of his (former) comrades? That they are committing murder when they fire their guns, and that they are not responsible for the murder they commit. The officer in charge is responsible, and those among his superiors who determined on the policy of killing hostages. Responsibility passes over the heads of the members of the firing squad, not because of their oaths, not because of their orders, but because of the direct threat that drives them to act as they do.

War is a world of duress, of threat and counter-threat, so we must be clear about those cases in which duress does, and those in which it does not count as an excuse for conduct we would otherwise condemn. Soldiers are conscripted and forced to fight, but conscription by itself does not force them to kill innocent people. Soldiers are attacked and forced to fight, but neither aggression nor enemy onslaught forces them to kill innocent people. Conscription and attack bring them up against serious risks and hard choices. But constricted and frightening as their situation is, we still say that they choose freely and are responsible for what they do. Only a man with a gun at his head is not responsible.

But superior orders are not always enforced at the point of a gun. Army discipline in the actual context of war is often a great deal more haphazard than the firing squad example suggests. "It is a great boon of frontline positions," writes Gray, "that . . . disobedience is frequently possible, since supervision is not very exact where danger of death is present."[18] And in rear areas as well as at the front, there are ways of responding to an order short of obeying it: postponement, evasion, deliberate misunderstanding, loose construction, overly literal construction, and so on. One can ignore an immoral command or answer it with questions or protests; and sometimes even an overt refusal only invites reprimand, demotion, or detention; there is no risk of death. Whenever these possibilities are open, moral men will seize upon them. The law seems to require a similar readiness, for it is a legal principle that duress excuses only if the harm the individual soldier inflicts is not disproportionate to the harm with which he is threatened.[19] He is not excused for the murder of innocent people by the threat of demotion.

It has to be said, however, that officers are far more capable than enlisted men of weighing the dangers they face. Telford Taylor has described the case of Colonel William Peters, an officer in the Confederate Army during the American Civil War, who refused a direct order to burn the town of Chambersburg, Pennsylvania.[20] Peters was relieved of his command and placed under arrest, but he was never brought before a court martial. We may admire his courage, but if he anticipated that his superiors would ("prudently", as another Confederate officer said) avoid a trial, his decision was relatively easy. The decision of an ordinary soldier, who may well be subject to summary justice and who knows little of the temper of his more distant superiors, is much harder. At My Lai, those men who refused to fire never suffered for their refusal and apparently did not expect to suffer; and that suggests that we must blame the others for their obedience. In more ambiguous cases, the duress of superior orders, though it is not "imminent, real, and inevitable" and cannot count as a defense, is commonly regarded as an extenuating factor. That seems the right attitude to take, but I want to stress once again that when we take it we are not making concessions to the need for discipline, but simply recognizing the plight of the common soldier.

There is another reason for extenuation, unmentioned in the legal literature, but prominent in moral accounts of disobedience. The path that I have marked out as the right one is often a very lonely path. Here, too, the case of the German soldier who broke ranks with his fellow executioners and was promptly executed by them is unusual and extreme. But even when a soldier's doubts and anxieties are widely shared, they are still the subject of private brooding, not of public discussion. And when he acts, he acts alone, with no assurance that his comrades will support him. Civil protest and disobedience usually arise out of a community of values. But the army is an organization, not a community, and the communion of ordinary soldiers is shaped by the character and purposes of the organization, not by their private commitments. Theirs is the rough solidarity of men who face a common enemy and endure a common discipline. On both sides of a war, unity is reflexive, not intentional or premeditated. To disobey is to breach that elemental accord, to claim a moral separateness (or a moral superiority), to challenge one's fellows, perhaps even to intensify the dangers they face. "This is what is most difficult," wrote a French soldier who went to Algeria and then refused to fight, "being cut off from the fraternity, being locked up in a monologue, being incomprehensible."[21]

Now, *incomprehensible* is perhaps too strong a word, for a man appeals at such a time to common moral standards. But in the context of a military organization, that appeal will often go unheard, and so it involves a risk that may well be greater than that of punishment: the risk of a profound and morally disturbing isolation. This is not to say that one can join in a massacre for the sake of togetherness. But it suggests that moral life is rooted in a kind of association that military discipline precludes or temporarily cuts off, and that fact, too, must be taken into account in the judgments we make. It must be taken into account especially in the case of common soldiers, for officers are more free in their associations and more involved in discussions about policy and strategy. They have a say in the shape and character of the organization over which they preside. Hence, again, the critical importance of command responsibility.

Command Responsibility

Being an officer is not at all like being a common soldier. Rank is something men compete for, aspire to, glory in, and so even when officers were initially conscripted, we need not worry about holding them rigidly to the duties of their office. For rank can be avoided even when service cannot. Junior officers are killed at a high rate in combat, but still there are soldiers who want to be officers. It is a question of the pleasures of command; there is nothing quite like it (so I am told) in civilian life. The other side of pleasure, however, is responsibility. Officers take on immense responsibilities, again unlike anything in civilian life, for they have in their control the means of death and destruction. The higher their rank, the greater the reach of their command, the larger their responsibilities. They plan and organize campaigns; they decide on strategy and tactics; they choose to fight here rather than there; they order men into battle. Always, they must aim at victory and attend to the needs of their own soldiers. But they have at the same time a higher duty: "The soldier, be he friend or foe," wrote Douglas MacArthur when he confirmed the death sentence of General Yamashita, "is charged with the protection of the weak and unarmed. It is the very essence and reason of his being . . . [a] sacred trust."[22] Precisely because he himself, gun in hand, artillery and bombers at his call, poses a threat to the weak and unarmed, he must take steps to shield them. He must fight with restraint, accepting risks, mindful of the rights of the innocent.

That obviously means that he cannot order massacres; nor can he terrorize civilians with bombardment or bombing, or uproot whole populations in order to create "free-fire zones," or take reprisals against prisoners, or threaten to kill hostages. But it means more than that. Military commanders have two further and morally crucial responsibilities. First, in planning their campaigns, they must take positive steps to limit even unintended civilian deaths (and they must make sure that the numbers killed are not disproportionate to the military benefits they expect). Here the laws of war are of little help; no officer is going to be criminally charged for killing too many people if he does not actually massacre them. But the moral responsibility is clear, and it cannot be located anywhere else than in the office of commander. The campaign belongs to the commander as it does not belong to the ordinary combatants; he has access to all available information and also to the means of generating more information; he has (or ought to have) an overview of the sum of actions and effects that he is ordering and hoping for. If, then, the conditions set by the doctrine of double effect are not met, we should not hesitate to hold him accountable for the failure. Second, military commanders, in organizing their forces, must take positive steps to enforce the war convention and hold the men under their command to its standards. They must see to their training in this regard, issue clear orders, establish inspection procedures, and assure the punishment of individual soldiers and subordinate officers who kill or injure innocent people. If a great deal of such killing and injuring takes place, they are presumptively responsible, for we assume that it lay within their power to prevent it. Given what actually happens in war, military commanders have a great deal to answer for.

General Bradley and the Bombing of St. Lô

In July 1944, Omar Bradley, in command of American forces in Normandy, was engaged in planning a breakout from the invasion beachheads established the month before. The plan that he worked out, code-named COBRA and approved by Generals Montgomery and Eisenhower, called for the carpet bombing of an area three and a half miles wide, one and a half deep, along the Périers road outside the town of St. Lô. "Air bombing, we calculated, would either destroy or stun the enemy in the carpet" and so permit a quick advance. But it also posed a moral problem, which Bradley discusses in his autobiography. On July 20, he described the coming attack to some American newsmen:[23]

> The correspondents listened quietly to the outline of our plan, craned their necks as I pointed to the carpet and . . . tallied the air strength that had been assigned to us. At the close of the briefing, one of the newsmen asked if we would forewarn the French living within bounds of the carpet. I shook my head as if to escape the necessity for saying no. If we were to tip our hand to the French, we would also show it to the Germans . . . The success of COBRA hung upon surprise; it was essential we have surprise even if it meant the slaughter of innocents as well.

Bombing of this sort, along the line of battle and in close support of combat troops, is permitted by positive international law. Even indiscriminate fire is permitted within the actual combat zone.[24] Civilians are thought to be forewarned by the proximity of the fighting. But as the correspondent's question suggests, this does not resolve the moral issue. We still want to know what positive measures might have been taken to avoid "the slaughter of innocents" or reduce the damage done. It is important to insist on such measures because, as this example clearly shows, the proportionality rule often has no inhibitory effects at all. Even if a large number of civilians lived in those five square miles near St. Lô, and even if all of them were likely to die, it would seem a small price to pay for a breakout that might well signal the end of the war. To say that, however, is not to say that those innocent lives are forfeit, for there may be ways of saving them short of calling off the attack. Perhaps civilians all along the battlefront could have been warned (without giving up surprise in a particular sector). Perhaps the attack could have been redirected through some less populated area (even at greater risk to the soldiers involved). Perhaps the planes, flying low, could have aimed at specific enemy targets, or artillery have been used instead (since shells could then be aimed more precisely than bombs), or paratroops dropped or patrols sent forward to seize important positions in advance of the main attack. I am in no position to recommend any of these courses of action, although, in the event, any of the last of them might have been preferable, even from a military point of view. For the bombs missed the carpet and killed or wounded several hundred American soldiers. How many French civilians were killed or wounded Bradley does not say.

However many civilians died, it cannot be said that their deaths were intentional. On the other hand, unless Bradley worked his way through the sorts of possibilities I have listed, it also cannot be said that he *intended not to kill them*. I have already explained why that negative intention ought to be required from soldiers; it is the domestic equivalent of what the lawyers call "due care" in domestic society. With reference to specific and small-scale military actions (like the bombing of cellars described by Frank Richards), the people required to take care are common soldiers and their immediate superiors. In cases such as the COBRA campaign, the relevant individuals stand higher in the hierarchy; it is on General Bradley that we rightly focus our attention, and on his superiors. Once again, I have to say that I cannot specify the precise point at which the requirements of "due care" have been met. How much attention is required? How much risk must be accepted? The line isn't clear.[25] But it is clear enough that most campaigns are planned and carried out well below the line; and one can blame commanders who don't make minimal efforts, even if one doesn't know exactly what a maximum effort would entail.

The Case of General Yamashita

The same problem of specifying standards comes up when one considers the responsibility of commanders for the actions of their subordinates. They are bound, as I have said, to enforce the war convention. But even the best possible system of enforcement doesn't preclude particular violations. It proves itself the best possible system by seizing upon these in a systematic way and by punishing the individuals who commit them so as to deter the others. It is only if there is a massive breakdown of this disciplinary system that we demand an accounting from the officers who preside over it. This, in effect, is the demand formally made upon General Yamashita by an American military commission in the aftermath of the Philippine campaign in 1945.[26] It was said of Yamashita that he was responsible for a large number of specified acts of violence and murder inflicted upon unarmed civilians and prisoners of war. That these acts had in fact been committed by Japanese soldiers no one denied. On the other hand, no evidence was presented to show that Yamashita had ordered the violence and murder nor even that he had known about any of the specified acts. His responsibility lay in his failure "to discharge his duty as commander to control the operations of the members of his command, permitting them to commit brutal atrocities . . ." Defending himself, Yamashita claimed that he had been entirely unable to exercise control over his troops: the successful American invasion had disrupted his communication and command structure, leaving him in effective charge only of the troops whom he personally led, in retreat, into the mountains of northern Luzon; and these troops had committed no atrocities. The commission refused to accept this defense and sentenced Yamashita to death. His appeal was carried to the U.S. Supreme Court, which declined to review the case, despite memorable dissents by Justices Murphy and Rutledge. Yamashita was executed on February 22, 1946.

There are two ways of describing the standard to which Yamashita was held by the commission and the Court majority. The defense lawyers argued that the standard was one of strict liability, radically inappropriate in cases of criminal justice. That is to say, Yamashita was convicted without reference to any acts he committed or even to any omissions that he might have avoided. He was convicted of having held an office, because of the duties said to inhere in that office, even though the duties were in fact undo-able under the conditions in which he found himself. Justice Murphy went further: the duties were undo-able because of the conditions that the American army had created.[27]

> . . . read against the background of military events in the Philippines subsequent to October 9, 1944, these charges amount to this: "We, the victorious American forces, have done everything possible to destroy and disorganize your lines of communication, your effective control of your personnel, your ability to wage war. In these respects we have succeeded . . . And now we charge and condemn you for having been inefficient in maintaining control of your troops during the period when we were so effectively besieging and eliminating your forces and blocking your ability to maintain effective command."

This is probably an accurate description of the facts of the case. Not only was Yamashita unable to do the things that commanders should do, but if we push the argument back, he was in no sense the author of the conditions which made those things impossible. I should add, however, that the other judges did not believe, or did not admit, that they were enforcing the principle of strict liability. According to Chief Justice Stone, the question was "whether the law of war imposes on an army commander a duty to take such appropriate measures *as are within his power* to control the troops under his command . . ." It is easy to answer that question affirmatively, but not at all easy to say what measures are "appropriate" under the adverse conditions of combat, disorganization, and defeat.

One wants to set the standards very high, and the argument for strict liability is utilitarian in character: holding officers automatically responsible for massive violations of the rules of war forces them to do everything they can to avoid such violations, without forcing us to specify what they ought to do.[28] But there are two problems with this. First of all, we don't really want commanders to do everything they can, for that requirement, taken literally, would leave them little time to do anything else. This point is never as telling in their case as it is in the case of political leaders and domestic crime: we don't require our leaders to do everything they can (but only to take "appropriate measures") to prevent robbery and murder, for they have other things to do. But they, presumably, have not armed and trained the people who commit robbery and murder, and these people are not directly in their charge. The case of military commanders is different; hence we must expect them to devote a great deal of time and attention to the discipline and control of the men-with-guns they have turned loose in the world. But still, not all their time and attention, not all the resources at their command.

The second argument against strict liability in criminal cases is a more familiar one. Even doing "everything" is not the same as doing it successfully. All we can require is serious efforts of specific sorts; we cannot require success, since the conditions of warfare are such that success isn't always possible. And the impossibility of success is necessarily an excuse—given serious effort, an entirely satisfactory excuse—for failure. To refuse to accept the excuse is to refuse to regard the defendent as a moral agent: for it is in the nature of moral agents (of human beings) that their best efforts sometimes fail. The refusal disregards the defendant's humanity, makes him into an example, *pour encourager les autres*; and that we have no right to do to anyone.

These two arguments seem to me right, and they exonerate General Yamashita, but they also leave us with no clear standards at all. In fact, there is no philosophical or theoretical way of fixing such standards. That is also true with regard to the planning and organization of military campaigns. There is no sure rule against which to measure the conduct of General Bradley. The discussion of double effect in chapters 9 and 10 pointed only in a fairly crude way toward the sorts of considerations that are relevant when we make judgments about such matters. The appropriate standards can emerge only through a long process of casuistic reasoning, that is, by attending to one case after another, morally or legally. The chief failure of the military commission and the Supreme Court in 1945, aside from the fact that they failed to do justice to General Yamashita, is that they made no contribution to this process. They did not specify the measures that Yamashita might have taken; they did not suggest what degree of disorganization might serve as a limit on command responsibility. Only by making such specifications, again and again, can we draw the lines that the war convention requires.

We can say more than this, I think, if we turn back briefly to the My Lai case. The evidence brought forward at the trial of Lieutenant Calley and the materials collected by newsmen carrying on their own investigations of the massacre clearly suggest the responsibility of officers superior to both Calley and Medina. The strategy of the American war in Vietnam, as I have already argued, tended to put civilians at risk in unacceptable ways, and ordinary soldiers could hardly ignore the implications of that strategy. My Lai was itself in a free-fire zone, routinely shelled and bombed. "If you can shoot artillery . . . in there every night," one soldier asked, "how can the people in there be worth so much?"[29] In effect, soldiers were taught that civilian lives were not worth much, and there seems to have been little effort to counteract that teaching except by the most formal and perfunctory instruction in the rules of war. If we are fully to assign blame for the massacre, then, there are a large number of officers whom we would have to condemn. I cannot put together a list here, and I doubt that all of them could have been or ought to have been legally charged and tried—though this might have been a useful occasion to apply, and improve upon, the Yamashita precedent. But that many officers are morally chargeable seems certain, and their blameworthiness is not less than that of the men who did the actual killing. Indeed, there is this difference between them: in the case of the ordinary soldiers, the burden of proof lies with us. As in any murder case, we must prove their knowing and willful participation. But the officers are presumptively guilty; the burden of proof, if they would demonstrate their innocence, lies with them. And until we find some way of imposing that burden, we shall not have done all that we can do in defense of the "weak and unarmed," the innocent victims of war.

The Nature of Necessity (4)

I have left the hardest question for last. What are we to say about those military commanders (or political leaders) who override the rules of war and kill innocent people in a "supreme emergency"? Surely we want to be led at such a time by men and women ready to do what has to be done—what is *necessary*; for it is only here that necessity, in its true sense, comes into the theory of war. On the other hand, we cannot ignore or forget what it is they do. The deliberate killing of the innocent is murder. Sometimes, in conditions of extremity (which I have tried to define and delimit), commanders must commit murder or they must order others to commit it. And then they are murderers, though in a good cause. In domestic society, and particularly in the context of revolutionary politics, we say of such people that they have dirty hands. I have argued elsewhere that men and women with dirty hands, though it may be the case that they had acted well and done what their office required, must nonetheless bear a burden of responsibility and guilt.[30] They have killed unjustly, let us say, for the sake of justice itself, but justice itself requires that unjust killing be condemned. There is obviously no question here of legal punishment, but of some other way of assigning and enforcing blame. What way, however, is radically unclear. The available answers are all likely to make us uneasy. The nature of that uneasiness will be apparent if we turn again to the case of British terror bombing in World War II.

The Dishonoring of Arthur Harris

"He will perhaps go down in history as a giant among the leaders of men. He gave Bomber Command the courage to surmount its ordeals . . ." So writes the historian Noble Frankland about Arthur Harris, who directed the strategic bombing of Germany from February 1942 until the end of the war.[31] Harris was, as we have seen, the determined advocate of terrorism, resisting every attempt to use his planes for other purposes. Now, terror bombing is a criminal activity, and after the immediate threat posed by Hitler's early victories had passed, it was an entirely indefensible activity. Hence Harris' case isn't really an example of the dirty hands problem. He and Churchill, who was ultimately responsible for military policy, faced no moral dilemma: they should simply have stopped the bombing campaign. But we can take it as an example, nonetheless, for it apparently had that form in the minds of British leaders, even of Churchill himself at the end. That is why Harris, though of course criminal charges were never brought against him, was not treated after the war as a giant among the leaders of men.

He had done what his government thought necessary, but what he had done was ugly, and there seems to have been a conscious decision not to celebrate the exploits of Bomber Command or to honor its leader. "From this work," writes Angus Calder, "Churchill and his colleagues at last recoiled. After the strategic air offensive officially ended in mid-April [1945], Bomber Command was slighted and snubbed; and Harris, unlike other well-known commanders, was not rewarded with a peerage." In such circumstances, not to honor was to dishonor, and that is exactly how Harris regarded the government's action (or omission).[32] He waited a while for his reward and then, resentfully, left England for his native Rhodesia. The men he led were similarly treated, though the snub was not so personal. In Westminster Abbey, there is a plaque honoring those pilots of Fighter Command who died during the war, listing them all by name. But the bomber pilots, though they suffered far heavier casualties, have no plaque; their names are unrecorded. It is as if the British had taken to heart Rolf Hochhuth's question:[33]

> Is a pilot who bombs
> population centers under orders
> still to be called a *soldier*?

All this makes a point, though it does so indirectly and in so equivocal a fashion that we cannot but notice its moral awkwardness. Harris and his men have a legitimate complaint: they did what they were told to do and what their leaders thought was necessary and right, but they are dishonored for doing it, and it is suddenly suggested (what else can the dishonor mean?) that what was necessary and right was also wrong. Harris felt that he was being made a scapegoat, and it is surely true that if blame is to be distributed for the bombing, Churchill deserves a full share. But Churchill's success in dissociating himself from the policy of terrorism is not of great importance; there is always a remedy for that in retrospective criticism. What is important is that his dissociation was part of a national dissociation—a deliberate policy that has moral significance and value.

And yet, the policy seems cruel. Stated in general terms, it amounts to this: that a nation fighting a just war, when it is desperate and survival itself is at risk, must use unscrupulous or morally ignorant soldiers; and as soon as their usefulness is past, it must disown them. I would rather say something else: that decent men and women, hard-pressed in war, must sometimes do terrible things, and then they themselves have to look for some way to reaffirm the values they have overthrown. But the first statement is probably the more realistic one. For it is very rare, as Machiavelli wrote in his *Discourses*, "that a good man should be found willing to employ wicked means," even when such means are morally required.[84] And then we must look for people who are not good, and use them, and dishonor them. Perhaps there is some better way of doing that than the way Churchill chose. It would have been better if he had explained to his countrymen the moral costs of their survival and if he had praised the courage and endurance of the fliers of Bomber Command even while insisting that it was not possible to take pride in what they had done (an impossibility that many of them must have felt). But Churchill did not do that; he never admitted that the bombing constituted a wrong. In the absence of such an admission, the refusal to honor Harris at least went some small distance toward re-establishing a commitment to the rules of war and the rights they protect. And that, I think, is the deepest meaning of all assignments of responsibility.

Conclusion

The world of necessity is generated by a conflict between collective survival and human rights. We find ourselves in that world less often than we think, certainly less often than we say; but whenever we are there, we experience the ultimate tyranny of war—and also, it might be argued, the ultimate incoherence of the theory of war. In a troubling essay entitled "War and Massacre," Thomas Nagel has described our situation at such a time in terms of a conflict between utilitarian and absolutist modes of thought: we know that there are some outcomes that must be avoided at all costs, and we know that there are some costs that can never rightly be paid. We must face the possibility, Nagel argues, "that these two forms of moral intuition are not capable of being brought together into a single, coherent moral system, and that the world can present us with situations in which there is no honorable or moral course for a man to take, no course free of guilt and responsibility for evil."[35] I have tried to avoid the stark indeterminacy of that description by suggesting that political leaders can hardly help but choose the utilitarian side of the dilemma. That is what they are there for. They must opt for collective survival and override those rights that have suddenly loomed as obstacles to survival. But I don't want to say, any more than Nagel does, that they are free of guilt when they do that. Were there no guilt involved, the decisions they make would be less agonizing than they are. And they can only prove their honor by accepting responsibility for those decisions and by living out the agony. A moral theory that made their life easier, or that concealed their dilemma from the rest of us, might achieve greater coherence, but it would miss or it would repress the reality of war.

It is sometimes said that the dilemma ought to be concealed, that we should draw the veil (as Churchill tried to do) over the crimes that soldiers and statesmen cannot avoid. Or, we should avert our eyes—for the sake of our innocence, I suppose, and the moral certainties. But that is a dangerous business; having looked away, how will we know when to look back? Soon we will avert our eyes from everything that happens in wars and battles, condemning nothing, like the second monkey in the Japanese statue, who sees no evil. And yet there is plenty to see. Soldiers and statesmen live mostly on this side of the ultimate crises of collective survival; the greater number by far of the crimes they commit can neither be defended nor excused. They are simply crimes. Someone must try to see them clearly and describe them "in express words." Even the murders called necessary must be similarly described; it doubles the crime to look away, for then we are not able to fix the limits of necessity, or remember the victims, or make our own (awkward) judgments of the people who kill in our name.

Mostly morality is tested only by the ordinary pressures of military conflict. Mostly it is possible, even when it isn't easy, to live by the requirements of justice. And mostly the judgments we make of what soldiers and statesmen do are singular and clearcut; with whatever hesitations, we say yes or no, we say right or wrong. But in supreme emergencies our judgments are doubled, reflecting the dualist character of the theory of war and the deeper complexity of our moral realism; we say yes *and* no, right *and* wrong. That dualism makes us uneasy; the world of war is not a fully comprehensible, let alone a morally satisfactory place. And yet it cannot be escaped, short of a universal order in which the existence of nations and peoples could never be threatened. There is every reason to work for such an order. The difficulty is that we sometimes have no choice but to fight for it.

Afterword: Nonviolence and the Theory of War

The dream of a war to end war, the myth of Armageddon (the last battle), the vision of the lion lying down with the lamb—all these point toward an age definitively peaceful, a distant age that lies across some unknown time-break, without armed struggle and systematic killing. It will not come, so we have been told, until the forces of evil have been decisively defeated and mankind freed forever from the lust for conquest and domination. In our myths and visions, the end of war is also the end of secular history. Those of us trapped within that history, who see no end to it, have no choice but to fight on, defending the values to which we are committed, unless or until some alternative means of defense can be found. The only alternative is nonviolent defense, "war without weapons," as it has been called by its advocates, who seek to adjust our dreams to our realities. They claim that we can uphold the values of communal life and liberty without fighting and killing, and this claim raises important questions (secular and practical questions) about the theory of war and the argument for justice. To treat them as they deserve would require another book; I can offer only a brief essay, a partial and tentative analysis of the ways in which nonviolence relates, first, to the doctrine of aggression, and then to the rules of war.

Nonviolent defense differs from conventional strategies in that it concedes the overrunning of the country that is being defended.

It establishes no obstacles capable of stopping a military advance or preventing a military occupation. "Although minor delaying actions against the incursions of foreign troops and functionaries may be possible," writes Gene Sharp, "civilian defense . . . does not attempt to halt such entry, and cannot successfully do so."[1] That is a radical concession, and I don't think that any government has ever made it willingly. Nonviolence has been practiced (in the face of an invasion) only after violence, or the threat of violence, has failed. Then its protagonists aim to deny the victorious army the fruits of its victory through a systematic policy of civilian resistance and noncooperation: they call upon the conquered people to make themselves ungovernable. I want to stress that it is not war but civilian resistance that has usually been regarded as a last resort, because war holds out at least the possibility of avoiding the occupation that evokes or requires the resistance. But we might reverse this ordering were we to decide that resistance is as likely to end the occupation as military action is to prevent it, and at a much lower cost in human lives. There is as yet no evidence that that proposition is true, "no cases in which . . . civilian defense has caused an invader to withdraw."[2] But no nonviolent struggle has ever been undertaken by a people trained in advance in its methods and prepared (as soldiers are in the case of war) to accept its costs. So it might be true; and if it is, we should have to regard aggression very differently from the way we do at present.

It might be said that nonviolence abolishes aggressive war simply by virtue of the refusal to engage the aggressor militarily. Invasion is not morally coercive in the ways I described in Chapter 4, men and women cannot be forced to fight, if they have come to believe that they can defend their country in some other way, without killing and being killed. And if there really is some other way, at least potentially effective, then the aggressor cannot be charged with forcing them to fight. Nonviolence de-escalates the conflict and diminishes its criminality. By adopting the methods of disobedience, noncooperation, boycott, and general strike, the citizens of the invaded country transform aggressive war into a political struggle. They treat the aggressor in effect as a domestic tyrant or usurper, and they turn his soldiers into policemen. If the invader accepts this role, and if he responds to the resistance he encounters with curfews, fines, jail sentences, and nothing more, the prospect is opened up of a long-term struggle, not without its difficulties and painfulness for civilians, but far less destructive than even a short war, and winnable (we are assuming) by those same civilians. Allied states would have no reason to intervene militarily in such a struggle; which is a good thing, since if they too were committed to nonviolent defense, they would have no means of intervening. But they could bring moral and perhaps also economic pressure to bear against the invaders.

This, then, would be the position of the invaders: they would hold the country they had "attacked," could establish military bases wherever they pleased, and enjoy whatever strategic benefits these yielded them (vis-à-vis other countries, presumably). But their logistics problems would be severe, for unless they brought along their own personnel, they could not depend upon the local transportation or communication systems. And since they could hardly bring along an entire workforce, they would have great difficulty exploiting the natural resources and the industrial productivity of the invaded country. Hence the economic costs of the occupation would be high. The political costs might well be higher. Everywhere their soldiers would encounter sullen, resentful, withdrawn, and noncooperative civilians. Though these civilians would never take up arms, they would rally, demonstrate, and strike; and the soldiers would have to respond, coercively, like the hated instruments of a tyrannical regime. Their military élan might well fade, their morale erode, under the strains of civilian hostility and of an on-going struggle in which they never experienced the release of an open fight. Eventually, perhaps, the occupation would become untenable, and the invaders would simply leave; they would have won and then lost a "war without weapons."

This is an attractive, even though it is not a millennial, picture. Indeed, it is attractive precisely because it is not millennial, but conceivable in the world we know. It is only just conceivable, however; for the success I have described is possible only if the invaders are committed to the war convention—and they won't always be committed. While nonviolence by itself replaces aggressive war with political struggle, it cannot by itself determine the means of struggle. The invading army can always adopt the common methods of domestic tyrants, which go well beyond curfews, fines, and jail sentences; and its leaders, though they are soldiers, may well be tempted to do that for the sake of a quick "victory." Tyrants will not, of course, lay siege to their own cities or bomb or bombard them; nor will invaders who encounter no armed opposition.[8] But there are other, probably more efficient, ways of terrorizing a people whose country one controls, and of breaking their resistance. In his "Reflections on Gandhi," George Orwell points out the importance of exemplary leadership and wide publicity in a nonviolent campaign and wonders whether such a campaign would even be possible in a totalitarian state. "It is difficult to see how Gandhi's methods could be applied in a country where opponents of the regime disappear in the middle of the night and are never heard from again."[4] Nor would civilian resistance work well against invaders who sent out squads of soldiers to kill civilian leaders, who arrested and tortured suspects, established concentration camps, and exiled large numbers of people from areas where the resistance was strong to distant and desolate parts of the country. Nonviolent defense is no defense at all against tyrants or conquerors ready to adopt such measures. Gandhi demonstrated this truth, I think by the perverse advice he gave to the Jews of Germany: that they should commit suicide rather than fight back against Nazi tyranny.[5] Here nonviolence, under extreme conditions, collapses into violence directed at oneself rather than at one's murderers, though why it should take that direction I cannot understand.

If one faces an enemy like the Nazis, and if armed resistance is impossible, it is virtually certain that the men and women of the occupied country—those who have been marked out for survival, at any rate, and perhaps even those who have been marked out for death—will yield to their new masters and obey their decrees. The country will grow silent. Resistance will be a matter of individual heroism or of the heroism of small groups, but not of collective struggle.

The success of nonviolent resistance requires that soldiers (or their officers or political leaders) refuse at some early point, before civilian endurance is exhausted, to carry out or support a terrorist policy. As in guerrilla war, the strategy is to force the invading army to bear the onus of civilian deaths. But here the onus is to be made especially clear (especially unbearable) by the dramatic absence of any armed struggle in which civilians might be collusive. They will be hostile, certainly, but no soldiers will die at their hands or at the hands of partisans who have their secret support. And yet, if their resistance is to be broken decisively and quickly, the soldiers will have to be prepared to kill them. Since they are not always prepared to do that, or since their officers are not always sure that they will do it again and again, as might be necessary, civilian defense has had a certain limited effectiveness—not in expelling an invading army, but in preventing the attainment of particular goals set by its leaders. As Liddell Hart has argued, however, these effects have only been possible[6]

> against opponents whose code of morality was fundamentally similar [to that of the civilian defenders], and whose ruthlessness was thereby restrained. It is very doubtful whether non-violent resistance would have availed against a Tartar conqueror in the past, or against a Stalin in more recent times. The only impression it seems to have made on Hitler was to excite his impulse to trample on what, to his mind, was contemptible weakness—although there is evidence that it did embarrass many of his generals, brought up in a better code . . .

If one could count on that "better code" and look forward to a nonviolent test of wills—civilian solidarity against military discipline—there would, I think, be no reason to fight: political struggle is better than fighting, even when victory is uncertain. For victory in war is also uncertain; and here it might be said, as it cannot easily be said in the case of war, that the citizens of the occupied country will win if they deserve to win. As in the domestic struggle against tyranny (so long as the struggle doesn't degenerate into massacre), we judge them by their capacity for self-help, that is, by their collective determination to defend their liberty.

When one cannot count on the moral code, nonviolence is either a disguised form of surrender or a minimalist way of upholding communal values after a military defeat. I don't want to underestimate the importance of the second of these. Though civilian resistance evokes no moral recognition among the invading soldiers, it can still be important for its practitioners. It expresses the communal will to survive; and though the expression is brief, as in Czechoslovakia in 1968, it is likely to be long remembered.[7] The heroism of civilians is even more heartening than that of soldiers. On the other hand, one should not expect much more from civilians confronted with a terrorist or potentially terrorist army than brief or sporadic resistance. It is easy to say that "Non-violent action is not a course for cowards. It requires the ability and determination to sustain the battle whatever the price in suffering . . ."[8] But this sort of exhortation is no more attractive than that of a general telling his soldiers to fight to the last man. Indeed, I prefer the exhortation of the general, since he at least addresses himself to a limited number of men, not to an entire population. The case is similar with guerrilla war, which has this advantage over civilian resistance: it recapitulates the military situation where only a relatively few people are asked "to sustain the battle"—though the others will suffer too, as we have seen, unless the opposing army fights in accordance with the war convention.

The comparison with guerrilla war is worth pursuing further. In an armed insurrection, the coercing and killing of civilians by enemy soldiers has the effect of mobilizing other civilians and bringing them into the insurgent camp. The indiscriminate violence of their opponents is one of the major sources of guerrilla recruitment. Nonviolent resistance, on the other hand, is possible on a significant scale only if civilians are already mobilized and prepared to act together. The resistance is simply the physical expression of that mobilization, directly, in the streets, or indirectly, through economic slowdowns and political passivity. Now the coercion and killing of civilians is likely to break the solidarity of the resistance, spreading terror through the country and eventually producing a dulled acquiescence. At the same time, it may demoralize the soldiers who are called upon to do what appears to them—if it appears to them—indecent work, and it may undercut support for the occupation among the friends and relatives of those soldiers. Guerrilla war can produce a similar demoralization, but the effect is compounded by the fear soldiers must feel in the face of the hostile men and women among whom they are forced to fight (and die). In the case of nonviolent defense, there will be no fear; there will only be disgust and shame. The success of the defense is entirely dependent upon the moral convictions and sensibilities of the enemy soldiers.

Nonviolent defense depends upon noncombatant immunity. For this reason, it is no service to the cause to ridicule the rules of war or to insist (as Tolstoy did) that violence is always and necessarily unrestrained. When one wages a "war without weapons," one appeals for restraint from men with weapons. It is not likely that these men, soldiers subject to military discipline, are going to be converted to the creed of nonviolence. Nor is it critical to the success of the "war" that they be converted, but only that they be held to their own putative standards. The appeal that is made to them takes this form: "You cannot shoot at me, because I am not shooting at you; nor am I going to shoot at you. I am your enemy and will remain so as long as you occupy my country. But I am a noncombatant enemy, and you must coerce and control me, if you can, without violence." The appeal simply restates the argument about civilian rights and soldierly duties that under-

lies the war convention and provides its substance. And this suggests that the transformation of war into a political struggle has as
its prior condition the restraint of war as a military struggle. If we
are to aim at the transformation, as we should, we must begin by
insisting upon the rules of war and by holding soldiers rigidly to
the norms they set. The restraint of war is the beginning of peace.

NOTES

Preface

1. The most concise and forceful exposition of these reasons is Stanley Hoffmann, "International Law and the Control of Force," in *The Relevance of International Law*, ed. Karl Deutsch and Stanley Hoffmann (New York, 1971), pp. 34–66. Given the present state of the law, I have most often cited positivists of an earlier age, especially W. E. Hall, John Westlake, and J. M. Spaight.

2. The pioneering work of this sort is Myres S. McDougal and Florentino P. Feliciano, *Law and Minimum World Public Order* (New Haven, 1961).

3. For a useful study of these writers, see James Turner Johnson, *Ideology, Reason, and the Limitation of War: Religious and Secular Concepts, 1200–1740* (Princeton, 1975).

1   Against "Realism"

1. This and subsequent quotations are from *Hobbes' Thucydides*, ed. Richard Schlatter (New Brunswick, N.J., 1975), pp. 377–85 (*The History of The Peloponnesian War*, 5:84–116).

2. Dionysius of Halicarnassus, *On Thucydides*, trans. W. Kendrick Pritchett (Berkeley, 1975), pp. 31–33.

3. See F. M. Cornford, *Thucydides Mythistoricus* (London, 1907), esp. ch. XIII.

4. *The Trojan Women*, trans. Gilbert Murray (London, 1905), p. 16.

5. Werner Jaeger, *Paideia: the Ideals of Greek Culture*, trans. Gilbert Highet (New York, 1939), I, 402.

*6. H. W. Fowler, *A Dictionary of Modern English Usage*, second ed., rev. Sir Ernest Gowers (New York, 1965), p. 168; cf. Jaeger, I, 397.

7. *Plutarch's Lives*, trans. John Dryden, rev. Arthur Hugh Clough (London, 1910), I, 303. Alcibiades also "selected for himself one of the captive Melian women . . ."

8. *Hobbes' Thucydides*, pp. 194–204 (*The History of the Peloponnesian War*, 3:36–49).

9. Thomas Hobbes, *Leviathan*, ch. IV.

10. *The Charterhouse of Parma*, I, chs. 3 and 4; J. F. C. Fuller, *A Military History of the Western World* (n.p., 1955), II, ch. 15.

11. C. W. C. Oman, *The Art of War in the Middle Ages* (Ithaca, N.Y., 1968), p. 137.

12. Raphael Holinshed, *Chronicles of England, Scotland, and Ireland*, excerpted in William Shakespeare, *The Life of Henry V* (Signet Classics, New York, 1965), p. 197.

13. *Henry V*, 4:7, ll. 1–11.

14. David Hume, *The History of England* (Boston, 1854), II, 358.
15. René de Belleval, *Azincourt* (Paris, 1865), pp. 105–06.
16. See the summary of opinions in J. H. Wylie, *The Reign of Henry the Fifth* (Cambridge, England, 1919), II, 171ff.
17. For an excellent and detailed account, which suggests that Henry's action cannot be defended, see John Keegan, *The Face of Battle* (New York, 1976), pp. 107–12.

2   The Crime of War

1. Clausewitz should now be read in the new translation by Michael Howard and Peter Paret, *On War* (Princeton, 1976). But this book appeared after my own work was finished; I have quoted Clausewitz from a graceful, though abridged version by Edward M. Collins, *War, Politics, and Power* (Chicago, 1962), p. 65. Cf. Howard and Paret, p. 76.
2. Press conference, January 12, 1955.
3. Clausewitz, p. 64. Cf. Howard and Paret, pp. 75–76.
4. Clausewitz, pp. 72, 204. Cf. Howard and Paret, pp. 81, 581.
5. John Ruskin, *The Crown of Wild Olive: Four Lectures on Industry and War* (New York, 1874), pp. 90–91.
6. Wilfred Owen, "Anthem for Doomed Youth," in *Collected Poems*, ed. C. Day Lewis (New York, 1965), p. 44.
7. Thomas Hobbes, *Leviathan*, ch. XXI. For a description of primitive warfare of this sort, see Robert Gardner and Karl G. Heider, *Gardens of War: Life and Death in the New Guinea Stone Age* (New York, 1968), ch. 6.
8. Quoted in J. F. C. Fuller, *The Conduct of War, 1789–1961* (n.p., 1968), p. 16.
9. Machiavelli, *History of Florence* (New York, 1960), Bk. IV, ch. I, p. 164.
10. Ruskin, p. 92.
11. *War and Peace*, trans. Constance Garnett (New York, n.d.), Part Two, III, p. 111.
12. "A Terre," *Collected Poems*, p. 64.
13. Fuller, *Conduct of War*, p. 35.
14. Thomas Sackville, Earl of Dorset, "The Induction," *Works*, ed. R. W. Sackville-West (London, 1859), p. 115.
15. This and the following quotations are from William Tecumseh Sherman, *Memoirs* (New York, 1875), pp. 119–20.

3   The Rules of War

1. Louis Simpson, "The Ash and the Oak," *Good News of Death and Other Poems*, in *Poets of Today* II (New York, 1955), p. 162.
2. See for example, Fuller, *Conduct of War*, ch. II ("The Rebirth of Total War").
3. Edward Rickenbacker's *Fighting the Flying Circus* (New York, 1919) is a lively (and typical) account of the chivalry of the air. In 1918, Rickenbacker wrote in his flight diary: "Resolved today that . . . I will never shoot at a Hun who is at a disadvantage . . ." (p. 338). For a general account, see Frederick Oughton, *The Aces* (New York, 1960).

Notes

4. Quoted in Desmond Young, *Rommel: The Desert Fox* (New.York, 1958), p. 137.

5. Eisenhower, *Crusade in Europe* (New York, 1948), pp. 156–57.

6. Ronald Lewin, *Rommel as Military Commander* (New York, 1970), pp. 294, 311. See also Young, pp. 130–32.

7. Quoted in Robert W. Tucker, *The Law of War and Neutrality at Sea* (Washington, 1957), p. 6 n. Tucker's discussion of the legal issues is very useful; see also H. Lauterpacht, "The Limits of the Operation of the Law of War," in 30 *British Yearbook of International Law* (1953).

8. *Henry V*, 4:1, ll. 132–35.

9. Francisco de Vitoria, *De Indis et De Iure Belli Relationes*, ed. Ernest Nys (Washington, D.C., 1917): *On the Law of War*, trans. John Pawley Bate, p. 176.

10. Randall Jarrell, "The Death of the Ball Turret Gunner," in *The Complete Poems* (New York, 1969), p. 144.

11. See below, ch. 18. For a historical account of these issues, see C. A. Pompe, *Aggressive War: An International Crime* (The Hague, 1953).

12. Quincy Wright, *A Study of War* (Chicago, 1942), I, 8.

13. Gardner and Heider, *Gardens of War*, p. 139.

14. *First Samuel*, 17:32.

15. Johan Huizinga, *Homo Ludens* (Boston, 1955), p. 92.

16. *War and Peace*, Part Ten, XXV, p. 725.

17. For a discussion of this agreement, see my essay "Prisoners of War: Does the Fight Continue After the Battle?" in *Obligations: Essays on Disobedience, War and Citizenship* (Cambridge, Mass., 1970).

18. *Moltke in Seinen Briefen* (Berlin, 1902), p. 253. The letter is addressed to J. C. Bluntschli, a noted scholar of international law.

4   Law and Order in International Society

1. *Henry V*, 1:2, ll. 24–28.

2. The judges distinguished "aggressive acts" from "aggressive wars," but then used the first of these as the generic term: see *Nazi Conspiracy and Aggression: Opinion and Judgment* (Washington, D.C., 1947), p. 16.

3. Quoted in Michael Howard, "War as an Instrument of Policy," in Herbert Butterfield and Martin Wight, eds., *Diplomatic Investigations* (Cambridge, Mass., 1966), p. 199. Cf. *On War*, trans. Howard and Paret, p. 370.

4. John Westlake, *Collected Papers*, ed. L. Oppenheim (Cambridge, England, 1914), p. 78.

5. See Ruth Putnam, *Alsace and Lorraine from Caesar to Kaiser: 58 B.C.–1871 A.D.* (New York, 1915).

6. Henry Sidgwick, *The Elements of Politics* (London, 1891), pp. 268, 287.

7. *Leviathan*, ch. 30.

8. *Leviathan*, ch. 15.

9. For a critique of this analogy, see the two essays by Hedley Bull, "Society and Anarchy in International Relations," and "The Grotian Conception of International Society," in *Diplomatic Investigations*, chs. 2 and 3.

10. See Vitoria, *On the Law of War*, p. 177.

11. Lenin, *Socialism and War* (London, 1940), pp. 10–11.

12. Edmund Wilson, *Patriotic Gore* (New York, 1966), p. xi.

13. It is worth noting that the United Nations' recently adopted definition of aggression closely follows the paradigm: see the *Report of the Special Committee on the Question of Defining Aggression* (1974), General Assembly Official Records,

29th session, supplement no. 19 (A/9619), pp. 10–13. The definition is reprinted and analyzed in Yehuda Melzer, *Concepts of Just War* (Leyden, 1975), pp. 26ff.

14. *On the Law of War*, p. 170.

15. See L. Oppenheim, *International Law*, vol. II, *War and Neutrality* (London, 1906), pp. 55ff.

16. C. A. Pompe, *Aggressive War*, p. 152.

17. Quoted in Pompe, p. 152.

18. Quoted in Franz Mehring, *Karl Marx*, trans. Edward Fitzgerald (Ann Arbor, 1962), p. 438.

19. *Minutes of the General Council of the First International: 1870–1871* (Moscow, n.d.), p. 57.

20. Roger Morgan, *The German Social-Democrats and the First International: 1864–1872* (Cambridge, England, 1965), p. 206.

21. "First Address of the General Council of the International Working Men's Association on the Franco-Prussian War," in Marx and Engels, *Selected Works* (Moscow, 1951), I, 443.

22. "Second Address . . . ," *Selected Works*, I, 449 (Marx's italics).

23. *Selected Works*, I, 441.

24. See the arguments made by Churchill at the time: *The Gathering Storm* (New York, 1961), chs. 17 and 18; also Martin Gilbert and Richard Gott, *The Appeasers* (London, 1963). For a recent scholarly reappraisal somewhat more sympathetic to Chamberlain, see Keith Robbins, *Munich: 1938* (London, 1968).

25. Gerald Vann, *Morality and War* (London, 1939).

26. Max Jakobson, *The Diplomacy of the Winter War* (Cambridge, Mass., 1961), p. 117.

27. Jakobson reports an admission by the Swedish prime minister that had Sweden been publicly committed to assist Finland in the autumn of 1939, the Soviet Union would probably not have attacked (p. 237).

5 Anticipations

1. D. W. Bowett, *Self-Defense in International Law* (New York, 1958), p. 59. My own position has been influenced by Julius Stone's critique of the legalist argument: *Aggression and World Order* (Berkeley, 1968).

2. Quoted from the *Annual Register*, in H. Butterfield, "The Balance of Power," *Diplomatic Investigations*, pp. 144–45.

3. Francis Bacon, *Essays* ("Of Empire"); see also his treatise *Considerations Touching a War With Spain* (1624), in *The Works of Francis Bacon*, ed. James Spedding *et al.* (London, 1874), XIV, pp. 469–505.

4. *Oxford English Dictionary*, "threaten."

5. M. D. Vattel, *The Law of Nations* (Northampton, Mass., 1805), Bk. III, ch. III, paras. 42–44, pp. 357–78. Cf. John Westlake, *Chapters on the Principles of International Law* (Cambridge, England, 1894), p. 120.

6. Jonathan Swift, *The Conduct of the Allies and of the Late Ministry in Beginning and Carrying on the Present War* (1711), in *Prose Works*, ed. Temple Scott (London, 1901), V, 116.

7. As late as the eighteenth century, Vattel still argued that a prince "has a right to demand, even by force of arms, the reparation of an insult." *Law of Nations*, Bk. II, ch. IV, para. 48, p. 216.

8. Compare the argument of Hugo Grotius: "The danger . . . must be immediate and imminent in point of time. I admit, to be sure, that if the assailant seizes weapons in such a way that his intent to kill is manifest, the crime can be fore-

Notes

stalled; for in morals as in material things a point is not to be found which does not have a certain breadth." *The Law of War and Peace,* trans. Francis W. Kelsey (Indianapolis, n.d.), Bk. II, ch. I, section V, p. 173.

9. Walter Laquer, *The Road to War: The Origin and Aftermath of the Arab-Israeli Conflict, 1967–8* (Baltimore, 1969), p. 110.

10. Edward Luttwak and Dan Horowitz, *The Israeli Army* (New York, 1975), p. 212.

11. Luttwak and Horowitz, p. 224.

6 Interventions

1. "A Few Words on Non-Intervention" in J. S. Mill, *Dissertations and Discussions* (New York, 1873), III, 238–63.

2. See Irving Howe, ed., *The Basic Writings of Trotsky* (New York, 1963), p. 397.

3. John Norton Moore, "International Law and the United States' Role in Vietnam: A Reply," in R. Falk, ed., *The Vietnam War and International Law* (Princeton, 1968), p. 431. Moore addresses himself specifically to the argument of W. E. Hall, *International Law* (5th ed., Oxford, 1904), p. 289–90, but Hall follows Mill closely.

4. For a brief survey, see Jean Sigmann, *1848: The Romantic and Democratic Revolutions in Europe,* trans. L. F. Edwards (New York, 1973), ch. 10.

5. Charles Sproxton, *Palmerston and the Hungarian Revolution* (Cambridge, 1919), p. 48.

6. "Non-Intervention," p. 261–62.

7. See S. French and A. Gutman, "The Principle of National Self-determination," in Held, Morgenbesser, and Nagel, eds., *Philosophy, Morality, and International Affairs* (New York, 1974), pp. 138–53.

8. This is the general position of R. J. Vincent, *Nonintervention and World Order* (Princeton, 1974), esp. ch. 9.

9. Sproxton, p. 109.

10. See, for example, Hall, *International Law,* p. 293.

11. "On the Principle of Non-Intervention" (Oxford, 1860), p. 21.

12. See Hugh Thomas, *The Spanish Civil War* (New York, 1961), ch. 31, 40, 48, 58; Norman J. Padelford, *International Law and Diplomacy in the Spanish Civil Strife* (New York, 1939) is an incredibly naive defense of the nonintervention agreements.

13. A useful statement of this position can be found in the essay by John Norton Moore already cited; see note 3 above. For an example of the official view, see Leonard Meeker, "Vietnam and the International Law of Self-Defense" in the same volume, pp. 318–32.

14. I shall follow the account of G. M. Kahin and John W. Lewis, *The United States in Vietnam* (New York, 1967).

15. "On the Principle of Non-Intervention," p. 16.

16. See Gregory Henderson, *Korea: The Politics of the Vortex* (Cambridge, Mass., 1968), ch. 6.

17. Kahin and Lewis, p. 146.

18. Ellery C. Stowell suggests some possible examples in *Intervention in International Law* (Washington, D.C., 1921), ch. II. For contemporary legal views (and newer examples), see Richard Lillich, ed., *Humanitarian Intervention and the United Nations* (Charlottesville, Virginia, 1973).

19. Quoted in Philip S. Foner, *The Spanish-Cuban-American War and the Birth of American Imperialism* (New York, 1972), I, 111.

20. Quoted in Stowell, p. 122n.

21. See, for example, Julius W. Pratt, *Expansionists of 1898* (Baltimore, 1936) and Walter La Feber, *The New Empire: An Interpretation of American Expansion* (Ithaca, 1963); also Foner, I, ch. XIV.

22. Foner, I, ch. XIII.

23. F. E. Chadwick, *The Relations of the United States and Spain: Diplomacy* (New York, 1909), pp. 586–87. These lines are the epigraph to Walter Millis' account of the war: *The Martial Spirit* (n.p., 1931).

24. Millis, p. 404; it should be noted that Millis also writes of the American decision to go to war: "Seldom can history have recorded a plainer case of military aggression . . ." (p. 160).

25. For a contemporary account by a British journalist, see David Loshak, *Pakistan Crisis* (London, 1971).

26. John Westlake, *International Law*, vol. I, *Peace* (2nd ed., Cambridge 1910), pp. 319–20.

27. Thomas M. Franck and Nigel S. Rodley, "After Bangladesh: The Law of Humanitarian Intervention by Military Force," 67 *American Journal of International Law* 304 (1973).

28. Julius Stone, *Aggression and World Order*, p. 99.

7   War's Ends, and the Importance of Winning

1. "The Range in the Desert," *The Complete Poems*, p. 176.

2. B. H. Liddell Hart, *Strategy* (2nd rev. ed., New York, 1974), p. 339: Liddell Hart himself holds a different, and a much more sophisticated, position.

3. *War, Politics and Power*, p. 233; cf. the new translation of Howard and Paret, p. 595.

4. The work of Reinhold Niebuhr was the major inspiration of this group, Hans Morganthau its most systematic theorist. For works more immediately relevant to my purposes in this chapter, see George Kennan, *American Diplomacy: 1900–1950* (Chicago, 1951); John W. Spanier, *The Truman-MacArthur Controversy and the Korean War* (Cambridge, Mass., 1959); Paul Kecskemeti, *Strategic Surrender: the Politics of Victory and Defeat* (New York, 1964). For a useful critique of the "realists," see Charles Frankel, *Morality and U.S. Foreign Policy*, Foreign Policy Association Headline Series, no. 224 (1975).

5. Spanier, p. 5.

6. Kecskemeti, pp. 25–26.

7. On the connection between Wilson's "world view" and his desire for a compromise peace, see N. Gordon Levin, Jr., *Woodrow Wilson and World Politics: America's Response to War and Revolution* (New York, 1970), pp. 43, 52ff.

8. *The Hinge of Fate* (New York, 1962), p. 600.

9. Kecskemeti, pp. 217, 241

10. *Hinge of Fate*, p. 600; see also Churchill's cabinet memorandum of January 14, 1944, p. 599.

11. *American Diplomacy*, pp. 87–88.

12. Robert Phillimore, *Commentaries Upon International Law* (Philadelphia, 1854), I, 315.

13. Kecskemeti, p. 219.

14. See Raymond G. O'Connor, *Diplomacy for Victory: FDR and Unconditional Surrender* (New York, 1971).

15. Kecskemeti, p. 240.

Notes

16. For a general view of punishment as public condemnation, see "The Expressive Function of Punishment," in Joel Feinberg, *Doing and Deserving* (Princeton, 1970), ch. 5.
17. Glen D. Paige, *The Korean Decision* (New York, 1968), pp. 218–19.
18. *Strategy*, p. 355.
19. Quoted in Spanier, p. 88.
20. Quoted in David Rees, *Korea: The Limited War* (Baltimore, 1970), p. 101.
21. *Concepts of Just War*, pp. 170–71.
22. Liddell Hart, *Strategy*, p. 338.
23. Hume, *Theory of Politics*, ed. Frederick Watkins, (Edinburgh, 1951), pp. 190–91.

8 War's Means, and the Importance of Fighting Well

1. *Elements of Politics*, pp. 253–54.
2. *Elements of Politics*, p. 254; for a contemporary statement from a roughly similar point of view, see R. B. Brandt, "Utilitarianism and the Rules of War," 1 *Philosophy and Public Affairs* 145–65 (1972).
3. Byron Farwell, *The Great Anglo-Boer War* (New York, 1976), p. 209.
4. *The Law of Land Warfare*, U.S. Department of the Army Field Manual FM 27–10 (1956), para. 3. See the discussion of this provision in Telford Taylor, *Nuremberg and Vietnam* (Chicago, 1970), pp. 34–36, and Marshall Cohen, "Morality and the Laws of War," *Philosophy, Morality, and International Affairs*, pp. 72ff.
5. *Elements of Politics*, p. 264.
6. For an example of the "morality" of the feud, see Margaret Hasluck, "The Albanian Blood Feud," in Paul Bohannan, *Law and Warfare: Studies in the Anthropology of Conflict* (New York, 1967), pp. 381–408.
7. The story is told in Ignazio Silone, "Reflections on the Welfare State," 8 *Dissent* 189 (1961); De Sica's film *Two Women* is based on an incident from this period in Italian history.
8. *On the Law of War*, pp. 184–85.
9. *Deuteronomy* 21:10–14. This passage is ignored in Susan Brownmiller's analysis of the "true Hebraic concept . . . of rape" in *Against Our Will: Men, Women, and Rape* (New York, 1975), pp. 19–23.
10. See, for example, McDougal and Feliciano, *Law and Minimum World Public Order*, p. 42 and *passim*.

9 Noncombatant Immunity and Military Necessity

1. S. L. A. Marshall, *Men Against Fire* (New York, 1966), chs. 5 and 6.
2. Wilfred Owen, *Collected Letters*, ed. Harold Owen and John Bell (London, 1967), p. 458 (14 May 1917).
3. *Good-bye to All That* (rev. ed., New York, 1957), p. 132.
4. *The Collected Essays, Journalism and Letters of George Orwell*, ed. Sonia Orwell and Ian Angus (New York, 1968), II, 254.
5. *The Fortress: A Diary of Anzio and After* (Hammondsworth, 1958), p. 21.
6. *Sardinian Brigade: A Memoir of World War I*, trans. Marion Rawson (New York, 1970), pp. 166–71.

7. Archibald Forbes, quoted in J. M. Spaight, *War Rights on Land* (London, 1911), p. 104.

8. *Instructions for the Government of Armies of the United States in the Field*, General Orders 100, April, 1863 (Washington, 1898), Article 69.

9. M. Greenspan, *The Modern Law of Land Warfare* (Berkeley, 1959), pp. 313–14.

10. G. E. M. Anscombe, *Mr. Truman's Degree* (privately printed, 1958), p. 7; see also "War and Murder" in *Nuclear Weapons and Christian Conscience*, ed. Walter Stein (London, 1963).

11. See Sir Frederick Smith, *The Destruction of Merchant Ships under International Law* (London, 1917) and Tucker, *Law of War and Neutrality at Sea*.

12. H. A. Smith, *Law and Custom of the Sea* (London, 1950), p. 123.

13. Tucker, p. 72.

14. Tucker, p. 67.

15. Doenitz, *Memoirs: Ten Years and Twenty Days*, trans. K. H. Stevens (London, 1959), p. 261.

16. *The Destruction of Convoy PQ 17* (New York, n.d.), p. 157; for other examples, see pp. 145, 192–93.

17. *Nazi Conspiracy and Aggression: Opinion and Judgment*, p. 140.

18. Doenitz, *Memoirs*, p. 259.

19. *Old Soldiers Never Die* (New York, 1966), p. 198.

20. Kenneth Dougherty, *General Ethics: An Introduction to the Basic Principles of the Moral Life According to St. Thomas Aquinas* (Peekskill, N.Y., 1959), p. 64.

21. Dougherty, pp. 65–66; cf. John C. Ford, S. J. "The Morality of Obliteration Bombing," in *War and Morality*, ed. Richard Wasserstrom (Belmont, California, 1970). I cannot make any effort here to review the philisophical controversies over double effect. Dougherty provides a (very simple) text book description, Ford a careful (and courageous) application.

22. For a philosophical version of the argument that it cannot make a difference whether the killing of innocent people is direct or indirect, see Jonathan Bennett, "Whatever the Consequences," *Ethics*, ed. Judith Jarvis Thomson and Gerald Dworkin (New York, 1968).

23. Reginald Thompson, *Cry Korea* (London, 1951), pp. 54, 142–43.

24. I have been helped in thinking about these questions by Charles Fried's discussion of "Imposing Risks on Others," *An Anatomy of Values: Problems of Personal and Social Choice* (Cambridge, Mass., 1970), ch. XI.

25. Quoted from the published text of Marcel Ophuls' documentary film, *The Sorrow and the Pity* (New York, 1972), p. 131.

26. Thomas Gallagher, *Assault in Norway* (New York, 1975), pp. 19–20, 50.

10   War Against Civilians: Sieges and Blockades

1. *The Works of Josephus*, trans. Tho. Lodge (London 1620): *The Wars of the Jews*, Bk. VI, ch. XIV, p. 721.

2. See, for example Elena Skrjabina's remarkable memoir, *Siege and Survival: The Odyssey of a Leningrader* (Carbonville, Ill., 1971).

3. Charles Chaney Hyde, *International Law* (2nd rev. ed., Boston, 1945), III, 1802.

4. *The Works*, p. 722.

5. M. H. Keen, *The Laws of War in the Late Middle Ages* (London, 1965), p. 128 for an account of aristocratic obligations in such cases.

Notes

6. *The Art of War*, trans. Ellis Farneworth, rev. with an intro. by Neal Wood (Indianapolis, 1965), p. 193.

7. Spaight's discussion is the best: *War Rights*, pp. 174ff.

8. *The Works*, p. 718.

9. I shall follow the account of Leon Goure, *The Siege of Leningrad* (Stanford, 1962).

10. Goure, p. 141; *Trials of War Criminals before the Nuremberg Military Tribunals* (Washington, D.C., 1950), XI, 563.

11. The citation is from Hyde, *International Law*, III, 1802–03.

12. Spaight, pp. 174ff.

13. Spaight, pp. 177–78.

14. Hall, *International Law*, p. 398.

15. *The Code of Maimonides: Book Fourteen: The Book of Judges*, trans. Abraham M. Hershman (New Haven, 1949), p. 222; Grotius, *Law of War and Peace*, Bk. III, ch. XI, section xiv, pp. 739–40.

16. See Skrjabina, *Siege and Survival*, "Leningrad."

17. *Deuteronomy* 20:20.

18. *Hobbes' Thucydides*, pp. 123–24 (2:19–20); *War Commentaries of Caesar*, trans. Rex Warner (New York, 1960), pp. 70, 96 (*Gallic Wars* 3:3, 5:1).

19. A. C. Bell, *A History of the Blockade of Germany* (London, 1937), pp. 213–14.

20. Spaight, p. 138.

21. Hall, *International Law*, p. 656.

22. B. H. Liddell Hart, *The Real War: 1914–1918*, (Boston, 1964), p. 473.

23. The studies were carried out by German statisticians, but the results are accepted by Bell. He is a little reluctant, however, to regard these results as a sign of the "success" of the British blockade: see p. 673.

24. Bell, p. 117. Cf. the same argument made by a French historian, Louis Guichard, *The Naval Blockade: 1914–1918*, trans. Christopher R. Turner (New York, 1930), p. 304.

11   Guerrilla War

1. *The Sorrow and the Pity*, pp. 113–14.

2. For a useful survey of the legal situation, see Gerhard von Glahn, *The Occupation of Enemy Territory* (Minneapolis, 1957).

3. See, for example, W. F. Ford, "Resistance Movements and International Law," 7–8 *International Review of the Red Cross* (1967–68) and G. I. A. D. Draper, "The Status of Combatants and the Question of Guerrilla War," 45 *British Yearbook of International Law* (1971).

4. Quoted in Draper, p. 188.

5. Quoted in Douglas Pike, *Viet Cong* (Cambridge, Mass., 1968), p. 242.

6. Mao Tse-tung, *Selected Military Writings* (Peking, 1966), p. 343.

7. Dickey Chapelle, "How Castro Won," in *The Guerrilla—And How to Fight Him: Selections from the Marine Corps Gazette*, ed. T. N. Greene (New York, 1965), p. 223.

8. Draper, p. 203.

9. See Michael Calvert, *Chindits: Long Range Penetration* (New York, 1973).

10. Draper, pp. 202–04.

11. *Guerrilla Parties Considered With Reference to the Laws and Usages of War* (New York, 1862). Lieber wrote this pamphlet at the request of General Halleck.

12. Jeffrey Race, *War Comes to Long An* (Berkeley, 1972), pp. 196–97.

13. See *The Guerrilla—And How to Fight Him*; John McCuen, *The Art of Counter-Revolutionary War* (London, 1966); Frank Kitson, *Low Intensity Operations: Subversion, Insurgency, and Peacekeeping* (Harrisburg, 1971).

14. *Seven Pillars of Wisdom* (New York, 1936), Bk. III, ch. 33, p. 196.

15. For a graphic description of soldiers going beyond these limits, see Victor Kolpacoff's novel of the Vietnam war, *The Prisoners of Quai Dong* (New York, 1967).

16. Race, p. 233.

17. Jonathan Schell, *The Military Half* (New York, 1968), pp. 14ff.

18. For an account of forcible deportation, see Jonathan Schell, *The Village of Ben Suc* (New York, 1967).

19. *The Other Half*, p. 151.

20. Orville and Jonathan Schell, letter to *The New York Times*, Nov. 26, 1969; quoted in Noam Chomsky, *At War With Asia* (New York, 1970), pp. 292–93.

21. See the description of the camps that the British set up for Boer farmers: Farwell, *Anglo-Boer War*, chs. 40, 41.

22. Sir Robert Thompson, *Defeating Communist Insurgency* (New York, 1966), p. 125.

23. Don Oberdorfer, *Tet* (New York, 1972), p. 202.

24. Schell, *The Other Half*, pp. 96, 159.

25. Kitson, p. 138.

26. *Street Without Joy* (New York, 1972), ch. 7.

27. See the account of Regis Debray, *Che's Guerrilla War*, trans. Rosemary Sheed (Hammondsworth, 1975).

12 Terrorism

1. But Liddell Hart, the foremost strategist of the "indirect approach," has consistently opposed terrorist tactics: see, for example, *Strategy*, pp. 349–50 (on terror bombing).

2. Rear Admiral L. H. K. Hamilton, quoted in Irving, *Destruction of Convoy PQ 17*, p. 44.

3. *Politics*, trans. Ernest Barker (Oxford, 1948), p. 288 (1314a).

4. *The Just Assassins*, in *Caligula and Three Other Plays*, trans. Stuart Gilbert (New York, 1958), p. 258. The actual historical incident is described in Roland Gaucher, *The Terrorists: from Tsarist Russia to the OAS* (London, 1965), pp. 49, 50 n.

5. J. Bowyer Bell, *The Secret Army: A History of the IRA* (Cambridge, Massachusetts, 1974), pp. 161–62.

6. Gerold Frank, *The Deed* (New York, 1963), pp. 248–49.

7. James E. Bond, *The Rules of Riot: Internal Conflict and the Law of War* (Princeton, 1974), pp. 89–90.

8. Pike, *Viet Cong*, p. 248.

9. Race, *War Comes to Long An*, p. 83, which suggests that it was precisely the *best* public health officers, teachers, and so on who were attacked—because they constituted a possible anti-communist leadership.

10. Pike, p. 250.

11. Pike, p. 251.

12. The argument, I suppose, goes back to Machiavelli, though most of his descriptions of the necessary violence of founders and reformers have to do with the killing of particular people, members of the old ruling class: see *The Prince*, ch. VIII and *Discourses*, I:9 for examples.

Notes

13. *The Wretched of the Earth*, trans. Constance Farrington (New York, n.d.), pp. 18–19.

14. *Gillo Pontecorvo's The Battle of Algiers*, ed. Piernico Solinas (New York, 1973), pp. 79–80.

13   Reprisals

1. G. Lowes Dickinson, *War: Its Nature, Cause, and Cure* (London, 1923), p. 15.

2. H. Brocher, "Les principes naturels du droit de la guerre," 5 *Revue de droit international et de legislation comparée* 349 (1873).

3. Robert B. Asprey, *War in the Shadows: The Guerrilla in History* (New York, 1975), I, 478.

4. Frits Kalshoven, *Belligerent Reprisals* (Leyden, 1971), pp. 193–200.

5. Kalshoven, pp. 78ff.

6. See, for example, the essays of H. J. McCloskey and T. L. S. Sprigge in *Contemporary Utilitarianism*, ed. Michael D. Bayles (Garden City, New York, 1968).

7. Spaight, *War Rights*, p. 120.

8. Spaight, p. 462.

9. McDougal and Feliciano, *Law and Minimum World Public Order*, p. 682.

10. See Robert Katz, *Death in Rome* (New York, 1967) for an account of one of the most brutal Nazi reprisals.

11. Spaight, p. 463n.

12. Greenspan is typical: "Only in exceedingly grave cases should there be resort to reprisals." *Modern Law of Land Warfare*, p. 411.

13. Lieber, *Instructions*, Article 27 (emphasis added).

14. Kalshoven, pp. 263ff.

15. McDougal and Feliciano, p. 684.

16. Churchill, *The Grand Alliance* (New York, 1962), p. 359. A distinction similar to the one I am defending here is suggested by Westlake: ". . . the laws of war are too deeply rooted in humanity and morality to be discussed on the footing of contract alone, except it may be some parts of no great importance which convention might have settled otherwise than it has." *International Law*, II, 126.

17. See Kalshoven on "non-belligerent reprisals," pp. 287ff.

18. Luttwak and Horowitz, *The Israeli Army*, p. 110.

19. For accounts and evaluations of the raid, see Richard Falk, "The Beirut Raid and the International Law of Reprisal," 63 *American Journal of International Law* (1969) and Yehuda Blum, "The Beirut Raid and the International Double Standard: A Reply to Professor Falk," 64 *A.J.I.L.* (1970).

20. See the general condemnation voted by the Security Council on April 9, 1964, cited in Sydney D. Bailey, *Prohibitions and Restraints in War* (London, 1972), p. 55.

21. Hans Kelson, *Principles of International Law*, 2nd ed., rev. Robert W. Tucker (New York, 1967), p. 87.

14   Winning and Fighting Well

1. *The Chinese Classics*, trans. and ed. James Legge, vol. V: *The Ch'un Ts'ew with The Tso Chuen* (Oxford, 1893), p. 183.

2. *Military Writings*, p. 240.

3. Quoted in Arthur Waley, *Three Ways of Thought in Ancient China* (Garden City, New York, n.d.), p. 131.

4. *Military Writings*, pp. 81, 223–24.

5. *Basic Tactics* (New York, 1966), p. 98.

6. *The Chinese Classics*, V, 183.

7. *The Need for Roots*, trans. Arthur Wills (Boston, 1955), p. 159.

8. *A Theory of Justice* (Cambridge, Mass., 1971), p. 379. Compare Vitoria: ". . . whatever is done in right of war receives the construction most favorable to the claims of those engaged in a just war." *On the Law of War*, p. 180.

9. This seems to be G. E. M. Anscombe's position in the two essays already cited: *Mr. Truman's Degree* and "War and Murder."

10. For a discussion of what it means to "override" a moral principle, see Robert Nozick, "Moral Complications and Moral Structures," 13 *Natural Law Forum* 34–35 and notes (1968).

15 Aggression and Neutrality

1. Philip C. Jessup, *Neutrality: Its History, Economics, and Law* (New York, 1936), IV, 80 (emphasis added).

2. W. E. Hall, *The Rights and Duties of Neutrals* (London, 1874) is the best account of the laws of neutrality.

3. Westlake, *International Law*, II, 162.

4. The speech is reprinted in *The Theory and Practice of Neutrality in the Twentieth Century*, ed. Roderick Ogley (New York, 1970), p. 83.

5. *Theory and Practice of Neutrality*, p. 74.

6. Liddell Hart, *The Real War*, pp. 46–47.

7. For an example of the American response, see James M. Beck, *The Evidence in the Case: A Discussion of the Moral Responsibility for the War of 1914* (New York, 1915), esp. ch. IX.

8. *Socialism and War*, p. 15.

9. Nils Oervik, *The Decline of Neutrality: 1914–1941* (Oslo, 1953), p. 241.

10. Oervik, p. 223.

11. Churchill, *The Gathering Storm* (New York, 1961), Bk. II, ch. 9.

12. *Assignment to Catastrophe* (New York, 1954), I, 71–72.

13. *Time Unguarded: The Ironside Diaries 1937–1940*, ed. Roderick Macleod and Denis Kelly (New York, 1962), p. 211.

14. *Ironside Diaries*, p. 185.

15. *Ironside Diaries*, p. 216.

16. *History of the Second World War* (New York, 1971), p. 53.

17. *Ironside Diaries*, p. 238.

18. *The Gathering Storm*, p. 488.

19. Oervik, p. 237.

20. For an account of the campaign, see J. L. Moulton, *A Study of Warfare in Three Dimensions: The Norwegian Campaign of 1940* (Athens, Ohio, 1967).

21. *History of the Second World War*, p. 59. Cf. General Ironside's entry for February 14, 1940: "Winston is now pressing for his laying of mines in neutral Norwegian waters as the only means of forcing the Germans to violate Scandinavia and so give us a chance of getting into Narvik." *The Ironside Diaries*, p. 222.

Notes

16 Supreme Emergency

1. Quoted in George Quester, *Deterrence Before Hiroshima* (New York, 1966), p. 67.

2. See J. Glenn Gray, *The Warriors: Reflections on Men in Battle* (New York, 1967), ch. 5: "Images of the Enemy."

3. But the claim that one can never kill an innocent person abstracts from questions of coercion and consent: see the examples cited in chapter 10.

4. See Quester, *Deterrence* and F. M. Sallagar, *The Road to Total War: Escalation in World War II* (Rand Corporation Report, 1969); also the official history by Sir Charles Webster and Noble Frankland, *The Strategic Air Offensive Against Germany* (London, 1961).

5. Noble Frankland, *Bomber Offensive: The Devastation of Europe* (New York, 1970), p. 41.

6. The Story of the Cherwell minute is told, most unsympathetically, in C. P. Snow, *Science and Government* (New York, 1962).

7. Quester, pp. 117–18.

8. Quoted in Quester, p. 141.

9. Quoted in Angus Calder, *The People's War: 1939–1945* (New York, 1969), p. 491.

10. Calder, p. 229; the same poll is cited by Vera Brittain, a courageous opponent of British bombing policy: *Humiliation with Honor* (New York, 1943), p. 91.

11. ". . . it was not [Cherwell's] ruthlessness that worried us most, it was his calculations." Snow, *Science and Government*, p. 48. Cf. P. M. S. Blackett's postwar critique of the bombing, worked out in narrowly strategic terms: *Fear, War, and the Bomb* (New York, 1949), ch. 2.

12. Sallagar, p. 127.

13. Sallagar, p. 128.

14. Frankland, *Bomber Offensive*, pp. 38–39.

15. Frankland, *Bomber Offensive*, p. 134.

16. Sir Arthur Harris, *Bomber Offensive* (London, 1947), p. 74.

17. Calder, p. 229.

18. *The Hinge of Fate*, p. 770.

19. For a detailed account of this attack, see David Irving, *The Destruction of Dresden* (New York, 1963).

20. Quoted in Quester, p. 156.

21. *Memoirs of a Revolutionist* (New York, 1957), p. 178.

22. Robert C. Batchelder, *The Irreversible Decision: 1939–1950* (New York, 1965), p. 38. Batchelder's is the best historical account of the decision to drop the bomb, and the only one that treats the moral issues in a systematic way.

23. A. Russell Buchanan, *The United States and World War II* (New York, 1964), I, 75.

24. "The Decision to Use the Atomic Bomb," *Harpers Magazine* (February, 1947), repr. in *The Atomic Bomb: The Great Decision*, ed. Paul R. Baker (New York, 1968), p. 21.

25. *Speaking Frankly* (New York, 1947), p. 261.

26. *Atomic Quest* (New York, 1956), p. 247.

27. *Mr. Citizen* (New York, 1960), p. 267. I owe this group of quotations to Gerald McElroy.

28. Batchelder, p. 159.

29. Batchelder, p. 149.

30. *Triumph and Tragedy* (New York, 1962), p. 639.

31. "The Decision to Use the Bomb," p. 21.

32. *Speaking Frankly*, p. 264.

33. The case would be even worse if the bomb were used for political rather than military reasons (with the Russians rather than the Japanese in mind): on this point, see the careful analysis of Martin J. Sherwin, *A World Destroyed: The Atomic Bomb and the Grand Alliance* (New York, 1975).

17 Nuclear Deterrence

1. "The Decision to Use the Bomb," in *The Atomic Bomb*, ed. Baker, p. 21.

2. *Reflections on the Revolution in France* (Everyman's Library, London, 1910), p. 75.

3. See, for example, *Nuclear Weapons and Christian Conscience*, ed. Stein; *Nuclear Weapons and the Conflict of Conscience*, ed. John C. Bennett (New York, 1962); *The Moral Dilemma of Nuclear Weapons*, ed. William Clancy (New York, 1961); *Morality and Modern Warfare*, ed. William J. Nagle (Baltimore, 1960).

4. "Moral Urgencies in the Nuclear Context," in *Nuclear Weapons and the Conflict of Conscience*, p. 101.

5. *The Just War: Force and Political Responsibility* (New York, 1968), p. 171.

6. "Explorations into the Unilateral Disarmament Position," in *Nuclear Weapons and the Conflict of Conscience*, p. 130.

7. See the novel *Fail-Safe* by Eugene Burdick and Harvey Wheeler (New York, 1962) for a possible scenario.

8. Paul Ramsey, "A Political Ethics Context for Strategic Thinking," in *Strategic Thinking and Its Moral Implications*, ed. Morton A. Kaplan (Chicago, 1973), pp. 134–35.

9. George Urban, "A Conversation with George F. Kennan," 47 *Encounter* 3:37 (September, 1976).

10. For a review and critique of this literature, see Philip Green, *Deadly Logic: The Theory of Nuclear Deterrence* (Ohio State University Press, 1966).

11. *Nuclear Weapons and Foreign Policy* (New York, 1957), p. 180.

12. *On War*, trans. Terence Kilmartin (New York, 1968), p. 138.

13. See the article "Warfare, Conduct of" in the *Encyclopaedia Britannica* (15th ed., Chicago, 1975), *Macropaedia*, Vol. 19, p. 509.

14. *On War*, p. 138.

15. Bernard Brodie, *War and Politics* (New York, 1973), p. 404 (author's emphasis).

16. The bulk of Ramsey's articles, papers, and pamphlets are collected in his book *The Just War*; see also his earlier work *War and the Christian Conscience: How Shall Modern War Be Justly Conducted?* (Durham, 1961).

17. "War and Murder," p. 57.

18. *The Just War*, p. 252; see also p. 320.

19. *The Just War*, p. 303.

20. *War and Politics*, p. 404.

21. *The Just War*, p. 253 (author's emphasis); see also p. 328.

22. "Warfare," p. 568.

23. *The Just War*, p. 254; see also pp. 333ff.

24. *The Just War*, p. 364. Ramsey is paraphrasing Anscombe's critique of pacifism: see "War and Murder," p. 56.

Notes

18 The Crime of Aggression: Political Leaders and Citizens

1. Joseph W. Bishop, Jr., "The Question of War Crimes," 54 *Commentary* 6:85 (December, 1972).

2. See the suggestion of Sanford Levinson, "Responsibility for Crimes of War," 2 *Philosophy and Public Affairs* 270ff. (1973).

3. For a useful account of this doctrine, tracing it back to the jurisprudence of John Austin, see Stanley Paulson, "Classical Legal Positivism at Nuremberg," 4 *Philosophy and Public Affairs* 132–58 (1975).

4. Quoted in Noam Chomsky, *At War With Asia*, p. 310.

5. Stanley Kunitz, "Foreign Affairs," in *Selected Poems: 1928–1959* (Boston, 1958), p. 23.

6. *Trials of War Criminals Before the Nuremberg Military Tribunals*, vol. 11 (1950), pp. 488–89; see the discussion in Levinson, pp. 253ff. and in Greenspan, *Modern Law of Land Warfare*, pp. 449–50.

7. *Trials of War Criminals*, vol. 14 (n.d.), p. 383; see Levinson, p. 263.

8. *Trials of War Criminals*, vol. 14, p. 472; see Levinson, p. 264.

9. For a discussion of the Vietnam cases, see Edward Weisband and Thomas M. Franck, *Resignation in Protest* (New York, 1976).

10. *Kurt Gerstein: The Ambiguity of Good*, trans. Charles Fullman (New York, 1969).

11. *Trials of War Criminals*, vol. 14, p. 346.

12. *King John* 4:2, ll. 231–41.

13. For the contemporary law of reparations, see Greenspan, pp. 309–10, 592–93.

14. *The Warriors*, 196–97.

15. *The Warriors*, p. 198.

16. *The Warriors*, p. 199.

17. In thinking about these issues, I have been greatly helped by the essays in Joel Feinberg's *Doing and Deserving*.

18. *The Warriors*, p. 199.

19. See Richard A. Falk, "The Circle of Responsibility," in *Crimes of War*, ed. Falk, G. Kolko, and R. J. Lifton (New York, 1971), p. 230: "The circle of responsibility is drawn around all who have or should have knowledge of the illegal and immoral character of the war."

20. *American Power and the New Mandarins* (New York, 1969).

19 War Crimes: Soldiers and Their Officers

1. *The Seventh Day: Soldiers Talk About the Six Day War* (London, 1970), p. 126.

2. I owe this point to Dan Little.

3. Guy Chapman, *A Passionate Prodigality* (New York, 1966), pp. 99–100.

4. Richard Wasserstrom, "The Responsibility of the Individual for War Crimes," in *Philosophy, Morality, and International Affairs*, p. 62.

5. *The Thin Red Line* (New York, 1964), pp. 271–78.

6. On the difficulties of surrender in the midst of a modern battle, see John Keegan, *The Face of Battle*, p. 322.

7. See the discussion of this point by Samuel David Resnick, *Moral Responsibility and Democratic Theory,* unpublished Ph.D. dissertation (Harvard University, 1972).

8. Seymour Hersh, *My Lai 4: A Report on the Massacre and its Aftermath* (New York, 1970); see also David Cooper, "Responsibility and the 'System'" in *Individual and Collective Responsibility: The Massacre at My Lai,* ed. Peter French (Cambridge, Mass., 1972), pp. 83–100.

9. Hersh, p. 42.

10. *The Warriors,* p. 181.

11. *The Measures Taken,* in *The Jewish Wife and Other Short Plays,* trans. Eric Bentley (New York, 1965), p. 82.

12. The best account of the present legal situation is Yoram Dinstein, *The Defense of Obedience to Superior Orders in International Law* (Leiden, 1965).

13. McDougal and Feliciano, *Law and Minimum World Public Order,* p. 690.

14. Quoted in Kurt Baier's analysis of the Calley trial, "Guilt and Responsibility," *Individual and Collective Responsibility,* p. 42.

15. See Wasserstrom, "The Responsibility of the Individual."

16. Quoted in Telford Taylor, *Nuremberg and Vietnam,* p. 49.

17. *The Warriors,* pp. 185–86.

18. *The Warriors,* p. 189.

19. McDougal and Feliciano, pp. 693–94 and notes.

20. *Nuremberg and Vietnam,* p. 55n.

21. Jean Le Meur, "The Story of a Responsible Act," in *Political Man and Social Man,* ed. Robert Paul Wolff (New York, 1964), p 204.

22. Quoted in A. J. Barker, *Yamashita* (New York, 1973), pp. 157–58.

23. Omar N. Bradley, *A Soldier's Story* (New York, 1964), pp. 343–44.

24. For the relevant law, see Greenspan, *Modern Law of Land Warfare,* pp. 332ff.

25. See Fried, *Anatomy of Values,* pp. 194–99.

26. I shall follow the account of A. Frank Reel, *The Case of General Yamashita* (Chicago, 1949).

27. Reel, p. 280: the appendix of this book reprints the Supreme Court decision.

28. On strict liability, see Feinberg, *Doing and Deserving,* pp. 223ff.

29. Hersh, p. 11.

30. "Political Action: The Problem of Dirty Hands," 2 *Philosophy and Public Affairs* (1973), pp. 160–80.

31. Frankland, *Bomber Offensive,* p. 159.

32. Calder, *The People's War,* p. 565; Irving, *Destruction of Dresden,* pp. 250–57.

33. *Soldiers: An Obituary for Geneva,* trans. Robert David MacDonald (New York, 1968), p. 192.

34. *The Discourses,* Bk. I, ch. XVIII.

35. 1 *Philosophy and Public Affairs* (1972), p. 143.

Afterword: Nonviolence and the Theory of War

1. *Exploring Nonviolent Alternatives* (Boston, 1971), p. 93; cf. Anders Boserup and Andrew Mack, *War Without Weapons: Non-Violence in National Defense* (New York, 1975), p. 135.

2. Sharp, p. 52.

Notes

3. But an enemy state might threaten to bomb rather than invade; on this possibility, see Adam Roberts, "Civilian Defense Strategy," in *Civilian Resistance as a National Defense*, ed. Roberts (Hammondsworth, 1969), pp. 268–72.

4. *Collected Essays, Journalism, and Letters*, vol. 4, p. 469.

5. Louis Fischer, *Gandhi and Stalin*, quoted in Orwell's "Reflections," p. 468.

6. "Lessons from Resistance Movements—Guerrilla and Non-Violent," in *Civilian Resistance*, p. 240.

7. For a brief account of Czech resistance, see Boserup and Mack, pp. 102–16.

8. Sharp, p. 66; but he believes that the degree and extent of suffering will be "vastly smaller" than in regular warfare (p. 65).

INDEX

Index

Index

Index